It Didn't Mean Anything

It Didn't Mean Anything

A Psychoanalytic Reading of American Detective Fiction

ALEXANDER N. HOWE

McFarland & Company, Inc., Publishers
Jefferson, North Carolina, and London

LIBRARY OF CONGRESS CATALOGUING-IN-PUBLICATION DATA

Howe, Alexander N., 1973–
    It didn't mean anything : a psychoanalytic reading of American detective fiction / Alexander N. Howe.
        p.   cm.
    Includes bibliographical references and index.

    ISBN 978-0-7864-3454-1
softcover : 50# alkaline paper

    1. Detective and mystery stories, American — History and criticism.   2. Psychoanalysis and literature — United States.   3. American fiction — 20th century — History and criticism.   4. American literature — Psychological aspects.   I. Title.
PS374.D4H69   2008
813'.0872093561—dc22   2008003190

British Library cataloguing data are available

©2008 Alexander N. Howe. All rights reserved

No part of this book may be reproduced or transmitted in any form or by any means, electronic or mechanical, including photocopying or recording, or by any information storage and retrieval system, without permission in writing from the publisher.

On the cover: Photo illustration based on the portrait in the Freud Museum, London

Manufactured in the United States of America

McFarland & Company, Inc., Publishers
   Box 611, Jefferson, North Carolina 28640
      www.mcfarlandpub.com

For Brigid,
Because all of me wants to...

Acknowledgments

Like all works of criticism, this study is indebted to the assistance of many individuals — more than I could possibly mention here. I am grateful for the numerous comments and words of support that I received from colleagues and others I met while giving presentations of portions of these arguments over the past few years. I would also like to thank Professors Brett Levinson and William Spanos of Binghamton University for guiding my early thoughts surrounding this project. As an American reader of Lacan — one with only an average reading knowledge of French — I am especially indebted to the work of all the critics and clinicians that are discussed and cited throughout this book. I am certain that my own misunderstandings and limitations are present in these pages, as well. Naturally, for this I accept full responsibility. I would like to express my gratitude for the funding provided by the Provost's Office and the Office for Sponsored Research and Programs at the University of the District of Columbia. This aid was instrumental for completing the project. I thank my parents, Timothy Howe and Diane Howe, for their encouragement and for having such high standards of low literature. Finally, I would like to thank my wife, Brigid Nuta Howe, for her love and support throughout the many long nights that were required to finish this work. Her patience and understanding with me during this time was invaluable and likely more than I deserve.

Contents

Acknowledgments vii
Introduction: Reading the Detective and the Analyst Encore! 1

ONE   The Classical Detective: Truth, Knowledge, and the Imbecility of the Master   11

TWO   "Protective Thinking": Obsessional Neurosis, Analysis, and the Hard-Boiled Detective   67

THREE   Hysteria, Paranoia, and Love in Philip K. Dick's Anti-Detective Fiction   122

FOUR   Remembering, Repeating, and Working Through: Traumatic Narrative in the Hard-Boiled Fiction of Marcia Muller   172

Afterword 237
Notes 241
Bibliography 269
Index 277

Introduction:
Reading the Detective
and the Analyst *Encore!*

Detective fiction and psychoanalysis are two of the most powerful and popular discourses to emerge in the nineteenth century. Poe is said to have founded detective fiction when he published the stories "The Murders in the Rue Morgue," "The Murder of Marie Roget," and "The Purloined Letter" between the years 1841 and 1844. Undeniably, in these tales, the author establishes conventions that are still evident today, even within the myriad of subgenres that have emerged within detective and crime fiction. First and foremost among these practices is the exploration of mystery through a self-conscious use of Reason. The result: illumination and the end of mystery. Of course, Freud is the undisputed father of psychoanalysis. As a matter of convenience, we might take the publication of *Studies in Hysteria* in 1895, a text co-authored with Freud's colleague and confidant Joseph Breuer, as the "advent" of psychoanalysis. It is in this early text that the term "the talking cure" is coined, and Freud and Breuer outline a therapy that stakes its curative powers on speech itself. If the patient and analyst can articulate in words the hidden cause of the symptom, suffering will be alleviated. The result: cure and the end of affliction. Or so the story goes.

The similarity of these two practices has long been a topic of critical interest. Indeed, it is possible to argue that Freud himself was the first proponent of the detective-analyst analogy. Freud was born in 1856, seven years after Poe's death in 1849. However, the science of psychoanalysis gains momentum during the heyday of Poe's greatest disciple, Sir Arthur Conan Doyle. The first Sherlock Holmes adventure, *A Study in Scarlet*, is published in 1887, and over the next three decades — the final Holmes adventure, "Shoscombe

Old Place," is published in 1921—Conan Doyle's detective will become perhaps the most famous fictional character in the history of publishing. These years coincide with a bulk of Freud's greatest production. Given the ubiquity of Sherlock Holmes even very early on, it is not surprising to learn that Freud was familiar with Conan Doyle's fiction. Beyond this general acquaintance, there is evidence to suggest that the father of psychoanalysis was in fact an admirer of Conan Doyle's famous detective. In the biography of one of Freud's famous patients, the "Wolfman," we are told:

> Once when we happened to speak of Conan Doyle and his creation, Sherlock Holmes, I had thought that Freud would have no use for this type of light reading matter, and was surprised to find that this was not at all the case and that Freud had read this author attentively. The fact that circumstantial evidence is useful in psychoanalysis when reconstructing a childhood history may explain Freud's interest in this type of literature.[1]

Indeed, Freud seems to authorize the patient's supposition regarding the similarity between analysis and detective. As he wrote in the *Introductory Lectures on Psychoanalysis*, speaking of the importance of small details, "And if you were a detective engaged in tracing a murder, would you expect to find that the murderer had left his photograph behind at the place of the crime, with his address attached? Or would you not necessarily have to be satisfied with comparatively slight and obscure traces of the person you were in search of? So do not let us under-estimate small indications; by their help we may succeed in getting on the track of something bigger."[2] Like the detective, the analyst reads these "obscure traces," relying upon the inadvertent content of a patient's story, rather than the actual account offered.

A final mention of detection worthy of note is found in an address given by Freud to law students at the University of Vienna. In this text, he suggests the similarities between criminal investigations and the analysis of hysteric patients:

> In both we are concerned with a secret, with something hidden.... In the case of the criminal it is a secret which he knows and hides from you, whereas in the case of the hysteric it is a secret which he himself does not know either, which is hidden from himself.... The task of the therapist, however, is the same as the examining magistrate. We have to uncover the hidden psychical material; and in order to do this we have invented a number of detective devices, some of which it seems that you gentlemen of the law are now about to copy from us.[3]

Here again, the analyst, like the detective, seeks the "truth" that lies beyond deceptive coverings. We can surmise that these "detective devices" in question focus upon the knowledge available in even the smallest, most "obscure traces." Available, at least, to those who have eyes to see — or ears to hear.

Given the frequency with which he uses this metaphor, it is clear that the similarities between analysis and detection were not lost on Freud himself.

It should be noted that each of these passages dates to a fairly early period in Freud's career. In fact, the theory of interpretation that is suggested in both selections (i.e., there is a real traumatic cause that must be excavated) will subsequently be abandoned.[4] Despite the insight of previous studies affirming the correspondence between detection and analysis, these inquiries often remain at the level of this early work, making use of clinical criteria that was ultimately discarded.[5] Generally speaking, analysis of this kind proceeds from a space of mastery whose therapeutic goal is to expertly identify and then return to the analysand those "forgotten" memories that have resulted in the pain of the symptom. Admittedly, such an ambition is entirely amenable to the manifest goal of the detective, which is always to provide a coherent narrative account of what at first seems an unsolvable mystery. However, as Freud quickly discovered, the presumption that there is a definitive solution to the mystery plaguing the analysand actually hinders analysis and, ultimately, therapeutic effects. Patients who gratefully accepted such oracular interpretation arrived at the next session with fresh symptoms demanding that analysis continue. In the end, expert interpretation cannot keep up with this will-to-pathology. Indeed, analysis from this position only lends itself to such production. These impasses required not only that therapeutic practices be rethought, but likewise that the psychical structures utilized by analysis to understand the patient be amended.

Within the history of detective fiction, a similar revision of investigative practices is found. This reconsideration begins with the passage from the classical detective text, typified by the work of Poe and Conan Doyle, to the work of the hard-boiled school of detective fiction. In this development, the self-assured certainty of the classical detective's indubitable methods is radically called into question. The hard-boiled "dick" has neither the classical detective's intelligence nor his cultural cachet, two crucial aspects of character that always reduce the murder or crime to an intellectual puzzle and ensure the classical sleuth's victory. Quite opposed to this, the hard-boiled detective is no longer a master in any sense. He is forced to enter the city's underworld, thus experiencing an ever-present threat to life and limb. The tools of the trade become the brute force of body and gun, and the use of intuition as it perhaps springs from both these items. In the mid–twentieth century, the anti-detective text will augment this criticism of authority and more fully implicate the detective in the crime under investigation. In this space, conventional methods of detection yield nothing but paranoia, which culminates in the revelation that the detective has become the very object of his own search. In other words, he has become criminal. In both the hard-boiled and anti-detective worlds, then, knowledge and interpretation remain in a state of crisis — or even failure.

Acknowledging this history, it seems a dubious proposition to assert a correspondence between the detective and the analyst based upon interpretative mastery. In the current study, I will reassess the affinity of the detective and analyst using the work of the French psychoanalyst Jacques Lacan. Over the course of Lacan's seminar (given annually for nearly thirty years), one encounters a theoretical modification similar to those already identified within Freud and the development of detective fiction. Though Lacan begins with the insight of Freud's later clinical work, he will himself revise his own theory of the clinic drastically throughout the 1950s, '60s, and '70s. This reformation will center around the position of the analyst in respect to the analysand's discourse, an alteration that will move the analyst from the position of the Other, or the unconscious, to the "object-cause" of the analysand's desire. In this way, the analyst embodies what Lacan will term the position of "truth" within the patient's psychical economy, that place where "knowledge" (or interpretation) fails. As will be shown, though there is much to be gained from the detective-analyst comparison, from this later Lacanian perspective, psychoanalysis in fact begins where the discourse of the classical detective ends. This is all the more curious as the methods of psychoanalysis might be said to culminate in "literature," an insight that is, I argue, shared by later manifestations of the detective genre.

This study is, then, an excursus on this adequation: the method of the fictional detective is *like* that of the psychoanalyst, and the vice versa. It is intended as an introduction for students and others interested in the meeting point(s) of these discourses. While addressing these issues, I will not provide a comprehensive history of detective fiction. (There are many wonderful histories of the genre available.) However, I will locate my argument throughout the development of detective fiction, largely in the American context. I will do this by reading a variety of canonical texts and some lesser-known works, as well. These will be examined alongside primary texts from Freud and Lacan, in addition to a number of secondary texts from scholars of the Lacanian clinic.

Naturally, this project raises the issue of a much-maligned practice: applied psychoanalysis. In brief, applied psychoanalysis assumes that it is possible to "diagnose" an author and, thereby, find the truth of an author's work, which is subsequently used in support of the original diagnosis. Though Freud himself is frequently guilty of this practice in his studies of literary and artistic texts, there is a long history of criticism that works against the simple application of psychoanalysis to literary texts. Lacan himself was a frequent critic of applied psychoanalysis, despite the fact that he often made "use" of literary texts in his own work. Indeed, in an account of his famous "Seminar on 'The Purloined Letter,'" given in the essay "Lituraterre," he suggests that in his reading of Poe, he had no interest in getting involved in the "literary smoochy-woochy" that is applied psychoanalysis.[6] In other words, he has no desire to valorize literature or analysis by unlocking literature's secrets through the knowledge of psychoanalysis. To these ends, he asserts that psychoanalysis cannot "motivate the least of literary judgments."[7]

In the introduction to the famous special edition of *Yale French Studies* on Literature and Psychoanalysis, published in 1977, Shoshana Felman addressed this issue of applied psychoanalysis, calling for the reappraisal of the conjunctive *and* of "literature and psychoanalysis." In this brief piece, entitled "To Open the Question," she argues that, despite the recognition of the similarity of literature and analysis, there remains in practice a well-entrenched hierarchical relation between these two discourses. Literature is always reduced to a passive object upon which the knowledge of psychoanalysis operates. To reinvigorate the conversation of this connection, she hopes to use literary insights to express the intimate relation between the two fields. Irony, that specifically literary insight, is the key. Necessarily corrupting textual boundaries (i.e., irony is present only in the difference of a statement from itself), irony refuses to act as a graspable object for knowledge understood in the conventional sense. Thus, the limits of critical authority are revealed, and its power is shown to have been a rhetorical effect of language. This insight is likewise the goal of analysis, which always confronts the analysand with the imaginary nature of fantasy:

> Psychoanalysis tells us that the fantasy is a fiction, and that consciousness is itself, in a sense, a fantasy-effect. In the same way, literature tells us that authority is a *language* effect, the product or the creation of its own *rhetorical* power: that authority is the power of fiction; that authority, therefore, is likewise a fiction.[8]

As each discourse seeks to curb the effects of authority with insight into the tautological nature of all discursive power, clearly the concurrence in question can no longer be thought of in terms of subject and object. For Felman, this requires that the previous relation of application be rethought in terms of *implication*, which etymologically suggests "being folded within." Psychoanalysis and literature, then, are "'enfolded within' each other, since they are, as it were, at the same time outside and inside each other," each is the "interiority of the other [...] the border between them is undecidable since they are really *traversed* by each other."[9] In the space of the other, each discourse functions as its *otherness-to-itself* or its *unconscious*, as Felman suggests.

The concluding thought of the author's prologue is an invitation to consider the way in which literature offers insight into the unconscious of psychoanalysis just as psychoanalysis has offered insight into the unconscious processes of literature. In this way, the insight of the irony inherent in the literary process demands not merely a reformation of the conjunction of "literature and psychoanalysis," but also a restructuring of analytic knowledge and its use.

While I have endeavored to follow Felman's recommendations, I do not for a moment pretend to have done so with complete success. In this study I am interested in using Lacanian clinical psychical structures to categorize various stages of detective fiction. In this sense, I will engage in diagnosis (and likely application), but I would like to suggest that this is a "diagnosis" that is ambiguous in all the senses implied in analytic practice. As Dor says of Freud's theory of diagnosis: "He shows us, among other things, how 'wild' interpretation always stems from an overhasty causalistic reasoning grounded in a hypothetico-deductive approach that does not take into account the distance separating the act of utterance from what is being said."[10] To avoid this pitfall, psychoanalytic diagnosis remains, then, provisional and open to "proof" or refutation in the future, but this always begins with a first step that views the patient from the perspective of a given psychical structure (e.g., hysteria, obsessional neurosis, etc.).[11] For my current purposes, I will take "psychical structure" as the way in which an individual has "chosen" to encounter the trauma of the unconscious. (Admittedly, in the case of psychosis, this becomes a bit more complicated.) Put very simply, the trauma of the unconscious necessarily marks the place where knowledge fails — even the indubitable knowledge of the detective. To put this in Dor's terms, the unconscious marks that point where "causality" falters. Consequently, the psychical structures do not offer a definitive "truth" or cause in the traditional sense. Rather, we might think of the psychical structures as strategies for organizing the inevitable failure of reading and interpretation. The detective is often said to be *the* representative of the powers of Reason. Knowing all possibilities before these occur, he or she plainly sees effects as they move seamlessly from their causes — even if she or he "reasons backwards" from effects to causes. In viewing detective fiction through the various lenses of the Lacanian psychical structures, what I hope to uncover in each case is the limit of such causality and, thus, the failure of the detective's interpretation.

To these ends, I will read the detective alternately according to hysteria, obsessional neurosis, perversion, and psychosis. Of course, this is an "open" diagnosis that is intended as provisional in the sense described above. Hysteria holds a special place in this inquiry. For analysis to begin, Lacan tells us that an individual must become "hystericized," either by an accidental trauma or through the intervention of the analyst. When "hystericized," the subject is suddenly confronted with what has been repressed in the production of "self" or "ego."[12] Quite simply, identity is shaken to the core. The bulk of my study, then, examines the way the originally cocksure detective becomes increasingly hystericized throughout the twentieth century. The structure of hysteria is particularly well suited for the criticism of knowledge and mastery. As we shall see, the hysteric's demand is always a demand for more interpretation, a protest that is in part suggested by the *encore!* in the title of Lacan's *Seminar XX*. In asking for more interpretation, the hysteric will unmask the master (be this analyst or other self-assured interpreter), showing that she or he is in the end incapable of offering a convincing knowledge. As I will argue, this hysterical strategy is privy to that distinctly "literary" insight — that is, the rhetorical or fictional dimension of all authority — suggested by Felman.

Chapter One works through prominent stories of the founding authors of detective fiction, Poe and Conan Doyle. I begin by reviewing criticism that assumes the totalizing knowledge of the classical detective. In response to such work, I argue that the detective's proficiency is in fact compromised by his frequent literary entanglements. This insight is read in terms of the "Bi-Part" soul of C. Auguste Dupin, Poe's great detective, who perhaps more readily acknowledges his connection with criminal and irrational forces — and, of course, the force of fiction. Holmes, on the contrary, professes to read the criminal solely through the proxy of clues, a position of clarity and distance that mimics the disinterest and privilege of the scientist. While this is the explicit discourse of the detective, more "obscure traces" reveal a literary impulse at the heart of Holmes' method, as well.

To conclude this chapter, I take up the detective-analyst analogy, an argument typically made in the context of the classical detective. Contrary to this assumption, I claim that this comparison is not suitable in the classical case, as the analyst refuses interpretation that offers a unified narrative. To these ends, I briefly return to Lacan's own "Seminar on 'The Purloined Letter,'" which establishes a clinical paradigm that places the analyst in the position of the Other. Making use of subsequent clinical models in comparison, I argue that even with Poe's Dupin, the detective-analyst analogy is not appropriate.

Chapter Two traces the development of the hard-boiled detective's code of honor through the work of Dashiell Hammett, Raymond Chandler, and Mickey Spillane. The often paradoxical nature of this code and its methods is read in terms of the psychical structure of obsessional neurosis. As this new detective is presented as both honorable and mercenary, I argue that these texts support and criticize their own hard-boiled version of masculinity, a conflicted stance that is representative of the sexual politics of America at the time. At its most basic level, what this version of masculinity privileges is the man who is beholden to no one. This stance is entirely comprehensible from the perspective of obsessional neurosis, as the fundamental desire of the obsessional is to annul the existence of the Other.

In Chandler's work, I argue, we find the "hystericization" of the obsessional hard-boiled detective, a condition that Lacan claimed was absolutely prerequisite for analytic work to begin. To these ends, Chandler's inclusion of "sentiment" within the tough guy form is read as a criticism of the precipitately failing masculinity upon which the genre is founded. The greater argument of this chapter is that, insofar as these detectives forsake knowledge in its previous forms, one encounters a potential insight into knowledge as it functions within later analytic paradigms. This makes the hard-boiled genre the appropriate site for an amended version of the detective-analyst analogy.

In Chapter Three, I analyze the science fiction of Philip K. Dick in terms of anti-detection. The anti-detective text works to "evoke the impulse to 'detect' ... in order to violently frustrate it by refusing to solve the crime."[13] The anti-detective project is, then, much like the work of the analyst that prompts the dissolution of unity in fantasy. The loss of such consistency is the obligatory starting point of Philip K. Dick's fiction, a gesture that frequently leaves the protagonist an inadvertent detective. Naturally, though the world remains full of presentiment, solutions remain wanting. To provide a greater context to this inventive use of detection, I view Dick's own writing on paranoia and respond to criticism that has lionized the author's work as productively subversive.

Throughout this chapter, I read the novels *Time Out of Joint* (1959), *Do Androids Dream of Electric Sheep?* (1968), and *Flow My Tears, the Policeman Said* (1974) from the perspective of paranoid psychosis and hysteria. As I demonstrate, Dick's own interest in the paranoia that so readily plagued America during the Cold War years is itself paranoid through and through. Curiously, this is best exemplified in Dick's emphasis upon love and empathy in response to contemporary malaise. Though his work does, indeed, in anti-detective fashion, work toward the illumination of paranoid tendencies within culture, his privileging of love and empathy duplicates the alienation — and therefore the paranoid structure — that is the object of his critique.

In Chapter Four, I return again to the question of hysteria, read through the female hard-boiled detective of Marcia Muller. Muller's first novel, *Edwin of the Iron Shoes* (1977) breaks ground for this sub-genre that flourished during the 1980s, as Sue Grafton and Sara Paretsky (and others) become hugely successful. From the beginning, the female hard-boiled detective is read as a transgressive figure that runs roughshod over the constraints of a masculine-inspired genre and the concomitant misogynist stereotypes that dominate this form and culture at large. The critical productivity of such work is undeniable, and certainly the recent spate of texts reassessing gender and sexuality within detective fiction (e.g., Abbott, Forter, Plain) owe much to these earlier studies. However, this framing is not without its own considerable strictures that limit inquiry into the question of sexual difference — an issue that has always been at the center of the hard-boiled genre.

Working from the insights of Chapter Two, I argue that the hard-boiled genre is always already a hystericizing form. In other words, structurally and aesthetically, the genre reveals the failure of the symbolic order to adequately account for the subject, male or female. In response to this silence, the subject will offer the Other any number of compensatory objects — including itself—in an effort to maintain the possibility of (full) meaning within that space. Strategically, then, Muller's works repeat a fascination with such objects, history's trophies, and foreground the utter inability of narrative to finally account for these items and the subjects whose identity they are to anchor. In creating the female hard-boiled detective, I argue, Muller expertly appropriates not a masculine genre, but a hystericizing structure that confronts us with the constitutive trauma of the subject. In so doing, the author ceaselessly interrogates characteristic masculine and feminine fantasies produced to elide this fact, and, further, shows the productivity of hysteria as a paradigm of investigation.

ONE

The Classical Detective: Truth, Knowledge, and the Imbecility of the Master

The Typology of the Classical Detective:
Science and Fiction

At the beginning of Sir Arthur Conan Doyle's story "The Resident Patient" (1893), Sherlock Holmes amazes Dr. Watson with a trick that perfectly demonstrates the detective's gifts at observation and deduction: He reads Watson's mind. Naturally, the detective does not actually establish a psychic connection that allows him to gain entrance into his counterpart's thoughts. Indeed, there is no need for such an intrusion because Watson's thoughts are written upon his face. As Holmes explains the ease of this process, "The features are given to man as the means by which he shall express his emotions, and yours [Watson's] are faithful servants."[1] By observing Watson's expressions, behavior, and reading material (the morning paper), Holmes is able to follow Watson's thoughts as these move from the simple contemplation of an unframed portrait of Henry Ward Beecher sitting atop a bookshelf, to the intricacies of Beecher's career. After a description of the circuitous path of Watson's reflections, a description that defies belief, Watson offers an exclamation that in some way appears in nearly all the Sherlock Holmes stories: "Absolutely!... And now that you have explained it, I confess that I am as amazed as before" (*CSH* 424). Naturally, the reader shares in this astonishment and admiration. Even after Holmes' patient explanations, we are left wondering, how could he possibly have known?

The trick performed here, which is of course repeated in a variety of forms throughout the detective genre, might be traced to its modern origin in the detective stories of Edgar Allan Poe. In fact, Holmes explains that he demonstrates this strange power to Watson because he (Watson) had doubted the possibility of reading thoughts through facial expressions when the concept was first explained to him during a discussion on Poe! As he will do frequently, Holmes defends the work of his investigative predecessor — while at the same time claiming to have improved upon his methods. And rightfully so. This defense is no small matter, as the experiment in thought reading reveals the most fundamental assumptions of the detective's practice. Namely, for those with a carefully trained eye, the world is a transparent chain of causality. Causes seamlessly produce effects, and, because of the relentlessness of this teleology, it is likewise possible to use this reason in reverse, from effects to causes. This unfailing mechanism is at the heart of the classical detective's worldview.

The so-called "classical detective story" typically refers to the work of Edgar Allan Poe, Sir Arthur Conan Doyle, and their immediate successors.[2] Reduced to its barest essentials, the classical detective story might be described as an account of the way in which a mystery is uncovered and solved by an amateur detective. Quite simply, it recounts the way a seemingly impossible story comes to be told. In "The Typology of Detective Fiction," Todorov argues that the detective story presents the two levels of text that are present within any literary work: "plot," the way a story is told; and "story," the way the event occurred in actuality.[3] As the author suggests, in the detective story this conjuncture has the somewhat paradoxical effect of making the second narrative appear largely "excessive," or "insignificant."[4] The telling of the investigation (plot) is only important insofar as it tells us how it all really happened (story).[5] However, because this first event occurred prior to the second telling of the plot, it must remain an absence within the detective's own narrative. In the "whodunit" of the classical story that revolves around murder, this "loss" is underscored in the violence of the original crime. The detective can give an account of the crime (i.e., the plot, or the second narrative), but he cannot raise the dead, just the structure of the genre cannot make present the "story" (i.e., the event in its actuality) as such. We are left only with stories of that missed event.

Convention demands that the detective narrative skew these limitations in a variety of ways. For example, the chronicler of the story will make regular assurances to the reader that very little embellishment will interfere with this final (re)telling. The assumption is, in other words, that a retelling (or re-presentation) is possible. Naturally, the reader is left to conclude that events happened "just as they occurred"— that is, that the narrative offers fact rather than fiction. In a similar vein, in the Sherlock Holmes stories, for instance, Holmes often chides Watson for his literary embellishments to what are supposed to be scientific case studies. As the reader of the detective story always identifies with the greater insight of the detective, she or he must then heed this caution and aspire to see beyond Watson's (fictional) indulgences. The result of these pretensions is an odd sleight of hand that extinguishes the second narrative, or plot, in the telling of a prior narrative, or story, that cannot be delivered. It goes without saying that, despite this apparent paradox, the structure of the detective genre remains comfortable — even comforting — to legions of readers throughout the world.[6]

Naturally, Todorov does not wish to suggest that the reader of the detective story is solely concerned with the solution and has, therefore, no interest in the second narration. As was suggested at the outset, the classical detective narrative is an account of the *way* the detective comes to learn the solution to the crime. Revealing the object of the solution — the "who" of the whodunit, for example — is satisfying, to be sure. However, per convention, the story remains incomplete until the detective shares *how* he arrived at the solution. As Barzun suggested long ago, the classical detective story is truly the "romance of reason."[7] Hence the importance of the detective painstakingly explaining at the end not merely what happened, but how and when he came to the correct conclusions. The classical detective story is, in this sense, a story of method and the limits of method. It is the story of the rhetoric of all narrative, which is, allegedly, a process of reducing things just as they happened, to the *account* of things just as they happened. In this way, the detective narrative is a story about interpretation, as such.

The taxonomy of the various types of detective fiction developed in Todorov's study is helpful for fleshing out this notion. As the title of his article suggests — "The Topology of Detective Fiction"— Todorov is interested in analyzing the shape and structure of the detective narrative. By studying the building blocks of the genre, it will be possible to construct sub-genres of the form.[8] At the core of the detective story, argues Todorov, are these two narratives that surround the lost, traumatic event that is presumably the center of the story. This is true even of the variations that will develop from the original classical, or whodunit, form. For example, in the thriller, the first narrative of the actual traumatic event functions merely as a pretext for greater focus upon the second narrative of the investigation. The retrospection of the whodunit form is left by the wayside, and the narrative focus turns to the present. "We are no longer told about a crime anterior to the moment of the narrative; the narrative coincides with the action."[9] This alteration allows the possibility of character development that is forbidden in the classical detective story, and ensures that the detective is more vulnerable to his surroundings. Apropos this question of danger, Todorov suggests that the two narratives might be further distinguished by the differing effects they have on the reader.

In the classical story, the reader experiences "curiosity." The narrative proceeds from "effect to cause: starting from a certain effect (a corpse and certain clues) we must find its cause (the culprit and his motive)."[10] Inversely, the thriller inspires "suspense" in the reader. Here, interest moves from cause to effect: "[W]e are first shown the causes, the initial *donnees* (gangsters preparing a heist), and our interest is sustained by what will happen, that is, certain effects (corpses, crimes, fights)."[11] To complete his topology, Todorov speaks of a third category as well: the suspense novel. This form in a sense unites the first two varieties. The reader experiences a curiosity about how past events are to be given meaning, and suspense as to what will happen next.[12] However, while the reader could always expect an erudite solution at the end of a classical detective story, the suspense novel does not offer this security.

These distinctions raise an issue that is crucial to understanding the classical detective and his interpretative method: his invulnerability. Conan Doyle's Sherlock Holmes is especially instructive here. The great detective's failures are small in number, and he rarely experiences a genuine threat to life or limb. Further, the very structure of the genre — which is narrated by the detective's confidant — always allows Holmes to have the final word in the case. Indeed, Holmes in effect survives his own death, which occurs in "The Final Problem" (1893), as we discover in "The Adventure of the Empty House" (1905). As Todorov explains, "suspense," which is based upon the possibility of violence, is strictly impossible in the classical detective story as the detective and his narrator are "by definition, immunized: nothing [can] happen to them."[13] The classical detective is strictly immune to the violence that he explains.

In his "Murders in the Rue Morgue" (1841), the tale frequently taken as the first modern detective story, Poe establishes many of the conventions that will ensure the classical detective his safe distance from the violence he explains. For example, Poe's detective, C. August Dupin, and his friend, the unnamed narrator, live on the outskirts in Paris in a "time-eaten and grotesque mansion, long deserted through superstitions into which we did not inquire, and tottering to its fall in a retired and desolate portion of the Faubourg St. Germain."[14] Far from being an uncomfortable residence, this mansion is furnished in a style that "suited the rather fantastic gloom of our common temper," as the narrator explains (*CEAP* 144). These details are perhaps unsurprising as the pair met at "an obscure library in the Rue Montmartre" while searching for the same "very rare and remarkable volume" (*CEAP* 143). Clearly suggested in each of these elements is a withdrawal from the common society of the city. Like their mansion that is out of joint with the times and "tottering to its fall" — as houses so often do in Poe's work — the detective and his companion remain out of step with their surroundings.

The intellectual nature of this remoteness is marked by their meeting place at an obscure library, and their subsequent penchant for spending days in a "little back library, or book closet" in the home, as the reader is told at the beginning of "The Purloined Letter" (*CEAP* 208). Presumably, this habit of study has led to the "fantastic gloom" of their shared temperaments, but the two find it a comfortable, if isolated, existence: "Our seclusion was perfect," and "We existed in ourselves alone," as the narrator assures the reader (*CEAP* 144). Of course, this seclusion will be disrupted, for a time, with the intrusion of a crime. However, as Todorov's comments on structure suggest, we always begin from the safety of the drawing room or book closet, as it were. All beginnings necessarily depart from the end. Indeed, for the tale to be narratable, the crime must already have been solved, and the story carefully encapsulated within the narrator's plot. In other words, for the classical detective, the solution to mystery is always guaranteed. Nothing is wagered.

The general aloofness of the classical detective suggested in each of these details is sustained by a much more basic requirement: The story must be documented by a devotee of the detective. This character's amazed admiration for the work of the ingenious sleuth represents the position of the reader and, more generally, the status quo. Obviously, this arrangement is vital for establishing the detective's acumen. He always arrives at solutions long before the reader and his even more confused companion. Because the detective does not narrate events in the first person — as the hard-boiled detective often does — his thought processes need not be shared with the reader, allowing the solution (and its explanation) to be revealed only after the proper denouement. Always deferred to in narration, but never present himself, the classical detective functions as a sort of absent center around which the drama of the mystery unfolds. He is an organizing principle outside the space he surveys, what Derrida would call a "center elsewhere."[15] Though suspicion may be cast upon all that appears within the text, the detective's perspective is finally beyond reproach. In this way, the classical detective remains outside the confusion and danger inherent in the disrupted (urban) space of the tale. Here one thinks of the many Sherlock Holmes stories that end with Holmes narrating his solution to the crime, comfortably seated in his drawing room at 221B Baker Street, and safely distanced in time and space from the danger recounted. The crime has all along been a puzzle for his amusement, or more data for his detecting mania.

Turning to another foundational text within detective fiction criticism, S. S. Van Dine's frequently referenced "Twenty Rules for Writing Detective Stories" (1928) illustrates well the expectations of mastery that accompany the classical detective's immunity. As the title suggests, Dine's essay is essentially a twenty-point manifesto. Followed to the letter, these demands will ensure that the detective is the hero of his own epistemological fable and a champion of Reason. The pleasures of this quest are, as Freeman famously claimed, an "intellectual satisfaction."[16] For Dine, the most basic requirements are the following: the criminal must be found by "logical deductions — not accident or coincidence or unmotivated confession"; this must occur through "naturalistic means" (i.e., the supernatural has no place within detective fiction); and, "The method of the murder, and the means of detecting it, must be rational and scientific." Finally, the result of such measured conduct will ensure Dine's primary rule: "The reader must have equal opportunity with the detective for solving the mystery."[17] To put this more simply, and to use a well-worn phrase: the reader reads like a detective.

These analytical requirements are understandably couched in the terms of a scientific confidence that had already become the dominant measure of textual authority in the nineteenth century.[18] However, even within Dine's rationalist "literary" manifesto, the wages of this authority and its method are all too evident. Literature must conform to reality as revealed by science. The extremity of such limitations is most distinct in the dual requirement that motives (e.g., for a murder) should be "personal," yet the text should engage in neither "literary dallying with side-issues [nor] subtly worked-out character analyses."[19] In other words, all human motivations must be reduced to an algebra of types (e.g., when confronted with Situation X, a Type Y person will always perform Act Z). Dine does include the proviso that "there must be a sufficient descriptiveness and character delineation to give the novel verisimilitude," but it is clear that characterization will be done in service of the intellectual "problem" presented.[20]

This lack of interest in developing character is plain in the way the detective himself is presented. Dine requires that the detective's relations with others be strictly limited: the detective can have no peers, as there can be only one detective, just as there can only be one master; and there can be no love interest, as such entanglements would immediately show the limitations of the master.[21] Similarly, Dine demands that the detective himself cannot be the murderer — a quibbling point that is perhaps obvious, if conservative.[22] If the detective escapes suspicion, he is spared even the modicum of character development recommended with the rules. Here again, Sherlock Holmes is instructive. Though he is perhaps one of the most famous literary characters in all history, even avid readers would struggle to answer the question "Who is Sherlock Holmes?" on a personal level.[23] Undeniably, the detective repeatedly gives a human face to the most impossible of perplexities. Nevertheless, he himself remains decidedly inhuman given the lack of development his character receives.

It is just these aspects of the detective narrative that critics have read as a conservative defense of the status quo. The detective orders the city according to a repressive logic that demands that everything (and everyone) remain in its place. Naturally, as figure of this ordering power, the gumshoe himself escapes such scrutiny. The classical detective's relation to the police bears this out perhaps more explicitly. Though more insightful than his official colleagues, the (amateur) detective gladly hands off his query to the proper authorities at the end of the day. The assumption is, of course, that the law, which defends the state, is fair and just. Its wisdom remains beyond reproach as does the detective's skill and judgment. Thus, the detective becomes another cog — albeit an expert cog — in the machinery of the state as it endeavors to perfect its methods of policing in the nineteenth-century industrial city.

Making a similar argument, Walter Benjamin links the detective narrative to photography — a crucial technology for the rise of criminology in the nineteenth century. As Benjamin observes: "Photography made it possible for the first time to preserve permanent and unmistakable traces of a human being. The detective story came into being when this most decisive of all conquests of a person's incognito had been accomplished. Since then, the end of efforts to capture a man in his speech and actions has not been in sight."[24] As is his custom, Benjamin here makes a subtle argument linking technological and artistic practices to the lived experience of individuals in urban centers — in this case, Paris. We might read the detective story as a sort of relay for this greater liquidation of the individual in this context. Indeed, the detective story both marks and disperses the "commonsense" notion that there is nothing unseen by power. In this, the person's "incognito" is truly liquidated. Spanos, in his famous essay "The Detective and the Boundary: Some Notes on the Postmodern Literary Imagination" (1972), reads such aspects of the detective as endemic to Western Reason itself. This totalizing reason, which the detective figures so well, is "the rational or rather the positivistic structure of consciousness that views spatial and temporal phenomena in the world as 'problems' to be 'solved.'"[25] Just as the detective story attempts to reduce the accidents of the world to the terms of its own posthumous account, so too does reason always endeavor to catch creation by the tail, to name the unnamable, and establish a human order where there is only an inhuman chaos.

Naturally, the point to be taken is that interpretation is always a violent enterprise that covers over and creates as much as it describes or represents. While at first glance this operation appears largely repressive in nature — both physically and conceptually — as Freud identified early on, to speak of the repressed is to necessarily speak of its return.[26] To be sure, such returns are symptomatically written throughout the detective genre. In the remainder of the chapter, I will attempt to recuperate such returns in the case of the classical detective.

The Classical Detective: The Power and Knowledge of Vision

God is in the details, a secular adage (often attributed to Flaubert) that effectively summarizes the aspect of nineteenth century epistemology that the work of the classical detective so aptly figures. As Michel Foucault has suggested, it is the "detail" that is the fundamental currency within the panoptic disciplinary society that emerges at the end of the eighteenth century. As he writes, "For the disciplined man, as for the true believer, no detail is unimportant, but not so much for the meaning that it conceals within it as for the hold it provides for the power that wishes to seize it."[27] As trusted representative of the ruling order, or the disciplinary apparatus, the detective reduces individuals to knowable types based upon details that might be charted, or mapped, and thus grasped hold of by knowledge.

The above passage comes from Foucault's famous *Discipline and Punish: The Birth of the Prison* (1975), a project that reads the development of prison technology and forms of institutionalized punishment in the late eighteenth and nineteenth centuries. However, as the author argues, the corrective strategies developed during this time reach far beyond the prison walls. During the years in question, power must readjust itself to the changing structure of contemporary experience, particularly the rise of the modern city. When "Power," understood in an abstract sense, adjusts to regulate larger groups of people living in greater concentrations, the result is what Foucault calls the "disciplinary society." In the disciplinary society, power does not manifest itself in open confrontations. Rather it insinuates itself into the farthest recesses of the social order, surreptitiously training individuals to behave in a prescribed fashion. The result is the production of what Foucault calls "docile bodies," whose greater efficiency (in the factory, school, home, etc.) is in inverse proportion to political efficacy. In other words, though a trained body results in increased production, this at the same time equals increased subordination:

> In a word, the disciplines are the ensemble of minute technical inventions that made it possible to increase the useful size of multiplicities by decreasing the inconveniences of the power which, in order to make them useful, most control them. A multiplicity, whether in a workshop or a nation, an army or a school, reaches the threshold of a discipline when the relation of the one to the other becomes favorable.[28]

Training populations through the relays of various institutions (e.g., family, schools, work, etc.), the disciplines make it possible to order the chaos of urban populations.

To elaborate upon the shared strategies of these various disciplinary mechanisms, Foucault references Jeremy Bentham's panopticon, the ideal prison. As the word itself suggests, the panopticon is a structure that is "all-seeing." The prison conceived by Bentham is a circular structure, with individual cells lining the outside wall. A central tower surveys all that occurs within the smaller units. Ideally, inmates have no clear view of the guard within the tower—perhaps all the inmate sees is the shadow of a guard pacing. However, because they could potentially be observed at any moment, prisoners must behave as though they are being observed at all times. The efficiency of this system is clear enough. One guard can keep watch over any number of prisoners—indeed, as Foucault suggests, after a time, an actual guard is no longer necessary. (A simple cardboard silhouette running along a mechanized track would be sufficient. The moving shadow cast by this device would give the prisoners the illusion that they are always under observation.) Importantly, this is done by breaking down the larger crowd into smaller components (i.e., individuals) that might be known and controlled: "The crowd, a compact mass, a locus of multiple exchanges, individualities merging together, a collective effect, is abolished and replaced by a collection of separated individualities" (201). This is done by using the very force of the crowd — differently organized — against itself. Power is not in the tower, then, but in the prisoners themselves who have internalized its directives and act accordingly. While Foucault is interested in reading the larger context of the panopticon, he makes it clear that it is not a metaphor for the functioning of society. Rather, "it is the diagram of a mechanism of power reduced to its ideal form," a "generalizable model of functions; a way of defining power relations in terms of everyday life of men."[29]

The panopticon — and the disciplinary apparatuses it exemplifies — works by ensuring the continued visibility of bodies, while at the same producing knowledge about these bodies. In this sense, power is not simply repressive, or reprimanding. On the contrary, power is productive. Naturally, the possibility of a single gaze observing everything at all times is not possible. This requires the "gaze" of power to be broken down into various relays that function as the traveling eye, as it were, of power as such. As is often indicated, this notion of seeing without being seen, through disguise and networks of informants, is the basis of Vidocq's innovation of police practices in the Sûreté in Paris.[30] Perhaps a more famous symbol of this tactic is the Pinkerton's logo that features an eye with the inscription: "We Never Sleep."

As these emblems suggest, the detective is a prominent relay extending power's gaze through knowledge production. Indeed, there is no shortage of criticism reading the detective as the eye of power, *par excellence*. Such a conclusion is brought into focus using Foucault's notion of the "examination," a generalized strategy for the coupling of vision and knowledge within a disciplinary apparatus. As Foucault explains:

> The examination combines the techniques of an observing hierarchy and those of a normalizing judgment. It is a normalizing gaze, a surveillance that makes it possible to qualify, to classify and to punish. It establishes over individuals a visibility through which one differentiates them and judges them. That is why, in all the mechanisms of a discipline, the examination is highly ritualized. In it are combined the ceremony of power and the form of the experiment, the deployment of force and the establishment of truth [...] it manifests the subjection of those who are perceived as objects and the objectification of those who are subjected. The superimposition of the power relations and knowledge relations assumes in the examination all its visible brilliance.[31]

Foucault uses the institutions of the hospital and school to illustrate the ways in which examination becomes integrated into a disciplinary apparatus, from its architecture to its function. While the detective is obviously not a representative of a single institution, he is for that reason all the more easily taken as a figure of discipline, or knowledge, generally. Here one thinks of the voracious reading of Sherlock Holmes, and his assertion that he likes to maintain an "exact knowledge" of London.[32] The detective's gaze differentiates and normalizes as it gathers knowledge and then judges accordingly. His purview stretches far beyond London, reaching to all of Europe.

A final detail to be taken from Foucault's notion of the examination is the issue of documentation. The reduction of individuals to objects of knowledge obviously requires the documentation of that process. It must be put in writing. Maintaining scrupulous records of "ordinary individuals" is a unique turn in history, as Foucault suggests, as biography was formerly reserved for "great men." Their tales served as a monument to their power in life. Quite the opposite, the reduction of the individual to a "case study" is a mark of subordination, "a document for possible use."[33] As Foucault elaborates:

> The examination as the fixing, at once ritual and "scientific," of individual differences, as the pinning down of each individual in his own particularity ... clearly indicates the appearance of a new modality of power in which each individual receives as his status his own individuality, and in which he is linked by his status to the features, the measurements, the gaps, the "marks" that characterize him and make him a "case."[34]

In the end, this is precisely what the classical detective strives to produce: case studies that reveal the way in which individuals are made useful to power. Though Holmes objects to the manner in which Watson documents his cases, he certainly cannot object to the need for their publication. Like the various indexical monographs that Holmes has authored, these are of "great practical interest to the scientific detective" and discipline as such (*CSH* 91). If "The Book of Life"— the title of an article Holmes publishes on his own method in *A Study in Scarlet*— can be read, it must, of course, be written.

Franco Moretti has analyzed the classical detective according to many of these Foucauldian insights, going so far as to claim that "Detective fiction is a hymn to culture's coercive abilities: which prove more effective than pure and simple institutional repression."[35] The author reads the detective as the great defender of monopoly capital, which demands de-individuated collections of wealth. To be an individual in this space is to upset the very foundation of class society, which remains much more static than it may first appear. This, says Moretti, is exactly what detective fiction teaches us regarding the individual. To fall on the outside of the greater system of registration and encoding is to fall into the realm of the criminal. The individual's best hope is to "conform to a stereotype: in this way, one will never be a victim or a criminal."[36]

Naturally, this places the classical detective in a unique position. (I will continue throughout this chapter to use Holmes and Dupin as working models of this position.) Without hesitation, he gives up his individuality in favor of his work, while at the same time he must retain traces of "individuality" (or an understanding of individuality) if he is to pursue the criminal. Yet at the end of the day, it is his work that matters above all else, a point which Holmes makes clear when he recalls Flaubert's statement: "L'homme c'est rien — l'oeuvre c'est tout." ("A man is nothing; it is his work that matters.") This statement is doubly appropriate. Flaubert's point is that the personal details of an author are ultimately irrelevant to the work of art — these personal trifles should interfere neither with the production nor the reception of a work. In other words, art can never be reduced to its author. An artist labors, then, as Holmes suggests, on behalf of the greater "Work," although it is doubtful that the mechanistic reason represented by Holmes is quite what Flaubert had in mind. Moretti expresses similar apprehensions, going so far as to claim that the entirety of the Sherlock Holmes opus "reiterates Bentham's Panopticon ideal," precisely by showing that individual existence is always articulated in terms of social existence.[37]

While it is clear that the classical detective is the perfect figure for the totalizing nature of knowledge and power within a disciplinary society, Moretti claims that it is for this very reason that the detective's lessons must be looked at in askance. In other words, in the detective's brilliant defense of his methods and insight, he protests too strongly, as it were. Again, the context of these stories is the emergence of the modern city, a time of great anxiety as traditional forms of observation and management are challenged. To parry this danger, the detective offers the power of science — as Moretti notes, the frequent appearances of transportation and communication technologies in detective fiction are crucial figures to establish such optimism. Like the trains and telegrams that so frequently connect individuals (and ideas), the detective's narrative will connect all points within the undifferentiated crowd.

The science he represents promises not simply an explanation of one event, but a law upon which all such events might be understood — this is the basis of deduction.

In this way, detective fiction strives to:

> keep the relationship between science and society unproblematic: It creates a problem, a "concrete effect" — the crime — and declares a sole cause relevant: the criminal.... In finding one solution that is valid for all — detective fiction does not permit alternative readings — society posits its unity, and, again, declares itself innocent.... Because the crime is presented in the form of a mystery, society is absolved from the start: the solution of the mystery proves its innocence.[38]

In so doing, the detective unifies society and all its competing mechanisms into one great chain of causality that he sees without interruption. Knowing all possible causes (i.e., laws of nature), it is but a small step to reading their effects. Or so the detective would like us to believe.

It is on this point that Moretti's argument takes a turn that will be of great interest to my current purposes. Moretti concludes that the detective's work is best understood as that of a physician. Holmes is just that: "the great doctor of the late Victorians, who convinces them that society is still a great organism: a unitary and knowable body. His 'science' is none other than the ideology of this organism."[39] Capable of discerning the causes of the minutest of ailments, or symptoms, the detective administers over the body of the social in a bureaucratic and medical sense. He brings science down to the level of common sense and at the same time produces a myth about the grandeur of its functioning. Again, for Moretti, the extreme confidence portrayed in the detective's powers of reasoning is merely a mark of the cultural anxiety that surrounds these issues. Referencing Max Weber on this point, Moretti indicates that science, particularly the emergent "human" sciences, cannot produce a general agreement on the matter of cause.

In this ideological sleight of hand, the status of the clue (or symptom) becomes quite interesting. These are "not facts," as Moretti underlines, "but verbal procedures — more exactly *rhetorical figures*."[40] While we are left to conclude, then, that there is a good deal of rhetoric in the physician's work as well, the greater point to be taken is the rhetorical nature of the detective story. Crime might best be understood as a "semantic ambiguity" that has disrupted "the usual forms of human communication and interaction."[41] The criminal has interjected ambiguity, which must be reversed by the detective. In so doing, he will make certain that words again mean as they should, or that signifiers once more match their signifieds.

Looked at in this way, crime is an apt analogy for literature. Of course, the most basic premise of literature is that its words might mean something else. In this indeterminacy of textuality, there remains a schism between signifiers and signified that cannot be liquidated — even by the great detective. As Moretti suggests, in committing the crime, the criminal "has composed an audacious *poetic work*."[42] The detective's goal lies in the opposite direction — against literature, as it were. However, as Moretti suggests by emphasizing the rhetorical aspects of the "science" of the detective, literature is never so far removed from the detective's occupation.

The Rhetoric of Mastery

To examine more closely these issues of science, rhetoric, and literature in detective fiction, I turn to the celebrated "deduction" practiced by Sherlock Holmes. "The grand thing," as Holmes tells Watson, "is to reason backward," that is, from effects to causes, a process that is "founded upon the observation of trifles," details, or clues (*CSH* 83). When one knows what to look for, there is no event, no cause, that can remain hidden from the detective's eye. A famous figure of such scientific optimism is the paleontologist Cuvier who, Holmes claims, was capable of describing an entire animal by the mere observation of a single bone (*CSH* 225). As Conan Doyle knew well, Cuvier was a fellow traveler of Holmes for a number of compelling reasons. In the early nineteenth century, the French scientist pioneered the fields of comparative anatomy and paleontology. In the process, he authored classificatory systems that encompass all the creatures of the Earth — or so was Cuvier's aspiration.

It is not difficult to understand Holmes' admiration for the scientist. Cuvier understood an organism to be a logically constructed system in which each part contributed equally to the whole. Each piece of the system implied the totality of the system itself, just as the most insignificant clues can betray the most complex plots. Indeed, this is precisely how Cuvier "read" the fossil record to support his systems of classification of life on the Earth.[43] For the scientist, the remains of former species provided invaluable clues to the story of life itself. Both detective and scientist, then, read traces and clues to reconstruct an object or event lost to history.[44] Interestingly, at one point within his 1825 treatise, *Discourse on the Revolutionary Upheavals on the Surface of the Globe*, Cuvier makes reference to another precursor of the detective, Voltaire's character Zadig. Zadig, a young Babylonian scholar, was capable of reading prior events (e.g., the passing of a dog or a horse along a road) by observing minute traces, just Holmes and Dupin did subsequently. Speaking of the explanatory power of his own classification system, Cuvier suggests that a track upon the road reveals not merely what type of animal passed, but all aspects of its physiology. "That mark is more certain than all of Zadig's," he boasts.[45]

A well-known example of this method is found in Conan Doyle's story "Silver Blaze" (1892). The mystery surrounds the disappearance of the famous racehorse for which the story is named, the murder of a horse trainer, and a plot to fix the Wessex Cup. As his investigation is drawing to a close, Holmes remarks upon a detail seemingly irrelevant to the disappearance of the racehorse — the sheep kept near the stables. Apropos of nothing, Holmes asks Colonel Ross, the owner of Silver Blaze, if anything odd had happened to his sheep recently. The owner responds that in fact three of them had gone lame. Inspector Gregory, a local official assisting with the case, finds this detail interesting and asks Holmes if there is any other point to which he should draw his attention. "To the curious incident of the dog in the night-time," says Holmes, to which Gregory responds, "The dog did nothing in the night-time." "That was the curious incident," is the detective's terse response (*CSH* 347).

The conclusion of the story is quite interesting, as Holmes reveals that the murderer of the Colonel's stableman is in fact the horse, Silver Blaze.[46] Through his shrewd analysis of clues that at first glance lead to a more conventional solution (e.g., the trainer had been killed by a rival trainer), Holmes is able to ascertain that John Straker had planned on maiming Silver Blaze and betting against the horse. The proceeds of this venture would then be used to support his demanding mistress. Holmes admits that the curious item of the sheep falling lame was a guess on his part. Straker's body had been found with only a cataract knife (a small doctor's instrument), something that clearly could not serve as a weapon though this was the police's assumption. Suspecting that such an instrument might be used for invisibly maiming the racehorse, Holmes then imagined that Straker would likely practice the task before performing it on Silver Blaze. Hence his question about the sheep falling lame. The curious incident of the dog in the nighttime was, of course, the dog's silence as the horse was originally stolen. As Holmes deduces, "Obviously the midnight visitor was someone whom the dog knew well" (*CSH* 349).

Though Holmes' assumption is logical enough, it remains to be seen how he arrived at this conclusion, as well as the solution to the larger case. Speaking in very general terms, both deduction and induction are types of reasoning used to work with causes and effects. In the case of induction, one reasons from effects to causes, or from occurrences to rules of occurrence. Scientific practice, which views things in the world and then formulates laws that govern these things, is a sound example of this method. Deduction works in the opposite direction. It begins with the rule and concludes the consequence. In other words, deduction works from causes to effects, or from rules of occurrence to occurrences. While Holmes is known as the master of deduction, he uses both induction and deduction throughout his pursuits, and Silver Blaze is no exception. Taking the example of the dog in the nighttime, Holmes begins with an individual occurrence — or rather the absence of an occurrence; that is, the dog's silence as Silver Blaze is stolen. However, to explain this incident, Holmes relies upon the rule dogs do not bark at those they know, or dogs always bark at strangers. The logic in play here is finally deductive; however, to arrive at this deductive conclusion, it was necessary for Holmes to formulate a potential rule governing the incident. To do so, he gathers evidence, hypothesizes rules, and then imagines their consequences. In this way, the "grand thing" is not simply to reason backwards, but to reason backwards then forwards and back again, testing the validity of one's hypotheses along the way. His method is, then, not quite deductive, nor is it purely inductive. Of course, this "not quite" is a large qualification, requiring us to conclude that these "indubitable" methods of reasoning are finally rhetorical.[47] I will take these issues up momentarily.

In "Silver Blaze," Holmes goes so far as to admit that there is always a supplement necessary for his genius — something beyond his knowledge of the incontrovertible laws of nature and society. When Holmes and Watson arrive in Dartmoor to assist Colonel Ross and Inspector Gregory in locating the missing horse, Holmes reasons (long before he arrives) that the horse must still be alive and well in the area. Returning to the scene of the crime — the location on the moor where Straker was murdered — Holmes finds two additional items that he already expected he would find: the remains of a match, and the trail of a horse leading to the stable of a rival horse breeder (*CSH* 343). Regarding the former, the amazed Inspector Gregory admits that he is embarrassed that he overlooked such a thing. However, Holmes suggests that he only saw the match because he was looking for it (*CSH* 343). After finding the tracks of the missing horse (this without the aid of the Inspector or Colonel), Holmes explains to Watson: "See the value of imagination.... It is the one quality which Gregory lacks. We imagined what might have happened, acted upon the supposition, and find ourselves justified" (*CSH* 344). (While Inspector Gregory had hypothesized that the horse had either been killed or removed from the area, possibly by gypsies lurking about on the moor, Holmes offers a much simpler solution: after the murder, the horse sought shelter.) For Holmes, science is necessarily supported by imagination.

During Holmes' explanation of his reasoning after the conclusion of the case, he reveals to Watson that originally he himself had drawn the wrong conclusion from the evidence presented in the newspapers. However, when Holmes arrived on the scene, he was able to correct his misperceptions (i.e., that Fitzroy Simpson, the rival horse trainer was the murderer). His chain of reasoning runs from the curried meat fed to the stable boy on the night of the murder — its strong flavor hiding opium — to a bill found on Straker's body — suggesting the expensive tastes of a woman. As Holmes suggests, "One true inference invariably suggests others" (*CSH* 349). Naturally, the "causal" chain described by Holmes is a brilliant series that dazzles the reader. However, to arrive at this point, Holmes begins with possibilities — not with certainties. Though Holmes is quick to criticize Watson's penchant for literature when chronicling their adventures, it seems that there is an element of fiction in Holmes' own "science" of deduction.

This recalls a similar moment in "The Crooked Man." In this story, Holmes arrives at Watson's house — this after the latter has been married — and immediately remarks that Watson must be doing a great business recently. Explaining his observation, the detective notes that when the doctor's rounds are brief (i.e., when he has few patients), he walks. When he has many patients, he takes a Hansom cab. As the doctor's boots are not dirty, Holmes can only conclude that Watson had been doing a good business of late. Watson admits his usual admiration for his companion's insight, but Holmes, as is his wont, suggests that his trick is actually quite obvious:

> "Elementary," said he. "It is one of those instances where the reasoner can produce an effect which seems remarkable to his neighbour, because the latter has missed the one little point which is the basis of the deduction. The same may be said, my dear fellow, for the effect of some of these little sketches of yours, which is entirely meretricious, depending as it does upon your retaining in your hands some factors in the problem which are never imparted to the reader" [*CSH* 412].

The detective's brilliance is an effect of narrative "emplotment" — in other words, it is rhetoric. Indeed, Holmes goes on to explain that with his current case, he is in the position of his readers. That is to say, he is blindly searching for one or two threads that will pull "one of the strangest cases which ever perplexed a man's brain" together at last (*CSH* 412). Acknowledging this rhetorical aspect of the Holmes adventures, one is reminded of Raymond Chandler's comment: "Sherlock Holmes after all is mostly an attitude and a few dozen lines of unforgettable dialogue."[48] Similarly, Poe himself, in a letter to Cooke, was not shy to make an identical pronouncement regarding the ratiocination of his own detective, C. Auguste Dupin: "These tales of ratiocination owe most of their popularity to being something in a new key. I do not mean to say that they are not ingenious — but people think them more ingenious than they are — on account of their method and *air* of method."[49] Elementary, perhaps, but meretricious nevertheless.

The essays collected in Eco and Sebeok's *The Sign of Three: Dupin, Holmes, Peirce* (1988) offer great insight into this literary aspect of the classical detective's method. Each of the essays in the collection confronts the apparent authority of reason represented in Holmes or Dupin with the American semiotician Charles Peirce's notion of "abduction." According to Peirce, abduction is a form of reasoning that is distinct from induction and deduction: "Abduction is the process of forming an explanatory hypothesis"; "[It] is the step in-between a fact and its origin; the instinctive, perceptual jump which allows the subject to guess an origin which can then be tested out to prove or disprove the hypothesis."[50] Clearly, "guessing" is not compatible with the science of deduction and ratiocination practiced by Holmes and Dupin, respectively. As Holmes avers in *The Sign of the Four*, "I never guess. It is a shocking habit — destructive to the logical faculty" (*CSH* 93). (Apparently, guessing and "imagination," as mentioned in the "Silver Blaze," are quite distinct for Holmes.) Conversely, in abduction, a performative — or literary, as I have been suggesting — element is undeniable. Indeed, abductive logic effectively assumes the cause of a given result "out of thin air." Granted this hypothesis is always carefully, even "scientifically," wagered, but it is wagered nevertheless. Therefore, the imaginative and tentative nature of this activity must inhere. As Peirce summarizes, "Deduction proves that something *must* be; Induction shows that something *actually is* operative; Abduction merely suggests that something *may be*."[51] Abduction is, then, simply a guess (or hypothesis) that explains a given result.

In "reasoning backward," the detective seeks, in abductive fashion, a theory — and, ultimately, an incontrovertible rule — for a given set of contingent facts or clues. As Moretti suggests, the detective is himself a myth that promises that the infinite number of causes and effects might actually be reduced to the simple, contained order of reason. To be sure, Dupin and Holmes gallantly defend the efficacy of this method and its scientific base.[52] Even so, Holmes' claim that "when you have excluded the impossible, whatever remains, however improbable, must be the truth" depends upon an abductive leap of faith that does not so much discover as hypothesize (*CSH* 315). What is truly remarkable about Sherlock Holmes is his skill at making such assumptions. As Sebeok and Umiker-Sebeok conclude, "What makes Sherlock Holmes so successful at detection is not that he never guesses but that he guesses so well."[53] The apparently self-effacing claim that he is involved in is nothing more than "commonsense" rings true from this perspective. What Holmes is doing is providing a theory by excluding the least likely of all causes for a given fact, a daily activity for us all.[54] He is a master at divining *likely* possibilities from minute indexes, such as clay on shoes, the age of boots, the condition of shirt cuffs, and the like. However, because these observed facts are used retroactively to reason back to a rule or principle, and then an individual cause, Holmes is always involved in the guesswork of his readers — a situation that he himself at times admits.

In the end, the detective hermeneutic does indeed demand a doubled relation between the reader and detective, that is, the reader is invited to read like the detective. However, the playing field is far more level than we might at first assume. The reader may aspire to read like the great detective. However, in this aspiration, the reader does not seek absolute knowledge of causes and effects. Rather, the reader wishes to be as skilled in guesswork as the perhaps not-so-inimitable sleuth.

Interestingly, these discussions of abductive reason again raise the question of medical diagnosis and its relation to detective work. However, as the authors Ginzberg and Sebeok and Umiker-Sebeok suggest, medicine and detection are not alike in their scientific objectivity. Quite the contrary, medicine and detection are alike in their shared use of a sort of divination beyond so-called impartiality. Sir Arthur Conan Doyle was, of course, a practicing physician before becoming a full-time writer, and Sherlock Holmes is in large part drawn from Conan Doyle's own instructor, Dr. Joseph Bell. Bell was renowned for his keen ability at diagnosis. More amazingly, while completing medical examinations, the doctor was able to assay a patient's biography from the smallest pieces of information presented in their appearance.[55] Needless to say, this process is identical to the speculation of detection routinely demonstrated by Holmes. While Bell's process was renowned, his brilliance, like that of all physicians at the time, relied upon his ability to engage in "inspired guessing." Without twentieth-century visioning technologies, it was necessary for nineteenth-century medicine to "read" the disease only in its effects. The cause, the "disease" itself, is blindly theorized much like the solution to a mystery. Indeed, just as clues point to an object or an event that can never be made present, so too must symptomatology (i.e., medical diagnosis) read indexes that are not themselves the disease, but rather the result of the disease. As Sebeok and Umiker-Sebeok summarize, "To the extent that the character Sherlock Holmes himself practices the methods of medicine, an element of art and magic is blended into the logic of scientific discovery that he pursues."[56]

Ginzberg reads this "semiotic" (i.e., the reading objects through the proxy of signs and traces) turn in medicine as indicative of a larger "conjectural paradigm" that emerges in the nineteenth century, fueled by power's need to identify its citizens as suggested by Foucault.[57] This notion that "[r]eality is opaque; but there are certain points — clues, symptoms, which allow us to decipher it,"[58] remains at the core of the human sciences, which likewise participate in this greater surveillance project. However, because individual clues and symptoms are used to read larger cultural entities, error and variance will always plague assertions of scientific rigor. This fractured relation between part and whole, or law and exception, necessarily keeps the sciences from achieving the Galilean ideal of a rigorously scientific knowledge beyond the data collected.[59] Such a perspective can know nothing about the individual, if for no other reason than its aims are far greater. That is, science of this variety searches for larger rules governing systems beyond the individual. With the detective, it is just the opposite: the individual can be known entirely. In a sense, we might, then, read the detective as "completing" the project of science itself. The sleuth makes it possible, once and for all, for part and whole to at last be equal — a premise that again recalls Moretti's claim that the detective is essentially a myth about science. Interestingly, Ginzberg and Sebeok and Umiker-Sebeok conclude their arguments by stressing the importance of "intuition" in the abductive reasoning of the detective. Such intuition is always linked to the senses and, therefore, the body. For Ginzberg, in particular, there is a democratizing force here, as this type of knowledge is never restricted to a ruling elite. Further, this links us with other species, taking us beyond the human, as such.[60] Arguing in a similar direction, Sebeok and Umiker-Sebeok emphasize Holmes the "necromancer," to these ends.[61]

To flesh out further implications of the classical detective's scientific mythology, I turn now to Conan Doyle's story "The Red-Headed League" (1891). In this story, the owner of a small pawnshop, Mr. Jabez Wilson, "average [and] commonplace" in appearance, brings forth one of "the most singular" cases Holmes had ever encountered (*CSH* 176). Watson arrives at Baker Street in the midst of Wilson's initial explanation of the story. Holmes asks Wilson to retell the predicament for Watson's benefit, but also for Holmes, as well. As the detective says, "[T]he peculiar nature of your story makes me anxious to have every possible detail from your lips. As a rule, when I have heard some slight indication of the course of events, I am able to guide myself by the thousands of other similar cases which occur to my memory" (*CSH* 176–177). Here again, Holmes is himself "The Book of Life." If he can reduce the mystery (or effects) to his encyclopedic knowledge of causes, all details will be made clear.

Wilson's predicament began when he discovered a curious advertisement in the local paper calling for "nominal" employment within "The Red-Headed League" (*CSH* 181). The story of the organization is told to Wilson by Vincent Spaulding, one of his clerks at the pawnshop. The league was founded by an eccentric American millionaire, Ezekiah Hopkins, who was himself red-headed and had, therefore, a good deal of sympathy for men with hair of this color. After being hired by the league, Wilson is asked to sit daily from ten until two o'clock and copy pages out of the Encyclopedia Britannica. For this task he will be paid the rather large sum of four pounds per week. The duties of this job are obviously quite moderate, but the vocation does come with one curious stipulation: Wilson is required to remain within the league's offices in Pope's Court for the entire length of his shift. If he fails in this, or misses even a single day of work, his position will be lost forever (*CSH* 181).

After learning of his duties, Mr. Wilson becomes sadly apprehensive that the League is a hoax of some kind. Still somewhat curious, and welcoming the money that is potentially to be had, he begins his work copying. During the early days of his employment, Wilson's progress is checked by a Mr. Duncan Ross, a supervisor who stops by the office at regular intervals. As Wilson's work is always found agreeable, Ross's presence becomes less frequent, and then finally falls off altogether. Shortly after this latter occurrence, Mr. Wilson reports to work only to find a sign upon the door announcing the dissolution of the Red-Headed League. Though he makes inquiries for a forwarding address, he turns up little. The superintendent of the office building knows nothing about the league or its activities. However, he does give Wilson the forwarding address of a William Morris, who matches the description of Duncan Ross. As this likewise turns out to be a dead end, the pawnbroker brings his case before Sherlock Holmes.

The recital of this amusing situation is met with laughter from Holmes, though he does agree to take the case for the sake of its unusualness. Reflecting upon the story, Holmes asks about Wilson's assistant, Vincent Spaulding, who had originally noticed the advertisement for the League. It seems that Spaulding had only been employed at the pawnbroker's for a month. Wilson was actually reluctant to take him on; however, Spaulding agreed to work for half the salary others expected. Holmes then curiously inquires whether or not the clerk had pierced ears. The answer is affirmative. With this, Holmes promises a solution shortly, though the case is "a three pipe problem," requiring solitude for reflection (*CSH* 184).

The detective's procedure hereafter is a fitting, if abbreviated, representation of the abductive method described above. Immediately following the initial recitation of the mystery, it is clear that Holmes already has formulated a working hypothesis. As he explains, much to Wilson's consternation, there are possibly "graver issues" at stake than what "might at first sight appear" (*CSH* 183). After considering the case for the duration of "three pipes," Holmes suggests a trip into the city, ostensibly to attend a concert to aid his introspection. On the way, Holmes and Watson visit Wilson's pawnshop to gather data. Holmes excitedly views not only the shop but also the buildings up and down the block surrounding it. In the process, he deliberately bangs his walking stick over the road in front of the shop, finally knocking on the door to ask for directions in order to meet Mr. Wilson's assistant. Watson's typically slow-witted mimicking of Holmes' method leads him to ask about the importance of the assistant to the case. The detective assures him, somewhat dismissively, that it was not the assistant but the knees of his trousers that were of interest. Further, this was a "time for observation, not for talk" (*CSH* 184). Continuing on the way to the concert hall, Holmes remarks that a series of well-to-do shops abut the shabbier square in which the pawnshop is located. After a peaceful afternoon spent at the concert — an important detail that I will take up below — Holmes declares that a serious crime is to be committed that very night, and he and Watson have only limited time to stop its progress.

After dark, Watson and Holmes, along with Mr. Jones of Scotland Yard and a Mr. Merryweather depart for the crime scene. The men briefly discuss the exploits of the evening and engage in a terse yet derisive exchange regarding the relative intelligence of the police — an obligatory detail whenever the classical detective is forced to work with such official agents. In the midst of more casual conversation, the men also happen upon the topic of "John Clay," an accomplished criminal in the London underworld who is still at large. Both the night and the case end in the basement of local a London bank, the Coburg branch of the City and Suburban Bank. (Mr. Merryweather turns out to be the bank's president.) From the meager evidence given by Wilson, Holmes was able to conclude that Wilson's employment in the Red-Headed League was to ensure that he was out of the pawnshop while Spaulding — who is, of course, actually John Clay — and his accomplices tunneled into the basement of a neighboring bank that had recently shored up its reserves. The men lay in wait for the criminals and finally succeed in apprehending them with little fanfare.[62]

As convention demands, there is a postscript to the story that explains the detective's reasoning. Holmes explains to Watson that it was obvious from the first that Wilson's odd employment was to ensure that he was absent from the house for a given period during the day. Watson agrees but still wonders how Holmes so quickly determined a motive. Interestingly, and in support of Van Dine's rules of detection, Holmes mentions the impossibility of a "vulgar intrigue" (i.e., a sexual motive), which was simply "out of the question" as there was no woman in the house (*CSH* 190). After meeting the assistant Spaulding and learning that he was actually dealing with the criminal mastermind John Clay, Holmes reasons that the time spent by this man in the cellar is the key to the case. After imagining all possibilities, Holmes concluded, "I could think of nothing save that he was running a tunnel to some other building" (*CSH* 190). This hypothesis is then proved to Holmes by looking at the pant legs of the aptly named Clay.[63]

The final question that troubles Watson is Holmes' certainty that the crime was to be committed that very evening. Holmes avers that, as the

"League" had been closed, it was clear that the tunnel was soon to be used. If the culprits waited, they risked that their underpass would be discovered, or that the additional bullion within the bank might be moved elsewhere. In addition to this, they would obviously wish to allow optimal time for a getaway before their crime was discovered. So, since it was Saturday, and the banks did not open again until Monday, the band must strike that very night. As Watson concludes, and certainly the reader is here in agreement, "You reasoned it out beautifully.... It is so long a chain, yet every link rings true" (*CSH* 190).

Much like the single fossil uncovered by Cuvier, much can be learned about the structure of the Conan Doyle's version of the classical detective story from this one case. At the beginning of the tale, Holmes claims interest in the case because it is entirely out of the ordinary and, on the surface, resistant to his usual methods which are based upon probability and precedent. "As a rule," claims Holmes, "when I have heard some slight indication of the course of events, I am able to guide myself by the thousands of other similar cases which occur to my memory" (*CSH* 177). In the case of the Red-Headed League this is not possible, we are told, given its singularity. However, this wonderment hardly lasts beyond Wilson's initial telling of the story, as Holmes immediately remarks, "As a rule ... the more bizarre a thing is the less mysterious it proves to be" (*CSH* 183). The detective's method works by making the "bizarre" conform to the rule.

Indeed, the completeness of the detective's knowledge always ensures a reduction of the individual to a type, or category of knowledge. The reader is given a sense of this procedure as Holmes and Watson visit the area behind Saxe-Coburg Square during their trip to the pawnshop. Holmes asks Watson to slow his pace so that he (Holmes) might commit the order of the houses and businesses to memory. As Holmes plainly says, "It is a hobby of mine to have an exact knowledge of London" (*CSH* 185). Here the detective is speaking of geographic and architectural knowledge, but this can be appropriately generalized to all activities and items within the city. The detective's comprehensive understanding reduces even the capriciousness of humanity to a static, chartable knowledge. This ensures the radical determinism that is at the base of Holmes' method. Even the smallest detail can, when "all" possibilities are known, reveal the causal chain in which it is caught. At the end of the story, Holmes claims that the case has saved him from ennui, but he laments, "Alas! I already feel it closing in upon me. My life is spent in one long effort to escape from the commonplaces of existence. These little problems help me to do so" (*CSH* 190). Naturally, it is just the opposite. Holmes actually labors on behalf of "commonplaces" by reducing the bizarre and unordinary to a more mundane object of knowledge. For this reason, Jabez

Wilson's task of copying the Encyclopedia Britannica is hardly incidental, as it figures the work of the detective himself. Wilson complains of the mindlessness of the task, but Holmes congratulates him on acquiring minute knowledge on all subjects found under the letter "A." (Wilson's copying of the encyclopedia only preceded this far before its interruption.) Naturally, the reader can assume that Holmes' own encyclopedic knowledge extends far beyond this. Indeed, as his success in the case indicates, his knowledge is total.

A final detail from "The Red-Headed League" that supports this alleged "total" knowledge of the rationalist Holmes is found in a description of the detective that is a borrowed from Poe. In Poe's first detective story, "The Murders in the Rue Morgue," the narrator famously describes the "Bi-Part soul" of his detective companion, Dupin. The "creative and resolvent" sides of the detective spoken of in that first story are elaborated in "The Purloined Letter" (1844) insofar as Dupin is described as sharing Minister D's talents as both poet and mathematician (*CEAP* 218). At the risk of preempting a later discussion, this bifurcation of the detective's soul is actually what makes him a more astute investigator.

What must immediately strike the reader is the combination of two qualities that seemed irresolvable for the classical detective: calculation and literature.[64] Indeed, in Conan Doyle's repetition of Poe's well-known description — Watson describes Holmes as part "sleuth-hound" and part artist — the former is more a hindrance than an asset. As the doctor writes, "In his singular character the dual nature alternately asserted itself, and his extreme exactness and astuteness represented, as I have often thought, the reaction against the poetic and contemplative mood which occasionally predominated in him" (*CSH* 185). For Holmes, the sleuth-hound rises up in response to the danger of indulgence brought on by the poetic side of the detective's character. Importantly, Watson makes this description while he and Holmes enjoy a concert in London, seeing the legendary Spanish musician and composer Sarasate (*CSH* 185). This figure of the musician/composer is appropriate for a number of reasons. Obviously, an interpretative musician is guided by already scripted compositions and their performance history. However, as a composer, the musician becomes capable of "bending the rules," as it were, and creating the musical text anew. One wonders if "Holmes the musician" is a reaction against "Holmes the composer," as Watson's analogy would seem to suggest. More to the point, the sleuth-hound *and* artist seem to be equally represented in Holmes the "musician and composer"— the aspect that the sleuth-hound was to rise against. This odd repetition of the very characteristic that Watson wishes to pit Holmes against is duplicated again at the end of this description. Watson remarks that the detective's mood swings from "extreme languor to devouring energy" (*CSH* 185). After languishing in his "improvisations and his black-letter editions" for days, we are told, Holmes was suddenly seized with the "lust of the chase" and his "brilliant reasoning power would rise to the level of intuition, until those who were unacquainted with his methods would look askance at him as on a man whose knowledge was not that of other mortals" (*CSH* 185). The pleasure spoken of here, and the description of the detective's method as "intuition" — an abductive term, to be sure — seems again to undercut the very distinction that Waston makes. The Bi-Part soul of Holmes is perhaps more integrated than first assumed.

A final detail to be taken from the story in support of this claim occurs as Watson and Holmes foray into the neighborhood behind the pawnshop on Saxe-Coburg Square. Watson describes this area as presenting "as great a contrast to it [i.e., the adjoining neighborhood] as the front of a picture does to the back" (*CSH* 185). While this is perhaps an idle description given in jest by the Doctor, I wish to take it as emblematic of the relation between literature and reason in the classical detective story. Of course, this passage behind the scenes, from a neighborhood to its underside, is the basic process of detection. The detective sees beyond banal surfaces to the causal mechanisms that occur out of frame, so to speak. This is figured again in the literal "excavation" carried out by Holmes and his colleagues at the end of the story. To catch the criminals, they must go underground. However, Watson's analogy complicates the archeological metaphor that is suggested. A picture has neither back nor depth, just as a literary text has no "bottom," or underground space that might be mined for the ore of deep meaning. In literature, there is only a play of surfaces, a fact that Conan Doyle seems to be aware of when he names his burrowing master criminal John Clay. The name of the criminal gives away his location and occupation long before Holmes has a chance to examine the knees of his trousers. As the Bi-Part soul of Holmes and the analogy of the picture suggest, the classical detective's rhetoric of reason is a literary play of surfaces.

A discussion of scientific determinism and literature within Conan Doyle's Sherlock Holmes is not complete without mention of the curious history of the story, "The Final Problem" (1893). As the title implies, this was intended to be the final Sherlock Holmes story. By 1893, Conan Doyle had already grown tired of the formulaic stories featuring his by then famous detective — fame that ensured that his other work would remain forgotten.[65] Unfortunately, both commercial and conceptual problems ensured that the text failed miserably. However, these failings are quite instructive to my argument. First and foremost, Conan Doyle failed to realize the consuming power of the market demand that had been created for Holmes. When the detective was killed off in this story, the public responded with outrage and disbelief. Letters were sent to the author and his publishers demanding the swift return of the beloved character. These pleas proved to be so persistent that, in the end, Conan Doyle could only relent. The story's conceptual failure is more simple and bold: Conan Doyle had the audacity to work the totalizing assumptions of Holmes' methods to their logical conclusion. The public's ardent fascination with the detective clearly demonstrated that the myth of science that Holmes offered was convincing when worked out in a piecemeal, per case fashion. However, when Holmes promises to rid the whole of Europe itself of crime in "The Final Problem," what emerges is the more disturbing symptom of his Reason.

"The Final Problem" tells the story of Holmes' final encounter with his nemesis, Professor Moriarty and his henchmen. This confrontation promises to be dangerous like no other case before it. In pursuit (and in retreat) from Moriarty, the detective is actually removed from the physical and epistemological safety of his sitting room at 221B Baker Street. However, if successful, his plan promises to rid all of Europe of crime and evil. This broad stroke of justice is possible because the fiend Moriarty is the architect of nearly all of organized crime within the underworld of Europe (and beyond). I will quote at length from the passage describing this endgame. Holmes' assessment of Moriarty, not so much as an adversary but as a concept, is quite revealing:

> For years past I have continually been conscious of some power behind the malefactor, some deep organizing power which forever stands in the way of the law, and throws its shield over the wrong-doer. Again and again in cases of the most varying sorts — forgery cases, robberies, murders — I have felt the presence of this force, and I have deduced its action in many of those undiscovered crimes in which I have not been personally consulted. For years I have endeavoured to break through the veil which shrouded it, and at last the time came when I seized my thread and followed it, until it led me, after a thousand cunning windings, to ex–Professor Moriarty [*CSH* 471].

It is clear that Moriarty functions as a sort of double for the detective. The ex-professor is the only other individual that Holmes deems of equal mettle. A common literary device especially prevalent in gothic literature — that near relative of detective fiction — the presence of the double always guarantees anxiety and threatens disaster, as this figure embodies not only similarities, but also more sinister qualities that at first glance appear foreign to the doubled character. Naturally, such foreign elements are often most intimate to the subject, and this is certainly true of Holmes' Moriarty. Conceptually, the totalizing mechanism that is imagined in Moriarty is a mortal incarnation of the logical convenience assumed by the totalizing knowledge of Holmes. He is the underwriting order of criminality and its deviances, the whole to which all parts in the end refer. In other words, Professor Moriarty is the symptom of Sherlock Holmes' *modus operandi*, which must assume that all crime is knowable through a grand design. He is, then, the principle element that guarantees the consistency of Holmes' character and world.

The structural imperative that the evil professor represents is made all the more manifest in the drama that his presence ensures. Indeed, even before Holmes knows the arch-criminal's identity, the existence of such an individual is already assumed. If Moriarty did not exist, Holmes surely would have had to invent him, a humorous possibility that is explored within Nicholas Meyer's *The Seven Percent Solution* (1974), a novel that stages a meeting between an ailing Holmes and Sigmund Freud.[66] Meyer's portrayal of Moriarty as a kindly old retired professor who has been groundlessly persecuted by the mad Holmes in many ways provides an appropriate assessment of the situation. As Meyer understands well, the unambiguous paranoia in the above quotation is the seamy underside of Holmes' self-described method of deduction.

The relation between Holmes and Moriarty is, then, certainly more uncanny than the former would care to admit. The Professor's intellectual faculties match Holmes to the letter, so much so that throughout "The Final Problem" the two are, in effect, engaged in a game of "odds and evens," the amusement described by Poe in "The Purloined Letter" to figure detection. The player of this game is forced not simply to make moves based upon a single game strategy, but to make moves that take into account the opponent's knowledge of what they will do next. (I will discuss this at length in the conclusion of this chapter.) In this case, Holmes attempts to out-run the Professor and his accomplices to allow enough time for the trap he has set for the criminals to be sprung. This chase will lead the two characters throughout Europe. The pursuit is appropriately made in the figure of nineteenth-century technology *par excellence*: the locomotive. Running along its iron tracks, the train suggests the inevitability of scientific inquiry, as well as the detective's own self-described "science of deduction." In the famous conclusion to the story, Holmes chooses to abandon this waiting game, deciding instead to engage in a hopeless battle with Moriarty alone. Locked in combat that can have no winner, the characters meet their end at the bottom of Reichenbach Falls — a scene so memorably captured in one of the more famous illustrations done by Sidney Paget. Naturally, this is the only possible conclusion to the story, for the moment that Holmes set his infallible trap for Moriarty, likewise was his own doom sealed. This is true quite simply because of their coupling, not merely as doubled characters, but further, as conceptual relays within the practice of knowledge that they represent. If there is no more crime — the possibility promised with the end of Moriarty — there can be no more Sherlock Holmes.

The extremes of the Sherlockian method make it only reasonable that Conan Doyle's detective stories — and perhaps detective fiction in general —

came to be reductively defined as "a literature of reassurance and conformism," as Porter has suggested.[67] This chapter has thus far claimed that such a unilateral reading ignores a significant division within the texts themselves; that is, the so-called science of detection has much in common with the rhetoric of literature — this is a schism upon which even Conan Doyle self-consciously capitalized. In other words, the classical detective has far more in common with the criminal and madness than we might at first assume. (Here, the reader will recall Moretti's assertion that the criminal, working against the law, produces a sort of poetic work with his crime, which offers something "new" beyond convention.)

In the remainder of the chapter, I will turn to the work of Edgar Allan Poe, the reputed father of detective fiction. As my presentation of Conan Doyle suggests, I hesitate to read the Sherlock Holmes stories as a strict gentrification of the detective form as developed by Poe. That being said, Poe's work deals more directly with the linkage of science and art that I suggest is found (more often implicitly) within Conan Doyle's detective stories. This is perhaps not surprising given Poe's gothic inheritance, and his interest in madness that consumed him until his own mysterious death in 1849. In comparison with Conan Doyle, Poe was perhaps more attentive to the complications of the detective fiction formula and its methods. This focus, here at the "origin" of detective fiction, makes the claim that the genre is a transparently ideological, and therefore a straightforwardly "conformist," enterprise far more difficult to defend.

Ratiocination: What Doesn't Permit Itself to Be Read

A genealogy of the development of the detective within Poe's work most often begins with a discussion of "The Man in the Crowd" (1840), a well-known story that was published immediately prior to the author's detective stories.[68] This tale depicts the alluring chaos met by the individual living in the new metropolis, placing a particular emphasis on the dangerous obscurity at the margins of the city (i.e., slums). In the essay "On Some Motifs in Baudelaire," a work that offers an elaboration of Poe's story, Walter Benjamin cites the original context of the detective story as the loss of the individual and the haunting anonymity of the crowd in this new urban space: "Fear, revulsion, and horror were the emotions which the big-city crowd aroused in those who first observed it. For Poe it has something barbaric; discipline just barely manages to tame it."[69] However, for Poe and Benjamin, the cruelty of the city is not to be dismissed outright. On the contrary, as is the case for the narrator of Poe's story, the crowd remains an object of fascination that enlivens the heart of the observer.

As "The Man in the Crowd" begins, the narrator is watching the evening crowd pass before a café window. He entertains himself by expertly categorizing the passers-by according occupation, class, and errand. This talent is the hallmark of the *flâneur*, a figure that emerges with the modern city in direct response to the inhuman pace of the mass. The *flâneur* is an aristocratic observer, having no other occupation than passively taking in the sights of the city while strolling about the streets, out of step with those he views. As Benjamin suggests, the *flâneur* must always be disconnected from his surroundings. He is a philosophical meanderer without goal.

Leaving aside the aimlessness of this pose, the ideological assurances of such acts of reading are by now familiar. The narrator renders the chaos of the evening crowd legible by dividing and defining its component elements. As he begins this task, the narrator describes his viewing as taking "an abstract and general turn," through which he reduces the crowd to "their aggregate relations" (*CEAP* 475–76). However, this dispassionate stance quickly becomes more interested as his attention focuses on the "details" of the masses, that is, "the innumerable varieties of figure, dress, air, gait, visage, and expression of countenance" (*CEAP* 476). In a gothic fashion typical of Poe, it is when the narrator feels most "at home" in his method that a specter haunting his system of interpretation emerges.

In "The Man of the Crowd," such a ghost appears when the narrator's gaze is captured by a singular old man with a face of "absolute idiosyncrasy" (*CEAP* 478). Incapable of being reduced to one of the many classifications of the narrator's knowledge, the old man literally disrupts the narrator's reading of the crowd. Yet this illegibility is not for a lack of signification. The narrator states, "As I endeavored, during the brief minute of my original survey, to form some analysis of the meaning conveyed, there arose confusedly and periodically within my mind, the ideas of vast mental power, of caution, or penuriousness, of avarice, of coolness, of malice, of blood-thirstiness, of merriment, of excessive terror, or intense — supreme despair" (*CEAP* 478). Indeed, the enigma of the old man is the result of a surplus of signification.

Seized by the mystery of such uniqueness, the narrator imagines,

> "How wild a history," I said to myself, "is written within that bosom!" Then came a craving desire to keep the man in view — to know more of him. Hurriedly putting on an overcoat, and seizing my hat and cane, I made my way into the street, and pushed through the crowd in the direction which I had seen him take; for he had already disappeared. With some difficulty I at length came within sight of him, approached, and followed him closely, yet cautiously, so as not to attract his attention [*CEAP* 478].

This passage is worth quoting at length as it plainly marks the interpellation, or calling, of the narrator *as* a detective. His observation begins as a sedate diversion that enjoys the distance and safety afforded by the café window through which he views the crowd. However, as he turns his attention to *details*, more exacting clues that promise more sophisticated designations, he is pulled into the crowd itself.

Thus begins the work of the detective, although at this early stage of development, it is clear the investigator is not up to the task. Poe emphasizes this fact in the dubiousness of the narrator's self-proclaimed acuity. His skills as an observer are recounted with frequent mention of his "peculiar mental state" that apparently is the result of a recent illness (*CEAP* 478). This condition, and the "garish luster" of all things under the light of the gas-lamps, immediately compromises the veracity of the scene recounted. With this reported illness as pivot, there remains, then, a disunity between the *flâneur-*narrator's observations and the scene surveyed (*CEAP* 478).

The strangely isolating effects of the crowd underscore these misapprehensions. In other words, when the narrator enters the crowd, he feels the same "solitude on account of the very denseness of the company around" that he formerly observed in others (*CEAP* 476). The likelihood of understanding the mass — or the old man who figures its mystery — is quite unlikely, for the individual has no place there in the throng. Naturally, the narrator will do his best to reduce the enigma to the codes of his narrative, as was his method behind the café window. This occurs, for example, when the now frantic narrator swears that he catches the glimpse of a "diamond and of a dagger" beneath the old man's cloak (*CEAP* 478). However, the old man's status as a romantic villain — or hero — cannot be verified. Reason remains unable to penetrate the mysteries of the city and the individual.

Poe's scrutiny is all the more clear in the famous conclusion to the story. Finally exhausted from following the man throughout the evening and on into the following day, the narrator surmises: "This old man ... is the type and the genius of deep crime. He refuses to be alone. *He is a man of the crowd*. It will be in vain to follow, for I shall learn no more of him, nor of his deed ... and perhaps it is but one of the great mercies of God that '*er lasst sich nicht lesen*' [It does not permit itself to be read]" (*CEAP* 481). In his detective-like reductions of the world to simple categories of representation, to knowable types, the narrator must relegate the unknown man to the class of the anomalous. His case, in other words, remains unsolved. Importantly, it is his very singularity — his greater individuality — that disrupts the narrative. Given this singularity, the old man becomes "a man of the crowd," that is, the unknown that precipitately threatens the order of the city. Any such enigma must be read as criminal, a fact that suggests that the mercy spoken of by the narrator must be understood at the level of epistemology. It is, as he says, one of God's mercies that reading cannot penetrate here. Were the aporia of this unknown man allowed its full repercussions, his entire system of categorization would be in ruins (i.e., if it is possible for one case to deviate, why not another?).

The epigraph to the story, taken from La Bruyere's *Characters*,[70] sheds light on these issues of individual, enigma, and illumination. As the text reads in translation: "All men's misfortunes spring from their hatred of being alone." Obviously, this statement speaks to an inescapable solitude. However, this seems to contradict the narrator's conclusions about the old man at the end of the story. As the former indicates, the old man "refuses to be alone," and it is because of this that nothing can be known about him. Given the narrator's comments and behavior, only isolation from the crowd makes an individual readable. To be known is, in effect, to be alone. While Foucault's work suggests that this procedure is a function of disciplinary mechanisms that are designed to reduce multiplicities to individuals, we might take Poe's conclusion in a more general sense. Knowledge allows us to categorize our relations with others and the world around us. However, of necessity, knowledge at the same time bars a union with other individuals and the larger community because it must organize the world by abstract terms that betray singularity. We are capable of producing knowledge about any number of things, but this will never bring us closer to our fellow human beings. Read in this way, La Bruyere's statement seems to suggest that if we recognized this impasse, it would perhaps spare us some misery.

As the narrator is first drawn into the crowd through his detective-like deliberations, he clearly wishes not to be alone, to belong. In other words, the *flâneur*-narrator wishes to establish a knowable connection with his surroundings. However, by the time the story concludes, the narrator has come to understand that what the enigmatic old man represents cannot be breached by knowledge of any kind. Beyond that line is the madness that he calls "criminality." Incapable of knowing others apart from this individuating process, the narrator's hermeneutic process fails to bring him any closer to his neighbors. He remains alone. I would go so far as to argue that such a misunderstanding remains at the heart of the detective genre itself. For the hard-boiled detective, this loneliness will become an orienting experience.

In Dana Brand's reading of this story, it is only with the emergence of Poe's detective, C. Auguste Dupin, a reader whose abilities surpass those of the *flâneur*-narrator, that this failed reading of the city is corrected.[71] The detective is capable of reading the multiplicity of voices of the city, as well as the multiplicity of interpretative perspectives this space requires. As Brand emphasizes, though the detective remains an absolute master capable of solving the mystery of "urban experience itself," his story at the same time provides an invigorating encounter with the "shock and dislocation" of the city.[72]

While I agree with much of Brand's argument, in my own reading of Poe, I would like to emphasize the "shock and dislocation" that reverberates well beyond Dupin's mastering the city through the synecdoche of the crime.[73]

Unlike the average Sherlock Holmes story, Dupin's solution to a crime never seems to delivery the peace of interpretative conclusion. Indeed, the efficacy of producing identity through the solution of a crime is often beside the point in Poe's detective stories. For example, in "The Murders in the Rue Morgue," there is in fact no "who" that did "it." On the contrary, the crime committed by the escaped orangutan is entirely random, and therefore incalculable, at least according to "motive." In "The Mystery of Marie Roget," the multiplicity of accounts of the murder do not keep Dupin from arriving at a hypothesis. However, the story ends only with the detective's hypothesis. The actual identity of the murderer is not given, although the reader is told in an "editor's note" that "the desired result [i.e., solution] was brought to pass" (*CEAP* 206). Nevertheless, without an unmasking, the criminal remains, effectively, nameless "criminality." That much the reader knew at the beginning of the case. In a final note appended by the author, he warns that his fictional account of an actual murder (that of Mary Cecilia Rogers) cannot be taken as instructive.[74] He intends no parallels between real life and fiction, a telling admission to be sure. Finally, in "The Purloined Letter" the "who" is known from the beginning, leaving all exposed and, thereby, the whodunit form inoperative. Suffice it to say, in each story, Poe is quite deliberately equivocating the very concept of "mystery." If, as Benjamin claims, the origin of the detective story lies in the anxiety surrounding the loss of the individual's trace within the city — presumably making the charge of the genre the *re*-inscription of the individual — then Poe's work does little, if anything, to dispel this anxiety.

This fundamental undecidabilty found within Dupin's short case history immediately distinguishes this detective's methods from those of Holmes. In Poe, an aspect of the irrational inevitably accompanies every successful act of "ratiocination," Dupin's term for his investigative methods. In distinguishing this practice from Holmes' "deduction," Harrowitz is quite right to call attention to the sense of *process*— much like an artistic process — that inheres within the etymology of "ratiocination." This sense of progressive construction speaks to a tentative seriality that is unavailable to the more totalizing Holmesian hermeneutic, the "science of deduction."[75] Dupin certainly reasons abductively, but when compared to his famous successor, there seems to be an excess in his method that remains unaccountable.

This comparison is illustrated well when considering the two descriptions of the inherent contradictions within Dupin and Holmes. As described above, for Watson, the "dual nature" of Holmes is an ongoing battle between artistic and logical forces — the former always threatening to outrun the latter. For Dupin, it is quite different. In "The Murders at La Rue Morgue," Poe's narrator discusses the "Bi-part Soul" of Dupin as a way to come to terms with the eccentricity of Dupin when engaged in the study of mental puzzles. To quote the famous passage, "His manner at these moments was frigid and abstract; his eyes were vacant in expression; while his voice, usually a rich tenor, rose into a treble which would have sounded petulant but for the deliberateness of the enunciation" (*CEAP* 144). Given these states, the narrator imagines a "double Dupin" whose "Bi-Part Soul" is composed of both "creative" and "resolvent" elements (*CEAP* 144). For Dupin, there is a complimentary relation between these elements that is not found in the dual nature of Sherlock Holmes. Holmes' split soul provides little insight into his methods. On the contrary, its duality must be overcome by reason if the detective is to be effective. Admittedly, this characterization differs throughout Conan Doyle's opus, and Priestman has gone so far as to argue that the apparent confusion on this point represents the paradoxical requirements of both "reproducibility and uniqueness" within emergent serial literature.[76] But within the Poe stories, it is clear that the detective does not succeed in spite of this division. Rather, he succeeds because of it.

Dupin's Bi-Part Soul is elaborated upon in "The Purloined Letter," Poe's final detective story featuring Dupin. As is well known, the story presents the detective's recovery of the stolen letter of the title. The culprit, Minister D—, is known as the guilty party from the beginning. Thus, the real mystery becomes the location and recovery of the letter. The story devotes considerable time to descriptions of the police's methods of investigation. Though they have searched the Minister's apartments twice with great care, they cannot find the letter in the apartments or in the Minister's possession. A great criminal and intrigant, he is clearly a match for the police who, already per convention, have a tendency to remain rigid in the methods. As Dupin says, the Prefect (the head investigator) "perpetually errs by being too deep or too shallow for the matter at hand" (*CEAP* 215). Rather than adapting their methods to the specificity of an individual case, the police vary their methods only in intensity. They merely "extend or exaggerate their old modes of practice, without touching the principles" (*CEAP* 216). The police see only what they are prepared to see, and this is exactly why they are blind to the purloined letter. They assume that it must be hidden.

At the base of the Prefect's misjudgment of the Minister's cunning is the assumption that the Minister must be a fool because he is a poet. On the contrary, as Dupin explains, the Minister is both a poet *and* mathematician, and he is all the more menacing because of this. Following conventional wisdom espoused by Watson in "The Red-Headed League," the narrator claims that poetic skills would only hinder the process of cold, disinterested analysis. Against this perception, Dupin adamantly maintains that abstract truths cannot be taken for *general* truths (*CEAP* 218). When dealing with abstract space in which the boundaries between two bodies are finite, determining relations between entities is straightforward enough. Here, Dupin gives the example of a mathematical equation. However, when these abstract truths are applied to relations in the real world (e.g., morals), it is no longer possible to arrive at definitive conclusions. Dupin describes this impasse in terms of parts and whole, the very terms that Holmes will use to describe the perfection of his own method in comparison with the scientist Cuvier. Against such mediation, Dupin suggests that in human enterprises, "it is very usually *un*true that aggregated parts equal the whole" (*CEAP* 218). To imagine that the aggregate parts of the world equal an ideal whole is effectively to fall into the realm of myth, just as Moretti argued.

To these ends, Dupin mentions the common anthropological practice of assuming the validity of fables and folklore. Though the pagans themselves did not believe in these mythical stories, anthropologists "make inferences from them as existing realities" (*CEAP* 218). The dogmatic notion that mathematics is the highest form of knowledge is in a sense to believe the pagan fable of algebra. Unlike mathematics, in ratiocination, two plus two does not always equal four. As Dupin summarizes, "two motives, each of a given value, have not, necessarily, a value when united, equal to the sum of their values apart" (*CEAP* 218). Naturally, the point to be taken is that abstract knowledge does not necessarily correspond to the reality it purports to explain — despite what mathematicians or their defenders may claim.

While unreflective rationalists (the police, for example) may believe in such a calculable order to the world, the Minister D— and Dupin, as poet *and* mathematician, escape this blunder. Their poetic side offers insight into the constitutive nature of fiction in actuality. In a related context, Dupin explains: "The material world ... abounds with very strict analogies to the immaterial; and thus some color of truth has been given to the rhetorical dogma, that metaphor, or simile, may be made to strengthen an argument as well as embellish a description" (*CEAP* 219). The mathematician's claim that actual things in the world correspond absolutely to abstract truths is false, to be sure. However, the poet realizes that analogies with the "beyond" are necessary. Indeed, the poet understands that common opinion takes the pagan fables as truth, as it were. In other words, the poet is attentive to the rhetorical structuring of all experience.

This "poetic" knowledge is the basis of Dupin's methodology, which is based upon an often uncanny identification with the criminal. To "get into the head" of his adversary, the detective will attempt to think like a criminal, a trope that is of course all too familiar within the detective genre. In "The Murders in the Rue Morgue," the narrator begins his tale with a discussion of the differences between calculation and analysis. Calculation is based upon the measure of finite variables, whereas analysis engages the infinite possibilities of human motive and intellect. To elaborate, the narrator compares the game of chess with whist. Though chess is often assumed to be a crowning achievement of the intellect — much like the study of mathematics — the game merely tests the player's concentration. There are several possible moves in a game, but this number is always finite. In comparison, whist has an infinite number of "moves" as players are always engaged in analyzing not only what an opponent shows, but also what an opponent hides. In other words, the whist player is forced to consider his partner's method (or strategy) of play, which is itself always a method of deception. To these ends, "the analyst throws himself into the spirit of his opponent, identifies himself therewith, and not unfrequently sees thus, at a glance, the sole methods (sometimes indeed absurdly simple ones) by which he may seduce into error or hurry into miscalculation" (*CEAP* 142). The analyst does this by observing everything — not simply the "game" alone. Expressions, gestures, conversation, responses to success and failure, the handling of cards. These are all details that might be made useful to the whist analyst, as he looks for moments when an opponent's strategy is betrayed. Because of this, the game goes far beyond rules. As Sherlock Holmes suggested, the detective — or "analyst" — must have a powerful imagination. Poe's narrator concurs, affirming "it is in matters beyond the limits of mere rule that the skill of the analyst is evinced"; he concentrates both on the game (and its rules), as well as signs beyond these limits (*CEAP* 142).

In "The Purloined Letter," the analyst's skill of identification is further developed in Dupin's description of the clever schoolboy's expertise at the game "odds and evens." This schoolyard game is played simply by guessing whether the number of marbles held by the opposing player is odd or even. If one guesses correctly, the prize is the adversary's marbles. As there are but two "moves" in the game, strategy depends entirely upon determining how duplicitous a given opponent will be. For example, if an even number of marbles is used upon the first turn, the question becomes whether the opponent will then utilize a simple variation on the next turn and hold an odd amount. The player must take into consideration the other's knowledge of this simple variation and may choose to do just the opposite of what is expected, or perhaps even opposite of this expectation, *ad infinitum*. Interestingly, too clever a strategy seems to leave a player with no strategy at all.

When the clever school boy is asked about his unmatched success, he responds, "When I wish to find out how wise, or how stupid, or how good, or how wicked is any one, or what are his thoughts at the moment, I fashion the expression on my face, as accurately as possible, in accordance with the expression of his, and then wait to see what thoughts or sentiments arise in my mind or heart, as if to match or correspond with the expression" (*CEAP* 215–216). Much like Holmes' conclusion in "The Resident Patient," our thoughts are transparently written upon our faces. Indeed, Poe's example seems to go further and suggest that not only thoughts, but also our very soul is made visible in this way.

However, though this similarity inheres, I would argue that the methods the detectives use to "read thoughts" are not identical. In Poe's story, we are told that the success of the identification fundamental to this process depends upon the "admeasurement" of the challenger's intellect. This anachronistic term actually helps to clarify the topic at hand. A glance within the OED offers the following definition: "To assign a measure or limit to (a thing), to keep in measure; to moderate, limit, control," and likewise is the sense of "apportionment," "to assign each claimant his rightful share," apparent within the term.[77] Both the detective and the marble-winning boy are clearly involved in assigning claimants their rightful share, and they measure in the spatial and numerical senses of the term. In so doing, they likewise moderate, limit, and control. However, given Poe's linkage of the poetic and mathematical, it is certain that this analysis far exceeds the act of counting or measure. Indeed, I would suggest that this surplus is in fact essential to identification as it is described in Poe's story. The clever schoolboy does not "identify" in the manner usually expected, that is, by reducing another to the self. Thus difference becomes sameness through the categories of thought and expectations — an ever-present danger as Poe had already suggested in "The Man of the Crowd." This is of course the mistake of the police whose "non-admeasurement" reduces the Minister's intellect to their own. They erroneously assume that the Minister would hide the letter, which is of great value, in a deep recess. In other words, they assume him to behave according their principles of behavior. The schoolboy, as his technique is described, avoids this mismeasure by reversing the process. He makes himself identical with his opponent. He becomes another.

To be sure, there remains something mystical in this assessment of one's opponent. To "throw oneself" into the spirit of one's adversary, "to identify himself [fully] herewith," comes far too near subjective erasure, or the utter loss of self. Insofar as this practice of identification is to be taken as the *modus operandi* of the detective, he very clearly succeeds in becoming criminal himself. In this practice, the self is lost to another — something neither the police nor Sherlock Holmes could abide. Holmes' power, for example, is predicated upon the careful boundaries through which he maintains a discrete notion of the self. While the reader is admittedly never given a consistent content of Holmes as a person, it is nevertheless necessary that he remain distanced from the scenes and subjects he surveys. Only with the benefit of such limits is it possible to imagine oneself a master.

The equivocation of the boundaries between the body and intellect suggested here are equally as disquieting. The identification described by Poe's narrator is largely visceral in nature. It is an embodied knowledge, in that the boy *feels* what his opponent is thinking. These intuitions are won by first mimicking the facial expressions of his opponent. When this is done, he will "wait to see what thoughts or sentiments arise in my mind or heart, as if to match or correspond with the expression" (*CEAP* 216). The boy's gaming decisions are then made accordingly. There is certainly an intellectual identification at work here, one that importantly stresses the dubious process of metaphor, or the way in which knowledge operates by establishing equivalences between objects (or individuals). Significantly, in Poe's demonstration, this is mediated through the unknown of the body. He "feels" what his opponent will do next, but this is not quite the "knowing" of Sherlock Holmes. In the end, we are left to assume that it is this mediation of the irrational (i.e., bodily) insight that works so well for both Dupin and the boy. With reason thus eschewed, Poe's detective in several respects remains a sort of conjurer, as his romantic affinities would imply.[78]

The gulf between the methods of Dupin and Holmes that I have been describing is incontrovertible when one compares the following telling moments of disguise. In "The Purloined Letter," Dupin succeeds in recovering the lost missive of the story's title when, behind green-tinted spectacles, he calls upon the Minister D—. Having arranged for a diversion to occur outside the windows of this apartment, Dupin waits for his adversary's attention to be drawn to the street below. The detective then carefully replaces the stolen letter, which is hidden in plain view, with a decoy. In this way, he repeats the initial scene of the story (i.e., the original theft of the letter) and thereby becomes a criminal himself. Indeed, Dupin cannot avoid the temptation of signing the facsimile he leaves in place of the original letter in such a way that the Minister will know who has bested him.

Two notable comparisons in the Holmes opus immediately present themselves. In the first case, "A Scandal in Bohemia" (1891), the scene just described from "The Purloined Letter" is repeated in corresponding detail, no doubt in homage to Poe. In Conan Doyle's tale, it will be remembered that a lower-class upstart named Irene Adler is blackmailing the King of Bohemia with a photograph of the two together, which was taken during their recent, chaste affair. As the King is about to be married, he naturally wishes for the photograph to be returned as quickly as possible. Disguised as a clergyman, Holmes visits Adler and, like Dupin, arranges for a disturbance in the street. This is done according to the rather misogynist assumption that "When a woman thinks that her house is on fire, her instinct is at once to rush to the thing which she values most" (*CSH* 173). True to form, as is the point, Holmes' ruse works. However, the reconnaissance operation is not successfully followed by a second visit of recovery, as was true for Dupin. After the disturbance of Holmes' visit, Adler realizes that she has been duped and makes arrangements to leave London. The result is one of Holmes' famous failures.

It is certainly not incidental that Holmes is defeated by a female, and it is for just this reason that she comes to occupy such a prominent place in Holmes' libidinal economy. Women remain beyond the limits of the science of deduction. They are "naturally secretive" and mercurial, qualities exemplified when Adler comes — naturally, in disguise — to Baker Street to wish Sherlock Holmes a good night near the end of the case (*CSH* 171; 173). Though he had tricked her into betraying the hiding place of the photograph, Adler has the final word. In "The Adventure of the Second Stain" (1904), Holmes makes his complaint more explicit. As he laments: "And yet the motives of women are so inscrutable.... How can you build on such a quicksand? Their most trivial action may mean volumes, or their most extraordinary conduct may depend upon a hairpin or a curling tongs" (*CSH* 657). Nevertheless, Holmes is not immune to the charm of this feminine irrationality. At the conclusion to "A Scandal in Bohemia," he forsakes a large reward and asks the king only for the photograph of Adler. As Watson says in the very first line of the story, "To Sherlock Holmes she is always *the* woman" (*CSH* 161).

Though critics frequently read Holmes' easy manipulation of women, particularly of the lower classes, as representative of the violence and misogyny of his deductive method, this case seems to provide an alternative insight. As biographical details indicate, Conan Doyle was fascinated by limits of the rationalism that he himself helped to popularly disseminate. Irene Adler, "*the* woman," names the limit of that which can be known by reason, a conclusion that is, as we shall see, entirely amenable to psychoanalytic theory. In keeping with my distinction between the methods of Holmes and Dupin, it cannot be accidental that this story depicting the limits of Holmes' knowledge makes explicit reference to Dupin's success. Dupin outwits the womanly Minister D— whereas Holmes fails utterly in reading the woman. This leaves Holmes to conclude — admittedly, in a somewhat insincere fashion — that women and literature are the province of his colleague, Dr. Watson.

A second case that helps to distinguish the methods of Holmes and Dupin is Conan Doyle's story "The Adventure of Charles Augustus Milverton" (1904). The title is clearly a play upon the name C. Auguste Dupin, and the story itself lampoons the more suspect aspects of identification that I have been describing. Like the Minister D—, Charles Augustus Milverton is the "king of all blackmailers" (*CSH* 572). The story begins with a familiar prologue in which Watson explains the singularity of the case that is about to be told. However, this narrative platitude is here appropriate. In this story, Lady Eva, who is shortly to be wed to the Earl of Dovercourt, employs the services of Holmes to recover a series of indiscrete love letters that she had written before her engagement. Milverton arrives at Baker Street to negotiate a price for their return. When negotiations quickly break down, Holmes becomes uncharacteristically enraged, turning "gray with anger and mortification" (*CSH* 574). Out of sorts, Holmes goes so far as to attempt to forcibly detain Milverton while he searches him for the desired letters. The villain's protest explains the situation all too well. He admonishes Holmes for his forceful response, saying that he had hoped for "something [more] original" from the great detective (*CSH* 575). Indeed, in this action the detective has repeated the idiocy ascribed the police in "The Purloined Letter" by assuming that the letters must be hiding in an obvious place.

Presumably frustrated as never before, Holmes goes so far as to establish a false relationship with Milverton's housemaid, so that he might continue the investigation. He boasts to the astonished Watson that he has in fact become engaged to this woman, an extreme measure that he rationalizes as necessary given the pressing circumstances. As he explains in his typically cavalier fashion, "You can't help it, my dear Watson. You must play your cards as best you can when such a stake is on the table" (*CSH* 576). With the housemaid as his unknowing accomplice, Holmes plans to burglarize Milverton's home and retrieve the letters himself. It should be noted that even in "A Scandal in Bohemia," Holmes never intended to pilfer the compromising photograph. After ascertaining its location, he planned to return again with the King to bargain more forcefully for its restitution. This proposal of larceny is, then, absolutely unprecedented within the case histories.[79] The extremes of Holmes' plan is reflected in Watson's initial horror: "As a flash of lightning in the night shows up in an instant every detail of a wild landscape, so at one glance I seemed to see every possible result of such an action — the detective, the capture, the honoured career ending in irreparable failure and disgrace, my friend himself lying at the mercy of the odious Milverton" (*CSH* 576). From this description, it is clear that the possibility of Sherlock Holmes becoming criminal, even if this were in service of justice in the end, is absolutely unthinkable. Indeed, this conclusion is quickly magnified as the story takes a comedic turn.

It could be argued that the comedy begins when Holmes attempts to assure Watson that he is "never precipitate" in his actions, despite the extremes of his current behavior (*CSH* 576). The detective adamantly maintains that there is simply no other way to recover the letters. Because this is to be done on behalf of a lady, Holmes argues, both the risk and the illegality of the enterprise are pardonable. Watson, against his friend's protests, insists on accompanying Holmes, as in this case the master "can't tell what might happen" (*CSH* 576). In this venture he is out of his element — and, as in "The Final Problem," out of the sitting room at Baker Street. Attempting to quell Watson's anxieties, Holmes' professes, "I have always had an idea that I would have made highly efficient criminal" (*CSH* 577). This comment is a fitting preface for the comedy that follows.

A considerable portion of the burglary becomes a sort of misadventure, containing several slapstick elements. Upon first intruding into the house, Watson is nearly scared to death by a docile housecat. When the two "burglars" finally make their successful escape through the garden, Watson lags behind and is nearly apprehended by the gardener. The good Doctor initially professes to experience a "keener zest" in breaking and entering than he had ever felt while working on the side of the law (*CSH* 578). However, this zest is explained in the following sentence as belonging to the higher, "unselfish and chivalrous" character of their mission (*CSH* 578). The possibility of taking pleasure in becoming criminal is in the end the excitement of a doddering old man out to do a (unique) good deed.

The story takes an equally strange turn when Milverton enters the room in the middle of the robbery, forcing Watson and Holmes to hide behind the characteristic large velvet curtains of the country home. The tone now becomes that of melodrama as a woman enters from the garden, apparently keeping a preordained meeting time with the criminal. This woman turns out to be a former victim of the blackmailer posing as a chambermaid with compromising letters to sell. Apparently, her husband's heart had succumbed to the stress of the scandal that had followed the publication of her own indiscretions. After revealing herself, she promptly returns the favor, emptying a small revolver into Milverton's chest. The woman remains unknown until, at the end of the text, Holmes finally identifies the face he had only seen briefly in the dark. To reveal this to Watson, the two walk to a shop in Regent Circus displaying photographs of prominent families. Pointing to a photo of the bejeweled wife of a now deceased nobleman, Holmes puts his finger to his lips to swear Watson to secrecy.

The story is potentially very interesting as it depicts a woman willing to take violent revenge into her own hands. Similarly, the two adventurers choose, with great conviction, to operate outside the law they have vowed to uphold. Here again, at this limit of the law, they again encounter a woman scorned. However, this is sufficiently moralized, and quite literally supervised by Holmes and Watson, so as to limit the scope of the woman's deed. Unlike "A

Scandal in Bohemia," the woman in this case remains unnamed, and is respectfully pardoned by the two men. Her deed is ultimately just, and her social status further ensures discretion. The "disclosure" of her identity through the photograph seems to indicate a projected idealization that is quite similar to the position of Irene Adler. Though the conclusion of the story seems to show — somewhat dismissively — Holmes' expertise in containing the deadly (epistemological) potential of the woman, the comedic telling of his attempt at masquerade underscores his more conspicuous limitations.

The Detective and the Analyst: Psychoanalysis, Identification, and the Trauma of the Letter

I would like to turn now to the question of psychoanalysis and detective fiction to address these limits of interpretation that emerge in the classical detective — in Holmes and potentially Dupin, as well. As I will argue, this is appropriate for a number of reasons. Certainly, the historical contiguity of these two discourses, each rising to prominence during the latter half of the nineteenth century, makes this reading necessary. This analogy is likewise compelling given the similarity of the investigative and analytic techniques of the detective and analyst, as criticism has so frequently demonstrated. Each practitioner, it is argued, focuses upon the seemingly insignificant details found in clues and symptoms and, through these, reveals the cause of pathology — be this criminal or illness. However, this correlation is all too frequently spoken of in terms of the interpretative mastery that the conservative readings of the detective presented above espouse. To these ends, the detective and the analyst become mediators of the status quo, demanding the adaptation of the individual to "things as they are." While this is perhaps true of certain types of therapy, psychoanalysis does not ask individuals to become better adapted to the world around them. Quite the opposite, in fact. Psychoanalysis confronts the individual with the impossibility of this reconciliation. As has been demonstrated throughout this chapter, the classical detective's interpretative power is not quite so seamless, or indubitable, as it may at first appear. Much like psychoanalysis, then, classical detective fiction, particularly when read through the model of Poe, suggests as often as not that knowledge matches the world only with the greatest difficulty.

I will address these issues that surround the detective-analyst analogy through the work of the French psychoanalyst Jacques Lacan. His reading of the "The Purloined Letter" has an illustrious history within literary criticism, inspiring a number of responses from other academics, many of which have become famous in their own right.[80] Interestingly, Lacan turns to Poe's story during a time when his ongoing seminar takes up the topics of traumatic memory and identification in analysis. The "thought reading" of Dupin's clever schoolboy becomes quite important to this discussion, and will, ultimately, serve as a figure for discussing the very notion of interpretation in psychoanalysis. Before turning to Lacan's "Seminar on 'The Purloined Letter,'" I would like to discuss the psychoanalytic conception of the uncanny as it relates to scientific inquiry and, importantly, Lacan's understanding of the "subject."

In his brilliant essay "I Shall Be with You on Your Wedding Night," Mladen Dolar describes the emergence of the Enlightenment's own uncanny double — its Moriarty, as it were — through a reading of *Frankenstein: Or, the Modern Prometheus* (1818). Shelly's acclaimed novel suitably marks the transforming position of the uncanny as it shifts from the province of the supernatural to "objective" reality, revealing in this way a "specific dimension of the uncanny that emerges with modernity."[81] As the author explains, gothic fiction, with its sundry ghosts and monsters, exhibits all too well the specters of uncertainty that will haunt the Enlightenment project. As its founding texts reveal, what this project sought most generally is the mechanization of all conceptions of life itself (from the biological to the psychological and sociological). The stake of detective fiction in this Enlightenment project is clear enough. Throughout such work — what will become the human sciences — there is a fascination with the linkage between matter and spirit, or nature and culture.[82] The "monster" of Shelly's text is the very object sought in this process as it marks the "point where the spiritual would directly spring from the material."[83] The monster, then, is that zero point before life becomes "bound," to follow the Promethean thematic, by culture.[84] In this way, it inhabits the space of first "cause," that original point in the great chain of being, much as Moriarty does within "The Final Problem."

In this regard, the unnamed monster is literally the embodiment of the Enlightenment's object of inquiry. Nevertheless, it remains unrecognized by the culture (i.e., its representative, Dr. Frankenstein) that gave it birth. It is the structural aspect of this dilemma that is, for Dolar, the mode of the uncanny that is particular to the Enlightenment. The peculiar position of the monster as both outside and inside the discourse of science — that is, it is the goal of this project, yet it is shunned all the same — speaks to the epistemological impasses that arise at this moment. The uncanny, or that mystery beyond knowing, is no longer openly recognized, as was perhaps the case when the doctrines of theology and the occult held greater commerce with the "unknown." However, this erasure is of course never total, as the presence of Frankenstein's monster attests. The repression of the uncanny by the insurgent rationalism of the Enlightenment ensures a violent return of the repressed. This mechanism explains the peculiar position of the "monster" as both goal and prohibition, for it is in the very method of the Enlightenment — a method, as we have seen, typified by detection — that these "new" monsters return. In seeking to drive all mystery from its field, the Enlightenment succeeds in producing its own limit as monstrous.

The interpretative productivity of Shelley's monster is undeniable, and thus seems to bear out Dolar's claim that this novel is indeed a foundational text of the modern era. Certainly, there is no critical discourse that cannot embrace the monster as a vicious return of what culture would otherwise like to forget. But, as Dolar is quick to qualify, a psychoanalytic reading of the novel ought to take an entirely different approach. Rather than engaging the monster as a forgotten content (e.g., society's repression of women or the working class), Shelley's fiend should be understood as the structural limit of interpretation itself. As Dolar writes:

> Psychoanalysis doesn't provide a new and better interpretation of the uncanny [or Frankenstein's uncanny monster]; it maintains it as *a limit to interpretation*. Its interpretation tries to circumscribe the point where interpretation fails, where no "more faithful" translation can be made. It tries to pinpoint the dimension of the object in that tiny crack before different meanings get hold of it and saturate it with sense, the point that can never be successfully recuperated by the signifying chain. In other words, psychoanalysis differs from other interpretations by its insistence on the formal level of the uncanny rather than on its content.[85]

Psychoanalysis, then, does not offer the individual a definable content, or ascribe a meaning to the symptom. In this sense, the monster, insofar as it embodies the structure of the uncanny, does not mean anything. Rather, it marks the limits of meaning, as such.

To anticipate a later discussion, I would suggest that the "object" spoken of here by Dolar is what Bruce Fink has called the "object-cause" of the subject.[86] (I will address the difference between the "individual" and the "subject" momentarily.) As the Peircian readings of detective fiction suggested, the possibility of ascribing a "cause" for a given effect is always dubious at best. On this score, psychoanalysis is in complete agreement. In fact, in *Seminar XI*, Lacan suggests "there is only cause in something that does not work."[87] This statement calls attention to the flimsiness of determining cause retroactively through knowledge — the great promise of the detective. This is the process, as Dolar describes, of "different meanings" getting hold of the uncanny object-cause and then attempting to "saturate it with sense." The analysand — and perhaps the detective, as well — makes the mistake of assuming that such knowledge somewhere exists. We might understand this "somewhere" according to the Lacanian concept of the big Other, which can be described as the realm of language, culture, tradition, and, importantly, authority and knowledge. This Other can be embodied by any number of "others" (parents, teachers, lovers, etc.); however, none of these figures ever adequately fleshes out the promise that the Other holds — that is, complete knowledge of the subject.

For example, in analysis, the patient assumes that their most intimate meaning is contained within the knowledge of the Other represented by the analyst. The Other, in this way, possesses knowledge about the subject's "cause" (i.e., the cause of suffering) — so the patient assumes. Just as there is always someone else responsible for the analysand's anguish (e.g., parents, spouses, coworkers), so too is it assumed that there is meaning elsewhere that might explain this suffering. As Dolar's account of Frankenstein's monster suggests, the greater horror is found when one acknowledges not only that one's uncanny monsters (or symptoms) cannot be explained by the Other's knowledge, but, more traumatic still, once reconciled to this limit, the patient must accept responsibility for this fissure between experience and meaning — rather than ascribing blame elsewhere. In this, the subject becomes its own "cause" by identifying with this very abyss that is present in the object (as cause).

To better understand this complex notion of the object-cause, I would like to refer to Freud's essay on the uncanny and discuss its relation to Lacan's "mirror phase." In the former, Freud displays the lexical coincidence, at a certain point in etymology, of the apparent German antonyms *heimliche*, the "at-home" or the familiar, and *unheimliche*, the "not-at-home" or that which is concealed. This coincidence of opposites is succinctly expressed in Schelling's definition of the term, which Freud cites: "According to him everything is uncanny that ought to have remained hidden and secret, and yet comes to light."[88] The uncanny is, then, an experience of the intimate as foreign, yet also the foreign as intimate. Indeed, it is the sort of short circuit between these two poles that accounts for an experience of the uncanny. Again using Shelley as an example, this is of course Dr. Frankenstein's reaction upon seeing "his" child. One can imagine the successful achievement of his goal (i.e., the creation of life) would be comfortably recognizable. However, though the monster certainly is familiar, he is all the more appalling because of this, and Frankenstein will spend the bulk of the story attempting to stave off encounters with his hideous progeny.

This unending wavering of the intimate and foreign will be read by Lacan as the very foundation of the subject. As there is no term for the "uncanny" within the French language, Lacan coins the term *extimité* (or, extimacy) to describe this structure. In an early account of the subject's emergence, "The Mirror Stage as Formative of the Function of the *I* Function, as Revealed in Psychoanalysis," Lacan focuses upon the specular aspects of identification through which the subject will come into being. As he explains, identification here is to be taken in its "fullest" sense, that is, "the transformation that takes place in the subject when he assumes an image" that is foreign to him.[89] Naturally, this is not to say that there is an image that is proper to the subject, for there is no subject as such before this initial misunderstanding, or *méconnaissance*, of identification. The subject becomes a subject by mis-recognizing itself in the image — be this the image in the mirror, the image of the caregiver standing over the crib, etc. Because it can never be equal to that Other found in the image of the mirror, the subject turns to the Other to fill this gap.

It is for just this reason that psychoanalysis speaks of the "subject" rather than the "individual." The latter term possesses the complex baggage of the Enlightenment that assumes that consciousness is transparent to itself, a notion emblematized in Descartes' *Cogito ergo sum*, I think therefore I am. Study and knowledge, such a position maintains, can help a person to become a better individual, aware of thoughts and motivations. On the contrary, psychoanalysis begins with the assumption that the "I" is another, which is misrecognized in an image. The "individual" is thus "subject to" this foreign image — and, therefore, subject to the Other — making self-transparency a misplaced notion, to say the least.

The essay on the mirror phase is helpful for understanding two of the three registers of the subject described by Lacan, the symbolic and the imaginary. (The third register, the Real, will be taken up in subsequent chapters.) The imaginary register is suggested in the wholeness of the mirror image itself. In that image, it is possible for the subject to imagine that it is complete — and, presumably, completely meaningful. Thus, the mirror provides a sort of idealized self-image toward which the subject is always striving. Unfortunately, the subject's experience cannot coincide with such completeness. We are never whole unto ourselves, requiring unending exchanges with others and the Other. We can understand the Other in this case as the symbolic order of the subject. Again, the Other is the realm of language, culture, authority, tradition, etc. In a vain attempt to flesh out its mirror image, so to speak, the subject adds language or other objects of culture to itself. This is done first by becoming fluent in language itself (i.e., when the child learns to speak), which is of course always the acquisition of the "foreign" language of the parents or caregiver(s). However, objects of language and culture are taken up throughout life's journey.

From the psychoanalytic perspective, this is always in part done to fill the more fundamental lack of the subject — that split that keeps the subject from equaling its mirror image. A consumer product, a higher education, or even a lover is always potentially the "it" that might finally offer completion. Taking the example of higher education, this "object" reveals all too well how this appeal to the Other at the same time binds the subject to the desire of the Other. In this search for the correct object, the subject asks, "What does the Other want from me?" which is to say, "What does the Other desire?" If the subject can determine this — by giving the parents a college-educated child, for example — wholeness might at last be won. Of course, such additions are to no avail, as the very notion of a lost wholeness that might be recovered is an effect of the subject's entrance into the symbolic order. There is no "before" this time because there was no subject before the misrecognition of itself in the mirror image — and the language of the Other. As Lacan summarizes, the ego is thus situated in a "fictional direction that will forever remain irreducible for any single individual ... no matter how successful the dialectical syntheses by which he must resolve, as *I*, his discordance with his own reality."[90] The intimacy of the "I" remains irreducibly foreign, then, as it is constructed in an alien language that promises — but never delivers — the fiction of authenticity.

It is not surprising that Freud relies on a literary device for explaining the uncanny effect of the intimately foreign image of the double. In his essay, Freud uses Rank's theory of the double to address the uncanny aspects of E. T. A. Hoffman's story "The Sandman." Summarizing Rank, the double is "originally an insurance against the destruction of the ego," whereby the infantile psyche essentially creates a "self" in reserve through the narcissistic creation of the figure of the double.[91] The logic at work here is in essence that of the mirror phase. The subject comes into being by imagining (or mis-recognizing) itself as another. Such "doubleness" is marked within literature in a variety of ways, but Freud calls attention to Hoffman's penchant for transferring thought processes between "two" characters, such that, "his self is confounded, or the foreign self is substituted for his own — in other words, by doubling, dividing and interchanging the self."[92] As readers of fantastic or gothic literature know well, the appearance of the double ensures destruction, leaving identity and reason utterly "confounded," as Freud suggests.

Far from being mere fictional exaggeration, this experience is actually a trenchant summary of the aspect of the double's most significant lesson: In the image of the other, the self (or ego) is lost. This explains Freud's claim that when this double is met later in life, it becomes a "vision of terror," or a "ghastly harbinger of death."[93] We might think of this in two ways. When the double appears, the logical sleight of hand at the subject's origin is revealed. Similarly, the emergence of the double results in the subject's mirror image being made "whole." The subject is built upon a constitutive lack that must be maintained. Without this split or gap, the subject is eradicated. Thus, the emergence of this other "me" reveals that the "I" has always already been epiphenomenal. Again, this is precisely how the unnamed monster of Shelley's text functions. Its uncanny presence discloses the contradictions at the heart of the world that gave it life by completing that world. In this way, that which should have remained hidden does indeed come to light.

As the nineteenth century drew to a close, the criminal joined the ranks of such menacing phantoms. The uncertainty and potential violence contained within these malefactors became an exceptionally powerful representation of the uncanny within popular fiction of the time. Naturally, the detective fared far better than his precursors in his confrontation with such figures. In Poe's detective tales, a gothic influence — and therefore a proximity to the uncanny — remains evident, a fact that complicates a conservative reading of Dupin's method, as I have been trying to suggest. With Conan Doyle, following Poe over forty years later, there can be no commerce with such legacy. Indeed, *The Hound of the Baskervilles* (1901-1902) is in many respects a defeat of gothic preoccupations by the scientific detective.[94] One could go so far as to claim that the basic premise of the Holmesian method — and his successors — is to quell the eruption of the uncanny by combating it in its various guises during the late nineteenth and early twentieth centuries. Certainly, there is some Gothic pleasure in the disjointed narratives shared by Holmes' clients. However, in the end, the masterful detective explains each recalcitrant moment of uncertainty. Yet, even to the intermittent reader, it is clear that there is a monstrousness that is at the same time produced in Holmes' expurgation of mystery. Examples of this range from the detective's drug addiction to the automaton that he himself becomes when "seized" by inspiration. Professor Moriarty must also figure prominently here, but it is clear that the monstrousness in this case is not the criminal's, rather belongs to Holmes himself.

To conclude this chapter, I would to take up these issues of the uncanny structure of the subject through a reading of Lacan's infamous "Seminar on 'The Purloined Letter.'" As is often noted, Lacan regarded this essay important enough to begin the French version of the *Écrits* (his collected writings published in 1966), making it the only essay in the volume to appear out of sequence. While this text certainly offers a development of much of what has been argued thus far, it remains to be seen whether or not Lacan himself was an adherent of the detective-analyst analogy.

Before beginning, it is perhaps wise to establish what Lacan is not doing with Poe's text. In his writings and seminars, Lacan's first task is always the training of analysts. In the seminar on Poe's text, he very clearly wishes to distance himself from literary criticism, particularly psychobiographical literary criticism, which always reads literature as a pathological construction of the author. If we can understand the symptoms of the author, we can understand the work, and vice versa. Such an approach takes an author's frailties as the "key" to her or his fiction, a reductive endeavor that was frequently practiced by Freud.[95] Repudiating such an approach, Lacan will interpret neither author nor fiction. Indeed, Lacan actually makes it a point to suggest that the choice of mystery fiction is not motivated by what might seem the obvious reasons, namely, the suggestion that the detective's work is like that of the analyst. As Lacan reminds, "In truth we should be right in judging that fact highly dubious as soon as we note that everything which warrants such mystery concerning a crime or offense — its nature and motives, instruments and execution, the procedure used to discover the author, and the means employed to convict him — is carefully eliminated here at the start of the episode."[96] In other words, there is in effect no mystery in Poe's story, making it a poor representation of illumination won through interpretation. Quite apart from the drama represented at the level of narration, Lacan wishes to read a second drama, which can be distinguished from the first as "persisting in the symbolic order" (*SPL* 34). To phrase this another way, in "The Seminar on 'The Purloined Letter,'" Lacan describes the way in which Poe's story might be read to emphasize the "decisive orientation which the subject receives from the itinerary of a signifier" (*SPL* 29). In other words, the way in which the subject is other through its determination in the Other. Again, as Lacan has already suggested, this has very little to do with a hidden meaning (of subject or mystery) revealed through brilliant interpretation.

Though Lacan claims that he is uninterested in Poe's story as a work of detective fiction, it is clear that the numerous uncanny aspects of Poe's tale make it all the more suited for his purposes. More specifically, the topic of Lacan's seminar at the time he first presents this work is repetition and memory, and the story obviously provides a perfect "case" for just these issues.[97] To these ends, "The Purloined Letter" will demonstrate the role of the "letter"— or signifier — in the construction of the subject, as well as within analytic treatment. The tale is the perfect figure for the vicissitudes of the signifier because it produces effects without a content. (Here, the reader will remember that the content of the purloined letter is never revealed in the story.) These effects are in turn organized according to a three-part structure that is itself thrice repeated each time the letter changes hands. The letter's grasp of the subject functions to demonstrate the way in which Lacan's notion of the letter is a function of the unconscious — that uncanny determinant of the subject. As the letter circulates among the various characters of the story, then, it plays the role of the unconscious: "It is his unconscious with all of its consequences ... in the symbolic circuit, each of them becomes someone else."[98]

To begin, it is necessary to understand what Lacan intends when he reads the letter of Poe's story as a signifier. For Lacan, a signifier is never a sign that clearly signifies a meaning to someone. A signifier is rather the (empty) structure that makes such an operation possible — though not definitively so. At this stage in Lacan's writing, the letter acts as the "material support" of the signifier, making the two concepts roughly identical. Serving as the "material support" of the signifier, the letter allows that the "signifier, by its very nature, always anticipates meaning by deploying its dimension in some sense before it."[99] In this way, meaning and the letter "insist," despite the fact that neither "consists" in any one particular signification.[100] This notion of the signifier as the empty structure of signification draws in part from the work of the Swiss linguist Ferdinand de Saussure. In his well-known *Course in General Linguistics* (1916), Saussure made the following claims about the signifier: 1. There is an arbitrary relation between the signifier and the signified (e.g., between "tree" the word and the green leafy entity that exists in the outdoors); 2. The signifier has no inherent value, that is, its meaning is determined by its difference in relation to other signifiers (e.g., the word "cat" has value as "cat" only because it is not "mat," "rat," "bat," etc.).[101] This relational value, and the potential of meaning, occurs only when signifiers are bound with others in a signifying chain. However, the final meaning of a signifier in a chain is never definitive, as this moment of "conclusion" (i.e., final meaning) is effectively displaced along the symbolic chain, which is structurally bound to all other signifiers in this system of difference. The purloined letter of Poe's story gives us a sense of this (necessary) incompletion. Even at the end of the story, Dupin's return of the letter to the Queen (via the Prefect) does not result in a "conclusion" (or terminus) that allows the meaning of the letter to be revealed to the reader. (That critics continue to discuss this story, as well as the whirligig of critical interpretations of this story, already suggests that such a possibility is misplaced.)

 Lacan suggests that the repetition of the letter is a type of memory, but it is unconscious, and therefore uncanny, in the strictest sense. To put this a different way, there is nothing "human" about this combination of signifiers that goes on repeating itself quite independently of the individual. It is for this reason that Lacan describes the unconscious as the discourse of the Other. The signifiers that circulate within that space behave in their own fashion, as even the most innocent parapraxis reveals. In the various supplements, or "Suites," published to "The Seminar on 'The Purloined Letter,'" Lacan produces an incredibly complex mathematical analysis of the development of three- and four-term series (or signifying chains) to illustrate these symbolic determinations of the subject.[102] The point of these exercises is to show how restrictions arise *ex nihilo* from the signifying chain itself. By combining the various terms, "a syntax is produced which allows certain combinations and prohibits others."[103] This simplest example of this is the tossing of a coin at random and then grouping the results together in pairs, resulting in a rudimentary symbolic chain. Three variations arise: 1. heads — heads; 2. heads — tails; and 3. tails — tails. When arranged in overlapping pairs, it is not possible for the tosses represented by number 1 to be followed by a number 3, nor can a 3 be followed by a 1. (Keeping in mind the second value of the first pair becomes the first value of the second.) The point to be taken is that the symbolic chain, or the unconscious, "remembers" the items within the series produced, and thereby maintains the strictures of its phantom syntax.[104]

As Fink indicates, this is not "memory" in the sense that we would ordinarily understand it, that is, it is not a "possession" of the ego. However, neither does the unconscious itself have anything to do with the ego, save for marking it with its interruption. There is "knowledge" of the signifying chain, but neither is this the subject's property: "This kind of knowledge has no subject, nor does it need one."[105] In *Seminar II*, Lacan describes this as an "acephalic" (i.e., headless) knowledge: "[T]he subject is decentered in relation to the individual. That is what *I is an other* means."[106] It is this "knowledge" that takes possession of the subject in moments when the repressed returns and the subject's determination by the signifying chain emerges presents itself. This is one of the intentions of Lacan's statement "a signifier is what represents the subject to another signifier."[107] In other words, the subject is an effect of the signifier.

This "headless" knowledge of the signifying chain is exactly what is encountered in Poe's story, according to Lacan's reading. The absence of meaning or content does not keep the letter from having very real effects on the subject, a fact that the queen, the minister, and perhaps even Dupin each learn in turn. In their "intersubjective" relations — that is, each subject is determined by the position of the others — the various characters of the story each fall into one of three positions that circulate around the empty letter. This is the symbolic chain of the text. The first position is blindness that looks for the letter in the real world, like the police or king. As the story reveals, the former are easily fooled when the letter is hidden in plain view, as they imagine that something precious would always be hidden. The second position sees the blindness of the first and makes use of this fact to hide the letter. The queen and the minister alternately occupy this position. Finally, the third position sees the first two positions and uses this to its advantage. The minister and Dupin are found here — and perhaps their critics, as well.[108] As the letter circulates among its various possessors, each falls into a position of blindness as they are effectively "possessed" by the letter. The apparent "objectivity" of the third position offers little refuge, even for Dupin who feels the need to let the minister know who has bested him by signing the letter with a quotation from Crébillon.

These positions might be taken as the varying levels of the subject: the first, the subject in the "real" world (i.e., the physical world, not the Lacanian "Real"); the second, the imaginary, which sees and imagines that the other is exactly like the self; the third, the symbolic, which provides a space outside the simple identification of the second position. Like the failure of the mirror image, the imaginary level is disrupted through the letter's repetition, which is to say that the imaginary register of the subject is disrupted by its symbolic determinants. This provides an interesting comment upon Dupin's method as previously outlined. Recalling the above discussion of "admeasurement," the trick of the clever schoolboy, based as it is upon identification, remains stuck within the second position. This position is, then, prone to the blindness that results from the circulation of the letter. The boy identifies himself with his opponent, but he does not account for the possibility of his opponent doing the same to him. In his reading of the odds/evens game, Lacan calls this "egomiming," in which the "subject adopts a mirror position, enabling him to guess the behavior of his adversary."[109] While Lacan admits the analogy effectively offers a touch of romance to the story, in the end, it is not a plausible method of interpretation, and certainly could not have offered Dupin the solution to the letter.[110]

Acknowledging this limit, the question then becomes, where is the analyst's position in respect to the letter? And how does the analyst escape from getting caught within its circuit? Likewise does the question with which I began this section still stand; that is, is the work of the detective and psychoanalyst similar for Lacan? To address these issues, I would like to take a small detour through the work of Slavoj Žižek.

In his *Looking Awry: An Introduction to Jacques Lacan Through Popular Culture* (1991), Žižek describes the symbolic determination of the subject in a presentation devoted to the classical detective. Here, the author argues that detection and analysis share a similar methodology in that each strategy of interpretation operates by resisting the interpretation suggested by a given object. At the crime scene, for example, a clever criminal will not simply remove all traces of his actions. He will leave false clues that will lead the police investigation in other directions — the so-called "false solution" that is so frequently present in the detective story. Žižek's claim is that this red herring is absolutely essential to the classical detective story and is in fact the basis of its appeal. Like the analyst reading a dream, the detective is not deceived by the completed "picture" of the crime scene, that is, the interpretation this scene in all its details (or clues) suggests. But neither does he attempt to find the "hidden truth" of the text by interpreting its details in hopes of finding a hidden meaning. To do this would be to fall into the idiocy the police, who are often fooled by such false lures.

What the detective and analyst see is not simply the odd object that stands out at the crime scene (e.g., a chair moved from its original position) or in the patient's discourse during an analytic session (e.g., a suggestive dream). They see the desire that such a text, already overdetermined by interpretation, implies. Making use of a Lacanian term found in our previous discussion, Žižek claims, "The truth lies not 'beyond' the domain of deception, it lies in the 'intention,' in the intersubjective function of the very deception."[111] Because of this, the clue (or symptom) must be isolated from the meaning that it imposes on the reader. It is through this ruse that the criminal (or patient) dissimulates. Again, the "truth" of a case is not found through an act of interpretative archeology that "uncovers" a hidden solution. Such a process suggests, using another metaphor at the heart of nineteenth-century epistemology, the removal of ore from dross. Rather than discarding this disguise (or dross), the detective and the analyst push this deception to the point of "self-reference," that is, "to the point at which it becomes obvious that its sole meaning consists in the fact that (others think) it possesses some meaning."[112]

To put this another way, what the detective and analyst analyze is not the consistency of a given text. Rather, they examine the intent (on the part of the criminal or analysand) to produce an image of such wholeness via the symbolic order, or in the register of meaning. As Copjec has phrased this strategy: "The detective does not refute the belief that the criminal author reveals himself completely and exclusively in his criminal works; he simply, but critically, denies that the evidence itself can account for the way it gives evidence. There is a gap, a distance, between the evidence and that which the evidence establishes, which means that there is something that is *not* visible in the evidence: the principle by which the trail attaches itself to the criminal."[113] A symptom or a clue is then never an entrance into another world of sense. Rather, they reveal the subject's desire to maintain that such sense exists. The difference may appear slight, but here again Poe's story is instructive. Because the police imagine that the letter must be hidden — like the "hidden" meaning assumed in the imaginary — they are incapable of seeing something hidden in plain view. Quite distinct from this approach, we might say, then, that both detective and analyst read at the level of the signifier rather than at the level of meaning.

As Žižek goes on to suggest, this inquiry occurs through the space of the transference that is opened in both the analytic session and the detective story. In transference, the patient assumes that the analyst possesses the secret knowledge of the symptom. Because this relation always circulates around the issue of knowledge, Lacan defines the analyst's position as the "Supposed-Subject-of-Knowing."[114] When reading a classical detective story, the reader in similarly entranced. In this transferential relation, the detective is the very seat of knowledge. His presence ensures the possibility that all apparently random "clues" will be made sense of, at least retrospectively. This is very similar to the position of Todorov and other critics of the genre who argue that the detective makes the traumatic core of the story narratable through plot. As Žižek points out, in detective fiction, this very typically occurs through the production of a scapegoat. When the criminal is discovered all the remaining *dramatis personae*, characters who had every reason to wish someone dead (no doubt the reader should be counted among these, as well) are allowed to have their desire without, effectively, "paying the price" for it.[115] However, it is at this point that the analyst and the detective part ways. While the classical detective unmasks a criminal, thereby absolving all others of guilt, the analyst does just the opposite: The analyst "confronts us precisely with the price we have to pay for the access to our desire, with an irredeemable loss."[116] In other words, rather than redeeming the subject from its stake in desire by producing a figure of totality (i.e., a mystery solved with everything returned to its rightful place), the analyst confronts the analysand with its own ineradicable division. In the first instance, the uncanniness of the crime is safely contained; in the second, the subject is challenged with its own uncanny structure.

This provides a good deal of insight into the meaning of Lacan's statement at the end of the "Seminar on 'The Purloined Letter,'" "a letter always arrives at its destination" (*SPL* 53). Derrida's critique of Lacan's reading of Poe centers around this issue of apparent destiny. Against this, he argues instead for the indeterminacy of literature that never arrives at an authoritative point of meaning. In response to Derrida, Žižek claims that the letter actually shows the paradox of teleology, an argument that he takes up using the three registers of the Lacanian subject: the imaginary, the symbolic, and the real.[117] A useful pivot here is Barbara Johnson's equally as famous entrance into the debate in her essay, "The Frame of Reference: Poe, Lacan, Derrida." Her response to this question of predestination is, simply: the letter always arrives at its destination because the letter's destination is wherever it arrives.[118] At the imaginary level, we see this in the misrecognition of the subject in the mirror image. In this case, the subject assumes it is the addressee of the letter (or image), but this "destiny" is only true after the contingent letter has been mistaken as necessary. Žižek describes the symbolic implications of the letter as revealing the "blind spots" of this misrecognition in the imaginary. These occur when the image of wholeness suggested in mirror identification is shown to be lacking.[119] Here, Žižek gives the example of applied psychoanalysis within criticism. In literary criticism of this variety, a text might be "unified" according to the Oedipus complex, or similar construction, as this is played out in the life of the protagonist — and perhaps the author, as well.

The letter returns "when we experience the utmost futility of this procedure, its utmost failure to touch the inherent logic of its object."[120] The letter arrives at its destination within the symbolic register, then, as a sort of "slip" or "success through failure."[121] In this instance, the psychoanalytic insight actually occurs in the failure of the application of psychoanalysis.

The relentless letter is perhaps more easily articulated within the register of the real. The Lacanian real is the space beyond the signification of the symbolic or the unity of the imaginary. Here, death must rank above all other examples. Indeed, as discussed above, detective fiction is in many ways an attempt to make sense of the meaninglessness our death must always be for ourselves. Our death can never be given an adequate sign, leaving us to content ourselves with the sleuth's piecemeal work at providing such meaning. However, as Žižek reminds, life is likewise foreign to the symbolic order, life taken here as enjoyment or *jouissance*. I will discuss this concept in greater detail in the following chapter, but suffice it to say that *jouissance* implies both pleasure and an alien, even painful, enjoyment that is never "possessed" by the subject—precisely because it cannot be symbolized, and thus grasped by knowledge. The letter as a mark of the Lacanian real is, then, the enjoyment that inheres within the symbolic order, contaminating sense. Consequently, Lacan will refer to *jouissance* with the *objet a*.[122] While this object has a number of guises in Lacan's work, here we might read the subject's object-cause and *jouissance*—each of which remains beyond articulation—as coinciding. Though described previously in this chapter, it should be noted that Lacan had yet to develop the concept of the *objet a* (or object-cause) at the time of "The Seminar on 'The Purloined Letter,'" an anachronism also noted by Žižek. This will become important to my subsequent argument.

The analytic praxis that is suggested in Lacan's reading of the letter depends upon the repetition of the symbolic register of the subject. Through this, the analyst disrupts the analysand's imaginary notions of wholeness with the symbolic coordinates that have produced this fiction. In this way, the intimate "meaning" of the subject (e.g., "I am this or that") is shown to be a construction made from the foreign language of the symbolic order. Through this, it will be possible to change the subject's relation to this order and alleviate symptomatic affliction — at least partially. In keeping with the insights of "The Purloined Letter," the analyst will *not* achieve this by giving the analysand an interpretation that offers meaning (or cause) to suffering. That is to say, analysis does not offer a meaningful content to the analysand's letters. Meaning stands quite apart from the signification that Lacan is here demonstrating. As Fink explains, quoting from Lacan's *Seminar XI*, "Interpretation brings forth an irreducible signifier, 'irreducible, signifying elements'.... What must be glimpsed by the analysand, beyond the meaning inherent in interpretation itself, is 'the signifier—which has no meaning, and is irreducible and traumatic—to which he, as subject, is subjective.'"[123] The subject is forced to confront the essential meaninglessness of those signifiers that formerly held him captive. Only after this might he take responsibility for the pathology that explained just this servitude.

It may be helpful to introduce the distinction between "knowledge" and "truth" as these terms are used by Lacan.[124] This distinction has much to do with his notion of understanding as an impediment to analysis; that is, analysts fool themselves by understanding "too much." As Lacan says in *Seminar II*, "One thinks one can do a good therapeutic analysis if one is gifted, intuitive, when one has made contact, if one puts to work the genius which each person deploys in an interpersonal relation."[125] In trying to "understand" the patient in this way (i.e., as an individual transparent to analytic paradigms), one is assured of missing the mark, precisely because this form of therapy stays in the realm of meaning. From this position, the analyst attempts to produce "knowledge" that exhaustively reads the symptoms of the patient, providing these with a fixed meaning. Thus, knowledge understood in this way seeks to adequately and accurately explain reality.

On the contrary, "truth," as it is understood by analysis, speaks to impossibility of such definitive meaning or illumination. This was in part Lacan's intention when he said, in *Television*, "I always speak the truth. Not the whole truth because there's no way to say it all. Saying it all is literally impossible: words fail."[126] The point to be taken is that, as speaking beings, we are always in the process of encountering the limits of our knowledge, and thereby our own subjectivity, if for no other reason than knowledge production always requires additional signifiers, *ad infinitum*. As Nobus has written, "The Lacanian truth emblematizes no more and no less than the very absence of definitive truths within human existence, owing to the fact that not all knowledge can be subjectified, that the enjoyment of fullness is forever excluded, that the symbolic law of castration compels (neurotic) subjects to desire until the end of their days."[127] What one encounters here is a structural "truth" based upon the lacking subject, which in the end is beyond interpretation that promises knowledge. Analysis thus works on behalf of truth rather than knowledge, curiously using interpretation to avoid the production of meaning.

If this is the goal of analysis, and "The Purloined Letter" is to teach us something about this practice, it seems clear that the most crucial question at the conclusion of the story is Dupin's escape from the "intersubjective triad" that will require, in turn, that he be reduced to a position of blindness (*SPL* 50). The detective is seized by the letter, if only for a short time, as Lacan indicates, suffering all the "feminizing effects" of such a position, before the epistle is sent back along its course. Thus removing himself from the triad as quickly as he entered, he turns the "medusoid face" of the signifier to the reader (*SPL* 51–52). This relation of the feminine and the letter (beyond the register of meaning), insofar as it relates to sexed identity, is a complex issue that I will address more directly in Chapter Three. In the current argument, I will read this "femininization" more simply as a mark of the passivity of the subject before the letter. Again, the subject does not possess the letter; rather, the letter possesses the subject.

In her brilliant reading of the Lacan-Derrida debate, Barbara Johnson claims that Dupin is cognizant of this emptiness of the letter. He seems to be capable, much like the analyst, of interpreting this truth without recourse to knowledge. This is not to say that Dupin discerns a content within the letter, or that he "understands" the letter in the sense that Holmes would conclude a case of his own. Rather, what Dupin understands is the letter in its effects — quite apart from its content — and with this insight he is capable of manipulating the misrecognition of the minister, by carrying out the repetition of these effects to his own ends. Rather than engaging in a straightforward act of identification to outwit his opponent, Dupin, much like the analyst, will instead confront Minister D—with the structure of repetition that is the letter. It is not so much that he knows what to "look for"; rather, "he knows what to repeat," and thus he escapes simple "egomiming" that Lacan identifies with imaginary identification.[128] Johnson's summary is especially useful for my current purposes: "Psychoanalysis is not the interpretation of repetition; it is the repetition of the *trauma of interpretation.*"[129] With this emphasis upon absence, Dupin does not seem to suffer from the delusion of "possessing" the letter, which is the height of "imbecility" of the master, figured by the king and the police, respectively (*SPL* 50).

Nevertheless, the danger of falling under the letter's spell always remains. Following Lacan's own conclusion, Žižek has asserted that Dupin's reward (given to him by the prefect) staves off the curse of the letter.[130] The exorbitant fee keeps the detective from becoming involved in the cycle of retribution, that is, keeps him from falling into the position of blindness within the symbolic circuit. As Lacan himself indicated, this is not unlike the analyst who receives (generous) compensation for acting as the "emissaries" for all of the analysand's purloined letters — at least for a time (*SPL* 49). This compensation refuses a personal relation between analyst and patient, significantly by confronting the patient with the emptiness of equivalences — monetary or otherwise.

In this sense, Poe's detective does seem to work *like* the analyst in Lacan's terms — at least at the time of the seminar in question. However, the precariousness of this positioning of the analyst (or detective) as emissary of the unconscious is evident in "The Purloined Letter" itself. Dupin, reading from the position of the Other, as the analyst, dramatizes the tremendous difficulties of removing oneself from the circuit of the letter. Though the letter is itself beyond meaning, the analysand will continue to attempt to make it meaningful, to give a content to the letter or meaning to the symptom. The analyst's very presence unfortunately seems to foster this response.

Indeed, as Lacan's thought develops, he removed the analyst from the position of the Other to avoid such complications.[131] Throughout his work in the 1960s and 1970s, Lacan continued to revise his understanding of clinical praxis, moving well beyond the exchange of letters that is suggested here. As Nobus indicates, this repositioning increasingly led Lacan to incorporate the question of desire into the session, through strategic means that worked against the analysand's reduction of this patient's demand for meaning.[132] Ultimately, Lacan placed the analyst in the position of the analysand's "object-cause" described above. Again, this notion stands quite apart from the "cause" that was sought after by the classical detective. Rather than over-running the analysand with signifiers in an unending interpretation, or symptomatology, as was the practice of the master, the analyst attempts to embody that most fundamental absence in the analysand's narrative, the analysand's truth — or object-cause. The analyst does not interpret this "truth." Rather, she or he holds this place open so that the mark of its absence might have effects on the subject. In other words, the analyst embodies the subject's absent "cause" as this term is described in *Seminar XI*, that is, "cause" taken to indicate something that doesn't work — that point where knowledge fails.[133] Cause in this sense marks the limit of discourses of mastery that one must ignore in order to imagine that everything "works" seamlessly, as it were.

In light of this subsequent clinical insight, the detective-analyst analogy is not appropriate in the case the classical detective, though this argument has all too frequently been made. This is true both for Holmes and Dupin as each, in their own fashion, desires to operate from a position of mastery — the latter in the complex way I have been trying to describe throughout this section. Each detective is, therefore, open to the "imbecility" of the master that necessarily results from such a vantage point. As I will argue in Chapter Two, from the perspective of Lacan's later clinic, the detective-analyst pairing only comes to make sense within the hard-boiled school of detection, a modality of the genre that rigorously works against the interpretative mastery of its classical predecessors.

TWO

"Protective Thinking": Obsessional Neurosis, Analysis, and the Hard-Boiled Detective

> "Let's stick around awhile. This excitement has put us behind in our drinking." "It's all right by me. What do you think will happen to Mimi and Dorothy and Gilbert now?" "Nothing new. They'll go on being Mimi and Dorothy and Gilbert just as you and I will go on being us and the Quinns will go on being the Quinns. Murder doesn't round out anybody's life except the murdered's and sometimes the murderer's." "That may be," Nora said, "but it's all pretty unsatisfactory."[1]

Introduction

In the 1920s, Carroll John Daly and Dashiell Hammett each published stories in *Black Mask Magazine* that inaugurated the hard-boiled detective genre.[2] Though Hammett's place within literary history is well known, Daly remains a largely forgotten figure at the origins of the hard-boiled detective. This is all the more curious as Daly's detective, Race Williams, possesses all the qualities that were made famous by later canonical figures of the genre: He is a lone wolf, a self-described "man of adventure," always operating according to a strict moral code of his own design. However, Race Williams possesses two distinct qualities that were, as the genre developed, banished from the hard-boiled world: he enjoys both violence and women.[3] It is no surprise that Mickey Spillane greatly admired Daly. Confessing his fond debt to the writer, Spillane went so far as to claim, "Mike [Hammer] and the Race Williams of the middle thirties could be twins."[4]

For Hammett and Chandler, the violent enjoyments of Race Williams and Mike Hammer, both sexual and murderous, are strictly unthinkable. Their detectives remain, generally, more calculating in their actions and more pious in their relations with women. The latter is true often to an extreme, particularly in the case of Chandler. However, despite the well-acknowledged literary acclaim of these two figures, in the 1950s Spillane became the most popular selling writer of detective fiction ever, much to the chagrin of the more intellectual supporters of the genre.[5] Within the same letter of admiration cited above, Spillane credits this success to Daly: "The public in accepting my books were in reality accepting the kind of work you have done."[6] In this chapter, I will address why this style and characterization took over twenty-five years to become popular, and why a detour through the more devout detectives of Hammett and Chandler was, apparently, necessary.

In 1929, just two years after the publication of the final Sherlock Holmes story,[7] Dashiell Hammett's much lauded *Red Harvest* appears on the literary scene, a moment that is frequently taken as the origin of the hard-boiled novel within American fiction.[8] This new version of the detective breaks with the refined nature of the classical formula, which, it is often said, sedately produces bodies so that the detective might have an intellectual puzzle to solve. In the famous essay "The Simple Art of Murder," Chandler claimed that the hard-boiled genre put murder back in the hands of those who were really good at it, "the kind of people that commit it for reasons, not just to provide a corpse."[9] Chandler's famous summary of this new figure indicates the great distance separating his own work from the classical detective:

> But down these mean streets a man must go who is not himself mean, who is neither tarnished nor afraid. The detective in this kind of story must be such a man.... He must be a complete man and a common man and yet an unusual man. He must be ... a man of honor — by instinct, by inevitability, without thought of it, and certainly without saying it. He must be the best man in his world and a good enough man for any world. ...[In] his private life ... I think he might seduce a duchess and I am quite sure he would not spoil a virgin; if he is a man of honor in one thing, he is that in all things.[10]

No longer a genteel dilettante remaining aloof from the world like Dupin or Holmes, the detective is now a common man in every respect. He does not possess the luxuries of means or intellect that were afforded his classical predecessors. More importantly, he is without what is perhaps the most characteristic aspect of the classical detective: his distance — and therefore safety — from the scene that he surveys. The hard-boiled detective is, in short, a man of the world.

This movement of the detective from the secure walls of the drawing room to the "mean streets," as Chandler phrases it, unsurprisingly requires an extreme shift in the detective's sanction and equally his goals. Indeed, the detective can no longer be taken as representative of larger, abstract concerns. In the chaos of the new metropolis in the early part of the twentieth century, he offers no guarantees of a shared justice but only his own idiosyncratic sense of honor.[11] As was shown in Chapter One, Sherlock Holmes tirelessly assures that the careful use of reason will bring all wrongdoings to light, restoring justice to the social order. In the world of the classical detective, murder does indeed out. His "scientific method of deduction" serves the law and Britain (and sometimes the lady) with an outcome as certain as the chemical experiments that he practices in the corner of the sitting room of 221B Baker Street. In the hard-boiled case, this causal relation misfires with a vengeance, and it is all the detective can do to maintain his own consistency — both bodily and psychically. Always "getting your man" remains the sleuth's credo, though "the man" referred to is now the detective himself. If his solution to the crime holds a criminal up to be seen before the law, there is no guarantee that justice will result. Often, the greater purpose of apprehending the criminal is so that the detective himself might remain unseen by the law, a dissemblance that is the basic structural characteristic of these novels. Inevitably, the gumshoe will take a relatively harmless case, through which he will then become *personally* implicated in a larger crime.[12] The solution to this crime in many ways becomes simply the detective's exculpation, a process that must abide by the strictures of his code, which demand above all else that he is never beholden to anyone. Thus, he can, at story's end, simply fade away.

This resolve is evident in the larger quotation taken from Chandler's essay, yet it is clear that the detective has found himself in a situation of forced choice. If he is a man of honor "by instinct, by inevitability, without thought of it," it is because he could not do otherwise. Choosing isolation perhaps offers some solace, and the illusion of mastery, but these desperate measures fail to achieve the redemption that remains his goal. No longer able to reorder the world itself, his only hope is to position himself against the city's disarray. Yet, this reprieve is won through a strict code of honor that places him ever distant from the social order he allegedly serves. With no authority to offer the detective sanction, he ultimately must wait for salvation, for a power capable of reestablishing community and recognizing the detective's place therein. He challenges not the structure of the social order, then, but rather its current players. He demands that a just authority replace the unjust. This conflicted relation to authority — paternal authority in particular — is the driving force of hard-boiled detective fiction. As I will argue, it is for this reason that the hard-boiled genre remains one of the more salient records of male hysteria in the first half of the twentieth century.

In Chandler's essay, it is clear that this ongoing discussion with the father — that is, with inheritance — is always paramount. At the surface, "The Simple Art of Murder" reads as a hard-boiled manifesto that celebrates American detective fiction over that of the English formula, or the classical form of the genre. These two forms are ostensibly distinguished by realism. The gritty American school describes things as they are, focusing its attention upon the creation of real characters, with only a token appeal to the logical puzzle that is commonly understood as the basic requirement of the detective story. On the contrary, the English formula labors over the staid convolutions of the whodunit, leading only to ever greater contrivance and flat, lifeless characters. Though the greater concern is the presentation of reason at work, this already seemed dated to Chandler in 1949. As he quipped, "The master of rare knowledge [i.e., the classical detective] is living psychologically in the age of the hoop skirt" (*SAM* 5).

In defense of the American school, Chandler celebrates the realism of Dashiell Hammett, the founding father. Though this gesture certainly expresses a genuine admiration, Chandler at the same time calls attention to the constructed nature of cynosure. Quality fiction must aspire toward the production of real characters, but these remain characters nevertheless. As he admits, "honesty is an art" (*SAM* 12). Hammett is clearly an adept author of such honesty, but he was merely picked from a group of many to represent the "founding" Father — a fact that Chandler is quick to admit. Indeed, despite Hammett's brilliant success, Chandler denies that he had any grand artistic ambition. Rather, he simply made a living by writing about something familiar to him. "He made some of it up; all writers do; but it had a basis in fact; it was made up of real things" (*SAM* 16). Yet, this tie to the real remains fleeting given the province of hard-boiled detective fiction delimited by the essay. The only items that detective fiction has "a right to be about," according to Chandler, are: "[M]ovement, intrigue, cross-purposes, and the gradual elucidation of character" (*SAM* 19). Initially "made up" of real things, these stories are quickly judged according to qualities quite apart from verisimilitude. Indeed, if there is anything "simple" about the art of murder, it is the selection of topic, for the story (in the sense of "story," or life as it happened, described in Chapter One) of the tale remains as artfully convoluted as ever.

The emphasis of character and movement suggested here certainly distinguishes the purpose of the American story from its English complement. However, Chandler still lists "redemption" and the search for a "hidden truth" among the goals of the genre, although it remains doubtful that either item can be achieved. This is true because the defining mark of the reality that is here celebrated — "[I]t is the world you live in," writes Chandler (*SAM* 20) — is its intransigence. The climactic list of examples of this social inertia near the conclusion of the essay echoes the individual's helplessness before a host of bad fathers: profiteers, gangsters, solicitors, corrupt judges and police, and murderous mayors (*SAM* 19–20). Many of these figures are immediately recognizable as the hard-boiled detective's patrons and, sometimes, accomplices.

Though Chandler's criticism of the genre (and contemporary society) presents the situation in Manichean terms, his fiction casts a much more ambiguous light upon these representatives of authority, and likewise upon the detective himself. The strict moral code of the detective potentially distances him from the debauchery of the fallen patriarch and the corrupt city. However, the specifics of this protocol remain wanting, leaving the detective's sense of "character" entirely prospective.

In the hard-boiled genre, then, there is no pact with the Father's authority that will mediate the detective's relations with the world. He is left with only a contested exchange with fathers that inscribes and repeats itself in the detective's troubled relation with women. This brings up the second great defining characteristic of the hard-boiled detective. Without the Father's sanction, the detective has no effective method of negotiating the sexual relation. Such confusion is found in the chaste nature of the detective's peculiar code, which Cawelti has described as an odd mixture of both honor and cynicism.[13] The conflictual nature of this stance will become all the more apparent when the detective is faced with the *femme fatale*, the obligatory hard-boiled device that promises both absolute fulfillment and lethal debauchery. Given this peril, the detective spoken of by Chandler in "The Simple Art of Murder" must be taken as the ideal rather than the rule, for the hard-boiled detective is never quite so commanding with his female counterparts.[14] The honor or chastity that he wishes to maintain is more often his own. The desiring women of this world have become monstrous killers that, quite literally, threaten the man's very being. But this dubious projection only thinly masks the fact that, in the hard-boiled realm, "the crime" is already in a sense the detective's own. Inevitably, the greater disruption of the narrative is the potentially unsettling effects of his desire — sexual or otherwise. As will be shown, both the menacing father and the *femme fatale* figure prominently among the number of strategies used by the detective to project the cause of his loss of mastery to the external world.

Despite the imperiled detective's skepticism and seclusion, a demand for meaning and reconciliation remain. The search for "redemption" and "hidden truth" remain objectives even in Chandler's account of the genre's fascination with entropy and dissolution. In psychoanalytic discourse, such paradoxical gestures or actions must be understood in the terms of obsessional neurosis. Above all else, the obsessive wishes to deny that he[15] has any implication within the Other. The obsessive subject imagines that he is whole unto himself, requiring nothing from the outside. This stance requires a never-ending series of rituals that, in the end, reduce the indeterminacy of language — and desire, which results from this — to a static, "obsessive thought." What results is the crippling anxiety and neurotic doubt that symptomatically accompanies the stasis that the obsessive has so carefully pieced together. It is for this reason that all obsessive acts are aborted, or "undone," by the obsessive himself.[16] The hard-boiled school is certainly the genre of "action," but insofar as this action is done in service of an aloof masculinity and self-sufficient toughness, it is an action that is undone time and time again by the obsessive detectives who play its game.

Reading the hard-boiled detective text according to the structure of obsessional neurosis, I will argue that here we encounter the "hystericization" of the detective, particularly when compared with the example of the classical detective. That is, the consistency of the obsessive detective's world is increasingly threatened by the encounters with the desire of the Other.[17] From this perspective, Chandler's description of the hard-boiled detective as a "complete man" must be met with the deepest scrutiny. This demand for detachment belies a desire for reconciliation, a fact found most readily in the detective's own first-person narration that seeks an interlocutor. Indeed, his words demand that someone listen. This chapter will focus upon such divided demands in the work of Hammett, Chandler, and Spillane. As will be shown, the clinical structure of obsessional neurosis provides an apt structure for placing the often divergent aspects of this version of detective fiction. Indeed, obsessional neurosis is nothing if not the practice of combining, in the dubious metonymy that is its mechanism, such heterogeneous elements.

Obsessional Neurosis: Strategies of Isolation

In *Inhibitions, Symptoms and Anxiety* (1926), Freud describes repression in obsessional neurosis according to repetition and isolation, mechanisms that each work at "undoing what has been done."[18] Given this objective, each process is likened to "negative magic," as the obsessional's defenses deny not merely the consequences of an event but the actual event itself. To phrase this in terms of the narrative theory discussed in Chapter One, the obsessional ritual is a counter-story aimed at the traumatic event in question. However, rather than revising stimuli so that the troubling story might be bound into a more comfortable plot, the ritual will eradicate both event and interpretation. Isolation supports this process and underscores the psychical annihilation that is here at stake. When an incident occurs that troubles the stasis of the obsessional, "he interpolates an interval during which nothing further must happen—during which he must perceive nothing and do nothing."[19] In this case, the ritual removes the obsessional from the experience as it is represented in memory and, in so doing, removes the affect associated with the precipitating trauma. Obsessional "thought," then, is purged of associative connections. Memories become unbound from affect, or the emotional response originally associated with a given event. However, these connections reassert themselves in the return in the subject's systems of inhibitions.

Importantly, Freud concludes this explanation by reemphasizing the magical aspect of these processes. To illustrate, he offers an exemplary primitive inhibition, the taboo of touching.[20] This commanding inhibition against contact symbolically expresses the obsessional's conflicted relation to others. On the one hand, he longs for sexual union that will do away with his distance from the Other, resulting in One, or sameness. At the same time, he imagines that such commingling will result in his own obliteration. The taboo will be generalized from a terror of sexual contagion to a fear of symbolic infection of any kind. The final outcome of this is a dread of the connection (i.e., touching) of thoughts themselves. The crippling results of these complimentary methods of repression are apparent, and it is hardly surprising that obsessional neurotics are notoriously feeble analysands. The isolation of thoughts at work in their inhibitions counters the demand for narrative production via free association.[21]

For Freud, the neurotic structures of obsessional neurosis and hysteria are defenses taken against the Oedipus complex, or the threat of castration. Lacan later reinterpreted these structures as two versions of separation, that is, two ways of entering language, or "castration" in the Lacanian sense. Separation is, in effect, a repetition of the trauma experienced in the development of the subject. Before separation from the Other, the subject is confronted with her or his "alienation" in the discourse of the Other. To receive items of need, the child must make use of the Other's language. Indeed, the child is well ensconced within the language of the Other long before birth. Expectant parents choose a name — that is, a place within language — and perform a host of other preparations for their child. Once born, the infant's mooring to the language of the Other is guaranteed insofar as all of the child's actions are interpreted as signs: Every cry becomes a demand for food, warmth, etc.

The point to be taken is that the child's alienation within the language of the Other is assured even before conception. This is the price of subjectivity. In separation, the subject is forced not only to react to this alienation, by learning to articulate its needs in this foreign tongue, but also to reconcile itself to the Other's lack. This lack is simply the Other's inability to adequately answer the appeals made by the subject. Each cry is a request for more than an object of need. Each demand that the infant makes to the Other is, for Lacan, always a demand for recognition, or a demand for love.[22] No sign can adequately express this recognition, to once and for all give the infant what it demands, if for no other reason than language is the very instrument of its loss. The differential that results, need minus demand, produces desire, a trauma in its own right, as a desiring subject is a lacking subject.[23]

The hysteric and the obsessive each respond to this trauma in a distinctive fashion, but they share a common goal: each wishes to ignore the lack within the Other. The hysteric subject will attempt to embody the object that has gone missing from this space. If she[24] is capable of becoming the object that the Other desires, all will remain well. Paradoxically, this requires that the hysteric remain ever attentive to the desire of the Other. She must constantly draw out the Other's limit so that she herself might embody it as object. The obsessive, on the contrary, will attempt to ignore the Other altogether. He assumes that everything is within its place, and that neither he nor the Other are lacking — that is, desiring — in any way. As was the case with the hysteric, the obsessive is likewise attentive to the Other, despite his claims to the contrary. Indeed, his imagined distancing from this figure can only take place if the Other is carefully watched.[25]

To adequately account for the obsessional's peculiar relation to the trauma of desire, it is necessary to introduce additional Lacanian terminology. Separation takes place under the aegis of what Lacan calls the Name-of-the-Father, which binds the child to the symbolic order through the phallic signifier.[26] Though it is constantly mistaken for the actual male organ — both by children working through the Oedipal stage, and often literary critics, as well — the phallus might be described as a tool used by the subject to enter language. As the founding metaphor, the Name-of-the-Father provides a place within the Symbolic order by naming the desire of the mother, thereby offering the infant distance from her sphere.[27] This "first" signifier holds a place open for the subject within the Symbolic order, that is, within the Other. It is the signifier to which all other signifiers will refer in the metonymy that is the desire of the subject. This is in part what Lacan means when he says "a signifier is what represents the subject to another signifier."[28] In other words, the subject is an effect of the signifying chain.

In this developmental drama, we might take the phallus as a mark of dissatisfaction that mediates the relation between the subject and the Other. The latter is never capable of giving the desired object that will at last fill the void opened by the originary cut of the signifier. And neither can the subject become the missing object desired by the Other. Lacan would describe this dialectic as the difference between *having* and *being* the phallus, a revision of Freud's theory of sexual difference according to a lack of the penis. I will return to this question of having and being the phallus and its relation to sexual difference below. Currently, what must be emphasized is that this complicated Oedipal triangulation results in the successful conclusion of separation, allowing the child to encounter the Other's lack. However, it is clear that speaking of the "conclusion" of separation is something of a misnomer, for separation marks the entrance of the subject into the structure of desire that is without end.

Because the obsessional wishes to deny that he is lacking (i.e., desiring), separation is met only with the greatest difficulty. Leclaire has suggested that rather than experiencing the *dissatisfaction* of the mother, which will then direct the child's desire beyond the bonds of the family, the obsessional subject encounters the mother's *satisfaction*.[29] This situation traps the neurotic in a regressive space that ensures that he will never possess the phallus, if for no other reason than because the dynamic of his Oedipal situation did not "show him" how such a thing was to be done. The mother's satisfaction, of course, cannot continue, although the obsessive would perhaps, in the end, prefer exactly this. Separation does begin for the obsessional.[30] Unfortunately, the Name-of-the-Father does not provide a more attractive answer to the imagined experience of wholeness that was enjoyed formerly. Again, this is hardly surprising, as the Name-of-the-Father marks the subject as lacking, thereby inaugurating desire. As object of the mother's satisfaction, the obsessional imagines that he is whole, without flaw, and lacking nothing. It is little wonder, then, that the obsessional will spend the remainder of his days in contemplation of his being, which is never again as certain as it seemed in these now lost moments of fulfillment. Precariously maintaining himself suspended between two Others (i.e., the Mother and Father), he denies that either has any consequence in determining his existence. In this suspension, the obsessional professes absolute separation, yet such a stance would be in all ways contrary to his general mode of indecision. In the obsessive ritual, this irresolution will take the form of conflicting actions that undo one another. By completing no actions, by asserting nothing, this subject attempts to fly beneath the radar, as it were, of the Other who wishes to bind him.

We might think of this in terms of the "object-cause" as described in Chapter One. This object refers to that empty space at the core of the subject, what is opened by way of the Paternal Metaphor or the phallus. It might be taken, then, as a piece carried over from the lost unity of the child and mother, or as that object which would complete the subject, making it identical with the (whole) image seen in the mirror.[31] What the neurotic subject disavows is that this "object" is lacking. Desire potentially offers this object; however, desire at the same time confronts the subject with the lack that was to be disavowed. This has everything to do with the curious place of the "object" of desire for Lacan. Again, as Fink explains, desire does not have an object; it possesses only a cause.[32] The child is initiated into desire both by the Other's (i.e., the parents' or caregivers') failure to adequately respond to demands, but also by the Other's attention that focuses beyond the child. Here, I will quote Fink at length:

> What arouses desire in a child is the Other's desire, not the Other's demand, nor even the Other's desire for this or that particular thing or person. The

Other's desire, as it alights upon specific objects and people, directs the child's desire but does not cause it. It is the Other's desire as pure desirousness — manifested in the Other's gaze at something or someone, but distinct from that something or someone — that elicits desire in the child.[33]

It is in this sense that the *objet a* is the "object" of desire. This is not an object that can be quantified or embodied, hence Lacan's suggestion that the gaze (i.e., the look and not the object looked at) and the voice (i.e., the grain of the voice itself and not the message it conveys) are privileged objects of desire. As Fink mentions, in this way, the *objet a* at the same time forces an encounter with the Lacanian Real, that space beyond the symbolization and meaning of the symbolic and imaginary registers of the subject. Taking the example of gaze and voice, neither of these objects possesses a mirror image or a signifier. They remain beyond signification, the very definition of the Lacanian Real.[34] When an object of the world fleshes out the *objet a*, it is given body, but only insofar as this object is made different from itself, resulting in desire, continuing its course, likely moving to embrace other objects in turn. This concept has a long and complex history within Lacan's thought. Consequently, I do not for a moment intend an exhaustive presentation of this object in its varying guises. For my current purposes, I will speak of the *objet a* as the object (a) cause of desire. As both cause and goal of desire, it is a paradoxical, uncanny structure, as described in Chapter One.

Lacan's formula of fantasy, $\$ \lozenge a$, represents the barred subject's relation to the object-cause of his desire.[35] (The subject is "barred" because language bars access to the object.) The diamond between the two terms, or "lozenge," as it is often called, suggests this barring. Thus, we might take it as a reference to alienation and separation. However, at the same time, the lozenge suggests the fantasy created by the subject to ignore this lack of the object — and, therefore, the lack within the Other. In the obsessional's fantasy, the *objet a* is covered by a fantasized relation with an object of the world through which the other (and Other) is approached. The Other is reduced to the other as object, an item that the obsessive can contemplate safely without fear of being asked anything in return. Should that object itself show any signs of life, any inkling of a desire of its own, this precarious economy will be upended. In other words, if the object reveals that behind it lies the *objet a*, the subject will be forced to confront the object as a limit rather than a compliment to the self. Fantasy in this way keeps the subject from experiencing the abyss that is always opened in an encounter with the *objet a*. In the latter instance, the obsessional will encounter not merely the Other's desire, but, no doubt more alarmingly, his own.

Perhaps the finest hard-boiled distillation of this obsessional necessity of desire scripted as impossible is found in Chandler's *The Big Sleep* (1939). Facing his own imminent death while being held prisoner in a remote location outside of town, the detective, Philip Marlowe, strangely "falls in love" with his inadvertent captor, Mona Mars.[36] Mars has been in hiding so that her husband will not be suspected of the murder of the man Marlowe claims not to be seeking, Rusty Regan. (With her missing, the police and others are led to suspect that Regan and Mona had run away together.) While talking with the captive Marlowe, she maintains that she loves her husband above all else, despite the fact that he is both a racketeer and murderer. In the strange scene that follows, Marlowe convinces the woman that her defense of her husband and denial of his murderousness is merely "protective thinking" that disavows actuality (*TBS* 194). Mars for a moment seems convinced by this — oddly timed — cajoling, and begins to criticize herself for her devotion. At the same time, Marlowe becomes increasingly smitten with his captor, despite his reproof. In this complex exchange, Marlowe criticizes the very logic that he himself is making use of, for in coming to desire Mona Mars, who must of course remain unattainable, he is likewise engaging in "protective thinking." By appealing to the inaccessible woman in this way, Marlowe ensures that his desire will be maintained as impossible. That is to say, it will not confront him in the manner in which he is more frequently assailed throughout the novel, notably in the form of Carmen Sternwood. A brief kiss before his exit seals the pact the two have established. Romantic love, which is always a form of impossible desire, in this case works, as Lacan describes, as a defense against *jouissance* and its disruptive, even fatal, potential.[37]

With this protective thinking comes the attendant defense of hard-boiled language. The detective's wit and insolence threaten physical violence at the slightest provocation. He means what he says and will translate his words into action if necessary — a promise in keeping with Chandler's edict to "make it real." Yet, this declared agency runs counter to the obsessional strategies of isolation and suspension, as these are designed to keep the subject from such confrontations by holding everything within its place. This stratagem is appropriately summarized in Roger Wade's lamentation found in Chandler's *The Long Goodbye*: "Goddam silly simile. Writers. Everything has to be like something else."[38] The obsessional detective's split gesture of action and detachment is a veritable criticism of literary interpretation itself. Indeed, it is safe to assert that the affinity between psychoanalysis and literature owes itself, largely, to the clinic of the hysteric. This is no accident, for, as has been well documented, the genesis of psychoanalysis, as well as its continued theoretical development throughout both Freud's and Lacan's careers, was inextricably bound with the desire of the hysteric.[39] The most basic analytic technique of free association privileges the hysteric because she is structurally predisposed to such a relation to language. Rather than the isolation of the signifier, as is the case for the obsessional, the hysteric translates symptomatic cathexis from signifier to signifier, a penchant that was initially a hindrance to Freud's own treatment of his patients.[40] Because she is all too attentive to the desire of the Other, the hysteric is predisposed to the production of ever more symptoms to win the attention of this figure.

Of course, this analogy depends upon a definition of literature as an ongoing translation of one kind or another, or a definition of literature as that which exceeds interpretation.[41] This is precisely Shoshana Felman's point in her well-known essay "To Open the Question," when she discusses literature as the unconscious of analysis itself. Literature becomes, in this way, an ongoing question through which psychoanalysis asks after the nature of its own being. Literature thus holds the place for what escapes analysis. Its "knowledge" is necessarily tentative and open to rereading, or a turn of the screw of interpretation.[42] The hysterical nature of this process is apparent precisely because desire is supported as *un*satisfied. It should not be assumed that the obsessive subject is any less predisposed to such an inquiry. Yet, there remains a marked difference between these two figures: while the hysteric questions, the obsessive subject finds an answer. From this perspective, one might say that it is not so much that the obsessive structure is not predisposed to the literary, but rather the obsessive subject takes the promise of literature literally. As Chandler advised, he will indeed make it real.

In *Television*, Lacan warned against the desire to speak *all* of the truth, in other words, to speak exhaustively the place of truth that marks the subject.[43] This is a warning that goes absolutely unheeded by the obsessive, as it is just this hope that orients this subject's relation to language. In short, language will be made his own, thus annulling the Other's presence. To put it simply, rather than recognizing his alienation within the language of the Other that is requisite for the first stage of this dialectic (i.e., alienation and separation), the obsessive curiously denies the Other's presence within language. As Lacan writes in *Seminar II*,

> [L]anguage is as much there to found us in the Other as to drastically prevent us from understanding him. And that is indeed what is at stake in the analytic experience. The subject doesn't know what he is saying, because he doesn't know what he is.[44]

This is exactly what the obsessional ignores. He will attempt to eliminate this encounter with language and his desire that is scripted there, refusing the interruption of the unconscious and his own "occultation by an ever purer [i.e., empty] signifier."[45] In other words, he will deny the most basic function of the unconscious, which is to unwind the symbolic network in which the subject is represented to another signifier. Naturally, questions of desire carry the greatest danger of the subject's loss or fading, but in this redirection, the thought process of the obsessive itself becomes sexualized. Forsaking an embrace of his object of desire, the obsessional will come to enjoy a distance from this object maintained through thought itself. All other forms of enjoyment must, then, be avoided, for if the obsessive is not thinking, so he imagines, he is then in mortal danger. As Soler concludes, "The obsessive is lost in thought, present in his thinking and not at the right place."[46]

This strategy against the effects of speech is amply demonstrated in the obsessional's practiced speech. Maintaining everything in its discrete place and disallowing thoughts of implication — that is, linkage and affect that would disrupt such an arrangement — his speech is neither tentative nor abundant. In the analytic session, the obsessional frequently maintains the demeanor of an expert, not asking the analyst for advice or opinion but rather *informing* the analyst, lecturing or discoursing without end to avoid the intrusion of the Other.[47] This speech is authoritative, taking no consideration of the Other's presence, and, largely, disjunctive. A lack of connective thoughts, what Freud termed, in a related context, "word bridges," is often symptomatically present in the pauses and breaks that so frequently punctuate his stilted discourse.[48] Such a symptomatic expression likewise represents the obsessive's relation to time, which always remains in suspension. A "little more thought" before action is always required, disregarding the demand of the Other, leaving this figure "waiting" for the obsessive himself.

The narration, tough-talk, and general aesthetic of the hard-boiled novel operate according to the split gesture of these obsessional tactics. The narration is typically in the first person, emphasizing the careful scripting of a story's plot according to the "lens" of the detective — he never stops talking, a situation that necessarily presents itself as a defense mechanism.[49] Throughout this speech, surroundings are tersely described, and there is little connective material indicating any sort of relation among what is surveyed.[50] This lends a fragmented character to the city, to be sure. However, this space remains at the same time full of presentiment and danger. In the classical detective story, though the city remains a primary feature, descriptively it is relegated to the background. The Wastonian narrator is more concerned with the detective's investigation and the presentation of clues in such a way that will allow the reader to participate in this inquiry. In the hard-boiled text, on the contrary, the city becomes much more a part of the narration, precisely because the detective's careful ordering of his world is crucial to maintaining his own innocence — as well as keeping his own desire at bay. The detective's narration, then, becomes an obsessive ritual whose structure and content keep all within its place, thereby minimizing outbreaks of violence and passion.

This program of abatement is found even in what would seem to be the most aggressive aspect of the genre, the detective's threats and wisecracks. Dialogue rife with sarcasm and menace is perhaps the most identifiable hard-boiled characteristic, and conventional wisdom reads this repartee at face value. As suggested above, it is as a sign that the detective is sure to "back up." Christianson describes this "tough talk" as "a linguistic assertion of power over experience" that always promises violence.[51] This link between hard-boiled speech and violence or aggression is imperative, for language is always a tool for the detective. Working as his own chronicler, he quite literally "orders" his narrative in the form of the manipulation of others. Similarly, at the heart of Chandler's own claim that hard-boiled fiction aspires towards realism is the "speech of the common man" (*SAM* 17). This populist-critical gesture also presumably underwrites the detective's wit and wisecracks, which flout authority and decorum. In so doing, this discourse represents a real discontent with such agencies. In Spillane this linkage of speech and aggression reaches the extreme in Mike Hammer's tendency to "narrate" his violence, and savor each moment of this speech before he (painfully) executes the criminal.[52] The violent power of language to (re)order the detective's own world is here made literal.

However, in the case of Chandler and Hammett, violence is simply not the way the hard-boiled detective wishes to do business. The force promised in the tough-guy dialect is most often virtual, a fact that undercuts the professed "action" and accompanying masculine demeanor of the genre. As Marlowe says in *The Long Goodbye*, "All tough guys are monotonous. Like playing cards with a deck that's all aces. You've got everything and you've got nothing. You're just sitting there looking at yourself" (*TLG* 64). The tough guy act is simply that, an act, and what Terry Lennox says of his marriage in that same novel applies here as well: The tough-talk is always a "[b]ig production, no story" (*TLG* 15).

The circuitous and sarcastic dialogue is appropriate to a genre that emerges, as Žižek has observed, when it is no longer possible to tell a story in a straightforward and linear fashion.[53] Clearly, this rift expresses changing relations to authority and the underlying fantasy structure of such exchanges. The hard-boiled genre meditates upon such issues above all else. If the classical detective story sought to redeem the individual and the social through the suture of narrative (i.e., to successfully bind story through plot), the hard-boiled novel represents the attempt to free the individual from such narrative necessities altogether. As suggested above, these concerns always implicate the detective in issues of inheritance, desire, and limit — elements of separation that the obsessional detective wishes to both disavow yet hold within reach. The classical detective story attempts to reestablish a linear story so that the reader, the detective, and the social order itself might be brought back within the narrative ordering of desire. In stark contrast to this practice, the hard-boiled text tells a story that will extinguish all desire itself—and presumably the need for such narration.

The divided gesture of this tactic inheres in historical readings of the genre, as well. This perhaps goes a long way toward accounting for the tremendous popularity of hard-boiled fiction.[54] To these ends, Porter's conclusion offers a familiar sentiment:

> The irony is in the circumstance that the private eye began to flourish in popular literature at a time that coincided with a major crisis of American individualism as the political philosophy of industrial capitalism. In the fiction, if no longer in life, the myth of heroic individualism persists. The Continental Op reaffirms his mastery over a city out of control in a way that the president [Herbert Hoover] signally failed to do for American society at large.[55]

This analysis offers a simple identificatory model. The assumption is that the reader takes pleasure in the enjoyment of a subjective position that remains prohibited in daily life, a judgment that raises the charge of escapism — an all-too-common complaint of popular literature. At a certain level, the genre does allow for the reaffirmation of (masculine) categories of experience that had become increasingly impracticable during the span of years from 1929 to 1947.[56] However, it would be hasty to conclude that readers of these popular texts were not aware, to a greater or lesser extent, that the joys of individualism proffered were rapidly becoming museum pieces. Indeed, I would go so far as to claim that hard-boiled detective fiction is explicitly self-conscious about the implausibility of the version of masculinity it appears to privilege.

This avowal is readily found in the aesthetic preoccupations contemporary with the publication of these novels. Marling sees hard-boiled detective fiction as representative of the dominant social aesthetic of the 1920s, which he describes as "metonymic."[57] This style is bound to the increasing mechanization of the smallest recesses of urban life. From architecture to consumer products, the lines of the skyscraper and the airplane represent the height of modernity and, above all else, speed. Machinery is metonymic, says Marling, as its fundamental purpose is to eliminate needless steps of production in favor of efficiency.[58] A play between exterior and interior (or presence and absence) is the necessary accompaniment to such metonymy, and here Marling finds Hammett's experience writing advertising copy to be a turning point in his development as an action writer.[59] Like the thought processes of the obsessional neurotic, the strategy of metonymy in the context of design is bound to the process of forgetting, if for no other reason than the synecdochal reference (i.e., parts suggesting a whole) that is demanded favors the inclusion of dissimilar elements according to a more general, and often quite "empty," abstraction.[60] Unlike the classical detective's world, parts are not always equal to the whole. The figure of "speed" illustrates this well. Though it often stands in for discourses of social progress, it figures nothing more than the idea of movement, quite apart from destination.[61] The veritable anonymity of the detective, whose mechanical rejection of human sentiment is based upon his abstract code of prohibition, owes much to these cultural tendencies. To assert anything about the detective requires one to analyze his actions, that is, to attend to his trajectory and its velocity throughout the text. This prohibits — or, at the very least, diminishes — the possibility of assigning him content.

However, at the same time, this new detective disrupts the logic upon which the aesthetic of motion is based. To these ends, it must be remembered that the hard-boiled detective is *self*-employed, underscoring his distance from the market economy that generates these demands, which always remain experienced as potential strictures on individuality. In this sense, the detective does not *produce* appropriately, and he remains a potential moment of stasis within his own aesthetics of motion.

Two hard-boiled conventions illustrate this fact, as well as underscore the detective's own idiosyncratic "protest" to these productive demands. First, ranking high atop the detective's code is his insistence that he will not take a case that is suspect or distasteful in any way — or suspect and distasteful in the wrong ways. He will choose the work that he does. This element of choice ensures the relative poverty of the detective and maintains his "non-production" between ventures. As a host of hard-boiled secretaries would affirm, he could always use a little more business. This non-production is typified by the frequent moments of reflection in the detective's office, which occur either after hours or during a business day that remains equally as quiet. The hard-boiled detective demands again and again this time for reflection, something that is unequivocally lost throughout individual experience during the historical period in question.

An additional item that illustrates this protest concerns a structural requirement at the level of plot. The hard-boiled novel typically begins as the detective, reluctantly, accepts an ordinary and otherwise uninteresting case. Unexpectedly, things go hopelessly awry as a larger crime erupts, calling into question the innocence of the detective himself. The greater portion of the novel will then work towards the extrication of the detective from such suspicion. However, after an alternate suspect has been provided and the detective's name has been cleared, he will continue his work to answer the queries elicited earlier. Per convention, these inquiries will lead the detective to discover criminality at the highest levels of society, emphasizing the all-pervasive corruption of contemporary culture and reestablishing the detective's need to distance himself from this vice. Here again, though the detective is warned not to continue with his investigation, he demands time for just this enterprise, the results of which become the greater narrative of the text itself. During this time, the Other is effectively made to wait, a customary obsessional strategy that works ostensibly to signify that the subject needs recognition from no one.

This "waiting game" is in turn indicative of the ongoing dialogue with paternal authority and the question of inheritance, fundamental pivots of the hard-boiled narrative. The detective's neurotic response to this situation is appropriate, as the father is always the father who fails. Importantly, this failure is scripted according to two dominant modalities: in the first instance, the father enjoys — that is, uses up — the inheritance that should belong to his offspring. Alternately, the father proves himself to be lacking in some fundamental way. He is not all-powerful and therefore cannot offer his progeny a stable point of identification. Rather than the ideal father who will preside over the compromise of symbolic order, ushering the child into the world to seek his desire thereby ensuring Oedipal peace, on the contrary, the detective encounters a lethal competitor. Despite the hard-boiled detective's insistence on his own selfishness, he actually remains suspended between a wish to sustain the father's flagging position and a desire to sever the ties of this relation. He may be in it for himself, but the needs of the father weigh heavily on the detective's mind.

An excellent example of this conflicted relation is the hard-boiled detective's peculiar demands on the issue of payment. As is well known, the hard-boiled detective frequently refuses to accept payment for his services — or, at the very least, he will not accept payment until something is truly owed him. Even in the latter instance, it is all-important that he never takes more than is "fair," which is often quite little. As Lacan suggested, it is by accepting the large reward that Dupin (potentially) keeps himself from becoming caught in the path of the purloined letter. In other words, this allows him to maintain his critical distance as classical detective. Attempting to maintain a similar detachment, the hard-boiled detective refuses extravagant retainers and rewards. However, this very refusal leaves him all the more indebted.

The failure of paternal authority encountered by the detective is frequently found in the literal reference to the father's desire. In the hard-boiled world, the patriarch's concupiscence inevitably damns his lineage and threatens the accord upon which the social order rests. The father presented within these texts is, then, the father who enjoys, the so-called "father of enjoyment," or "anal father."[62] His appearance is assured when the Oedipal father no longer functions as mediator between the subject and the symbolic order. This so-called anal father, as the developmental moniker indicates, represents a failure of the Oedipal structure through which the child enters the world. With the loss of an orienting point of identification in the symbolic order, or a strong ego ideal, the subject is left to engage with the real existing father, a potential rival and competitor.[63] As a plundering figure, he incessantly threatens to take the subject's enjoyment for himself. Given the obsessional's Oedipal difficulties, one might argue that this subject is always in some way dealing with the father who enjoys. In other words, the obsessive subject meets the father, in his various incarnations, always as a potential rival intent on disrupting the obsessional's own economy of enjoyment.

The Simple Art of Murdering the Father

This ambivalent relation with the father is perfectly articulated in Spillane's second novel, *My Gun Is Quick* (1950). The "father" in this case is Arthur Berin-Grotin, an aging captain of industry whom Hammer meets, apparently incidentally, while searching for the history of an unknown murdered woman. The aging man is himself quite preoccupied with names, telling Hammer, "I'd rather you only use the first half of my name.... Hyphenated family names always annoyed me, and since I am burdened with one myself I find it expedient to shorten it."[64] As this emphasis upon address makes clear, the father wishes to be whole, unmarked by a division of any kind, either in name or in memory. In a fashion typical of Spillane, this is figured through Berin's struggle against the ultimate limit, death itself. Throughout the story, he supervises the construction of an enormous mausoleum that prominently displays his un-hyphenated family name. This monolith effectively looms behind the actions of the father and the text itself, haunting the space of the narrative with the mark of this undead lasciviousness. In the Lacanian terminology I have been employing, the father's name is always an empty signifier without content. This originary, or pure, signifier marks the success of the Oedipal moment and the entrance of the subject into language according to the paternal metaphor (or Name-of-the-Father). However, this successful failure (i.e., it names the subject, but with an empty signifier) does not transpire for the obsessional subject, making the name a monument to the father's enjoyment.

This fallen father, the figure of such obscene enjoyment, is frequently encountered in Spillane's work, mediating Hammer's relation with women in need of rescue. Predictably, in *My Gun Is Quick*, "Berin" is the very name that Hammer seeks. The patriarch turns out to be the grandfather — and only remaining family — of the murdered girl that Hammer knew only briefly as "Red." By returning "Red's" name to her, Hammer (re)creates the ideal woman he imagines that he met shortly before her death. This veneration recalls another hallmark of the obsessional structure and Spillane's fiction: the Madonna-Whore binary. The question of the mother's satisfaction in the obsessive's problematic separation indicates why this would be the case. The mother marks, on the one hand, the space in which the obsessive enjoyed the greatest of satisfactions. However, given the obsessive's subsequent denial of his implication in the Other, the mother is always potentially a whore who threatens his consistency with her contagion. In Spillane's work, the ideal woman is often, like Red, met only for a moment, allowing Hammer's callow sexuality to create the woman as he sees fit.[65] *My Gun Is Quick* is an apt illustration of this penchant, as the entirety of the novel is presumably constructed upon this desire: to (re)build the perfect woman.[66] Given the well-publicized misogyny of Spillane's work, it hardly need be said that it is no coincidence that the ideal woman in this case is a dead woman. Even Hammer realizes this all too well. Indeed, *the* Woman that haunts Hammer throughout the first three books of the series (*I, the Jury*; *My Gun Is Quick*; and *Vengeance Is Mine!*) is a woman that he himself killed, Charlotte Manning. This hostile relation with the ideal will be pivotal to my discussion below.

It is clear, then, that the ideal woman is a screen upon which the detective negotiates his relation with death.[67] What bothers Hammer the most about the death of his redhead is what he terms the "senselessness" of it. It was a "messy death," as he says, "There was something unclean about it, like a wound that has healed over on top, concealing an ugly, festering sore brewing a deadly poison that will kill again" (*MHC* 189). Of course, Hammer's *modus operandi* is always, through his vengeance, to make sense of death. He will balance all accounts, acting as judge, jury, and executioner, as the title of Spillane's first Hammer novel suggests —*I, the Jury*. Critical response to the genre has long regarded this desire as one of the reader's greater pleasures. However, in the context of my current argument, the very notion of a "useful death," for reader or detective, reminds one of the obsessional's usage of this index for the arrangement of his life. As Leclaire summarizes, "the obsessional structure can be conceived of as the repeated refusal of the possibility of one's own death,"[68] which is to say that he will make his own "death" meaningful by making it impossible. This is accomplished primarily through "playing dead" at every moment, thus escaping the notice of the Other.

To be sure, with Mike Hammer, this characterization must appear fallacious. Spillane's detective does anything but play dead. Further, given his desire to draw out the Other, its law and its limitation, he might more adequately be diagnosed as a pervert according to the clinical terminology of psychoanalysis. I will return to this possibility in the conclusion to this chapter. Though this diagnosis may in fact be true, it does not in any way change the fact that Mike Hammer operates within the conflicted, obsessional demand that marks the hard-boiled genre itself. If he is indeed a pervert, this perhaps speaks to his popularity among the reading public who, partaking of an entirely neurotic structure in the hard-boiled text, dream of being perverts capable of such enjoyment. This will be returned to below.

Returning to the issue of the ideal woman, it is clear that this figure also acts as screen or proxy through which the detective's relation with the father will be played out. As is customary within the genre, the father at first elicits tremendous fascination, even respect, and Mike Hammer is not immune to this. He initially likes Berin a great deal, even going so far as to say that he admires the way in which the older man has lived his life. Singing his praises to an old cop buddy, Hammer remarks: "He's from another generation, Pat. Money, position, good manners ... everything you could expect of a gentleman of the old school. He's fiercely proud of his name; you know ... constantly alert that nothing should cloud the escutcheon of his family" (*MHC* 207).

In an act of benevolence cast as social consciousness, Berin hires Hammer to continue his search for the redhead's lost name. During preliminary investigations, the detective finds a ring that belonged to Red. Engraved on the ring is a cryptic set of initials, an undecipherable escutcheon, worn away by the passage of time. Naturally, the effaced sign of the ring is the family crest — which is itself an empty, purchased imitation of a hoary family legacy — that is replicated upon Berin's tomb. The redheaded woman, Nancy Sanford, was Berin's estranged granddaughter, who was cast out of the house when she became pregnant out of wedlock. Typically, Berin had squandered his fortune and was forced to team with gangsters in order to live in the manner to which he was accustomed. In this, he is the perfect representation of the utter corruption of the ruling elite, a generic hyperbole characteristic of Spillane. As is often the case in the Hammer series, the woman, even one idealized rather than vilified, serves as a sort of detour that ultimately reveals the father's enjoyment. Indeed, it is by allowing his granddaughter to fall from grace, to become a prostitute who moves freely about the city's underworld, that Berin himself participates in that "enjoyment" of her. For the "father of enjoyment," no woman is prohibited. Representative of this lasciviousness, the father Berin is revealed to be a criminal on a grand scale. In the final confrontation scene with the patriarch, Hammer repeatedly refers to the man's unnecessary pride for a name that had lost its depth of meaning and had, through his associations with known criminals, forced him to allow his granddaughter to be killed.

As punishment for this vile act, Hammer divines a method for taking away what is most precious to Berin, the immortality of his name. To do so,

Hammer explains that he will kill Berin and tell the police that the body belongs to one of his nameless thugs. This will ensure his burial in potter's field. Hammer then promises that the granddaughter's body will be placed within the mausoleum that was to be Berin's legacy. "They'll never find you even though they'll never give up looking, and whenever your name is mentioned it will be with a sneer and a dirty memory. The only clean thing will be the redhead. You'll die the kind of death you feared most ... lost, completely lost. Animals walking over your grave. Not even a marker" (*MHC* 343). In this way, the purification that so often concludes a Hammer mystery is achieved, and the ideal woman's memory is maintained. Indeed, the monument her corpse will occupy in actuality corresponds to the grandeur of her role within Hammer's fantasy life. Admittedly, the price of entrance is (a literal) death.

Interestingly, despite the violence of the father's murder, the very values that Hammer openly admired about Berin have been spared any direct criticism. The laudable aspects of "another generation" populated by "old school gentlemen" remain intact — though largely unnamed, and perhaps in need of rescue much like Nancy Sanford. In other words, Berin is represented as a gentleman fallen from grace. This is the curious paradox of Spillane's work, and *My Gun Is Quick*, in particular. Though power and authority are all too often shown to be corrupt and in need of the simple justice perpetrated by Hammer, the position of a benevolent father still remains. This nostalgia for an order that is now lost exists alongside a depiction of the city at its most chaotic.

Such relations with the father of enjoyment and the type of social order that this figure represents are complicated within the work of Hammett and Chandler, though the results may, in the end, be the same. This complication lies in the detective's inability to completely disassociate himself (i.e., through murder or retreat) from the social order and the charm of its representative patriarchs, despite the fact that this "separation" is what the detective's code calls for most fundamentally.

Hammett's Detectives: The Romance of "Stirring Things Up"

This is certainly true in the case of Hammett's Continental Op, the protagonist from the author's first complete novel, *Red Harvest*.[69] This unnamed detective, a precursor to Sam Spade, has a relation with the novel's sinister father, Elihu Willson, that bears all the struggles outlined above. At the beginning of the novel, the Continental Op is called to the anonymous mining town Personville — known as "Poisonville" to the locals — by Willson's son,

Donald, the editor of the local newspaper. Donald Willson had hoped to enlist the Op's aid in completing an exposé on the corruption within the town, an exposé that will almost certainly incriminate his father, Elihu Willson. As founder of Personville, the corrupt father had run the town unopposed for many years until the miners had organized against him. To combat organized labor, Willson brought in an army of hired thugs who unfortunately decided to remain in Poisonville after their job was complete.

After these former associates apparently murder his son and attempt to kill him as well, the older Willson hires the Continental Op to "clean up" Poisonville. When it is later discovered that his son has been killed by the bank clerk Albury in a banal crime of passion, Willson attempts to revoke his contract with the Continental Op. Standing firm against this request, the Op's professional code makes rescinding the agreement impossible. As he said to Willson originally, "[Y]ou're going to get a complete job or nothing. That's the way it'll have to be. Take it or leave it."[70] By this time, attempts have already been made upon the Op's life, one incident notably perpetrated by the chief of police himself. Deeply implicated in the violent struggles of the city, the Op again avows that terminating the investigation is impossible:

> Your fat chief of police tried to assassinate me last night. I don't like that. I'm just mean enough to want to ruin him for it. Now I'm going to have my fun. I've got ten thousand dollars of your money to play with. I'm going to use it opening Poisonville up from Adam's apple to ankles. I'll see that you get my reports regularly as possible. I hope you enjoy them [*RH* 64].

True to the hard-boiled detective's code of honor and cynicism, the Op promises a bloodletting and regular reports.

The imperative of a "complete job" is integral to the Op's code of conduct and will, in many ways, become the most basic ethic for all other hard-boiled detectives to follow. What we find here is a sort of "protective measure" to be used in his defense. By completing the narrative begun in his preliminary investigations (either in reports or the telling of *Red Harvest* itself), the Op will ensure that all has been safely put into place. He remains, ideally, neither threatened nor in debt. Yet, though this protection will act as prophylactic against the chaotic space of Poisonville, it can only do so by binding the Op to an order of another kind, to another father: the "Old Man," his boss at the agency. Hammett's "Op" is just that, a nameless operative for the San Francisco office. The limits of this bond are evident in the Op's insistence that Willson post a retainer of ten thousand dollars and letters of intention to the Continental Detective Agency of San Francisco. The latter will stipulate that "the Agency is to conduct the investigation as it sees fit" (*RH* 45). Though he acts without direct orders, and often illegally, in this administrative requirement he remains bound to this second Other, a linkage that will, he hopes, keep him from becoming imbricated in the violence and petty intrigue of Personville. The Op will not himself be "poisoned."

Of course, the Op is a remarkable exception in the history of the hard-boiled genre, as this figure will become an exclusively *private* investigator, unfettered by an institution and its restrictions. Indeed, this turn occurred even in Hammett's work with the introduction of the self-employed Sam Spade. We might read the emergence of Sam Spade and his abundant progeny as indicating a shift within the popular experience of the coherence of culture itself. Indeed, Spade's first novelistic appearance in *The Maltese Falcon* was published in 1930, a year after the market crash, and the beginning of a cultural malaise that would remain pervasive throughout the duration of World War II. With institutions, financial and otherwise, failing, the detective, like the average citizen, is now "on his own," without a ready benefactor of any kind. *Red Harvest*, published in 1929 — yet composed of much earlier material — seems already to be thinking the logic of this severance and the increased difficulty of positioning the individual in relation to an ever-chaotic social space. The Op's attempt to distance himself from the contagion of Poisonville through an alliance with a second Other (i.e., the Continental Detective Agency itself) fails, then, for a variety of reasons.

Hammett's attention to this dilemma must be taken as a meditation on the hermeneutic of detective fiction itself. In the novel in question, this inquiry begins with a radical divergence from the detective narrative that demands a denouement in which the reader discovers the true identity of the villain or killer and all is, it would seem, righted for a time. In *Red Harvest*, Donald Willson does not enlist the services of the Continental Operative to investigate a single crime, but rather to help him unmask the general corruption of Personville itself.[71] It is true that this vague request is quickly placed to one side as the Op stays on to investigate the murder of Donald Willson, but this crime is solved a third of the way through the novel. Not so incidentally, the solution to this crime concerns a lustful killing (i.e., a straightforward crime of passion), as a local bank teller, Robert Albury, murders Donald Willson out of jealously over the latter's relation with Dinah Brand. (The aptly named Dinah Brand is of course the "firebrand" that explosively motivates much of the narrative.)

Both the apparent randomness of this murder and its placement within the text underscore the implausibility of former methods and structures of detection. As the epigraph to this chapter, taken from Hammett's *Thin Man* (1933), reminds, "murder doesn't round out anyone's life." Neither, it seems, does it any longer "round out" the structure of the detective novel. In this way, the text self-consciously poses the questions of this "new" detective's procedures and capabilities. With Donald Willson's murder solved, the Op's remaining charge is to "clean up" Poisonville, a task that is exceptionally vague. Rather than looking for clues to a given crime, the detective is a further step removed: He must first search for a crime. As the Op discusses his "plan" to these ends with Dinah Brand, he jokes, "Maybe I'll advertise — *Crime Wanted — Male or Female*" (*RH* 84).

This disruption of more familiar versions of detection is further emphasized in the methods utilized by the Op.[72] Through a series of "experiments," as he phrases it — notably the unfixing of a fight to fuel distrust among the various factions of local gangsters — the detective dredges up the crimes that he seeks. As he explains, "Plans are all right sometimes.[...] And sometimes just stirring things up is all right — if you're tough enough to survive and keep your eyes open so you'll see what you want when it comes to the top" (*RH* 85). Gone is the superior intellect that views a crime from a privileged perspective and, thereby, reduces it to an intellectual puzzle. Through brute force and animal-like cunning, the hard-boiled detective endures where others fail. However, Brand's surly comments provide a pertinent criticism of the ultimate viability of this method: "So that's the way you scientific detectives work. My God! For a fat, middle-aged, hard-boiled, pig-headed guy, you've got the vaguest way of doing things I ever heard of" (*RH* 85).

The failure of the detective's former *modus operandi*, that is, the failure of the hermeneutic structure as such, closes the gap between the detective and Other in its various guises. In other words, the desired position of separation, an existence in which the detective owes no one anything, becomes untenable. Indeed, in the first novel of the genre, this stance is simply impossible, as the Continental Op quickly finds himself going "blood simple," and joining in the circuit of vengeance and violence that dominates Personville (*RH* 154). As the Op says of this contagion, "I've arranged a killing or two in my time, when they were necessary. But this is the first time that I've ever got the fever. It's this damned burg. You can't go straight here. I got myself tangled at the beginning" (*RH* 154). Summarizing this entanglement moments later, the Op suggests, "Play with murder enough and it gets you one of two ways. It makes you sick, or you get to like it" (*RH* 154–155). And, as he fears, he increasingly finds himself enjoying the latter reaction in his "cleansing" of Poisonville. The Op has fallen prey to the pleasure of violence, and Hammett makes it clear that this is an indulgence that must remain strictly off limits.

This failure and the perilous nature of its enjoyment are emphasized in the troubled relationship between the Op and the mercenary woman, and *femme fatale* prototype, Dinah Brand. In the terms of obsessional neurosis, the *femme fatale* is quite literally the emergence of the desire of the Other. Impossible desire suddenly made possible is utterly horrific for the detective, and the *femme fatale* thus becomes the harbinger of his doom. Indeed, it is always clear that the enjoyment of the pleasures offered by this figure will result in the detective's demise. It is neither incidental that the *femme fatale* is so often cast as a representative of the emerging market economy in which everything has its price. The desire of the Other always demands exchange, and an entrance into a figurative economy in which the uniqueness of items is reduced to a common index of trade. This is, of course, reprehensible for the detective. His code makes certain that everything — most importantly, himself — has a distinctive place and is not made dispensable with the emergence of the woman's demand.

The characterization of Dinah Brand is instructive to these ends. As she tells the Op, "I'm a girl who knows her Poisonville" — a sentiment that the Op will come to share — which is to say that she is fully adept at trading influences for money and selling out relations of whatever kind (*RH* 84). Brand has been the mistress of several leading figures within the various gangs of Poisonville, and she uses the information culled from this experience to her advantage. This is perhaps most evident in Brand's capitalizing on the Op's interference with the fixed boxing match. Much to the chagrin of her companion, Max Thayer, she exploits the information that she has, despite the fact that this is a clear act of betrayal. As she says, "He doesn't own me," no man does (*RH* 85).

Like Brigid O'Shaughnessy of *The Maltese Falcon*, Brand is a modern woman unfettered by any of the traditional requirements of sentiment and propriety that would quite literally "keep her in her place," that is, out of both sexual and monetary economies. Indeed, the inherent danger of the *femme fatale* is galvanized within the genre by the confluence of these two systems. Each woman is a small-time capitalist, and neither is shy about placing herself — that is, her body — into exchange. Further, each woman depends upon the fact that the men they encounter will still be prone to their more conventional wiles. Robert Albury, Brand's former lover and killer of Donald Willson, expresses this well when he describes her business savvy: "She's money-mad, all right, but somehow you don't mind it. She's so thoroughly mercenary, so frankly greedy, that there's nothing disagreeable about it. You'll understand what I mean when you know her" (*RH* 27).

Albury is in this way an exemplary "sap," to use Hammett's own terminology. In other words, the young bank teller allowed himself to believe that the promise of love from Brand, or any woman, is worth the asking price, which was all of Albury's savings and, potentially, whatever he could embezzle from his employer, the local bank. But in this world, love's banal fantasy is an anachronism. As Brand says, "It's not so much the money. It's the principle of the thing. If a girl's got something that's worth something to somebody, she's a boob is she doesn't collect" (*RH* 35). Money is her language, a fact that reduces all other appeals by the Continental Op, or any other man, to nonsense (*RH* 33). In Hammett's fiction, then, men and women no longer speak the same language, a point that I shall return to shortly.

The entrepreneurial nature of these women significantly compromises the detective in acts of love and lust. In Hammett's fiction, this distinction (i.e., love and lust) might be used as an index for classifying the differences between *Red Harvest* and *The Maltese Falcon*. In the former, the Continental Op spends one too many evenings drinking with Dinah Brand only to wake one morning holding an ice pick that has pierced her chest. For some time, the Op worries that he in fact killed Brand. He cannot adequately convince himself that he is innocent beyond a shadow of doubt, making lust, violence, and desire in this instance indistinguishable.[73] Near the conclusion of the story, it is discovered that Oliver "Reno" Starkey killed Brand, arranging the body and the murder weapon to incriminate the Op. Naturally, the point to be taken is that this innocence is only apparent. He is not Brand's killer, but neither is he blameless. By "stirring up" Poisonville, the Op set into motion numerous murders. He did not kill Brand, but he is nevertheless culpable. He has gone "blood simple" like the natives, effectively voiding his professional code of conduct despite the doctoring of the reports for the "Old Man" that he will complete at the end of the novel.

Sam Spade perhaps fares better in the *Maltese Falcon*, as he refuses to "play the sap" for Brigid, despite the fact that he "may" love her.[74] In the climactic conclusion of the novel, a scene that was so memorably captured in Huston's film version, he turns Brigid over to the police. Spade does this for a number of reasons, but what arises most prominently in his enumeration is, again, the detective's code:

> When a man's partner is killed he's supposed to do something about it. It doesn't make any difference what you thought of him. He was your partner and you're supposed to do something about it. Then it happens we were in the detective business. Well, when one of your organization gets killed it's bad business to let the killer get away with it. It's bad all around — bad for that one organization, bad for every detective everywhere [*MF* 214].

Brigid's machinations depended upon Spade's sentiment, but, as this speech indicates, the detective has none. He will not play the sap. Importantly, this greater bond to the fallen partner is something that utterly escaped Brigid's attention.

The triangulated relation of this scene lays bare the fantasy structure that is at the heart of the hard-boiled world. Recognizing her position as mediator between the detective and father or brother — that is, the (masculine) symbolic order itself — the *femme fatale* represents the impasse that keeps that masculine order from fulfilling itself. In this way, avoiding a simple reduction of this figure to a castrating, perverse woman of enjoyment, we might read the *femme fatale* as marking a significant moment of breakdown in the relationship between the hysteric and the obsessional. The failure of the obsessional male's objects to fill the lack in the symbolic order of the Other (and thus prevent an encounter with the *objet a*) results in the collapse of former methods of distancing. Indeed, the women that greet the hard-boiled detective in these places are perfectly willing to reduce all to the empty value of money. Everything (love, honor, the body, etc.) becomes reducible to currency and thereby becomes exchangeable. This the obsessional cannot tolerate as his very being depends upon the singularity of each object of exchange. Only in this way is it possible for him to imagine the objects he gives in effigy — not for exchange, but to avoid just this transaction — plug the hole in the Other, thereby maintaining desire as comfortably impossible.[75]

We have seen how love might be used as a defense against the *jouissance* that threatens to overrun the detective's consistency. As was evident in the example taken from *The Big Sleep*, the prohibitive structure of romantic love provides an apposite mechanism for marking the subject in a time when no credible authority will do so. It seems implicit in this explanation that the *femme fatale* is *the* figure of *jouissance* that lulls the detective into acts of disastrous transgression. Responding to her lure, he pulls the trigger, as it were. However, on the contrary, this figure must likewise be read as a defense against the *jouissance* that menaces the detective — though admittedly a less effective defense when compared with that of love. As Copjec has suggested,

> In order to *indemnify* himself against these dangers, he creates in the femme fatale a *double* to which he surrenders the *jouissance* he cannot himself sustain. That is, he tries to take some distance from himself, to initiate some alterity in his relation to himself — to split himself, we would say, not as the desiring subject between sense and being, but between knowledge and *jouissance*. Giving up his right to enjoyment, the hero contracts with the femme fatale that she will henceforth command it from him, as levy.[76]

Copjec is speaking of the noir "hero" (particularly in the work of James M. Cain), a figure at one remove from the hard-boiled detective in terms of the genealogy of detective fiction. Nevertheless, this statement is not without credence in the hard-boiled context. We enter the space of noir when the detective becomes the criminal, when his protective measures utterly fail. After such a transgression, the plausibility of this indemnification is remote at best. However, when reading the hard-boiled detective proper, the feasibility of these protective measures remains an ongoing question, resulting in the various ascetic hard-boiled codes that have been read in this chapter.

The "levy" demanded by the *femme fatale*, and the transferential relation that this indicates, is an excellent illustration of what has been called the "Subject-Supposed-to-Enjoy."[77] Žižek has written of this formulation in terms of "interpassivity," an "activity" of transferring one's enjoyment safely elsewhere. This fittingly describes the relation to Other in obsessional neurosis. The obsessional's father of enjoyment is not merely a prohibitive entity. He is likewise the subject who enjoys in the obsessional's stead and, therefore, spares him the entanglements of *jouissance*. In the formula of fantasy read on page 76 ($ ◇ *a*), this transfer of enjoyment, this "interpassivity," is indicated by the *objets a*. That is, the objects that will, through the screen of fantasy, cover over the *objet a*—which is always the threshold of *jouissance*. (I will discuss this point at greater length in Chapter Three.) Here again, it is only logical that the obsessional would so desperately wish to distance himself from the *objet a*, as this marks the lack that links him to the space of the Other. The *objet a* is quite literally "the inert passivity" of the subject.[78] In other words, it is that small piece of enjoyment that escapes meaning or, in Copjec's terms, knowledge. The result: the subject becomes the passive object of the Other's desire. The common obsessional fear that the Other is enjoying at his expense is a symptomatic expression of the truth that the Other does indeed enjoy the subject in this sense.

The *femme fatale* understood as defense in this way provides a compelling response to readings that interpret this figure as representative of the fundamental chaos and lack of meaning in the modern individual's life. This quasi-existential analysis misses the point by confusing the fantasy for the real, as it were. The *femme fatale* is not the representative of all that becomes unfathomable when at the beginning of the twentieth century the grand narratives formerly underwriting the social begin to fail. Rather, she must be understood as the sense made by the subject when confronted with just this confusion. Indeed, the *femme fatale*—in the hard-boiled context, as opposed to the world of noir — is in many ways a mark of the pact made by the obsessional detective with the declining father, hence the importance of their frequent entanglements. Far from being meaningless, she is the detective's attempt to make meaning of the sexual relation and enjoyment, as Copjec suggests. It is no accident that the detective will bar his relation to this figure with a highly personal code of honor. In so doing, he is regulating a relation to his symptom, which is always a compromise, in the fullest sense of the term, of *jouissance*. The answers that the detective will offer to these questions of sexual difference and enjoyment are always distinctive, that is, they are singular, which is the neurotic *méconnaissance* in its most pristine form: the subject imagines that their ailment is absolutely unique, if for no other reason than because the very object of their individuality has been taken away.

The vicissitudes of this relation are clear. The detective is alternately fascinated, tempted, and repulsed. If he draws too near the *femme fatale*, if he approaches his fantasy in actuality, it will become evident that the epiphany she promises, as either villain or lover, masked the fact that in the end she hid nothing. The depth of this figure was merely the ruse of the obsessional structure, a position that shows itself to be seriously compromised in the world of empty signs now inhabited by the hard-boiled detective.

Returning to *The Maltese Falcon*, it cannot be emphasized strongly enough that Hammett was — from the beginning of his work — well aware of these structural necessities and the relation of these to masculine desire.[79] Apropos of this, it is of course no accident that the absolute singularity of the Maltese Falcon is spoken of *ad nauseam* by the character Gutman. Importantly, Gutman has divined the existence of the falcon through a historical exegesis as there are no straightforward, extant records of this object. He traces its journey through the centuries by discerning veiled references, usually surrounding its loss, made by its various owners in often unrelated documents. Much like the reader of a detective novel, the falcon is Gutman's prized object that holds the solution to the historical mystery he has so assiduously studied. This character is clearly a romantic adventurer, and, appropriately, he is hesitant to tell Spade just how much he thinks the Maltese Falcon is worth. Naturally, the falcon can only be priceless, a fact that will not keep them from achieving an incredibly substantial sum in its actual sale.

During their first interview together, Spade is quick to question the ownership of this object, a query that is, presumably, made on behalf of his client, Brigid O'Shaughnessy, who is at the moment in possession of the falcon. But as Gutman describes the issue of ownership and the bird, "An article of that value that has passed from hand to hand by such means is clearly the property of whoever can get hold of it" (*MF* 128). However, bad luck has always fallen upon those that come to possess the black bird — another aspect of the story portrayed so well in Huston's film version. Like the purloined letter, its power seems to be more in its potential — that is, its promise — than in its use, an odd circumstance that renders this invaluable object in the end worthless, but nevertheless commanding.

Hammett's brilliance in *The Maltese Falcon* is to make literal this fact, as we discover in the end, along with Gutman, Cairo, and Brigid, that the *rara avis* is a fake. Furiously disappointed, the group theorizes that the Russian, from whom they originally stole the falcon, had played them by allowing them to pilfer a forgery. Yet Gutman, more charmed by the romance of the situation, is not as upset as the other members of the party. He immediately makes it clear that the continuance of his crusade is not a tremendous inconvenience, and even indicates that he would like to have a man of Spade's resources along for the trip (*MF* 203–204). The absence of the object of the search is, of course, what sustains these individuals as questing characters, a situation that is duplicated toward the end of Hammett's novel when Spade bargains for his life by possessing not the bird itself, but the location of the falcon.

As in all quest narratives, keeping the Maltese Falcon out of reach allows the narrative to continue and, in this conclusion, the logic of detective fiction is unmistakably commented upon. The object of the detective's own pursuit — be it of an identity, a stolen object, etc. — is ultimately only a forgery that sustains the desire of both the detective and reader. From the beginning, Spade refuses to take an interest in the search for the falcon. Rather, he chooses to manipulate the apparent romance — and likewise the simple greed — that enthralls the would-be possessors of the artifact. Not so incidentally, he plays upon this sentiment just as Brigid O'Shaughnessy hopes to play upon his own. The effects these reversals have on the genre itself are hardly slight. As Hammett casts aside the idealistic quest after rare objects (of whatever kind) as the appropriate mode of the hard-boiled detective, we are left to question what new directives will take this place.

As has been indicated, in *Red Harvest* Hammett made it perfectly clear that the detective no longer works to support the social order by facilitating justice. Even in this early text, the focus of the detective's fascination shifts to the question of woman and the desire of others. What he seeks is to know the truth about others' desire so that he might reveal their guilt and, more significantly, his own innocence. Like the splitting at work in the figure of the *femme fatale*, this transference of guilt guarantees the detective's life. However, at the same time, this transmission reduces his existence to a sort of death-in-life experience typical of the obsessional neurotic.

What distinguishes the conservative nature of this hard-boiled aspiration from the structure of the classical detective story is the inherent lamentation of the gesture. Moretti was quite right to conclude that the goal of the classical story is that nothing should happen.[80] The same could be said of the hard-boiled story, particularly regarding its terminally interrupted erotics. However, in the detective's always already compromised assertion that he needs nothing, he requests considerably more than he likes to admit. For example, at the conclusion of *The Maltese Falcon*, Spade claims to love Brigid, or that he "may" love her, but he emphasizes that she cannot go without punishment for the murder of his partner, Miles Archer. He must, therefore, turn her over to the police. If he indulges in his desire for Brigid, he is almost certain to be sentenced to death. Spade's assertion that letting the killer of his partner go free would be bad for business can be taken as an appeal to a filial order that would allow him protection from the very desire that threatens his stability.

Huston's film version of the novel perhaps shifts Spades' alibi more toward the register of romantic love, as the script removes many of Spade's more mercenary comments made during the climactic final confrontation with Brigid. The viewer is left, then, with what might appear as a less conflicted sense of (impossible) love, which nevertheless must be forsaken to be upheld — a point that I will return to in Chapter Three. As I have suggested, such doomed romance is readily reducible to the obsessional's desiring economy. Hence the greater pathos, I would argue, when in the film Spade tells Brigid, "I won't because all of me wants to regardless of consequences. And because you counted on that with me the same as you counted on it with all the others."[81] Thus, the object of his desire will be placed safely out of reach. The love that he declares, then, requires nothing of him and is, effectively, revoked at the same time that it is offered. The same is perhaps true of the filial order that is here used as alibi, for the plausibility of this brotherhood is significantly problematized given the simple fact that Miles Archer was an unlikable scoundrel. This difficulty underscores the suitability of an appeal to the structure of obsessional neurosis as the pact made with the father or the network of brothers (i.e., a symbolic order founded upon a stable, masculine authority) is ultimately a ruse that works to erase the detective's debt to these same figures.

This bid for radical separation from the symbolic order made by the obsessional is likewise emphasized in Spade's imperative never to be "duped," particularly by "playing the sap" for a woman, an aspect of the detective's code that again indicates the obsessional's ambivalent relation with the Other. What remains of the utmost importance is that the subject disavow any implication with the Other. If this implication is suddenly established, in other words, if the Other's desire suddenly appears, the obsessive will experience the urgent danger of being "enjoyed," of being the Other's passive object of satisfaction, a situation that will result in, so the obsessive imagines, his dissolution as a subject. As we have seen, it is by "playing dead" that the obsessive will attempt to ward off this more certain death at the hands of the Other, a stratagem that may yet seem, *prima facie*, ill-suited for describing the hard-boiled man of action. To weigh the plausibility of this assertion, it will be helpful to turn to a more explicit discussion of the subject and the Other, and the danger of being duped. We find this in Hammett's "parable of Flitcraft," which appears near the beginning of *The Maltese Falcon*.

This parable relating a seemingly inexplicable "life decision" made by a well-to-do real estate agent named Flitcraft is told to Brigid O'Shaughnessy by Sam Spade as they wait to hear from Joel Cairo regarding the location of *rara avis*, the Maltese Falcon itself. The reader is placed in a similar position as the parable is recited; that is, the reader is left awaiting the precious object offered by the tale. And like the characters of the text, we ultimately find ourselves without the promised objective, but only with a redundant forgery. Importantly, the reader is immediately told *how* Spade relates this story: "He talked in a steady matter-of-fact voice that was devoid of emphasis or pauses, though now and then he repeated a sentence slightly rearranged, as if it were important that each detail be related exactly as it happened" (*MF* 61). This is comparable to Hammett's own recounting of the story of the Maltese Falcon, and the legacy that this style will have in the history of hard-boiled fiction. In this way, *The Maltese Falcon*, Hammett's third completed novel, continues to explicitly raise questions regarding the limits and possibility of the genre. For this reason, the Flitcraft story must be read as a parable of the hard-boiled text itself.

Brigid O'Shaughnessy again doubles the questing metaphorics at play in this passage given her own particular interest in the narration. As the true hysteric of the text, she is, we are told, "more engaged with his purpose in telling the story than with the story he told," though in the end the subject matter does become of interest to her (*MF* 61). She is, then, more concerned with how the story potentially illuminates the nature of Spade's desire, and, by embodying this object, she will ensure her possession of the greater article at stake, the falcon. However, the style and manner of the retelling, much like the poetics of hard-boiled narrative generally, make such a sounding difficult to say the least. This requires that O'Shaughnessy herself turn to the object of the story, though this too seems to offer little help in her efforts to understand Spade's motivation.

Like all parables, the conclusion of the story ends in paradox. However, in this case, the paradox appropriately dramatizes the varying responses the subject can make in answer to the fretful presence of the Other. The parable is as follows: One day Flitcraft, a successful businessman, husband, and father, goes to lunch and utterly disappears. The state of his affairs shows no indication that this was premeditated: his accounts show no recent or large withdrawals, and there is no element of his primarily happy and content life that could possibly explain his vanishing. Several years later, a man matching Flitcraft's description is found in Spokane and Sam Spade, who is working for a Seattle-based detective agency at the time, is sent to question him. When confronted, the man does turn out to be Flitcraft. Spade finds that he is peculiarly more concerned about communicating the "whys" of his story — we are told that he had never before discussed this with anyone — than he is remorseful about leaving his family so abruptly. (His conscience is eased all the more by the fact that he had left his family more than well provided for.) As he tells Spade, during his lunch hour on the day of his disappearance, he was walking past a construction site when a beam fell almost ten stories and hit the sidewalk right next to him. This violent and random event shook him out of an otherwise complacent life. As he concludes, if it is possible for a good, honest family man to nearly be killed at random, "he would change his life at random by simply going away" (*MF* 64). To beat chance at its own game, he leaves immediately without giving any warning to anyone, and drifts about the Northwest for a time before finally settling in Spokane where he remarries and begins a new life.

There are several details here that are worthy of note. First, it must be emphasized that Flitcraft is a happily mundane individual. As Spade says, "Flitcraft had been a good citizen and a good husband and father, not by any outer compulsion, but simply because he was a man who was most comfortable in step with his surroundings.... The life he knew was a clean and orderly sane responsible affair" (*MF* 63–64). Flitcraft lived ensconced within the symbolic order that welcomed him by, we are free to conclude, offering him comfortable space within its boundaries. As Spade affirms, Flitcraft desired nothing else, in other words, his desire was successfully — and no doubt, given the evidence, obsessively — maintained in abeyance.

The randomness of the beam falling forces him to encounter, as Spade sees quite clearly, the randomness of the world and, therefore, the ultimate fallacy upon which he had formerly based his existence. In this accident, Flitcraft has encountered the lack in the Other and, therefore, the Other's desire that had previously been kept under wraps through his workaday, suburban rituals. A curious aside in Spade's tale authorizes this assumption — and here we should remember the careful manner in which he is telling the story so as to get every detail correct. As Spade recounts, "Going to lunch he passed an office-building that was being put up — just a skeleton" (*MF* 63). The structure, "just a skeleton," that supports the banal symbolic order of office buildings, new Packards, county clubs, etc., comes into focus and is, given the incident, shown to be anything but stable.

Importantly, though Flitcraft's life is spared, a piece of the broken beam strikes him across the face, giving him a lasting scar. Here again, a side comment underscores the importance of this mark: Spade tells the reader not only that Flitcraft rubbed the scar while telling the story, but that he rubbed it, "well, affectionately" (*MF* 63). In this way, the scar marks both the lack within the symbolic order and, therefore, within the subject himself. It is the mark of Flitcraft's subjectivity. Like the symptom, the scar marks the subject with the trauma of the Lacanian Real, or that which cannot be symbolized, much like his incident with chance.[82] Like all good symptoms, Flitcraft is shown to have a somewhat "pleasurable" relationship with this injury.

Were the story to end here, it would be of little interest and, no doubt, not qualify as a parable as such. However, the parabolic nature of the story becomes evident when Spade describes how Flitcraft ultimately rearranges his life. Flitcraft is obviously hystericized by his encounter with the Other's desire.[83] His wandering around the Northwest after this incident speaks to this fact when compared with his formerly well-ordered life. With the insight of his accident, he presumably comes to understand that this order was a sham. In his enlightenment, he is no longer "duped" by the Other, as it were. However, Spade's favorite part of the story, as he tells us, is the way in which Flitcraft chooses to reorder his life after this initial deviation.[84] He again settles and takes a wife who "didn't look like the first, but they were more alike than they were different. You know the kind of women that play fair games of gold and bridge and like new salad-recipes" (*MF* 64). As Spade concludes, "He adjusted himself to beams falling, and then no more of them fell, and he adjusted himself to not falling" (*MF* 64). In other words, though he took his near-death experience to be a radical insight into the utter fallibility and absurdity of existence, he has, quite in spite of himself, resettled into a comfortably ordered routine that is nearly identical to the one he left behind.

This story is a perfect illustration of Lacan's notion of *les nons dupes errent,* or "the non-duped err," a homophonic play upon the Name-of-the-Father, *le Nom du Père*. (This term, *le Nom du Père*, likewise suggests "No!"-of-the-Father, or the prohibition upon which the symbolic order is based.) This conception, developed late in Lacan's work, underscores, among other things, the formative role of fantasy in the construction of reality.[85] The individual who is not duped by the big Other would, like Flitcraft, not fall for the false promise, and false consistency, of the symbolic order. From this perspective, institutions, or their representatives, are recognized *not* as embodying authority or an institutional mandate (or any other ideal). Rather, they are viewed to be simply individuals playing a part that is, in the end, empty of any real sanction.

However, though the Name-of-the-Father — or any signifier that would come to occupy this place — is empty, this does not diminish the effectiveness of the signifier in either fantasy or reality. Those who are "not duped" err the most, as they do not recognize the dimension of fantasy that supports reality itself.[86] This is Flitcraft's mistake, for though he does indeed see the framework, the skeleton upon which reality is built, he does not recognize the part that he himself plays in this construction. Appropriately obsessive in this sense, he refuses to acknowledge the necessity of his own desire in support of the symbolic order. This failure is evident in many respects. Indeed, his response to randomness with a randomness of his own is deeply problematic. Describing this life change as a response immediately assumes an interlocutor, and his flight must then be read as an attempt to both hide from and, no doubt, be found by this same Other. In either case, it is of central importance that the Other itself be duped to spare Flitcraft this same injury. Just as he chooses to repeat his former life after his hystericization is quieted, his attempt to distance himself from the Other, simply to hide away, at the same time reveals itself as a transparent attempt to draw the Other closer. Flitcraft's action, then, becomes compromised in the obsessional fashion that is endemic to the hard-boiled narrative.

Both the obsessive subject and the (obsessional) hard-boiled detective are the "non-duped" who "err" insofar as each imagines that he requires nothing from the Other and escapes any sort of exchange with this space. The non-duped who err miss the point of what Žižek calls "symbolic efficiency," which is the structuring of reality *through* the fiction of the big Other.[87] As illustrative of this point, Žižek gives the example of a judge who is in person frail and unimposing. The judge's true physical characteristics matter little, as this person, when he speaks from the symbolic position of his charge, gives voice to the Law itself. To deny the force of the judge's speech is to deny the functioning of symbolic efficiency, which is nothing other than the way in which the subject participates in the fiction of the Other, and thus participates in a symbolic community.[88]

The hard-boiled search for realism immediately implicates the genre and its orienting male fantasy of self-sufficiency in such duping. Spade's telling of the parable might be taken as emblematic of this bind, and he, like Flitcraft, ultimately finds himself right back where he started at the beginning of his own story, stuck between two women: Iva Archer, his murdered partner's widow, and his secretary Effie Perrine.[89] By turning Brigid O'Shaughnessy over the police, Spade imagines that he has successfully liquidated both the love and violent desire — violent precisely because his own desire is implicated — that she represented. Indeed, love is perhaps the greatest example of symbolic efficiency, for, when in love, our partner becomes, despite all the flaws that accompany embodiment, that precious object that delivers all that was promised by the symbolic order in the first place. This is exactly what Spade turns his back upon. However, despite his denial of the fact that he is likewise "duped," or the sap he does not wish to be, at the conclusion of the novel he returns, we are left to assume, to his tired relationship with Iva Archer.[90] To put this another way, though he renounced Brigid to assert his own permanence, he in all ways depends upon this renunciation and, therefore, an exchange with the symbolic order. This is an excellent indication of how woman is the symptom of man, as the carefully scripted denial of the *femme fatale* as meaningless is the very way in which the detective continues to believe that there is sense to the symbolic order from which he distances himself.[91]

Raymond Chandler: Hystericizing the Hard-Boiled Detective

In the work of Raymond Chandler, these obsessional traits will undergo a marked revision, as his detective, Philip Marlowe, is, effectively, a "hystericized" version of his hard-boiled predecessors.[92] From this perspective it is not incidental that, all too frequently within criticism, Marlowe is charged with being a homosexual. Undeniably, one finds that Marlowe's narrative often reveals a fascination with men. Marlowe is quite sensitive to the details of their appearance, their manner, and, importantly, their relations with women. However, while such preoccupations certainly represent a significant shift in the detective's style, it is unclear as to why these should be taken as indicative of Marlowe's sexuality. By hystericizing his detective, Chandler is deliberately exploring aspects of the detective — and contemporary masculinity — that were formerly present in the muted, symptomatic discourse that this chapter has analyzed.[93] To these ends, Chandler raises the question of "sentiment," a quality that was fatal in Hammett's work, to the surface of Marlowe's own first-person narration. This fascination immediately places this new detective some distance from the mercenary figure of Sam Spade.

The sentimental narration of Marlowe is certainly a remarkable development in a genre that earned credibility for its "tough" honesty. Bordering at times on the maudlin, this style is part and parcel of what I am calling the hystericization of the hard-boiled detective. Unlike Spade and other detectives of this sort, Marlowe does not possess the same control over language in his narration or relations, a fact that speaks to the failing nature of the detective's former protective measures. This is especially true in *Farewell, My Lovely* (1940), a text that in many ways deals with the dissolution of Marlowe's drive to find a strong, male ego ideal, a point of identification that the detective desperately needs. Importantly, Marlowe is frequently preoccupied with the experience of his own voice. He confesses to an unnerving alienation from his speech and an accompanying loss of power; he admits to talking too much and not knowing either what he means or how to articulate it.[94] This loss of voice coincides with the increasing failure of the obsessional strategies in defense of desire that were, seemingly, possible in Hammett's fiction. The compromised authority of both the narration and detective, then, continue the critical examination of the detective's hermeneutic at work in the genre and the relation of this to contemporary mythologies of masculinity. Though Chandler was a tremendous admirer of Hammett's writing, it is clear that he is interested in pushing the logic of the detective's characterization well beyond the standards established by the latter.

To these ends, Chandler places his (obsessive) detective's desiring economy into a state of crisis. This requires Marlowe to question the very nature of his being, but he does so in a very specific direction: He questions his sexed identity. Throughout the Marlowe series, the detective is incessantly confronted with the question "What does it mean to be a man?"[95] The query of one's sexed identity is the orienting question of the hysteric.[96] With the hystericization of the hard-boiled detective, though he remains structurally an obsessive subject, I would like to suggest that the hysteric's inquiry necessarily weighs all the more heavily upon him. As with Spillane and Hammett, in Chandler's fiction one finds a frantic attempt to reestablish a pact of some kind with the father, a figure that prominently directs, either as patron or prohibition, all of Marlowe's actions.[97]

Marlowe's search for the "ideal male"—and the father is always potentially just that—differs from the obsessive pact that I have been examining as it is now acknowledged rather than covert. In other words, Marlowe actively seeks the father. Nevertheless, the detective approaches this figure through the compromised obsessional methods of repetition and isolation so common to the hard-boiled project. As has been shown, the manipulation of the (imagined) father's prohibition functions prominently to these ends. The detective maintains the authority of the father while at the same time questioning its sanction; that is, he continues to cower before the father's prohibition, while at the same time searching for an ever greater ideal.[98]

Marlowe's sentimental attachment to General Sternwood in *The Big Sleep* (1939) perfectly exemplifies this conflicted relation with the father. Though the patriarch remains in many ways a symbol of power, he is declining rapidly toward anachronism. Like the oil wells on the family's property, he is nearly used up. As Sternwood says himself, "You are looking at a very dull survival of a rather gaudy life.... There's very little that I can eat and my sleep is so close to waking that it is hardly worth the name. I seem to exist largely on heat, like a newborn spider, and the orchids are an excuse for the heat" (*TBS* 9). The plundering aspect required of a hard-boiled father is apparent though excusable to Marlowe if for no other reason than because this posturing gives him a sovereign to whom he might be subordinate. In Chandler, this is always the greater calling. Indeed, it is hardly incidental that Marlowe's knightly quests are, almost exclusively, the search for men.

The Big Sleep becomes such a quest, as Marlowe, in spite of himself, searches for General Sternwood's protégé, Rusty Regan. Regan had suddenly disappeared without leaving a trace, but Sternwood is not so concerned about the man as he is hurt by his desertion. This plea immediately wins the sympathy of the sentimental Marlowe who becomes a second Regan—a man whom Marlowe, we are told, resembles a great deal—and thereby a second son to the decrepit Sternwood. Marlowe's sympathy is further elicited in the short exchange that appropriately centers around the question of "tough talk" or dialect. Sternwood mentions that when he first met Regan he took him for "an adventurer who happened to get himself wrapped up in some velvet" (*TBS* 10). As Marlowe replies, "You must have liked him.... You learned to talk the language," and Sternwood has no hesitation in telling the detective that Rusty Regan was "the breath of life to me — while he lasted" (*TBS* 10–11). This adaptation of such lingo is a feeble gesture on the part of the aging patriarch, who should, like the more robust — and wealthier — Harlan Potter of *The Long Goodbye* (1953), rarely need to speak at all, let alone in the glib discourse of the street that is a rejection of the very authority that he represents. As is true of Sternwood, a diminution of the all-powerful father is typically the initial seduction of Philip Marlowe, drawing him into the folds of the narrative.

This novel famously begins with Marlowe's contemplation of the stained glass window above the Sternwood residence. The window depicts, it will be remembered, a knight trying to rescue a damsel who has fallen into the clutches of some appropriate villain or another. As Marlowe describes,

> The knight had pushed the vizor of his helmet back to be sociable, and he was fiddling with the knots of the ropes that tied the lady to the tree and not getting anywhere. I stood there and thought that if I lived in the house, I would sooner or later have to climb up there and help him. He didn't seem really to be trying [*TBS* 4].

As is often indicated, this is an economic rendering of Marlowe's chivalrous penchants. Equally as important in this passage is his qualification of the condition under which he would help the errant knight who remains trapped in the frozen time of the text of the stained glass. He would assist "if he lived in the house," which suggests both a desire to identify with Sternwood — this even before he meets the eerily charming invalid — and a reciprocal separation. In other words, Marlowe is not so much a knightly figure who will go about his business with the aid of his well-rehearsed code of honor. Rather, Marlowe is looking for an authority that could authorize such an arrangement in the first place. His knightly code, then, is an obsessive ritual that holds a place for a father powerful enough to respond to this demand, while simultaneously distancing the detective from that same figure, buying time until he might finally "live in that house," as he says.

This rendering of Marlowe's knightly code as a work in progress, as it were, is emphasized throughout Chandler insofar as Marlowe is most often not enlisted to rescue a woman in distress, but is rather hired to find a man. As Plain indicates, making use of the description of the character Moose Malloy from Chandler's *Farewell, My Lovely*, Marlowe is always looking for the "big man," that ideal figure of masculinity that would again allow the symbolic order be underwritten by masculine authority.[99] Time and time again, this ideal figure is betrayed by women — much to Marlowe's dismay. This is true of Sternwood who is, essentially, betrayed by his two daughters: the one, Carmen, kills Sternwood's adopted male heir, while the other, Vivian, helps hide this crime from her father.

In *Farewell, My Lovely*, this betrayal finds its greatest expression in the character Moose Malloy. After having been in prison for eight years, Malloy, much in the manner of Marlowe's chivalrous code, searches for the girl he left behind, "little Velma." The fact that she never once visited him in prison attests to the extreme devotion of the questing knight for his lady. While Malloy was away, Velma transformed herself into the aptly named Helen Grayle, the wife of a prominent, though aging and impotent, judge.[100] Perhaps the most venomous of Marlowe's women, she in the end kills Malloy — who would forgive her anything — without the slightest compunction.

By portraying the questing knight as the harsh, even animalistic, Moose Malloy, Chandler casts serious doubt on the possibility of this figure's return to prominence. In other words, the masculinity cast in the hard-boiled ideals of toughness and independence is deemed unserviceable. Chandler's final novel, *The Long Goodbye*, augments this doubt considerably as Marlowe's identificatory figure, Terry Lennox, is an embarrassing drunk. He has married into money, knowing all too well that his wife, Sylvia Lennox, is a conniving cheat. But far from hindering Marlowe's identification with Lennox, this frailty in fact fuels his feelings of attraction and debt to this character. Lennox was wounded in the war, requiring considerable plastic surgery that resulted in clearly visible scars running down one side of his face. Another distinguishing characteristic is Lennox's full head of white hair, despite his relative youth — this is presumably the result of trauma experienced during the war. The latter characteristic, a detail that is strangely repeated throughout the early sections of the novel, economically places Lennox in a paternal role. This position is likewise suggested by his marriage into the family of the greater father of the text, Harlan Potter, California's wealthiest multi-millionaire.

The detective first meets Lennox after he has fallen over drunk at The Dancers nightclub and is abandoned by his wife Sylvia. The two strike up a friendship for reasons that Marlowe is slow to elaborate upon. Lennox just "got to him," as he says, but in such a powerful way that Marlowe quickly wishes that he no longer had anything to do with Lennox (*TLG* 5, 8). During an evening of drinking, Marlowe presciently tells Lennox, "You're a problem that I don't have to solve. But the problem is there" (*TLG* 9). The context is a discussion of Lennox's assorted marriage problems, the details of which will make Lennox the primary suspect in the brutal murder of his wife that happens just a short time after this meeting. However, unlike the Continental Op who remains a man of few words, words that are most often carefully chosen, Marlowe's own speech is utterly symptomatic, requiring the careful attention of the reader. As he has been told on several occasions, he talks too much, and he never does say quite what he intends. Naturally, in this case, Marlowe's denial is as good as an assertion. Lennox is in fact a decisive problem that Marlowe must solve. Specifically, Marlowe must reconcile both his sympathy and disgust for his new friend. Though Marlowe takes him up as an ego ideal of sorts, Lennox all too frequently fails to live up to this confidence.[101]

Read as an obsessional construction, Chandler's sentimental version of the hard-boiled detective is neither a betrayal of the genre nor a tremendous innovation. The hard-boiled demand for separation has always already carried within it such sentiment: The detective's solitary ethic seeks camaraderie in isolation and then laments the situation that requires this fragmentation. *The Long Goodbye* is unique among Chandler's works as it most openly investigates the varying desires of assimilation and disintegration that are so tangible within this bifurcated demand. Forter has made the argument that the hard-boiled detective novel works towards subverting a conventional male desire for mastery in favor of the temptations of masochism and death itself.[102] This analysis is as brilliant as it is insightful — particularly in the case of Hammett, whose work remains Forter's primary example. However, in the case of Chandler, even in his final novel, it seems that the death drive functions, paradoxically, in favor of "life" or the preservation of the detective's desire for subjective consistency. For the obsessional, the drives of Thanatos and Eros cannot be read at face value.

Marlowe's alternating interest and disgust with Lennox's abjection (e.g., he is a cuckold, an alcoholic, a coward, etc.) certainly speaks to an interest in — and identification with — not the "big man," but rather a more piteous version of masculinity. Terry Lennox becomes exactly this when he asks Marlowe to help him flee the country after his wife has been brutally murdered. Marlowe is subsequently imprisoned on suspicion that he has aided this escape, although he refuses to give the police any information on the recent whereabouts of his friend. Shortly after Marlowe is released, he receives the news that Lennox has committed suicide in a cheap hotel room in Mexico City. Suspicious of such a convenient end to a high-profile murder case, Marlowe remains unconvinced of his friend's demise. As the detective quips, "A deadman is the best fall guy in the world. He never talks back" (*TLG* 57). This statement accurately sums the psychical structure here in question, for with the obsessional neurotic, the dead (and the living, as well) always play such a role. Refusing to give up his friend to the police, Marlowe again comes to Lennox's aid by trying to clear his name. The remainder of the text then becomes an imaginary conversation with Lennox. Throughout this prosopopoeia, it becomes clear that, despite his attraction to his friend's undoing, both symbolically and literally, the dead man remains Marlowe's own "fall guy."

Importantly, Marlowe's ongoing conference with the dead concerns the question of payment, or over-payment as the case may be. Lennox had given Marlowe five hundred dollars for his ride to Tijuana and, a few days after Marlowe's release from jail, a final letter from Terry arrives containing a five-thousand-dollar bill. While typically in command of these situations of payment, Marlowe here does not have the opportunity to refund Lennox's money as the latter's death prevents its return. This is especially troubling for Marlowe. He frequently takes the larger bill out of his safe to stroke its surface and bask in its presence. This is on the one hand sentimental, but this ritual of course at the same time calls into question Marlowe's debt to this other. The largesse indicates that Marlowe has always received something more from Lennox than a simple feeling of superiority. Indeed, the bill reveals just how meaningful Lennox has become in Marlowe's desiring economy.[103]

Marlowe refers to his exorbitant banknote by the name of the man whose face appears on the bill. Another founding father: Madison. The bill is obviously extremely rare, in fact, the reader is told that there are only about one thousand of these bills in circulation. This extreme scarcity — and, obviously, value — underscores the fragile pact made with the Other through this token, while at the same time it leaves Marlowe far too obligated to this same figure. Lennox's gross over-payment cannot be dismissed as "just business," requiring Marlowe to make the return of the money his most urgent task. In many respects, then, the text becomes a reversal of "The Purloined Letter." The detective works not to recover the phallic signifier, but rather to keep his distance from it at all costs. However, it should not be assumed that Marlowe has yet understood the lesson of the letter. Though the return of the bill promises to reconstitute the symbolic order of the text, this gesture is made with an indignity that nevertheless asks for a content behind the semblance, or a father behind the "flash money."

The "portrait of Madison," as Marlowe comes to call the five-thousand-dollar bill, in this way exemplifies the nature of the obsessional's relations with the world. As Marlowe says elsewhere, in a related context, "All tough guys are monotonous. Like playing with a deck of aces, you've got everything and nothing" (*TLG* 64). This comment refers to the threatening "tough" speech of the average hard-boiled thug, but I would like to suggest that this criticism be considered at the level of the genre, as well. The action of the tough guy detective — at least before the emergence of Spillane — is predicated upon tough talk and largely empty threats. As is the case with the obsessional, words are all that the detective has to assert his potency. These offer the pretense of power, but little else, as the portrait of Madison makes clear. The bill is exorbitantly large and, precisely because of this fact, it is doubtful that it will ever be put into circulation. Even Lennox used this item as a prop, an affectation that was, in the end, nothing but a sign of the excessive wealth into which he married. In each symbolic economy, Lennox receives everything and nothing. Indeed, after imagining that the bill — and all it represents — could be useful, his second great mistake is to think that he could effectively exchange this useless tender as some sort of compensation to his friend Marlowe. Similarly, one recalls Marlowe's penchant for describing objects, people, gestures, etc., as "meaningless," all the while trying to define the recalcitrant world around him.[104] Indeed, this odd resignation, "it didn't mean anything," runs like a refrain throughout the series.

Marlowe's well-known penchant for playing chess by himself doubles the impotence and isolation figured in the useless currency. (This solitary gaming is of course used to similar ends throughout the Marlowe series.) In these games, the detective "replays" famous matches of the masters, being carefully attentive to the "defenses" used by the respective players.

This must be taken as critical reflection upon the version of masculinity at stake in the detective genre. The repetition of the chess game, whose outcome has already been played out to a draw, clearly mirrors the detective's identification with the "big man." In each game, "defense" is of the utmost importance. Though Marlowe criticizes the impotence of such a contest as "elaborate a waste of human intelligence as you could find anywhere outside an advertising agency" (*TLG* 153), this "war without blood," it remains to be seen whether this stalemate can productively be avoided at other levels of his characterization.

The greatest hindrance to surmounting this identification, to traversing the fantasy of the "big man," is the fact that Marlowe's rejections are scripted entirely within the split discourse of sentiment. In the ambiguous note left by Lennox during his final hour, he asks Marlowe to light a cigarette and pour a cup of coffee in remembrance of him, a ritual that is to be followed with one last gimlet at their favorite bar, Ernie's. The detective performs each rite, earnest in its meaning.

This final farewell is the "long goodbye" for which the book is named. However, it is likewise ostensibly a goodbye to the sentiment, that intrusive bond to the dead, which troubles Marlowe. This valediction takes a detour through the lives of Eileen and Roger Wade, a sub-plot that ultimately yields the solution to the murder of Sylvia Lennox. It seems that Eileen Wade, in a fit of insane jealousy at her husband Roger's affair with Sylvia, killed Sylvia and then brutally mutilated the corpse beyond all recognition. After this is clarified, Lennox himself reappears — from beyond the grave, as it were —

admitting that his apparent suicide was a forgery that he pulled off with the aid of old army buddies. He has again undergone plastic surgery, but Marlowe is assured of his identity by the color of his eyes.[105] This purchase of a new life was done solely because Lennox was certain that he would take the blame for the murder of his wife. Naturally, this speaks to a not-so-unconscious wish that he had committed the murder, but what is of greater interest is Marlowe's jilted feelings in response to this. Lennox had not stayed to defend himself. Instead, he effectively surrenders, just as he has done all his life. For this, Marlowe chastises Lennox for being a moral defeatist. Marlowe indicts Lennox with the following comments: "For a long time I couldn't figure you at all. You had nice ways and nice qualities, but there was something wrong. You had standards and you lived up to them, but they were personal. They had no relation to any kind of ethics or scruples" (*TLG* 310).

It is here that Marlowe's refusal of sentiment becomes most sentimental. If Lennox has betrayed anything, it is Marlowe's own personal ethic that has transformed his friend into an ego ideal that potentially offers him a point of symbolic identification. Unsurprisingly, Marlowe's accusations turn to the issue of meaning: "You bought a lot of me, Terry. For a smile and a nod and a wave of the hand and a few quiet drinks in a quiet bar here and there. It was nice while it lasted. So long, amigo. I won't say goodbye. I said it to you when it meant something. I said it when it was sad, lonely and final" (*TLG* 311). Lennox is clearly the father who has failed Marlowe, but in a particularly obsessive manner: he has refused, like all good fathers, to remain dead. Rather than showing Marlowe how to avoid desire, Lennox is shown to be nothing more than an empty surface (i.e., he is revealed as lacking), as his thrice-reconstructed face indicates.

The detective is unquestionably hystericized in this encounter, but the repetition of Marlowe's sentiment in the midst of its renouncement shows that his fantasy structure remains in place. Plain reads this text as an end to Marlowe's search for the ideal father, or the "big man" who would make sense of masculinity itself. On the contrary, I would argue that what occurs in Marlowe's sentimental renouncement is merely another obsessive rejection of an individual father figure, a gesture that at the same time holds the place of the father open. In this way, Marlowe manages to maintain his personal "ethic" in suspension, predicated as it is upon his obsessional isolation. Indeed, this stance will be held indefinitely as this is the final novel written by Chandler.[106]

These difficulties with the father beget Marlowe's infamous difficulties with women. Though Marlowe makes frequent comments to the effect that "he knows nothing about women," it is clear that the opposite is in fact true: Marlowe knows nothing about men. Admittedly, this leaves him at a similar disadvantage when considering the opposite sex, as well. As is the case with the hysteric, Marlowe will attempt to answer the question of the sexual relation by making inquiries into the desiring relations of those around him. Naturally, in the end, masculine desire is of greater interest in his analyses.

For example, in *Farewell, My Lovely*, Marlowe will search for Moose Malloy who in turn searches for his lost love Velma Valento. This inquiry results in a series of murders committed by the latter, each presaging the inert, dead body that is at the heart of Malloy's fantasy itself—that is, the construction of "little Velma" in his own memory. The "farewell" of this novel speaks to the *pathos* elicited by Malloy's condemned love for a woman who long ago betrayed him and who will, finally, murder him. Marlowe looks to the "big man" to learn something of desire, but of course this will be done in order to sustain desire as impossible, thereby supporting the uncompromising portrait of a powerful masculinity. The distanced woman and the unrequited nature of Malloy's love for Velma appears to offer Marlowe a practicable erotics well suited to these ends.[107] However, Chandler appropriately indicts Marlowe's ideal for containing the seeds of its own destruction, notably through the animalistic frenzy of Malloy, who simply "does not know his own strength." The latter characteristic is important not only because this misunderstanding results in two unintentional murders. This quality likewise figures the character's fantasy life as well, a misapprehension that will cost him his life. As Malloy's fantasy proves to be truly lethal, the "farewell" of the title must at the same time refer to the abandonment of Marlowe's search for an effective strategy for distancing himself from the question of femininity.

Given his greater deference to the father, Marlowe, like Freud's famous obsessional case study, the so-called "Rat Man," will take the father's prohibition against the enjoyment of the mother and generalize it to all women.[108] As a result, Marlowe's brief encounters with women are, nearly without exception, unconsummated and traumatic for the detective.[109] The most famous example of this occurs in *The Big Sleep* when Carmen Sternwood, a character who remains perhaps more a succubus figure than a *femme fatale*, randomly appears in Marlowe's apartment, waiting for him in bed.[110] Before finding her, he senses that something is out of sorts, there is a scent in the air—one of several details signifying Carmen's animality—that is described as "cloying," a term that felicitously anticipates the excess of the scene that follows (*TBS* 153). Marlowe attempts to coax Carmen out of bed, saying that he cannot join her because he would be letting her, and no doubt her father, down (*TBS* 155). It is little wonder, then, that throughout his appeal, the detective addresses Carmen in fraternal terms, calling her "pal" and "friend" (*TBS* 155).

Needless to say, Carmen is entirely uncooperative, but it is the nature of her resistance that demands attention. As Marlowe describes her reaction: "I looked away. Then I was aware of the hissing noise very sudden and sharp. It startled me into looking at her again. She sat there naked, her face like scraped bone. The hissing noise came tearing out of her mouth as if she had nothing to do with it. There was something behind her eyes, blank as they were, that I had never seen in a woman's eyes" (*TBS* 157). What Marlowe encounters in this wonderfully described "blankness" is the *objet a*, here as that uncanny disembodied voice, which is never an "object" that might be grasped or signified — or definitely linked to a body. This "hiss" confronts Marlowe with his own object-cause, as his own *jouissance* transferred to Carmen in the manner suggested by Copjec above. The woman does indeed return to demand it from him as levy. Yet, from his vantage point, it remains a void that nevertheless seems to have an indescribable content of some kind. In a genre that is dedicated to the maintenance of masculine authority through the eradication of desire, it is entirely appropriate that the emergence of the woman's desire be cast in both these animal-like figures and images of the void. Given the anxiety with which this "mastery" is maintained, it is no accident that these women become predatory. In *The Big Sleep*, it is not merely those that follow the sirens call who are devoured, but likewise those who refuse. It will be remembered that Rusty Regan — who, like Marlowe, rejected Carmen's advances — is thrown into the void of an abandoned Sternwood oil well. He is, quite literally, a casualty of the abyss of the feminine.

Such events shake Marlowe's obsessional edifice to its very foundations. At one point during his confrontation with Carmen, Marlowe calmly tells the reader, "It's so hard for women — even nice women — to realize that their bodies are not irresistible" (*TBS* 156). Naturally, the point to be taken is that Marlowe is not the slightest bit aroused or interested in Carmen Sternwood. However, at the end of the chapter, after Carmen has finally left his apartment, Marlowe himself goes back to the bed and "savagely" tears it to pieces (*TBS* 159). The next morning he finds it necessary to have an extra cup of coffee, explaining, "You can have a hangover from other things than alcohol. I had one from women. Women made me sick" (*TBS* 159). Clearly, Marlowe's defenses are not as sound as he would make them appear. A similar event occurs in *The Long Goodbye*, as Marlowe describes his romantic encounter with Eileen Wade. "I lifted her and carried her the few steps to the bed and lowered her. She kept her arms around my neck. She was making some kind of a whistling noise in her throat. Then thrashed about and moaned. This was murder. I was as erotic as a stallion. I was losing control. You don't get that sort of invitation from that sort of woman very often anywhere" (*TLG* 173). This episode is cut short by the Wade's butler. After Marlowe turns the butler away, he returns to the bed but finds the "spell broken" and the noises made by Eileen all the more uncanny. He summarily leaves Wade and proceeds to drink until he passes out. Each encounter with the *objet a* returned to him through the *femme fatale* hystericizes Marlowe, requiring that he purify himself through various obsessional rites during the remainder of the respective stories.

It is the way in which this purification occurs that the obsessional structure which underlies the hard-boiled detective text is revealed all too well— even in the case of the more frequently hystericized Marlowe. In *The Big Sleep*, the encounter with Carmen opens the larger aporia of the text, that is, how Marlowe solves the disappearance of Rusty Regan. Criticism frequently claims that *The Big Sleep* cheats the reader by not *showing* how Marlowe concludes that Carmen murdered Regan in a violent fit after the latter had refused her advances. With this knowledge, Marlowe loads Carmen's gun with blanks, tricking the younger Sternwood into repeating the event of Regan's death, a repetition that requires a trip to the desiccated oil wells at the edge of the family's property.

The solution of this mystery demands that Marlowe himself repeat his own traumatic incident with Carmen in thought. Significantly, it is through the figure of the "big man" sought in this text, Rusty Regan, that he comes to signify the event in question, reducing it, essentially, to a clue in the mystery with which the novel began. This is the operation of obsessional knowledge *par excellence*. Through repetition and an unhinging of event from affect, the desire that had erupted in his encounters with Carmen is successfully dissipated. That this occurs "behind the scenes," as it were, is likewise appropriate to the obsessional structure of the hard-boiled narrative. If the obsessive ritual is to work properly, it is all-important that it not be brought under the scrutiny of a prying Other of any kind, and here that Other is of course the reader of the text.

I would like to return for a moment to a question that was central to my reading of the classical detective in Chapter One, that is, the critical analogy made between the detective and the psychoanalyst. It must be acknowledged that Freudian categories, at least as these are popularly absorbed by the time, are often quite present within hard-boiled fiction.[111] Indeed, one frequently finds discussion of the relation between the detective and analyst at the level of narrative in these texts. Given the antagonistic nature of these discussions, I find it productive to understand the genre itself as an obsessive response to the discourse of analysis. However, as I will briefly demonstrate by way of conclusion, this denial is not made without an accompanying illumination of the work of the analyst. Though their goals may be quite disparate, I wish to argue that knowledge functions in a similar way for the hard-boiled detective and analyst.[112]

The Detective Meets the Analyst: Perverse Disavowals of the Mike Hammer Series

The best example illustrating this tension between analysis and hard-boiled detection is found in Spillane's first novel, *I, the Jury* (1947). Indeed, the *femme fatale*, Charlotte Manning, is herself an analyst, an embodiment that is paradigmatic of the hard-boiled anxiety surrounding the analytic enterprise. This recalls Žižek's reading of *The Silence of the Lambs* as an example of the American difficulty in conceptualizing the Lacanian analyst.[113] Like Anthony Hopkins' character in that same film, the Lacanian analyst devours the subject, calling for her or his radical dissolution. This stance is in all ways opposed to the work of ego psychology, which aims to bolster the analysand's ego, typically through an identification with the analyst. Such therapy partakes of an adaptive metaphor that hopes to reconcile the patient's ego-thoughts with her or his *Umwelt*, a relation that is, as has been shown, fundamentally incompatible to Lacanian psychoanalysis.

As the obsessional attempts to simultaneously annul and appeal to the Other, an encounter with the analyst by the obsessional detective must be exceptionally uncomfortable as this confrontation reveals the over-determination of this split demand in the detective's fantasy structure. As has been suggested, only a catastrophe of the gravest magnitude will bring the obsessional to the analyst. Once there, it is most likely the hystericization that has prompted the decision — a condition that remains requisite for any productive analysis to begin — will be short lived.[114] If the hard-boiled detective is to be understood primarily within the obsessional structure, it is certain that he himself is not an analyst of the kind spoken of in Chapter One. However, this is not to say that this fiction does not reveal much about the analytic process.

A particularly telling reference to the similarities between the vocations of the analyst and the detective appear in Chandler's *The Long Goodbye*. As Marlowe tells Inspector Ohls near the conclusion of the novel:

> This ain't police business any more. It's getting to be a branch of the medical racket. Ten years from now guys like Hernandez and me will be doing Rohrschach tests and word associations instead of chin-ups and target practice. When we go out on a case we'll carry little black bags with portable lie detectors and bottles of truth serum. Too bad we didn't grab the four hard monkeys that poured it on Big Willie Magoon. We might have been able to unmaladjust them and make them love their mothers [*TLG* 267].

Marlowe's sarcasm echoes a criticism that occurs throughout the text of the therapeutic culture that was by this time already well entrenched in Southern California. Naturally, according to the measure of the hard-boiled ethic of seclusion and self-reliance, the patients, and Roger Wade in particular, are themselves cast as more reprehensible than the corrupt doctors that illegally practice psychopharmacology.[115] Even so, the similarity between the two practices remains, a fact that apparently bothers Marlowe the detective in much the same way that it bothered Freud the analyst. Admittedly, the latter was much more reticent about his attraction to the work of his (fictional) fellow travelers.

A second instance from *The Long Goodbye* that speaks directly to the omnipresence of Freudian categories is the following, spoken to Marlowe by the writer Roger Wade who is loath to entertain his party guests: "Every damn one of them knows I'm an alcoholic. So they wonder what I'm running away from. Some Freudian bastard has made that a commonplace. Every ten-year-old kid knows it by now. If I had a ten-year-old kid, which God forbid, the brat would be asking me, 'What are you running away from when you get drunk, Daddy?'" (*TLG* 142). As a criticism of this fashionable Freudian reduction is present at the level of narrative, it must be assumed that Roger Wade, and Marlowe as well, cannot adequately be diagnosed from such a "pop-psychology" perspective. The question of moving beyond this reduction must, then, remain ongoing for Marlowe.

Despite these limitations, there are significant similarities between the detective's methods and Lacan's definition of the function of the analyst.[116] The Lacanian analyst does not proceed by way of brilliant interpretation, although this may occur at appropriately punctuated moments within the analysis. On the contrary, to analyze exclusively from such a position of mastery would be to support the analysand's belief in the Supposed-Subject-of-Knowing, a fantasy that analysis will deny at every turn.[117] Rather than offering the patient a stable identification that might be taken in place of a faltering ego, the Lacanian analyst will attempt to embody the object-cause of the analysand's desire.[118]

By bringing the patient into contact with the emptiness of this structure, it is possible for the "traversal of the fantasy," or the giving up of fantasies regarding the promise and the prohibition of the Other. As Lacan describes, "It is a desire to obtain absolute difference, a desire which intervenes when, confronted with the primary signifier, the subject is, for the first time, in a position to subject himself to it."[119] In this "traversal," the analysand takes responsibility for, "subjects himself to," the emptiness of the signifier that was formerly the seat of the Other's (fantasmatic) power. The subject in this way takes responsibility for her or his own "cause," rather than waiting for the Other (the analyst, the detective, etc.) to give meaning to this absence. Rather than blaming some phantom Other for the ruins of one's life and character, one accepts responsibility for having chosen to respond to life's travails and tragedies in an idiomatic way. "Change" might now occur, as the oppressive demand of the Other is no longer present. However, it is just as likely that the analysand may now come to "enjoy their symptom."[120]

Like the analyst, the hard-boiled detective offers no global interpretations that lead to the incontrovertible solution of a crime. This detective is more concerned with questions of desire and guilt, matters that are seldom "solved," and indeterminacies from which he himself is never excused.[121] This attention to desire is evident in the Continental Op's method of "stirring things up," a technique that is fundamental to hard-boiled practice. The Op's methods attempt to bring both relations and (violent) desires to the surface, obviously a habit that is not without its perils. As he explains, "stirring things up is all right — if you're tough enough to survive, and keep your eyes open so you'll see what you want when it comes to the top" (*RH* 85). As is the case with the analyst, the detective will do his best not to let his own desire to become active, for this is the quickest way to ensure one's entrance into a losing battle. He must likewise keep himself sufficiently distanced from the paths of desire that he crosses. Spillane no doubt exaggerates this method to the extreme, but the overall technique and its goals are not so different from the Op, Spade, or Marlowe. Mike Hammer willingly becomes the "executioner" in addition to simply identifying the criminal by way of exculpating himself. He wishes, before vengeance is enacted, to confront the killer with his crime, to make the individual own up to their transgressive desire and, then, to pay the price.[122]

Such melodramatic confrontations are often made use of by Philip Marlowe, as well.[123] At the end of *The Long Goodbye*, the policeman Bernie Ohls accuses Marlowe of wanting Eileen Wade dead, given the way that he (Marlowe) roughly confronted her with the murder of both her husband and Sylvia Lennox. (Shortly after this confrontation, Wade commits suicide.) As Marlowe responds, "I wanted her to take a good long quiet look at herself. What she did about it was her business. I wanted to clear an innocent man. I didn't give a good goddam how I did it and I don't now. I'll be around when you feel like doing something about me" (*TLG* 278). As is decidedly the case with Spillane, the personal nature of this decision is betrayed by Marlowe's flagrant call to the Other, present here as the institution of the police. (As he says, he will be around if they wish to punish him for his actions.) As has been shown, this desire to be punished by some higher agency, to at last "get what one has coming to them," is a typical fantasy of the obsessional neurotic. Indeed, this veiled demand is evident in the hard-boiled convention, developed early on by Daly and Hammett, which requires that the detective himself be the victim of physical violence. However, the point to be taken apropos the current discussion is that, though the detective's personal interest precludes such moments from being analytic in a strict sense, insights of the analytic discourse are present here nevertheless.

A fitting expression of the uncanny similarity between analytic "knowledge" and that of a more interested, and therefore pathological, nature is again epitomized in Spillane's *I, the Jury*. Indeed, it seems as though the work of the detective and the therapist, Charlotte Manning, are most similar as each betrays (i.e., diverges from) the demands of analysis itself. The insatiable analyst uses her training in order to identify and make use of the weaknesses of her prey, who are, naturally, most often men. As Hammer summarizes the similarities between detective work and analysis in familiar terms, it is the "details that counted," the little things that work to reveal limitation and guilt (*MHC* 79). Putting this method into action, Charlotte describes her male patients: "But they are such little men. Either they have no character to begin with or what they had is gone. Their minds are frail, their conception limited. So many have repressions or obsessions, and they come to me with their pitiful stories; well, when you constantly see men with their masculinity gone, and find the same sort among those whom you call your friends, you get so you actually search for a real man" (*MHC* 82). Initially this is taken as charming flirting by Hammer, who is entirely consumed with Charlotte's beauty, though at the novel's conclusion the preying element of this admiration is evident.[124] Again, as is typical in Spillane, in this one finds an illuminating distillation of generic codes in its very exaggeration. Unlike many of her predecessors, Charlotte Manning literally wishes to enjoy Mike Hammer sexually — he is, after all, a "real" man — and then do away with him. Sentiment and symbolic exchange are here entirely out of place. And neither demure nor effigy are necessary as the proxy of mystery and its object are effectively abandoned.

Despite Manning's dissimulation, she is rather candid of her own limits and, perhaps, those of her profession. As she says of herself, "I'm used to personal conflict, the struggle that goes on within one's mind, not with differences between two or more people. I can notice things, put them in their proper places, but I can't do more than file them away" (*MHC* 85). Appropriately, she has trouble with relations and, contrary to vocational demands, she has difficulties in identifying intentions. In treating each patient as an island, so to speak, her theory of the psyche dwelling in isolation matches the obsessional detective's *modus operandi* all too well. Naturally, this likewise functions to bind Charlotte to the formal hard-boiled convention that demands that the woman misjudge the man's intention. Even in the highly sexualized world of Spillane, both man and woman continue to speak "different languages." In Hammett and Chandler, this misplaced presumption revolved around sentiment or romantic love, the sexualization of these relations often left either absent altogether or merely implicit. In Spillane, these former representations become explicit as Charlotte depends upon Hammer's lust for her body; hence the latter's perplexity after she is shot by Hammer while undressing before him in the infamous final scene of the novel. When she asks how he could have done such a thing, Hammer simply avers, "It was easy" (*MHC* 246).

From Spillane's perspective, the analyst is condemned, then, to the level of the descriptive, and becomes in this way little more than a bystander undeserving of the respect the profession, for some reason, popularly demands. In short, the analyst cannot be the "man" of action. However, these limitations did not keep Manning from using the tools of her trade to prey upon the weak men she describes, as she uses them as pawns in her various blackmailing and drug-trafficking schemes. Within the text she and her profession are condemned for plundering the weaknesses of others and using their desire against them. Of course, this is hardly novel within the genre, save for one item: Charlotte Manning openly enjoys this process, as is made evident in the preoccupation with her — often "manly" — libido. The deadly aspect of the woman's enjoyment is emphasized in a particularly heinous detail noticed by Hammer while investigating the initial murder (of his friend Jack) at the beginning of the text. The murderer, who we later discover is Charlotte, shot the victim in the stomach and then remained amusedly watching his death and suffering as he crawled across the floor, trying to reach his gun. As was the case even when this enjoyment was latent, it is for this reason that the woman must be eradicated.

But what is also more manifest in the work of Spillane is the detective's own enjoyment in these processes. This enjoyment has, as I have endeavored to show throughout this chapter, existed — albeit in a much different form — from the earliest moments of the genre, despite the obsessional detective's assertions to the contrary. In *I, the Jury,* the detective's enjoyment is hyperbolically rendered in the delight Hammer takes in Charlotte sexually and homicidally. That this is ultimately done in the name of justice throughout the Hammer novels clearly establishes his character as a pervert. The pervert is the subject for whom castration has not been fully completed, leaving the individual stranded between alienation and separation.[125] Suspended in this position, the pervert will attempt to enact the law of castration that failed him, as is the goal of every perverse ritual (i.e., to establish the Law). The police officer is always, in effect, a pervert, as this person repeatedly attempts to bring about the "true" existence of the law in their daily work. However, given that the perverse subject has not completely accepted the Law of the Father, this relation to the law is idiosyncratic, that is, unmediated by the symbolic order.

This is precisely what Mike Hammer expresses when he criticizes the law's inability to "remember," that is, to enact private vengeance: "The law is fine. But this time I'm the law and I'm not going to be cold and impartial. I'm going to remember all those things" (*MHC* 4). What the law refuses to remember, or rather allow — so the (neurotic) individual imagines — is the individual subject's own enjoyment. Symbolic castration — that is, alienation within the language of the Other — requires this for every subject. From the psychoanalytic perspective, each psychical structure (e.g., obsessional neurosis, hysteria, etc.) is a method of coming to terms with this imagined loss. The similarities between the obsessional and perverse structure are apparent as each attempts to deny the loss of castration. However, though the pervert would seem to be more straightforward in this disavowal, this is not the case. Pursuing pleasure at all costs, the pervert in the end works only for the enjoyment of the Other, seeking to bring this limit, and hence their own subjectivity, into existence.[126]

Spillane, then, does not mark the end of the hard-boiled genre of detective fiction. Rather, what one finds in his work is the manifestation of the (perverse) dream of the "real" man that has been present within the genre since its beginnings. As Freud identified long ago, the neurotic dreams of being a pervert, of acting out the transgressions the pervert enjoys. This neurotic fantasy misapprehends the place and function of this transgressive enjoyment, which actually attempts to establish the law's prohibition. Despite the indignant response to his popularity, both academic and popular, it is no accident that the sales of Spillane's Hammer novels exponentially surpassed the sales of any other detective writer in the history of the genre. If one adheres to the genealogy I have presented in this chapter, this popularity can be explained as Mike Hammer being the solution to the mystery of masculinity that had been posed by the hard-boiled genre from its beginnings. His perversion is enjoyed all the more by the reading public as it offers explicit versions of formerly implicit desires, while at the same time recalling the safe obsessional structure to which this same audience had grown so accustomed.

However, what is markedly changed with this entrance of perversion onto the hard-boiled stage is the detective's relation to knowledge. Again, the pervert is the subject who, by way of attempting to make the law itself exist, produces a knowledge of enjoyment. In treating neurotic patients, analysis must be entirely opposed to such a presumption. Analysis confronts the subject with erroneousness of the very structure that posits enjoyment as having been commandeered by the Other. (There can, then, be no symbolic law of enjoyment — indeed, *jouissance* is precisely what escapes this space.) Without the alibi of the latter, whose crime was the basis of the knowledge of *lost* enjoyment, the subject is forced to confront and subjectivize his relation to this aporia. In other words, the subject is called upon to ponder the place of "truth" rather than that of "knowledge."

Conclusion

As was discussed in Chapter One, in Lacan's realignment of the place of the analyst from Other to object-cause of desire, it is no longer possible for the analyst to use knowledge in any commonsensical way. Quite simply, knowledge cannot be understood as a tool that achieves results, such as providing meaning to the symptom. As object-cause of desire, the analyst must then bracket her or his knowledge and in so doing allow patients themselves to produce a new knowledge of their symptom.[127] Here, too, the content of this knowledge is unimportant provided the subject does effectively change her or his relation to this formerly traumatic piece of the real, that is, the *objet a*.

As Lacan says in *Seminar XX*, the analyst is the one who "makes his knowledge function in terms of truth," something that is impossible, leaving the analyst to proceed only by speaking "half-truths."[128] Rather than supplying the patient with signifiers in an unending interpretation, or symptomatology, the analyst attempts to embody the analysand's empty truth. The analyst does not interpret this "truth," rather, she or he confronts the patient with its absence. Here again, we arrive at the object-cause of the subject, that is, the traumatic core of the subject that is incapable of being symbolized. In many ways, the patient comes to analysis blaming this deficiency on the Other (in any number of guises), a gesture that at the same time allows the subject to imagine that their "cause" might be explained or symbolized. Indeed, that is precisely where the analyst comes in — she or he will at last articulate the enigma of suffering. Should the patient heed the emptiness of the place of truth — rather than demand its illumination — she or he will come to subjectify, or take responsibility for, this cause.

Interestingly, in the hard-boiled world, Žižek sees this possibility of subjectifying the cause in the *femme fatale*. As discussed above, in the end, the *femme fatale* cannot be reduced to the sexual enjoyment she promises, even in its more lethal dimension. Neither can she be reduced to the moral or ethical threat that her presence seems to ensure. Rather, "The real dimension of the threat is revealed when we 'traverse' the fantasy, when the coordinates of the fantasy space are lost via hysterical breakdown. In other words, what is really menacing about the femme fatale is not that she is fatal for *men* but that she presents a case of 'pure,' nonpathological subject fully assuming *her own* fate."[129] The *femme fatale*, then, takes responsibility for her own cause (or "fate"), embracing it even unto death. In this, she confronts the detective with the *objet a* as an empty cause and the possibility of identification with this space, a space that is beyond imaginary and symbolic coordinates — in other words, a space that is beyond the law of the father. Žižek goes on to conclude that, when confronted with the *femme fatale* in this way, the detective can do one of two things: He can forsake her, choosing any one of the variety of renunciations discussed throughout this chapter. Alternately, he can embrace her, and confront the emptiness of his own object-case.[130] This second option — so frequently shunned in the above examples — is typically the threshold of *film noir*, a world in which the detective perhaps more willingly becomes criminal.

While the *femme fatale* offers an excellent figure for the dissolution of the subject that occurs in "traversing the fantasy," or subjectifying the cause, I would like to suggest that hard-boiled detective fiction finds analytic insight elsewhere, as well. And it is here that I would like to reposition the detective-analyst analogy.

As has been shown, the hermeneutic of the classical detective presupposes a visibility, on some level, of all that is of importance. The criminal is always named and in this way the innocence of the group of potential subjects surrounding the murder is ensured. Though this latter operation is strictly impossible within the hard-boiled world, there remains nostalgia for such limpidity. This latter item perhaps complicates a reworking of the detective-analyst analogy. However, the fact that this nostalgia is effectively thwarted in nearly every case always already provides for the hystericization that is required of the analytic process.

This trauma at the level of epistemology that is experienced by the detective offers potential insight beyond the scientific discourse upon which investigation was formerly based. In this condition, the obsessional detective intuits that his former understanding of himself is meaningless and, given the globalizing aspects of his thought, this skepticism is further cast upon knowledge itself.[131] Admittedly, as has been evident throughout each of the literary works analyzed in this chapter, the detective all too often reenlists former obsessive rituals against such an insight. He continues to search for a systematic answer to what he imagines are the questions of desire and sexual difference, failing to recognize his symptomatic implication within these enigmas — in other words, he wagers knowledge against truth. However, such repetitions, and the version of masculinity that results, are constantly criticized within the genre itself. As the epigraph to this chapter reads, and these words — the last of Hammett's career as a novelist — are fittingly spoken by a woman, "It's all pretty unsatisfactory." Knowledge remains incapable of accounting for the place of truth, as the hystericized hard-boiled detective reveals all too well.

Such a confrontation with the empty place of truth is suggested at the conclusion of Chandler's *The High Window* (1942). After he has safely deposited the neurotic Merle Davis on her family's farm, he drives away, remarking: "I had a feeling as I saw the house disappear, as though I had written a poem and it was very good and I had lost it and would never remember it again."[132] As Lacan continues to develop his theory of interpretation, literature will increasingly be used to describe the end of analysis. Much like Freud's reliance on construction (a concept that I will take up in Chapter Four), Lacan will at times describe the subjectification of the object-cause in terms of literature, and poetry in particular: "Only poetry, as I've said to you, permits interpretation."[133] As Serge André explains,

> In contrast to the fraudulence of meaning, [Lacan] says, there is poetry, which can accomplish the feat of making a meaning absent. He invites his audience to find in poetry what psychoanalytic interpretation can hope to be. Instead of looking for a new signifier to replace the hole left in the unconscious by the lack of [the Other], the analyst should respond with "an empty word," modeled on poetry, "that is a meaning effect but also a hole-effect."[134]

I would like to suggest that Marlowe's poem, which he promptly forgets as he drives away, is such an interpretation.[135] It both opens the possibility for meaning, and at the same time reveals meaning as a literary effect. Here and elsewhere, the hard-boiled genre disrupts interpretative mastery, offering in its place, a poem — or literature, as such. For just these reasons, it is in these moments of interpretative breakdown that the detective-analyst analogy applies.

THREE

Hysteria, Paranoia, and Love in Philip K. Dick's Anti-Detective Fiction

Introduction

In the 2002 Hollywood production of Dick's short story "Imposter," there is one notable difference between the film and the original text. At the end of the film, Spence Olham finds that his murdered body lies among the wreckage of the alien spacecraft, certifying that he is an "imposter," an alien time-bomb that has been sent to assassinate high-ranking earth officials, but, unlike Dick's original story, there among the debris is also found the murdered body of Olham's wife, Mary, meaning of course that she too is an "imposter." The film's final sequence fantastically depicts the immolation of husband and wife, and the rising mushroom cloud that envelops miles of countryside and presumably the neighboring city.

This detail is hardly a drastic supplement. On the contrary, I would argue that it is the "truth" of Dick's work in the psychoanalytic sense discussed in chapters one and two. In other words, in this figure of violent eruption one finds the underwriting, repressed, yet organizing mechanism of the author's work: the failure of the sexual relationship. In Dick's fiction, this failure of the relation between man and woman is always linked to the failure of the social to produce consensus and to the resulting cultural symptoms of schizophrenia and paranoia. As will be shown in this chapter, such paranoia in the work of Philip K. Dick is comprehensible only through the index of woman, and it is precisely through this fascination that Dick's work is to be classified as "anti-detective" in nature. By calling attention to the masquerade of woman and the resulting consternation of the masculine subject, Philip K. Dick scripts the ultimate impossibility of knowledge production done according to the operations of detection that this study has examined.

To date, little scholarship has been done on Dick's debt to the detective genre. In criticism, one finds a trajectory that focuses upon the author's narrative innovations within the sci-fi genre. In early scholarship, there is often a negative reaction to the inconsistencies in plot and theme within the author's work. In subsequent criticism, these inconsistencies are read as brilliant excurses on the ideological bind into which the postmodern subject is thrown.[1] It is in service of this second perspective that Dick has been heralded as the great writer of "psychosis" or "paranoia," appellations that caused Dick a great deal of discomfort — even paranoia — during his own lifetime.[2]

In this chapter, I will read a small sample of Dick's work according to various clinical psychical structures. The sheer mass and inconsistency of the author's oeuvre makes this a dubious task, to be sure. This is further complicated by Dick's penchant for including a criticism of interpretation within the frame(s) of his fiction, a mirroring effect that results in a *mise en abyme* that is well known to all readers of Philip K. Dick. In an early but perspicacious essay, Stanislav Lem speaks of such difficulties that await when interpreting Dick's work. He concludes that in Dick's science fiction, "diagnosis comes to grief" for critics and presumably readers, as well.[3] Bearing in mind that psychoanalysis endeavors to mark interpretative failure, I will attempt to read Dick's work according to the categories of psychosis, neurosis, and hysteria in particular. These categories will in turn be utilized as points of reference for engaging three related preoccupations within the author's work: paranoia, love, and Woman.

The first two items (paranoia and love) readily present themselves as opposed terms within Dick's work, particularly if "love" is read, provisionally, as the equivalent of Dick's conception of "empathy." It is critically commonplace to claim that Dick's solution (for better or for worse) to the increasing alienation and paranoia of our utterly instrumentalized experience is the decidedly human reverence of life, the action of "empathy." My claim is just the opposite. In Dick's work, love does not redeem one from the paranoia of the contemporary moment. Rather, this paranoia is itself intimate to the very functioning of love. This version of love is founded not upon a communion with or dissolution into another being, but upon the construction of a necessary limit in respect to our relations with others. To these ends, Dick's fascination with objects (of handicraft or manufacture), a fascination that might otherwise be read as conflicted given his reverence of more human exchanges, becomes quite appropriate. For Lacan, love is always a love of objects. Indeed, when in love, one "gives the gift that one does not possess," that is, the *objet a*.[4] It is only insofar as one's partner gives body to the *objet a* that they are deserving of love, an embodiment that is, presumably, impossible — but an impossibility that does at times occur.[5]

The mediating force of the object in love is all the more apparent when one considers a second necessary pairing from the above trio of concepts, namely, paranoia and the Woman. Lacan is famous for making the inflammatory statement that the sexual relation does not exist.[6] Naturally, he is not suggesting that people do not couple, either physically or emotionally. What he wishes to suggest is that love is always weighted down by narcissism, ensuring the two people's love and desire never coincide. In other words, despite hopes to the contrary, there always remains something in between a couple, keeping them from love's promised union. Naturally, the impossibility of this relation does not keep it from illuminating the psychical economy of the subject. In this case, it is the *objet a* that distances the masculine subject from an encounter with *the* Woman, that is, a woman un-fractured by the veil of fantasy.[7] The Woman — unbarred — is, then, the Woman who would exist, who would make the sexual relationship possible.[8] In light of my topic, and for the sake of simplicity, in this chapter I will limit my discussion of these issues to the question of the masculine side of desire spoken of by Lacan in *Seminar XX*.

The undeniable paucity of female characters within Dick's work should not lead one to assume that the Woman is not a crucial determinant of his fictional worlds. Indeed, in several respects, this absence speaks to the Woman's sublime power. When these characters do appear, they are scripted in one of two guises: as either the absent, sublime object of fantasy, or as the woman (*the* Woman) who enjoys too much, and thereby threatens the subjective economy of the man. As will be shown, each manifestation is part and parcel of paranoia, both in a clinical and more general epistemological sense. From the neurotic's perspective, the "missing" woman, the sublime fantasy that necessarily remains displaced, is the promise of the sexual relationship completed elsewhere, in another world.[9] The case of the castrating female character (i.e., *the* Woman) uncannily duplicates this logic, but without the luxury of (neurotic) distance as the Woman appears in this world now, a fact that brings us to the threshold of a decidedly different psychical structure, namely, psychosis.

However, while this consideration of psychosis is indispensable given the author's preoccupations, it is my contention that criticism of Dick's work ought not to remain within this register. Dick's prescient delineation of radical changes in post-war American experience continues to ring true, that is, the "future" imagined by Dick continues to illuminate our present. Nevertheless, despite an often very explicit demand for social change and a return to intimacy in the face of post-industrial alienation, the work of Philip K.

Dick remains hesitant, even ambiguous, at the possibility of such changes actually coming to fruition. In other words, there remains a nostalgia for a return to a lost moment of cohesion, both within the social order and the sexual relationship, at the core of Dick's fiction. In this chapter, I will read the author's wavering on this score in terms of hysteria and paranoia. As will be shown, hysteria and paranoia are today common strategies for dealing with the failure of symbolic efficiency and, likewise, the vicissitudes of love. I will begin with a discussion of the structure of paranoia in Freud and Lacan's work. Following this, I will briefly examine Dick's own assertions on this topic, and elaborate the difficulties that his solution to the "problem" of paranoia encounters, largely through a reading of the early novel *Time Out of Joint* (1959). The chapter will conclude with a reading of the question of love and the Woman through an examination of *Flow My Tears, The Policeman Said* (1974), and *Do Androids Dream of Electric Sheep?* (1968), respectively. It is the latter text that explicitly reveals what is implicit elsewhere in the oeuvre, that is, that the directive of the anti-detective always informs Dick's science fiction.

The Structure of Paranoia: Lacking Lack

The structural invention within science fiction that Philip K. Dick frequently, and with great pride, claimed for his own was the plot in which an individual who, naturally having no reason to suspect otherwise, slowly discovers that he is not human, but a machine. Structurally, this contrivance, which has of course become quite commonplace in science fiction, is remarkably akin to the second great development of the genre that Dick achieved in *The Man in the High Castle* (1962). This text is the story of an alternate future, specifically the America that would exist if the Axis Powers had been victorious in World War II. The narrative is told from the multiple perspectives of various characters whose lives, as vastly different as they might be, touch each other in some significant, though often miniscule way. The narrative device in question here is the novel told from "multiple perspectives," abandoning — so it would seem — any sort of orienting center of narration.[10] The common element shared by these devices is that of radical alienation. In the first case, the protagonist is transformed into his own uncanny double, and left irreparably unequal to what was formerly imagined as "self." The second "innovation" is the performance of just this dilemma, and its concomitant anxiety, at the level of narration. In other words, structurally, the reader is plagued with a disorienting proliferation of narratives akin to those that trouble the characters of the text. Given this attention to the experience of alienation,

Philip K. Dick is perhaps the contemporary writer *par excellence* of what Lacan called the fundamental misrecognition (*méconnaissance*) of the subject. This misrecognition is, quite simply, the manner in which the subject is forced to find — with varying degrees of failure — its innermost being in the Other.

For Lacan, this fundamental alienation has far-reaching epistemological consequences. If the subject finds itself there in the place of the Other, the result can only be that the whole of knowledge is paranoid in nature, as the subject is left forever wondering what is occurring in that Other scene.[11] In this sense, Lacan will describe paranoia as part of "normal," neurotic functioning, whereas formerly this characterization was used to designate a primarily psychotic disturbance.

The difference between these two versions of paranoia (i.e., neurotic and psychotic) might quickly be summarized according to the concepts of alienation and foreclosure. Alienation, the situation of the neurotic subject, is the experience of feeling unendingly out of place in the world — an effect of the subject's search for an intimate signifier in the foreign space of the symbolic order. Never receiving recognition from that other space, the neurotic's experience is always plagued with doubt. For the psychotic subject, things are quite different. He remains foreclosed from the big Other, a situation that forces him to create his own symbolic order. Dwelling within a symbolic space expressly created for himself, the psychotic subject is not fraught with the doubt and alienation of the neurotic subject. This is why Lacan describes the orienting experience of the psychotic as that of certainty.[12] Lacan's implication of these two radically different subject positions through the term "paranoia" is crucial to his break from what he perceived to be the contemporary misunderstandings of psychotic functioning.[13] In a certain sense, Lacan's rereading of psychosis is remarkably akin to Dick's own thinking on the contemporary crisis of subjectivity.

Though paranoia has perhaps not received the same attention in theory and criticism as hysteria, it has likewise been a marked force in the development of psychoanalytic theory. As André has maintained, it is only against the paranoid theory of sexual relations authored by the rhinolaryngologist William Fliess, Freud's friend and mentor, that Freud's own theory of psychoanalysis was made possible.[14] Similarly, Lacan himself was quick to indicate that his entrance into psychoanalysis proper only began with a detailed study of paranoia in the form of his medical dissertation that was completed at the end of his training as a psychiatrist.[15]

This productive exchange is hardly surprising given the paranoiac's affinity for systematization and great acuity and inventiveness in reading. Both the psychoanalyst and the paranoid are nothing if not discerning readers, a kinship that initially discomfited Freud. In his analysis of the famous

Schreber case, Freud had remarked upon the uncanny similarity between Schreber's delusions of receiving divine messages and the libido theory with which he (Freud) was attempting to analyze these delusions.[16] Later in his career, Freud was much more accepting of this coincidence. For example, in the concluding paragraphs of "Constructions in Analysis" (1937), Freud went so far as to describe the analysand's delusions and the analyst's constructions as directed at the same goal. As he wrote, "The delusions of patients appear to me to be the equivalents of the constructions which we build up in the course of an analytic treatment.... Just as our construction is only effective because it recovers a fragment of lost experience, so the delusion owes its convincing power to the element of historic truth which it inserts in the place of the rejected reality."[17] Interestingly, Freud qualifies this statement in respect to psychosis, which, he says, "can do no more than replace the fragment of reality that is being repudiated in the present by another fragment that had already been repudiated in the remote past."[18] Analysis, on the contrary, potentially offers the analysand a *new* narrative arrangement of reality. However, this too is a fragment, one whose mechanism remains uncannily similar to that of delusions.

This implication of analysis and delusion recalls another discussion of imprecise (or extimate) boundaries in the brief piece "The Loss of Reality in Neurosis and Psychosis" (1924). In this essay, Freud remarks that while neurosis and psychosis would seem to be entirely distinct, each psychical mechanism shares the same goal. Neurosis and psychosis are each an "expression of a rebellion on the part of the id against the external world, of its unwillingness — or incapacity — to adapt itself to the exigencies of reality."[19] In this, both neurosis and psychosis turn away from reality so that the psyche might seek satisfaction elsewhere. For the neurotic, this will occur in fantasy; for the psychotic, in delusion. As Freud summarizes: "neurosis does not disavow the reality, it only ignores it; psychosis disavows it and tries to replace it."[20] In addition to sharing this departure from reality (the first step of illness), neurosis and psychosis likewise guarantee that the second step of illness — repression or disavowal, respectively — will be "partly unsuccessful."[21] In other words, inevitably, the patient's flight from reality will fail in some way. Elsewhere in the article, Freud offers the example of a former patient who was desperately in love with her brother-in-law. At her sister's deathbed, the woman suddenly thinks to herself that the brother-in-law is at last free to begin a relationship with her. This unpleasant thought, which is of course forbidden in reality, is immediately repressed. The result is a hysteric illness that ultimately brings the woman into analysis. The neurotic strategy of repression indeed is "partly unsuccessful." The psychotic response to this situation, as Freud suggests, would be to deny the death of the sister entirely.

No doubt, this strategy would be "partly unsuccessful," as well, resulting in the extreme anxiety that so frequently accompanies psychotic delusions. Here, Freud speculates, "Probably in a psychosis the rejected piece of reality constantly forces itself upon the mind, just as the repressed instinct does in a neurosis, and that is why in both the cases the consequences too are the same."[22] The point to be taken from Freud's discussion is that the limits between neurosis and psychosis are not as clear as we would at first assume. There is always an element of psychosis in neurosis — and neurosis in psychosis. As we shall see, this is an insight that is repeated throughout Philip K. Dick's oeuvre.

Returning to Lacan, we might identify this confluence in the paranoid nature of knowledge for the neurotic. The corollary of this paranoiac knowledge is what Lacan terms "aggressivity," the necessary accompaniment of the fundamental misrecognition (*méconnaissance*) of the subject. To recall a previous discussion, the "mirror phase" teaches that the subject is cut, or limited, by the signifier, and therefore unequal to the mirror image. The subject is, then, never "at home," even in its own skin, which is hardly a comfortable experience. If the "self is an other," Lacan concludes, this "structures the subject as rivaling with himself."[23] The double seen within the image of the mirror — that image the subject can never equal — is always uncanny, and must come to bear the subject's ill will and, hence, "aggressivity." Importantly, Lacan understands the ego as an object through which the subject will negotiate its relations with the world. The tension that results from this objectification "leads to the awakening of [the subject's] desire for the object of the other's desire," which is found in the aggressive rivalry shared among the subject, itself, others, and the world.[24] To phrase this in Freud's terms suggested above, the ego is itself a compromise formation that begins life as a flight from reality. And, naturally, it is always "partly unsuccessful," as Freud describes fantasy life and delusion.

This point might also be phrased according to another structure of antagonism developed subsequently in Lacan's thought, that is, the phallus. The phallus marks the subject's entrance into the realm of language as an absence, or as a subject of lack. As Fink has defined this structure: "It is the signifier of that loss or absence of being which is behind the subject's very relation to the signifier: there is no subject at the outset, and the signifier names the as yet empty space in which the subject will come to be."[25] In this way, the phallus, which remains actually empty, at the same time bears the promise of all that the subject imagines is lost with its entrance into language. "It is the signifier that is destined to designate meaning effects as a whole, insofar as the signifier conditions them by its presence as signifier."[26] As bearer of this promise, the phallus likewise underwrites the authority of the symbolic order, guaranteeing that at some undisclosed point in the future the signifier will at last be equal to the signified. The phallus is, then, that emptiness that provides a space of exchange between the subject and the symbolic authority of the Other.

This commerce, however, is always marked by an experience of contagion. As Žižek has written, "Insofar as phallus *qua* signifier designates the agency of the symbolic authority, its crucial feature resides in the fact that it is not 'mine,' the organ of a living subject, but a place where a foreign power intervenes and inscribes itself onto my body, a place where the big Other acts through me."[27] Though this describes a neurotic structure, the experience articulated sounds remarkably akin to a psychotic delusion. (That being said, the function of the Other for the neurotic and psychotic is quite distinct in Lacan. I will take this up momentarily.) This is the antagonism of the phallus, which marks the symbolic authority that, at least potentially, dwells within the subject. At the same time, the gap opened by the phallus allows for knowledge production, as such. In other words, because this signifier is lacking, the subject will attempt to produce knowledge about this lack through the symbolic order. However, this knowledge is bound to the subject's most basic alienation as it is produced not only *for* a "foreign power" but, as Žižek indicates, through the subject's veritable possession by that same entity.

We might approach the psychotic's experience of the Other and language through the formula suggested by Freud in his reading of the Schreber case. As Freud summarizes: "Paranoia decomposes just as hysteria condenses."[28] At first glance, the characterization of "decomposition" in paranoia seems to be counterintuitive. However, this notion of "decomposition" is quite similar to the Lacanian definition of psychosis as the result of the failure of the paternal metaphor, or Name-of-the-Father.[29] As discussed above, Lacan explains that paranoia *fixes* things (i.e., the subject, the other, objects, etc.). This definition would, then, seem to be more accurately described as condensation. Similarly, a foreclosure of the paternal metaphor would presumably spare one from the cut of the signifier and all its resultant disorientation. However, the decomposition of paranoid psychosis is done in the name of wholeness, of a total system, just as hysteria's condensation is done in the name of disintegration, that is, the disintegration of the Master's narrative.[30] The extremity of the psychotic's experience is clear: Psychosis begins with a radical foreclosure of the father (or phallic) function, that is, a disintegration of the entirety of the subject's libidinal ties to the world. This is followed by a rebuilding of a similar world that promises completeness.[31]

While the psychotic is not bound to language through the phallic function, as is the neurotic, Lacan's great contribution to the debates surrounding the psychotic was to insist that signifier was still operative in the case of psychosis — albeit in way that is radically different from the neurotic's experience. In his early readings of psychosis, Lacan emphasizes the continuing power of the signifier, even in its foreclosure, in the psychic life of the psychotic subject. Foreclosed from its operation within the symbolic register, "the signifier returns in the Real."[32] Lacan explains this "return" by making use of Jakobson's distinction between "code" and "message" phenomena.[33] A "code" might quickly be defined as an interpretative framework that transcends any individual text or "message." Messages, though they remain idiosyncratic and possess unique aspects of style, are only ever "readable" from the system of a code. For example, the neurotic subject is an adept translator of "messages" into "codes," precisely because the signifier, always split from itself, forces the subject to another signifier — and often another code — in order to decipher even the simplest of messages. Indeed, the neurotic subject is built upon the slippage involved in this process, so much so that a perfect translation of message to code (i.e., what would become of the presentation of that phantom "it") would result in great anxiety. Nevertheless, the gap involved in this process allows the neurotic to translate message into meaningful utterances via the code.

For the purposes of illustration, we might also think of this distinction in the terms suggested in Chapter One, story and plot. The message of a story (or history, as such) is unreadable apart from the code provided via plot. A plot type common within a fictional genre, like the whodunit, always already provides an interpretative framework for reading the meaning of the "message" of an individual text. As suggested in a previous discussion, detective fiction necessarily foregrounds this basic practice of knowledge formation, and, in light of my current discussion, the paranoia that accompanies this process. While the neurotic (and the reader of detective fiction) is perfectly adept at this translation of messages into code, the psychotic fails at this task. However, while the psychotic remains incapable of this translation, his language disturbances make the process more salient insofar as this structure of language is made ex-centric to "normal" neurotic functioning.

For Lacan, the failure of the psychotic to produce meaning in the fashion of the neurotic results in a domination of code phenomena in experience. Freud's famous analysis of the Schreber case demonstrates this well. Daniel Paul Schreber was a German judge in the nineteenth century who, upon being appointed to an influential position, suffered a psychotic breakdown.[34] During his recovery, his physician suggested to Schreber that he write an account of his illness and convalescence, an autobiography that came to be widely read, particularly in medical circles. (Freud's knowledge of the case is based solely on this account.) In his magnum opus, Schreber explains that his delusions revolved around the fantasy that he himself was a woman and that God would fertilize him, thereby producing a new race. Schreber communicated with the celestial world through what he called "divine rays"—these, apparently, also contained "divine seed"—which he described as bolts of light that carried absolute meaning. These divine rays, then, function at the level of "code." Though Schreber senses an ultimate meaning in each ray, these are without an orienting message that would allow metaphorical placement of the code and, thereby, the production of meaning. For example, in Schreber's delusion, it is of the nature of the "divine rays" that they speak, but only ever in an interrupted form. The rays remain depleted of significant predicates that would flesh out the (grammatical) subjects of the "messages." In other words, in the divine rays, there are only frames of interpretation and nothing to interpret. What is of importance here is that Schreber has no difficulty in completing these interrupted messages. For Lacan, the predominance of code begins to function as message, thereby inserting into the place of the enigma (i.e., the lack in the Other) a psychotic certainty where the neurotic would experience only doubt.[35]

This strange conjunction of enigma and certainty is itself structurally necessary given the lack of the phallic function (or paternal metaphor) for the psychotic. The enigma of the Other's message is tolerable in the neurotic case, as the subject remains sutured to the signifying chain and, therefore, seeking the meaning of the Other's message through language. The meaning of the Other's words is always promised, a promise that is sufficient in the metonymy of desire. Here, the rhetorical terms of Lacan's analysis are quite helpful. The phallus functions as a syntactic copula, that is, the linkage between subject and predicate of a proposition, folding the metonymic movement of the sentence back upon itself creating suture, and therefore meaning.[36] The phallus allows the (neurotic, or Oedipalized) subject to inhabit this syntactic fold, which is itself always the elision of a constitutive absence.[37] In the psychotic's case, the signifier (i.e., the Other's message) has no such relation to the signifying chain. Without the establishment of a relation between signifiers, which is the process of metaphor, the normal production of meaning cannot occur.

As Grigg has shown, this does not result in the utter failure of meaning for the psychotic, but rather the "proliferation of meaningfulness that manifests itself in the real in the form of verbal hallucinations, as well as in the enigma and conviction of the psychotic experiences."[38] While the neurotic's paranoid knowledge is a function of doubt, the psychotic's paranoia is always the expression of certainty. Lacking a signifier of difference afforded by the father function (i.e., the Name-of-the-Father), the paranoid makes the mistaken assumption that in the space of the enigma there must be an incontrovertible meaning. In the neurotic's case, neither the subject nor the Other possesses *the* object, or guaranteed meaning. As the psychotic does not possess such a (lacking) object to moderate its exchanges with the Other, the big Other loses its virtual status. The consequences of this are dire, to be sure. Without a structuring principle, the psychotic's "exchanges" with the Other are experienced as painful insurgences of *jouissance* on his body.[39] That lethal enjoyment that the neurotic keeps at a safe distance by transferring it to another (the *femme fatale*, for example) returns for the psychotic who cannot in turn disperse it through the symbolic order. Only with the greatest of efforts might the psychotic transform these random and often violent experiences into an orienting fantasy structure, one that typically casts the Other as malevolent agent.[40]

Returning to the realm of literature, a final helpful way to make this distinction between paranoia in neurosis and psychosis is through the opposed narrative structures of detection and anti-detection. As discussed in previous chapters, the detective narrative, classical or hard-boiled, is readily translated into the neurotic's fretful relation with desire. The detective forever chases a metonymy of clues on the way to the concluding metaphor of solution. Of course, exhaustive explanation remains forever out of reach, requiring the gumshoe, which is so frequently a serial character, to pick up the chase again and again. Like the neurotic, then, the detective orients his relation to the world through the absence of the definitive signifier—an absence that nevertheless affords the detective the possibility of producing knowledge.

Working against this knowledge production, the anti-detective text refuses the detective's (or reader's) demands for solution. While the conclusion of any good detective tale offers some form of resolution—even if this is fleeting—the anti-detective story offers only chaos, discontinuity, and non-solution. Tani has offered an economic summary of this form: "The anti-detective novel is basically an inverted detective novel."[41] Rather than successfully naming the threat and expurgating anxiety, the anti-detective finds that his investigation actually precipitates the crime he hoped to conquer. A well-known early example of the anti-detective story is Robbe-Grillet's *The Erasures* (1953), a tale that depicts a French inspector's quest to stop a murder from occurring. When, after careful investigation, the detective arrives at the crime scene on the appointed hour hoping to save the victim, he finds that he himself commits the crime. The detective is no longer *like* the criminal, as was formerly suggested in the mirror relation between sleuth and villain. On the contrary, the detective is criminal. The extremes of this gesture fall perfectly in line with Spanos's famous description of the goal of the anti-detective text, which is "to evoke the impulse to 'detect' and/or psychoanalyze in order to violently frustrate it by refusing to solve the crime (or to find the cause for neurosis)."[42] Rather than providing the reading with a solution to the crime, the anti-detective story suggests that the process of solution is itself a crime.

While my reading of the detective narrative has focused upon the perhaps "unconscious" aspects of detection that leave the investigator ever distant from his claims to mastery, the "anti-detective" impulse is, as Tani and Spanos indicate, directed at the detective's manifest discourse of cunning and expertise — a framing that more readily implicates the classical detective. The anti-detective text parodies the hubris of the detective's aspirations and faith in knowledge, as well as the Western Enlightenment tradition that supports this narrative of Reason triumphant. Not surprisingly, this sub-genre came into vogue after the carnage of World War II, the horrors of which squarely put the benefits of civilization in grave doubt.[43]

Leaving aside Spanos's implication of psychoanalysis and detection as discourses of mastery, the anti-detective text is quickly thought in terms of psychosis.[44] An "inverted" detective narrative surely leaves the detective and the social order he figures in a state chaos rather than resolution. This is of course a literal reversal of the linear narrative of detection. However, when looked at from a psycho-structural perspective, the "inversion" of the detective's narrative is much more straightforward. Indeed, one subverts the neurotic detective's paradoxical search for an object that must not be found by including *the* object within the narrative. Rather than an "empty" world that is incapable of being made sense of through conventional means, the world of the anti-detective might be understood as "too full." This is the parody of the anti-detective, if we understand parody in the terms suggested by Foucault in his essay "Nietzsche, Genealogy, and History." As Foucault suggests, the parodic mode of criticism proceeds by working the logic of the targeted text to its conclusion.[45] Again recalling Barzun's claim that detective fiction takes the object "seriously," the parodic strategy of the anti-detective story is to put that thesis to the test by delivering the object like never before.[46] In answer to the detective's (and reader's) quest for epiphany — a hysteric demand, to be sure, insofar as it wishes to remain unsatisfied — the writer of the anti-detective text presents this very miracle and, in so doing, reveals the violent paradox of detective narrative itself. As will be shown, this anti-detective impulse is the basic mechanism of the Philip K. Dick narrative, which gives literal body to the phantom Other whose absence formerly guaranteed detection as such.

Turning Paranoia Inside-Out: The Life and Times of Philip K. Dick

It hardly need be said that the question of paranoia oriented both the life and fiction of Philip K. Dick.[47] Twenty years after the author's death, rumors and stories continue to circulate regarding the exact nature of Dick's affliction. During his lifetime, however, the author was always remarkably canny on the topic in interviews, speaking of paranoia in his life and work quite openly. In any case, this much is clear: Philip K. Dick spent a good portion of his life certain that he was the mouthpiece of some Other from beyond this world.[48] The felicity of such an experience was not lost on Dick himself. In a letter written to Peter Fitting in 1974, Dick states: "It seems to me that by subtle but real degrees the world has come to resemble a PKD novel; or, put another way, subjectively I sense *my* typical universe which I used to merely create as fiction, and which I left, often happily, when I was done writing."[49] In an interview from roughly this same period, Dick jokes that he "used to be a paranoid," but no longer considered himself to be thus afflicted.[50]

Recent criticism indicates a darker, if amusing, component of Dick's delusional condition. It seems that the author sent numerous letters to the FBI claiming that various left-wing Marxist critics (Dick's greatest academic supporters of the time: Fredric Jameson, Peter Fitting, Richard Pinhas, and Stanislav Lem) had contacted Dick, asking that he encode various Communist communiqués in his fiction for agents working throughout Europe and North America. Heer appropriately identifies the importance of a visit paid to Dick by these admirers (i.e., Jameson, et al.), during which time he was asked to corroborate various Marxian readings of his own work that the men presented. Dick's anxiety at being "misinterpreted" by the "weird Marxist talk" offered by the individuals in question does indeed indicate an anxiety in the presence of metaphor (i.e., interpretation) that is the hallmark of the psychotic.[51] The failure of the father function results in a profusion of *fathers*, or those "malevolent" figures spoken of above that always threaten to enjoy at the psychotic's expense. The academics that wished to theoretically commandeer the author's fiction and, apparently, his lived universe as well, were experienced in just this way by Dick.

At first glance, the psychotic's difficulty with metaphor may seem paradoxical, as it is the neurotic subject who is "sutured" within language and should, presumably, therefore have a more "rigid" experience of meaning within language. However, for ambiguity within language to occur, it is first necessary that a single meaning be established, a possibility that is foreclosed to the psychotic subject.[52] As Fink has indicated, this lack of suture within language demands that the analysis of psychotics take a radically different form from the analysis of the neurotic patient. Because interpretation depends upon metaphor (i.e., interpretation, at its most basic level, always says that one thing means another), the analyst must curiously not engage in interpretation when working with the psychotic. Rather, the analyst attempts to bolster the psychotic's own makeshift "fundamental fantasy."[53] In such an analysis, all must remain "as is"—not the neurotic's "as if"—and not be indicative of something else. This is the paradox of the psychotic's fantasy: in order to ensure the existence of another world where their persecution "makes sense," nothing must be equivocal in this one.

This insight allows us to properly weigh the criticism that would lionize Philip K. Dick as a visionary whose work provides a sort of prolepsis for thinking oppositional strategies to ideological forces in our own time, insofar as these strictures alienate the subject's relation to its own experience of the world, its objects, and others.[54] To put this simply, it is exceptionally difficult to think of resistance according to the psychical structure of psychosis. Lacan's description of the subject's "choice" of subjectivity as a selection between *père ou pire*, bad or worse, underscores this fact. The acceptance of the Name-of-the-Father, or *père*, demands a life of servitude and alienation in service of the Other. However, the alternative, the refusal of this authority, is unquestionably worse, *pire*. This is true as, without the boundary of the signifier mediating the relation with the Other, the psychotic subject experiences the force of language in the form of the Other's *jouissance* that painfully bears down upon his body. Against this, he must labor to support an entire symbolic system on his own shoulders, as it were—a lost effort, to be sure.[55]

A sense of the structural impasse of paranoia that informs Dick's work is found in remarks made by the author in an interview conducted on November 2, 1974, with Paul Williams. In this interview, Dick spoke at length regarding the discomfort he felt at having been described as a "paranoid" writer by the interviewer and others. Like the episode describe by Heer, Dick here again betrayed an anxiety about how his work would be registered within the (critical, or academic) Other, and at the same time demonstrated the psychoanalytic insight of the necessity of the fiction of the big Other. Early in this interview, Dick suggested that "paranoia" had become an empty "jargon" word and offered a correction of such empty verbiage. He explains the (mistaken) commonsense understanding of the term as follows: "It's a pattern, Aha! It all makes sense, it fits into place, right? Aha! Right? The significance of this detail, and everything has meaning. There's the spread of meaning throughout everything. Nothing has been overlooked. But everything in a way is equally regarded, you know, as fitting into a gestalt. It's overgestalting."[56] While this response is common enough, particularly during the time of Cold War intrigue, he finds it both dangerous and inadequate.

Dick goes on to link this affect with a residual cosmology that persists, despite the failure of all grand narratives (particularly religion) in the contemporary, de-centered culture. This anachronistic yet lingering need for organizational systems results in a sense of malevolence behind things, says

Dick. Though there is no longer license for theories of transcendence, or anything beyond the "human," this explanatory convenience is, apparently, inevitable. A divine entity no longer remains as guarantor for the "patterns" that Dick assures us *are* there, but there remains a persistence of the sense of another space from which the inconsistencies of this world are orchestrated. As Dick explains, "you see a pattern of events, and if you have no transcendent view, no mystical view, no religious view, then the pattern must emanate from people. Where else can it come from, if that's all...? And you start sensing a kind of transcendent thing or mystical thing."[57] Clearly, this "emanation from people" is a difficult pill to swallow and the fantasy of ultimate meaning residing elsewhere — in the heavens or beyond — recurs without fail, so often resulting in the delusion of persecution that is readily identified with the paranoid.

As Dick warns, the greatest danger at stake in this misunderstanding is the loss of agency that results from delusions of invisible tyranny. Suggesting alternatives for thinking this concept that are not reducible to the conspiracy of a fiendish "them," Dick offers his practical response to the *hubris* of every paranoiac construction:

> You know what I think? I think the thing is that paranoia must be pulled inside out. Absolutely inside out. It's not that it should be destroyed. I mean, that the solution to paranoia is to convince the person there is no pattern to the universe, that everything is chaotic, chance, and that people have no intentions. And that he is unimportant.... Turn it inside out, rather than just abolish it. That it's benign, and that it transcends our individualities and so on. The way I feel is that the universe is actually alive, and we're in it as part of it.... It's not that individual objects are alive, it's the whole thing is an entity that is aware of itself, and we're part of it, and we're never outside of it.[58]

Naturally, one must remain skeptical of Dick's logic for turning paranoia "inside out." To support the alternate, quasi-new age cosmology that Dick offers in response to the hostile universe of the paranoid, it is necessary, he says, to maintain the structure in question. However, by inverting paranoia, the subject remains no less connected to all the objects of the world, which continue to function as signs to meaning behind things as they are. Another world continues to guarantee meaning in this one. The atavism resulting from this stance is structurally identical to the previous malevolent being or force that was assumed in the commonsense experience of the paranoid. As should be obvious, if the structure is left intact, Dick is not so much turning paranoia "inside out" as he is simply substituting one content for another. Just as Lacan spoke of the paranoid structure of all knowledge, the structure of paranoia, then, seems to be (ir)reversible, reducing Dick's response to simply another totalizing, and therefore paranoid, system.

Dick's inability to turn paranoia "inside out" without introducing a new ordering principle perhaps offers a more compelling explanation of the recalcitrance of this fantasy of the menacing Other. Indeed, as Dick's fiction demonstrates again and again, after the reign of the Father comes the reign of fathers. In other words, the failure of the Father and the symbolic order that his name founds results in the proliferation of any number of fathers, each more ominous than the next. (Here, I am speaking in terms of neurosis. However, it must be noted that the experience of the psychotic remains instructive when we are confronted with a disruption of the father function for the neurotic.) Žižek has described this insistence of the father — the Father of Enjoyment, or "Anal" father, rather than the former Father of Prohibition — in terms of the failure of a certain type of "symbolic efficiency."[59] The symbolic order is (or was) sustained by the semblance of its own completeness. The ruse is not on the side of the Other, naturally, but on the side of the subject who endeavors above all else to sustain this fantasy. Speaking of this duplicity, Žižek describes the big Other as the "order of lying sincerely," making use of an old Groucho Marx joke to illustrate this complex exchange.[60] The joke tells the story of a man who is caught in bed with another woman by his wife. Trying to avert an all but inevitable disaster, the husband assures his wife that there is nothing tawdry going on, but naturally the wife assures him that she sees the matter clearly with her own eyes. Continuing to swear to his innocence, the husband retorts: "Whom do you believe, my words or your eyes?" Žižek's point is that the subject's exchanges with the big Other formerly followed a similar logic. Though the subject was consistently confronted with the Other's lack, assurances of wholeness were believed every time. Were the subject to insist on believing its eyes, the authority and symbolic peace of the big Other would be lost.

The point to be taken is that with the increasing failure of the father function in contemporary culture — the starting point of Dick's fiction — this relation to the symbolic order is no longer possible. However, this does not for a moment mean the eclipse of the father's prohibition and the advent of a time where "anything goes." As the psychotic's experience indicates, freedom does not result when the prohibition of the Name-of-the-Father is absent. Rather, the father function returns in the guise of the violence that had always already guaranteed its functioning. It is from that very space that a new father, the Father of Enjoyment, as Žižek terms this figure, rises up to give his command.[61]

The shared context of the father's failure unites Dick's work with his hard-boiled predecessors discussed in Chapter Two. Not surprisingly, many of the contradictions within his science fiction duplicate the indecision the hard-boiled detective held for his own diminished patriarchs. Just as the hard-boiled project demanded freedom *and* recognition from the authority of the father, so too is Dick's work fraught with a desire for the new that is haunted by nostalgia. Csicsery-Ronay, Jr. has described this (dis)orienting feature of Dick's work as the "aesthetics of ambivalence," a concept that speaks to the "contradictions between technological ecstasy and anti-technological humanistic values, or between ideas as spectacle and ideas as ethical "substance," [that] are left necessarily unresolved."[62] More recently, Palmer has similarly suggested that Dick is a difficult author to synthesize precisely because he is simultaneously both a humanist and a postmodernist.[63] At the crux of this dilemma is the "hard-boiled father" so frequently found within Dick's fiction.[64] Here, Palmer is not speaking specifically of the hard-boiled patriarch as described in Chapter Two. Rather, he refers to the contentious status of the father in the nuclear family. Nevertheless, the embattled state of authority he describes is analogous to the crisis in symbolic efficiency described above. As he explains, here speaking of the short stories in particular, Dick inevitably has problems "reconciling existential openness, or relativity, with political or ethical closure," which results in "an instability that is not subject to dialectical analysis."[65] With the failure of symbolic efficiency, there is no longer a shared vision (or fantasy) of authority, ensuring that the father function doubly fails. I am in complete agreement with each critic's assessment of the inconsistencies at the heart of Dick's work. Beyond the ecstatic tropes of science fiction, both those invented and borrowed by Dick, beyond the importation of sundry philosophical debates, self-conscious diagnosis and the dizziness of the schizoid, Dick's fiction remains vacillating between a nostalgia for the lost individual and the fascinating vertigo of subjective dissolution.

Given this split gesture — a now familiar hard-boiled trope — we might read Philip K. Dick's opus in terms of hysteria, insofar as the hysteric subject suffers the ill-effects of the weakened father.[66] Verhaeghe describes the hysteric as the true "believer," who is "not so much revolutionary as serving a so-called alternative authority."[67] Hence the hysteric's own ambiguity: she is contentious, seeking to draw out the father's authority only to unmask its weakness. However, at the same time, the hysteric demands the recognition of the father — preferably a second, stronger father. As Verhaeghe concludes, the hysteric and the paranoid are the perfect contemporary couple, for the hysteric is the quintessential "believer," while the paranoid, despite his certainty, requires followers.[68] It is little wonder, then, that we find a proliferation of these couples throughout Dick's work.

In the following sections, I will analyze a novel from each of the productive periods of Dick's career, that is, within fiction written in the 1950s, 1960s, and 1970s. Over this span of years, one finds a marked development in the sophistication of this paradoxical, or "ambiguous," coupling of hysteria and paranoia. (Of course, I do not wish to suggest that the author's vast body of work is reducible solely to this development.) As will be shown, detection and anti-detection become featured modes of articulating this connection. Of particular interest for my purposes is the linkage of paranoia with the frustrations of the sexual relationship. In other words, paranoia within the work of the Philip K. Dick is increasingly bound to the questions of love and Woman. The often violent return of these issues designates the contemporary failure of symbolic efficiency, a determinant that is punctuated by the anti-detective impulse at the core of Dick's fiction.

Time Out of Joint: The Father's Failure and the Other of the Other

Dick's first hardcover, "mainstream" novel, *Time Out of Joint* (1959), was originally published by Lippincott not as a science fiction novel, but rather as a "novel of menace."[69] Like much of Dick's early work, the novel was not successful by any means, and Dick himself later described the text as "crude," particularly in its presentation of paranoia.[70] Here, one is tempted to agree with Dick's judgment, as the novel is little more than the substantiation of the protagonist's paranoid suspicions. In the novel, Ragle Gumm comes to suspect that life in his quiet, suburban 1950s town is not what it seems. This suspicion turns out to be entirely warranted, as Gumm discovers that this reality has been entirely constructed for him.[71] It is not 1956, but rather 1997, and Gumm is unwittingly working on the side of the Earth coalition in a civil war against Lunar colonists by participating in a local newspaper game, "Spot the Little Green Men." (By spotting the "little green men," the unsuspecting patriot predicts the targets of future missile attacks.) The entire movement of the text is directed without deviation toward a validation of Gumm's paranoia and a realization of his significance in this other world.

At first glance, this gesture would seem to be simply bad analysis. Rather than a sort of subjective justification, or instantiation, the goal of analysis is the dissolution of the subject's dependence upon narcissistic fantasies that guarantee the recognition of the Other and the continuity of the world. In *Time Out of Joint*, the opposite occurs. The subject's narcissism is not only facilitated, it is indisputably justified. In this way, Dick's text makes literal a classic paranoid delusion: not only does Ragle Gumm suspect that he is the center of the world that he knows — and possibly other worlds, as well — he in fact *is* the center of his world, as well as its savior. Dick's description of the text as "crude" no doubt has just this straightforwardness in mind, as in his later work, no such assurances will be given, and protagonists' paranoia will be left in a more or less "virtual" state.

However, Dick's dismissal of this work must not be taken at face value. Through this detour of a paranoid delusion (i.e., the onset of paranoid psychosis), the text soundly demonstrates the paranoid aspects of the "normal," neurotic subject. Indeed, read at the level of structure, *Time Out of Joint* ends not with a crude psychosis, but with a fascinating return to the neurotic structure of hysteria. This is perhaps what disturbed Dick most of all regarding *Time Out of Joint*, for, contrary to much of his later work, the text actually seems to move from psychosis to neurosis, which is to say that the afflicted protagonist actually succeeds at getting "well."[72] This rare, hopeful turn of events perfectly illustrates the ambiguity of paranoia within Dick's work, an issue that will remain unresolved throughout the author's fiction.

While the illumination that occurs at the end of *Time Out of Joint* is unique within Dick's opus, the onset of this realization occurs in a fashion that will become quite common to his fiction. The minimum requirement of a story by Philip K. Dick is an immediate symbolic crisis of one kind or another. The character's most basic experience of the social bond, of "reality" itself, is made impossible for reasons that remain just out of reach. In *Time Out of Joint* — the very title speaking to just such a disjunction — the apparent failure of the subject's bond to the social occurs through a very literal experience of the virtual character of social convention. This virtual aspect is deduced when the protagonist, Ragle Gumm, discovers numerous absences and inconsistencies within the banal, 1950s landscape of his small town life. These absences take the form of near-erasures of objects and landmarks that were formerly well known to Gumm. Appropriately, these items do not disappear entirely but leave the single trace of a small piece of paper on which appears the name of a given object (e.g., drinking fountain, soda stand, etc.), as though holding a place for a temporarily waylaid item.

Ragle Gumm secretly becomes a collector of these scraps of paper. However, he does not suspect the scale of the deception until his neighbor, Victor Nielson, tells the story of his constant, automatic reaching for the string of a non-existent light switch in his bedroom. (The room has a switch on the wall.) It is at this moment that Gumm's suspicions become more conspiratorial, as he assumes that these "missing items" do exist within another world, raising the question of his own significance within that other space. This revelation allows for the systematizing of numerous items of doubt that had formerly plagued Gumm. Like his vocation of "finding the little green men" in the local newspaper contest, he now looks for the answer to the hidden patterns of his own life. In other words, he becomes an inadvertent detective — an all-too-common occurrence within Philip K. Dick's work.

Strangely, it is difficult for Gumm to accept the fact that his discoveries of the paper slips and Vic's experience with the light switch have anything in common. This is perhaps explained in Gumm's very personal identification with these inconsistencies. Indeed, it seems as though he would like to take these small pieces of paper as a mark of an intimate knowledge about only himself. Only later is it amusingly discovered that these small pieces of paper, these holes in the big Other, were in fact used by the work crews moderating the simulation of the small town. "They," apparently, simply did not have enough props to decorate the entire area and moved items from place to place as the situation dictated.

Both the mechanism of this artifice and Gumm's intimate identification with the uncovered absences are Lacanian through and through. As has been shown, it is through the failure of the symbolic order to provide a satisfaction of desire that the Lacanian subject functions. The resultant lack requires that the subject continually search for meaning in the Other, in the detective-like fashion that becomes Gumm's own method. The subject is always a sleuthing metaphysician (i.e., a paranoid) insofar as she or he seeks to establish meaning in that other realm. Again, as Dick reveals so well, it is in this sense that "ordinary," neurotic paranoid knowledge bears an uncanny similarity with paranoid psychosis. However, the great difference between these two subjective structures swings upon the status of the big Other. In the case of the psychotic, the big Other takes on a real existence, and it answers the query of the subject with the harshest of commands. For the neurotic, the big Other is always silent and therefore virtual. It exists only insofar as we continue to participate in its fiction in generally agreed upon forms — believing the big Other's words and not our eyes, as Žižek describes. Through this consensus, the subject endeavors to find that which is most intimate to itself.

Despite the apparent progressive actualization of Gumm's paranoid "delusion," *Time Out of Joint* actually moves in the opposite direction: from an actual to a virtual big Other. While this vector reveals much about the intricate differences of neurotic and psychotic experience, at the same time it significantly problematizes the socio-political criticism contained within the text. Naturally, the obligatory sci-fi setting of a quasi-totalitarian state, in addition to the perhaps more novel manufactured "Old Town" of Gumm's fantasy, raises questions regarding the ideological implications of the subject's inevitable deferment to the big Other. Not surprisingly, various Marxist critics have seized *Time Out of Joint* toward these ends.[73] For example, Fitting reads the text as demonstrating ideology's incessant attempt to disguise its workings, erase its traces, and thereby secure the reproduction of the existing relations of production.[74] Pivotal to such a reading is the fact that Ragle Gumm's breakdown results neither from individual pathology nor even the pressures faced in a post-apocalyptic world. Rather the breakdown is caused by Gumm's growing realization that the moon Colonists' cause is just, that is, that the dominant ideology of the Earth forces operates according to a violent logic of exclusion.[75] Ideology successfully recuperates such moments of "insight" for its own enterprise, as Gumm's realization and protest change nothing. Though Ragle Gumm does "personally" create the regressive fantasy of the lost idyll of his 1950s childhood — this during a breakdown suffered after years of working for Earth's defense against the colonists — this reaction is quite readily made use of by the ideological apparatuses that continue to use Gumm as a human anti-missile system against Lunatic (i.e., colonist) attacks by supporting his delusion.

In this way, Fitting's reading is an apt illustration of Žižek's criticism of Althusser's understanding of ideological interpellation.[76] Psychoanalysis' entry point into the discussion of ideology occurs at a critical breakdown in Althusser's reasoning on this point in the author's famous essay, "Ideology and Ideological State Apparatuses."[77] Althusser's essay describes the way in which individuals come to be obedient ideological subjects. In a sort of Lacanian-Marxist reading of the ideological subject's genesis, Althusser suggests a moment of paradoxical origin in which the "individual" is "hailed," or interpellated, by ideology. As was true in Lacan's mirror phase, the individual misrecognizes itself in the hail of ideology, which provides a sort of mirror for identification. Prior to this ideal moment, the (ideological) subject is not a subject. The subject only emerges by assuming that it always already was the addressee of the hail, just as the Lacanian subject emerges by assuming that it always already was a subject in the first place. For Žižek, the weakness of Althusser's theory of ideology surrounds the internalization of the ideological command, which seems to assume the complete interpellation of the subject. Althusser assumes that the "hail" of ideology is fully internalized by the subject, as only in this way is it possible for the subject to make "sense" of the violence of this very imposition. The result is that the fully interpellated subject has no other frame from which to ask the question of her or his own existence and relation to the social order. Althusser's conclusion at the end of the essay speaks to just this totalizing requirement: Insofar as one is interpellated (fully) as a subject, one obeys.[78]

From a psychoanalytic standpoint, and this is the point of Žižek's criticism, it is incorrect to assume that a partial failure of interpellation would be an impediment to the functioning of ideology. Indeed, as Žižek counters, a certain failure in ideological interpellation is the very condition of ideology. Recalling the misrecognition of the mirror phase, the neurotic subject functions precisely because it is never equal to its mirror image. What is missing from Althusser's adequation, then, is the necessity of a "hysterical response" to all identifications or, likewise, to all interpellations.[79] As we have seen, the subject's problems — problems that save the subject from psychosis — begin because a complete identification is not possible. A remainder inheres, what Lacan calls the *objet a*, that for which neither the Other nor the subject can ever fully account. The presence of this excessive absence ensures that interpellation, like the progression of the mirror-phase, must be regarded as an ongoing process. It is never final. According to Žižek, the failure of ideology itself will ensure that the subject obeys, as the subject is always already bound to the other by the *objet a* as the (paradoxical) cause of desire. In other words, the Other's lack and not the Other's command (prohibitive or otherwise) is that which interpellates the now desiring subject.[80] The subject is perfectly willing to accept — or, more likely, to disguise or ignore, but nevertheless *make use of*— the lack in the Other as this saves the subject from contemplating a more fundamental lack at the kernel of their own being.

Žižek's debt to Laclau and Mouffe's text *Hegemony and Socialist Strategy* (1985) is plain when one considers the subject's subsequent relation to the social order. The more terrifying lack that must be mis-recognized at all costs by the interpellated subject is the Real of the social, that is, the fundamental antagonism of the social order that refuses any stable representation.[81] The orienting ideologies of a given social body do not create a "false reality" that is violently thrust upon the populace, but rather produces "a fantasy-construction which serves as a support for our 'reality' itself: an 'illusion' which structures our effective, real social relations and thereby masks some insupportable, real, impossible kernel."[82] Ideology, then, is not a prohibitive but rather a *protective* structure that allows social reality to escape, or misplace, this more traumatic Real. Ideological critique that demands the presentation of the "real" behind appearance misses this point entirely. Ideology does not keep us from a lost, "true" reality. On the contrary, ideology is that limit which allows us to imagine such a lost idyll in the first place. In so doing, it permits us distance from the trauma of the Real, the one operation facilitating the next. To actually "recover" lost reality is akin to psychosis insofar as that enabling absence (the *objet a*) is then missing — that is, the subject lacks its constitutive lack. The same is of course true of a perfect, or complete identification, a possibility that Althusser seems to privilege.

Apropos of this discussion, the final project of *Time Out of Joint* remains in question: Is Dick's novel a critique of ideology (as the Marxists suggest), or might it better be understood from a Žižekian perspective, that is, ideology here read as the support of "reality"?[83] It should not go unnoticed that this is essentially to recast my initial question regarding the neurotic or psychotic structure of the novel in different terms. To maintain a straightforward critique of ideology in favor of a "true" reality is to assume that there is an

Other of the Other, that is, beyond our "false" reality, there is a reality that is to be found again. Structurally, if this other world is found and the Other actualized, as it is in Ragle Gumm's case, the text cannot but fall into a psychotic discourse.

Yet, it is on the topic of ideological critique that Dick's novel is the most confused. At first glance, the text does seem to fall quite readily into demonstration of just how ideology is the support of reality. What is Gumm's breakdown if not a hysterical response to the ideology of the united Earth forces? Their slogan, "One Happy World," ironically underlines the impossibility of the individual's comfortable incorporation into the symbolic order of the text's fictional 1997. Rather than resulting in the loss of Gumm as an ideological subject, the breakdown and resulting fantasy construction are what ensure that Gumm becomes a perfectly operating ideological subject — "perfectly" operating in its failure. Gumm's very personal identification with the holes in the big Other, those small pieces of paper that quite literally indicate that a particular object has gone missing, are "holes" within the Other that the subject comes to desire. His collection of these scraps, these gaps, is akin to the manner in which the subject will organize her or his desire across the continuum of a metonymic series of objects that are, necessarily, missing. Indeed, what is desire if not "objects being evasive," as Gumm describes the disturbances in his world?[84] Like the desiring economy of the detective narrative, lack ensures that the subject participates in the (constructed) social order and the fantasy of its wholeness (i.e., ideology).

This curious crossing from a psychotic to neurotic structure is evident in the famous passage describing the vanishing of the soft-drink stand in the park while Gumm is attempting to make a purchase. In the midst of self-accusatory reflection, largely on his own failure to act in life, Gumm approaches a soft-drink stand and asks for a beer. Just then, "The fifty-cent piece fell away, down through the wood, sinking. It vanished.... Not again! It's happening to me again. The soft-drink stand fell into bits. Molecules. He saw the molecules, colorless, without qualities, that made it up. Then he saw through, into the space beyond it, he saw the hill behind, the trees and sky" (*TOJ* 54). Far from being either a random psychotic episode, or an error in the manipulation of the props populating Ragle's delusion, this moment marks an emergence from malady. Importantly, the opening of this gap in Gumm's experience occurs at the moment of an attempted transaction that meets with no reply. In this instance, one encounters the virtualization of the big Other. In other words, the absolute consistency of the psychotic's world begins to fade through the instantiation of a gap in the formerly airtight network. Only through the opening of this space is it possible for Gumm to function again as a desiring, and therefore divided, subject.

This situation is duplicated later when Gumm purposely wills the disappearance of his surroundings while riding on a city bus. In this case, the description of the incident is equally indicative of the necessity of boring a hole in the side of (psychotic) delusion. Only through this alteration in psychical structure is Gumm able to emerge into "reality," a passage that requires an enlarging of the hole he has begun digging, "a splitting rent opening up, a great gash," as he describes it (*TOJ* 109). The importance of this action and its promised naissance is not lost on Ragle. He actually goes so far as to describe this rupture as a "navel" (*TOJ 108*). For Freud, the navel is that space where the dream touches the unknown or, in Lacanian terms, it encounters the Real, the space beyond the meaning of the symbolic order.[85] In the above instance, Ragle Gumm is playing a sort of Dickian version of the *fort* and *da* game in which the subject is slowly sutured around emptiness, an operation that is always marked by the creation of a navel.[86] However, shortly after these insightful moments, this apparent understanding of the necessity of an internal gap for maintaining the link between the subject and the social is forsaken in favor of a second "outside," or reality, that will finally guarantee the truth. What is at issue here, I would suggest, is the question of symbolic efficiency, which requires an account of the father function.

An earlier short story, "The Father Thing" (1954), dating roughly to the same period as *Time Out of Joint*, perhaps better distills Dick's difficulties in coming to terms with the failure of the father. This story plays upon that trope that is so popular in the earlier short fiction, that is, the replacement of a living organism by a malevolent machine. As the title indicates, it is a boy's father who is killed and replaced by a homicidal replicant that is bent upon destroying the population, importantly, beginning with the family unit. At first glance, the story perhaps reads as an excursus into the status of our humanity and the danger of illusion at the level of appearances. To these ends, what enables the defeat of the "Father Thing" is the son's empathy that allows him to see the "emptiness" of the monster, revealing the impostor. This optimism is duplicated again in *Time Out of Joint*, insofar as the Ragle Gumm reclaims his own humanity in his empathy for the lunar colonists. Through his compassion, he comes to understand the decidedly "inhuman" ideology of the united Earth.

However, the conclusion of the short story is a good deal more unsettling. This is true, as we shall see, especially in comparison to the conclusion of *Time Out of Joint*. The uncanny, as it is represented within the "The Father Thing," moves far beyond the simple doubling and obscuring of egos. The appearance of the "father thing" results in the radical de-sublimation of the father that provided a peaceful pact with the symbolic order. Unlike the primal murder described by Freud in *Totem and Taboo* (1913), the death of the father in this case provides no access to libidinal organization, as the son is left with no identificatory link or prohibition to keep the requisite distance between the child and mother.[87] The description of the murdered "body" of the father in Dick's story is here illustrative. His dismembered remains—fished from a garbage can where they had been hidden—are described as flat, even two dimensional, both "colorless" and "transparent."[88] All that remains of the former father is his outline. He is "an empty skin," and "The insides were gone. The important part."[89] This could only be the case, as the failure of the symbolic father is the result of the disappearance of the gap upon which his "power" was predicated. It is not so much that the "content," depth, or power of the father is removed, for he never did possess such things. Rather, with the loss of this former structure, the symbolic efficiency that guaranteed the father's guise as authority, is left now reduced to depthless appearance. As Dick says, the insides are indeed gone.

As Žižek, following Lacan, has demonstrated, this failure is necessary given the position of the father in the modern bourgeois family.[90] In this single figure are combined the two basic components of symbolic mediation, a position of identification and a prohibitive superego. The failure of the father function is necessary—it is the "truth" of the Oedipus complex—as the father's power must remain virtual and unexercised. If the father attempts to make use of this power, the result is the unbridled emergence of an obscene enjoyment that was to be regulated by this very figure.[91] Here again, the "ordinary" functioning of the father is illustrative. The real existing father does not embody symbolic law because he *is* the embodiment of real authority, that is, because he is a strong or even all-powerful father. On the contrary, the real existing father situates himself in that space through his very distance from this embodiment. Again, it is not in spite of the real father's weakness, but *because of* this weakness, then, that the father occupies the place of symbolic mediation. This gap allows for the assumption that real authority lies elsewhere, an authority that then underwrites the actions of the actual father. Should the "father" forsake this enabling distance and actually attempt to embody the "real" father, the result is the return of the Real father, the Father of Enjoyment.

Žižek's description of the failure of the Paternal Function, as the "emergence of the Father of Enjoyment," or the "anal father," succinctly explains just this breakdown.[92] This nomenclature is of course taken from the mythology of the "primal father" that Freud produced in *Totem and Taboo*. This myth, it will be remembered, instantiates the father of prohibition—that is, the father of symbolic law—quite apart from the actual individual, insofar as the sons do not come to obey the father until after his murder. After this crime, the brothers make a pact that promises reverence to the father's memory, giving them an empty space with which to identify (i.e., a symbolic space) safely distanced from the bothersome presence of an actual father. This now surmounted figure is the true "forbidden object" of the Oedipus complex, not the incestuous desire for the mother. As Žižek felicitously phrases this, the "father Thing" must be killed for the symbolic pact of culture to be established.[93] When the reverse occurs, as it often does within contemporary experience, the killing of the symbolic father will result in the return of the primal, "anal," Father of Enjoyment.[94] As Žižek writes: "When the 'pacifying' symbolic authority is suspended, the only way to avoid the debilitating deadlock of desire, its inherent impossibility, is to locate the cause of its inaccessibility in a despotic figure which stands for the primordial *jouisseur*: we cannot enjoy because *he* appropriates all the enjoyment...."[95] Naturally, this speaks not to the return of some prehistoric monster, but rather to a marked change in the experience of the subject. Fathers are now engaged with in actuality, apart from the peace of symbolic substitution, making each "father" that the subject encounters a potential competitor. The subject is left to search desperately for a father that will provide a defense against this rapacious competitor, becoming all the more hysterical insofar as no Other can offer the consistency that the subject seeks.

The brilliance of Dick's story "The Father Thing" now comes into greater focus. The text addresses the violent core at the center of the always-fraught relation with the father and assesses the even more grim possibility of the father's demise. Appropriately, in the narrative, the "mechanism" which controls the father's possessed body is a sort of small external pod, which is described as an alien hybrid of both machine and flesh. The "father thing" is, then, in excess of the culture conventions that define not only familial relations, but the human as such. This control mechanism lives among the filth and decay of plant life that grows unattended on the "dark side of the garage." From this extimate position both in- and outside the banal symbolic order of the suburban setting, the pod controls and animates the "father thing." In this space of unformed life—a place that recalls Freud's own description of the navel arising like a mushroom from its "mycelium"—there likewise resides both a "mother thing" and a "Chris [i.e., son] thing."[96] This second set of imposters is necessary, as the destruction of the symbolic father voids the accord that formerly regulated the nuclear family (i.e., father, mother, son). Fortunately, son and mother are spared from their physical demise. At the end of the story, Chris and some boys from the neighborhood manage to defeat the father thing. However, this murder is of little use as the "Thing" that emerges in the place of the father is, as it is characterized in the story, neither human nor even of this world. With the absence of the father's orienting protection, it seems more than likely that "things" will return, as it were. In other words, as the boys at the end of the story fear, these monsters that infiltrate the body both from within and without will spread elsewhere.

This haunting of the father "thing" is helpful for understanding the failure of the father function in *Time Out of Joint*. Of course, such a failure is evident in the very title of the novel, which speaks to the general dis-jointedness that Ragle feels both in his experience of language and within his community. Lacking an orienting figure of authority with which to identify, the character feels himself to be a "child" that has in someway been abandoned (*TOJ* 54). This failure, as well as its accompanying malaise, is found in the earlier portion of the text when Ragle becomes aware that the "Little Green Men" contest is rigged in his favor. The subterfuge he actively participates in with the "contest promoters," albeit with a heavy heart, is a fitting representation of symbolic order's impotence to give the subject what it desires. (The gift of winning is not quite the "it" that Ragle seeks.) It is little wonder, then, that Gumm speaks of wishing to be punished in some way, an all too common neurotic desire that would require the silence of the big Other to be broken and the subject to at last be given an orienting demand (*TOJ* 23). The subject asks for the injunction of words, which might equal an operable symbolic law of any kind. Ragle Gumm wants "words" in which he can believe.

Yet Gumm's reflection on the power of the word is at the same time a realization of the absolute emptiness of all words. As he concludes, the "Word doesn't represent reality. Word is reality" (*TOJ* 60). However, lacking a suture within language, this possibility is hardly very comforting, and Gumm experiences the anxiety of this situation, realizing that "there is no right answer"—that is, there is no "one" word (*TOJ* 41). Without a credible point of symbolic identification to displace these anxieties, the result is an uncomfortable magnification of neurotic doubt. However, unlike the conclusion of "The Father Thing," Dick will attempt, in hysterical fashion, a final suture to reinstate some sort of father function.

As the novel draws to a conclusion, Dick seems to be incapable of accepting the possibility of the failure of the basic underpinning of the symbolic order.[97] To be sure, the author cunningly identifies a crisis of symbolic efficiency. However, in the end he refuses to accept this circumstance and likewise remains helpless to represent adequately this impasse. Here again, the category of hysteria is particularly suited to describe this hesitation. Verhaeghe asserts that there are two classic solutions to the difficulties encountered in both the experience of fathers and the subsequent silence of the big Other: the strategies of the paranoid and the hysteric.[98] (Ragle Gumm will take up each strategy before the conclusion of the novel.) To speak of the first example as a "solution" is in many ways a misnomer, as for the paranoid there never was a "problem" (i.e., with the failure of the father function), as such. As we have seen, the paranoid is afforded (painful) certainty. He does not "believe," he *knows*, and as a result, he looks for followers, a demand that the hysteric is perfectly willing to oblige.[99] In the face of the father's failure, the hysteric seeks a perfect father (i.e., a complete big Other), albeit with mixed motives. Dick's prescient pairing of these two figures perhaps accounts for the confused presentation of ideological criticism in *Time Out of Joint* and his difficulties with inverting the structure of paranoia. Like so much of his work, this novel maintains the ambiguity of the hysteric's criticism of authority in the name of another authority, along with an accompanying detour through paranoia. In each case, there remains an underlying romanticism even in the context of (potential) subjective disintegration akin to that found in hard-boiled detective.

The confusion of *Time Out of Joint* becomes more comprehensible if one accepts the centrality of this coupling (i.e., paranoia and hysteria) within Dick's work. At first glance, the strategy of the paranoid would seem the most appropriate for engaging the overall structure of the novel. In the beginning of the text, Gumm's break results in the creation of a delusion featuring his 1950s childhood that is subsequently seized by the appropriate ruling agencies. At the conclusion of the novel, Gumm does discover that he is the center of this delusion world, but likewise he is effectively the center of the "real" world to which he will ultimately escape. His successive attempts to escape to that other space, first alone and then with his brother-in-law Vic, are clearly a desire to see "outside," to see at last the "truth." As Gumm says after his first failed attempt, "I almost got over the edge and saw things as they really are" (*TOJ* 185). In this case, ideology might yet be seen as the support reality, insofar as Gumm finds nothing but desert and barren wilderness. In other words, beyond the fantasy structure of ideology, there is only emptiness.[100] His suspicion of the implausibility of this journey to the other side is appropriate: "Maybe I'm not moving. Caught in a between-place. Wheels of the pick-up truck spinning in gravel ... spinning uselessly, forever. The illusion of motion. Motor noise, wheel noise, headlights on pavement. But immobility" (*TOJ* 142).[101] Here, there is no outside.

However, when Gumm finally does escape to the "real world," the world of 1997, he discovers an Earth that has become a wasteland through years of war with colonists on the moon. Crossing the line into this other world, he slowly begins to remember his sympathies for the Lunatics and the part these feelings played in his initial breakdown. These sympathies, we learn, are the result of Gumm's first experience traveling into outer space, on furlough as an executive officer working for Earth's defense. This passage is worth quoting at length:

> For the first time in his life he found himself leaving Earth. Journeying out into space, between planets. Free of gravity. The greatest tie had ceased to hold him. The fundamental force that kept the universe of matter behaving as it did. The Heisenberg Unified Field Theory had connected all energy, all phenomena into a single experience. Now, as his ship left Earth, he passed from that experience to another, the experience of pure freedom [*TOJ* 244].

This experience to migrate, to travel beyond the known world, is characterized by Gumm as a "universal need," an "instinct, the most primitive drive, as well as the most noble and complex" (*TOJ* 245). The lunatics, in Gumm's mind, live this drive like no one else in history, and it is for this reason that the forces of Earth misunderstand them. This energy and insight is opposed to the insular world of Earth, a bounded space where one lives only according to basic needs.

I would argue that the conclusion to *Time Out of Joint* is inadequate and not in keeping with the spirit of the initial direction of the novel. As Gumm says of his decision to return to space with Mrs. Keitbein and the remainder of the Luna sympathizers, "I'm doing it because I know it is right. It comes first, my duty. Everyone else ... they all have done their duty; they have been loyal to what they believe in. I intend to do the same" (*TOJ* 254). With this, the novel apparently demonstrates the process through which Ragle "gets well," which here amounts to no longer being the dupe of ideology. However, in his privileging of the Lunatic "drive"—which here is nothing more than desire—to the beyond at the end of the text, the structure of the neurotic subject is all the more demonstrated.[102] In other words, Ragle has exchanged a psychotic paranoia for the ordinary neurotic paranoia that limits us all. In this way, Gumm refuses to allow ideology to script the object of his desire, to tell him what he wants. However, unfortunately, this stance is entirely amenable to the working of ideology, as the market demands infinitely desiring subjects. His trip into the emptiness of outer space interestingly becomes, then, a strategy for avoiding the emptiness of the *objet a* as cause of his desire. Further, what this text first offers and then ignores is the loss of the sanctioning authority that would allow one to ground this object choice in the first place. In other words, unlike the story "The Father Thing," Dick here ignores the fact that the paternal function is no longer operative.

This oversight is perhaps what Dick had in mind when he chastised the text as being too "primitive," requiring a more complex approach in the author's later fiction.[103] The point to be taken is not that the neurotic is ever more paranoid today, although such a thing might aptly be said of knowledge construction. Rather, with the decline in symbolic efficiency, one increasingly encounters the paranoid "truth" of the symbolic process. In other words, as Lacan suggested in his concept of "aggressivity," the subject is itself a paranoid construction. Without the peace of consensus formerly offered by the symbolic order, this fact becomes all the more apparent, and the subject experiences an ever-increasing antagonism with a variety of threatening others.

Romantic Love and the Limits of Empathy in the Work of Philip K. Dick

The most salient item linking *Time Out of Joint* with Dick's later work is the question of love. Given Dick's interest in the increasing failure of the more traditional authorities presiding over symbolic mediation of the social, it is not incidental that the question of love figures prominently in the author's work. What becomes clear in Dick's treatment of the topic is not simply that love has in some fundamental way been altered or made less accessible in the prohibitive times in which he wrote — as the author often claimed. Rather, in Dick's fiction, it becomes evident that love (of certain variety) itself is always dependent upon the construction of a limit or prohibition. It is actually the failure of this stricture — a failure of "closure," as it were — that hinders love's journey.

Psychoanalysis is not an idealism in the manner of romantic love, for example. The latter promises both totality and a union through exclusion, whereas psychoanalysis offers the subject dissolution through implication. This basic insight is operative in Lacan's suggestion that the "sexual relation does not exist," a claim that marks an inevitable disjunction between partners. While this distance is an unavoidable effect of our experience in language, in *Seminar XX*, Lacan will supplement his claim regarding this non-relation by asserting that love (of a very specific kind) makes up for this void: "What makes up for the sexual relationship is, quite precisely, love."[104]

It is in this same seminar (*Seminar XX*) that Lacan develops his graph of "sexuation," a table that demonstrates two different logics for approaching desire, *jouissance* and of course love.[105] *Jouissance* is a difficult term to translate into English. The term suggests pleasure, even orgasm. However, in French a sense of pain always inheres in *jouissance*, making this an alien "pleasure" to a certain extent. It is also worth noting that Lacan speaks of the *jouissance* as the time before the subject came into language — a time prior to the "mirror stage." As he writes, "*Jouissance* is prohibited to whoever speaks."[106] The point to be taken is that this "loss" of pleasure is the price of becoming a subject. Because of this, *jouissance* is a helpful focus for understanding the limits of the subject and knowledge.

Lacan's graph of sexuation appears as follows:

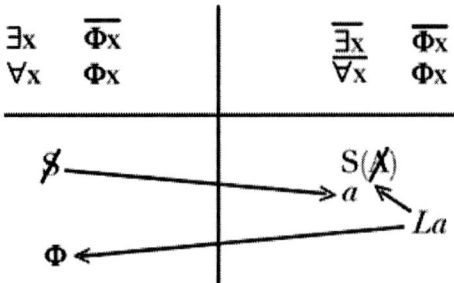

Figure 1. Lacan's graph of sexuation.

Though the two sides of the equation would seem to be broken down according to gender or biological sex — each half is frequently described in terms of "man" and "woman," respectively — Lacan does not for a moment intend this reduction. It is quite possible for a biological woman to situate herself on the left-hand side, just as a biological man might situate himself on the right-hand side of the graph. For the purposes of my discussion here, I will focus upon the masculine logic, or what Lacan has called "phallic *jouissance*," as represented on the left.

The terms found here are by now familiar. Near the top corner of the lower left quadrant, the barred S ($) stands for the split subject. From this symbol an arrow runs to the *a* on the right-hand, or feminine, side. Here again, we find the relation suggested in Lacan's graph of fantasy: $◇*a*. This *a* represents the man's object of enjoyment, which is based upon the logic of exclusion endemic to desire as described throughout chapters one and two. As Zupančič succinctly summarizes, "The inaccessibility of enjoyment is the very *mode of enjoyment* of the subject of desire," that is, the subject organized according to the masculine side of Lacan's graph.[107] In other words, the "man" will achieve enjoyment in a way that is akin to the logic of desire, which inevitably reduces the partner to an object of fantasy. This reduction demonstrates the larger point of Lacan's graph, which is to illustrate the way each side, or each partner, misses the other. The masculine subject misses his partner by approaching her only through the fantasy screening the *objet a*, which is to say that he does not really desire or enjoy "the woman." Rather he enjoys the object that she embodies, or the gift she gives yet does not possess.[108]

The logical equations found at the top left of the graph indicate why this would be the case. The first equation reads: There exists a subject that is not subject to castration. The second: All are subject to the law of castration. Obviously, there is a contradiction between these two statements. The point for Lacan is that the "whole" on the masculine side of the graph is presided over by the law of exclusion. Man can be considered a "whole" subject only through the exclusion of the one who is not subject to the law of castration. This latter subject is of course the primal father, the father of enjoyment who is not subject to the law of prohibition. For this father, all women are accessible. However, for the man subject to the law of castration, there are certain women who remain off-limits.[109] Unable to enjoy all the women, as does the father of enjoyment, the subject is forced to create a "set" of all Women by creating a complete sequence.[110] Here, it will be remembered that the man is wholly subject to the law of the signifier through castration. His *jouissance* is, then, found within the symbolic order. He must "make sense" of his experience through the knowledge produced in language. Unfortunately, there is no signifier for women, as is suggested by the barred woman on the right-hand side of Lacan's graph.[111] To make a complete "set" of women that will allow this concept at last to be written and understood, the man will, essentially, count women. He will produce a complete set. This is what Lacan suggests when he says that this subject experiences the woman "one by one," or part by part.[112] At the same time, this emphasis on a woman's "parts" suggests that it is not the woman that man encounters in the love relationship, but the *objet a*. The man enjoys the woman part by part, and in so doing, he ensures that his relationship with her is missed every time. This is the greater point to be taken. The relationship between men and women described by the graphs — and, again, this is *not* a biological distinction — is always missed, as each seeks something beyond their partner. On the masculine side of the graph in particular, we again encounter the logic of exclusion upon which desire — and often love — operates.

In her essay "I Can't Love You Unless I Give You Up," Salecl makes a distinction that will be quite helpful to this discussion. Here, she distinguishes between two types of love: romantic love, and love of sublimation. The first instance is characterized by prohibition, or the distancing of oneself from the love object, as is the case in courtly love, the exemplary experience of love for the masculine subject illustrated in Lacan's graph of sexuation described above.[113] The romantic lover endeavors to love the other as whole — as Other — a task that, as all failed romantic lovers know, is more easily accomplished without the actual presence of the beloved. Naturally, the other's vexing responses and demands thwart this fantasy every time. The goal of this variety of love, then, is actually to maintain an impossible relation with the other. Only by the maintenance of love's impasse might one imagine that it would truly be possible, in some other time or some other place, to love wholly the Other.[114] The love of sublimation is a much different category. In this case, perhaps counter-intuitively, the lover does *not* attempt to take the beloved as whole. Rather, the lover circles around the object that is the partner, "driven by the fact that the object can never be reached because of its impossible, horrifying nature."[115] In this case, it is through the part — as it were — that one (re)finds, and perhaps enjoys, the whole of the beloved. However, this is done in quite a different fashion than the "part by part" logic described above. I will return to this point shortly.

Again, it would be easy to describe the dominant register of romantic love as that of desire, given that each practice demands a quest without end. In the case of romantic (or courtly) love, not only must the consummation of the relationship be delayed, but likewise must correspondence with the beloved be kept only to the most basic requirements. It is for this reason that romantic love likewise follows the path of sublimation, although what one sublimates is the beloved in their entirety. Per convention, the beloved is placed upon a divine pedestal. The narcissism — indeed, even ventriloquism — that is at the heart of the "desire of the Other" is here all the more apparent, as the other's wants and needs are arranged according to the lover's own fantasy. The pleasure of romantic love depends upon this very absence of the beloved object of affection. Should the "Lady" actually be encountered, the likely result will be either impotence or flight back into the safe distance of desire.[116]

For Salecl, these plays of absence and presence require thinking of the relationship between love and the psychoanalytic concept of the drive. "We can even say that love is placed between desire and drive as an impossible mediator between the two," as she says.[117] The triangulation (i.e., of desire, drive, and love) that Salecl is suggesting is more readily grasped when one remembers that in *Seminar XI* Lacan describes the "object" of both desire and drive as one and the same: the *objet a*. In the case of desire, this object designates something that goes missing and, thereby, facilitates the subject's entrance into subjectivity through this absence. However, in the case of the drive, this object effectively becomes present, and it is this presence, not absence, which is then enjoyed.

Given the structural requirement of the absence of the object for the subject, it makes sense that Lacan describes the assertion of drive in terms of the subject's disappearance. When in the thrall of the drive, the subject becomes "acephalous," that is, a "headless subject."[118] The resulting enjoyment, or *jouissance*, can only be experienced as painful by the subject, as it requires its own erasure.[119] In other words, the emergence of the subject of the drive results in the dissolution of the subject of desire. (This is to move into a register that is distinct from the psychoanalytic "subject" that this study has addressed thus far.) Drive's paradox, or the paradox of sublimation, is the fact that any object can become an object of the drive, and thereby be enjoyed. As Lacan indicates: "By snatching at its object, the drive learns in a sense that this is precisely not the way it will be satisfied."[120] As he continues, here speaking of the oral drive: "Even when you stuff the mouth — the mouth that opens in the register of the drive — it is not the food that satisfies it, it is, as one says, the pleasure of the mouth."[121] The drive does not miss, as it effectively finds enjoyment beyond the object. Because of this, any object might serve as a missed target. Zupančič suggests, "In spite of the fact that the object we consume will never be 'it,' some part of 'it' is produced in the very act of consumption."[122] The drive is always satisfied though the subject experiences this satisfaction as an alien-enjoyment. And yet, because there is no identification involved here, the narcissism that is part and parcel of romantic love is avoided.

To put this distinction into context, as Zupančič has suggested, these two versions of love in Lacan's work surround just this question of sublimation. In the first instance, romantic love consists in "raising an object to the dignity of the Thing" in the act of sublimation.[123] The beloved becomes the cause of desire, therefore leaving the subject barred from any sort of communion with her. Indeed, as described in Chapter Two, because the subject's experience revolves around the absence of this object, meeting the cause of one's desire in actuality can result in disastrous consequences. However, love understood from the perspective of the drive is in many respects the reverse of this prohibition. Rather than the sublimation at work in desire, the mechanism of the drive results in a de-sublimation that allows the subject to enjoy the object — to find satisfaction different from its aim.[124] As Zupančič concludes: "In love, we do not find satisfaction in the other that we aim at, we find it in the space or gap, between, to put it bluntly, what we see and what we get (the sublime and the banal object)."[125]

Instead of a simple sublimation of the object to the level of transcendence, love works by recognizing that indiscernible distance between the beloved object as mundane and celestial. Of course, neither version is truly the beloved, but in the imperceptible distance that separates each image, the subject enjoys love. This is what Lacan intends with his cryptic statement, only love "allows *jouissance* to condescend to the realm of desire."[126] This second version of love moves beyond a narcissism based upon prohibition, prompting Salecl to conclude that in love (of this type), what one is attracted to is the very drive of the other. "Behind the Other's desire, what in the final instance keeps our desire in motion, is the unbearable *jouissance* of the Other."[127] The point to be taken is that love as sublimation, distinct from romantic love, allows the subject to enjoy the partner beyond the "part" offered in the relation of desire. Not so incidentally, it is this Other (capital "O") variety of love that is suggested on the right-hand side of the graph of sexuation. The arrow that runs from the barred Woman (W̶o̶m̶a̶n̶) to the S (A̶), or signifier of the lack in the Other, indicates the woman's bond to a *jouissance* beyond the symbolic order, an experience that potentially opens itself to this love of sublimation.

Returning to Philip K. Dick's work, it is easy to discern these issues played out on a grand scale. As Dick was writing throughout the years surrounding the sexual revolution, it is undeniable that his career spans a time of great unrest in the relationship between the sexes, as was likewise the case with the origin of hard-boiled detective fiction in the 1920s. This similarity no doubt in part accounts for Dick's reliance on the hard-boiled nostalgia and the ethic of separation, which he translates into the science-fiction genre through the device of psychotic paranoia. In light of this strategy, I would argue that Dick's fiction already foresees the failure (from a certain perspective) of discourses of the "emancipation" of sexuality, and the necessary failure of the "free love" movement of the 1960s. To cite an astute comment made at the time — a comment that is not entirely unrelated to this issue — Lacan famously told the student protesters disrupting his seminar in December of 1969: "What you aspire to as revolutionaries is a master. You will get one."[128] In other words, this demand for a "new" openness or freedom, for a break from tradition, is a hysteric desire for a new master. The same is true in the game of love, for, in the end, the call for libidinal freedom only thinly masks a call for prohibition. Far from thwarting love's endeavors, such a prohibition is the mainspring of amorous relations for psychoanalysis, as suggested above. This structural requirement ensures a unique place for love in a time when symbolic efficiency begins to falter.[129] Romantic love becomes an attractive, even urgent focus precisely because it provides a limit, and therefore gap, that thereby edges the subject's relation to the *jouissance* that always threatens the subject's consistency. Nevertheless, despite the comfort that love potentially offers in this context, contemporary difficulties of symbolic efficiency makes it that much more difficult to establish.

To take quickly the example of *Time Out of Joint* as preface to Dick's later exploration of these issues, one finds a characteristically brilliant portrayal of the banality of love's transcendence in the presentation of Ragle Gumm's "love" of his neighbor's wife, Junie Black. Gumm's often misogynistic description of June, though lengthy, will quickly elaborate this thesis. On a stolen afternoon as the two picnic in the park, Gumm looks at Junie as she reclines in the sun and wonders what she might be thinking. Pausing to answer his own question, he assumes that the most likely answer is "nothing." "The mind of a virgin, he thought. There was something touching about her ... the capacity to forget made her innocent all over again, each time. No matter how deeply she got involved with men, he conjectured, she probably remained psychically untouched. Still as she had been. Sweater and saddle shoes.... Her hair-style would alter through the years; she would use more make-up, probably diet. But otherwise eternal" (*TOJ* 51).

This description is interestingly given *before* the failure of Gumm's delusional construction. In this space, the requisite limit for love is present as June is married to Bill Black and, given the time and locale of "Old Town" (i.e., a conservative 1950s, suburban setting), the social prohibition forbidding their union is readily in place. It is quite telling, then, that Gumm's fantasy projection surrounding this woman doubles, even triples, such distancing through his sublimation of the otherwise utterly simple June Black. Indeed, she remains unaffected in all ways, despite her mortal entanglements. Neither Gumm, nor anyone, can "reach" her. Despite her embarrassing immaturity — or rather because of it — she remains "eternal," innocent "again" every time.

As Lacan indicated, love is the elevation of the "object to the dignity of the Thing."[130] In other words, the process of sublimation quite literally places the beloved into the space of the subject's lack — that is, the other comes to embody the subject's *objet a*, that missing piece lost in the process of subjectivization. In this way, the beloved promises a return of all that the subject imagines has been lost or prohibited through their inscription into the symbolic order. Obviously, the sublimation of the love object always involves a sort of writing, or a dressing of the "nothing" — that stupid, banal object from our everyday experience — into that more sublime entity. It is, then, not incidental that Ragle Gumm was formerly a "fashion designer," concerned with the question of dressing and giving body to the nothing that animates our desire (*TOJ* 223). He is clearly an adept romantic lover.

The emptiness that Gumm imagines there in the empty beyond of space — his goal as the text concludes — might, then, be thought in the terms of love that I have been describing. The vacuum of space is that emptiness inhering with the symbolic order itself, though it appears in this case without the "dressing" of fantasy. In the first instance (i.e., in the context of his first breakdown), his encounter with the real of his desire — namely, the emptiness of all desire, even when incarnated in any given object of fantasy — results in a regression back to formerly lost objects of comfort. To phrase this in Zupančič's terms, Gumm is not yet ready to accept the difference between what he sees and what he gets. In other words, though Gumm is attracted to the "thing" behind all the covering, he represses this desire and returns to former objects of stability. Nostalgia is nothing if not a clinging to the object in this fashion, a fact that bears strong similarities with the temporal inversion of the basic science fiction plot, a point that I will return to shortly.[131] The subtle hilarity of the text, then, is to privilege love within the sphere of Gumm's delusional construction. It seems that only there can he "love" Junie, an amusingly harsh indictment of the relation between romantic love and paranoid psychosis.[132]

After Gumm's awakening, June Black's appeal rapidly drifts away, and the sublimation of love is no longer possible:

> Hollow outward form instead of substance; the sun not actually shining, the day not actually warm at all but cold, gray and quietly raining.... In his mind he chased after her, across a hollow barren hillside. She dwindled, disappeared. The skeleton of life, white brittle scarecrow support in the shape of a cross. Grinning. Space instead of eyes. The whole world, he thought, can be seen through. I am on the inside looking out. Peeking through a crack and seeing — emptiness. Seeing into its eyes [*TOJ* 179–180].

Here one sees all too well the play of fantasy with the void to which it gives form. To lose this support is to lose the consistency of one's world and, as Dick expertly demonstrates, to lose the object that formerly distanced the subject from a traumatic encounter with the inconsistency of the symbolic order — or the lack in the big Other. As is true for Gumm, the object chosen for this task is so frequently woman herself, as idealized in love. However, with the failure of symbolic efficiency and its basic prohibition that is visited upon Ragle Gumm at the conclusion of the text, such a romantic love is no longer possible. Neither does love as sublimation seem to apply. He is unprepared to accept the difference between what he sees and what he gets in Junie Black, as his retreat into space shows.

The Horror of Impossible Love Made Possible

This struggle to "go on loving" in the face of such symbolic turmoil is found in the subsequent text, *Flow My Tears, the Policeman Said* (1974). The novel is set in a future where experience is in all ways mediated by the entertainment industry — a clear critique of Hollywood "culture" — and society is divided into a rigid caste system. The initial symbolic crisis of the text occurs when international celebrity Jason Taverner, the most recognized face in the world, awakens to find that no one remembers him. The anti-detective gesture of this predicament is clear, as Taverner literally loses every symbolic support that formerly oriented his life. As another detective by necessity in Dick's work, Taverner must find the cause of his predicament and attempt to return the social order to the its previous arrangement, thereby regaining the lavish life he has lost. However, unlike *Time Out of Joint*, *Flow My Tears* does not end with the promise of resolution. Indeed, the final cause of the "time warp" at the heart of novel is not so easily reversed, a fact that at the same time reveals the fundamental inconsistency of Taverner's previous existence.

Taverner can never go home again, a dilemma that makes the issues of love and empathy all the more urgent.

In *Flow My Tears*, we find a concise illustration of Dickian love when the character Ruth Rae tells the odd story of Emily Fusselman's rabbit.[133] Importantly, Rae's story is told after she and Taverner, who were acquainted in a previous time, have spent the night together in bed — neither feels especially "connected" to the other, despite the exertions of the evening. Rae's tale recounts the Fusselmans' pet rabbit's attempt to befriend the family cat and dog, only to be traumatized back into solitude after an incident with the German Shepherd. As Rae explains, what is so touching about this is the rabbit's attempt to overcome the limits of its "physiology," to become a "more evolved form of life" by playing with the other animals as equals (*FMT* 108). Of course, the analogy made here speaks to the transcendence of the self that occurs in love, a transcendence that frees us from the body and its mortality by binding us to another. This is the goal and beauty of love as described. As Rae explains with an apparent platitude, "When you love you cease to live for yourself; you live for another person" (*FMT* 110).

However, in keeping with Dick's reliance on the hard-boiled ethos, love in this text is always already predicated upon its own failure. In other words, we are clearly within the realm of romantic love. To these ends, Rae's monologue comes to privilege grief as the greatest of love's pleasures, and herein we find Dick's characteristic ambivalence in the face of his own insight. In grief, one encounters both the absolute loneliness of death *and* the vivification of life won through the connection with another living thing. "Grief reunites us with what you've lost," a reunion that demands a splitting of ourselves to accompany this lost piece, to "go part of the way with it on its journey," to "follow it as far as you can go" (*FMT* 112). The reunion is as precious as it is fleeting. From this unsustainable bliss, we are inevitably required to "phase back into this world," as Rae says (*FMT* 112). The lover returns irreparably wounded: "You don't ever completely come back from where you went with him — a fragment broken off your pulsing, pumping heart is there still" (*FMT* 113).

Rae's choice of vocabulary is interesting, as it is seems that the term "grief" is substituted where "love" would find a more common usage. Indeed, the "grief" of Rae's description is clearly a (lost) transcendent moment similar to the initial mother-child dyad that is sought by the questing, romantic lover. From this union, the subject can only "return" wounded in some way. This is the very condition of our humanity. To be human is to possess a broken heart and to battle the effects of this wound for a lifetime. This description is all the more appropriate given that Rae speaks of a love that is already lost in grief. Such an impossible love is of course the hallmark of romantic love. The mythic moment of unity with the lost object is always already lost — indeed, the real possibility of this encounter terrifies the lover, as it would abolish the fantasy structure that sublimates the beloved. The object only appears rendered in this form, just as the subject only enters the scene as fatally "wounded." It is for just this reason, then, that the love object spoken of by Rae is only known in its absence, through the mourning of this loss.[134] In other words, the Other of the love relationship is only known and experienced, as a lost object of fantasy. To these ends, Rae's phrasing is quite telling: "Grief reunites you with what you've lost. It's a merging; you go with the loved thing or person that's going away" (*FMT* 112). The beloved "thing" is granted privilege over the possibility of a lost "person."

This insistence of the object occluding the individual is familiar in Dick. For example, at the conclusion of *Flow My Tears, the Policeman Said*, a vase made by the character Mary Anne Dominic is the final object of the narrative gaze. Appropriately, the concluding line of the text indicates that the vase is "loved" (*FMT* 231). In *Seminar VII*, the figure of the vase is used by Lacan to illustrate the process of sublimation in its production of the Thing; as is the case in romantic love, the vase actively creates the very emptiness it encircles.[135] That Dick chooses to conclude his text with this figure already indicates that romantic love remains privileged, though this fact is lamented.

Apropos of this question of exclusion, it is no accident that Dick chooses to tell the story of a rabbit, a topic that resonates with the fable of the tortoise and the hare and, further, the famous paradox of the footrace between Achilles and the Tortoise.[136] In *Seminar XX*, Lacan uses the story of these runners as illustrative of the metonymy of the masculine side of desire: "It is quite clear that Achilles can only pass the tortoise — he cannot catch up with it. He only catches up with it at infinity."[137] While this assertion might be taken as an example of Lacan's famous pronouncement that "there is no such thing as the sexual relation," Zupančič reads this passage as referring to the masculine subject's relation to enjoyment and desire. As she writes, "What is incapable of being achieved by Achilles is his own *jouissance*"; in other words, what is indicated here is Achilles' relationship with his own *objet a*.[138] Hence, the radical limiting of enjoyment of the desiring subject on this side of Lacan's graphs of sexuation, which is characterized as follows: "Phallic *jouissance* is the obstacle owing to which man does not come (*n'arrive pas*), I would say, to enjoy woman's body, precisely because what he enjoys is the *jouissance* of the organ."[139] Though this passage is as opaque as any within *Seminar XX*, its logic has much in common with the play of objects within Dick's fiction.

This "organ" that Lacan speaks of is precisely what keeps Achilles from ever catching up with the tortoise, keeping him both from his enjoyment and, potentially, from "love." Between "man" and "woman" is the *jouissance* of "the organ," says Lacan. Though there is always a danger of mistaking the phallus for the penis, the "organ" spoken of here can only be the *objet a*, as it is produced through castration for the subject of male sexuation. If it is only through this "organ," or mechanism, that man will come to "enjoy" the woman, it is clear that he is incapable of enjoying his partner at all. He enjoys her only "piece by piece" (or "part by part") insofar as her body comes to be carved out by the process of fantasy — the very process of romantic love.

This is in part what Lacan intends elsewhere when he speaks of "a specific depreciation of love" in the dialectic between demand and masculine desire that causes a "divergence towards 'another woman.'"[140] Moving slowly towards the object of his desire, the man, like Achilles, can only approach her through the logic of exclusion, making each meeting only another play of distances. When an individual woman is found not to be *it*, the man pins his libidinal hope elsewhere. There is, then, an inherent difficulty in the desiring subject's ability to love, as we have seen. The man does desire the wholeness promised in love, and he remains (structurally) incapable of achieving this because of that interrupting object that remains both familiar and foreign, both desired and reviled. As Dick is clearly an adherent of the maudlin, hard-boiled ethos, this "failure" of love is so frequently represented in tragic terms in his work, despite the fact that this failure is the driving "truth" of his fictional worlds. In other words, without this prohibition, the chaotic futures of his fiction would be all the more unbearable.

In its solipsism, this desiring economy is remarkably resilient, ensuring the maintenance of boundaries that will support the subject's drive for isolation. As is the case in the detective narrative, where all objects are taken as a mark of enlightenment yet to come, little can shake its foundation, save for a lifting of the prohibition that marks its structuring impossibility. Again, this is the starting point of anti-detection, to provide the excluded object within the frame of inquiry. In the relation between the sexes, this shaking of the foundations occurs when, as we have seen, there is no longer a prohibition that might allow the lover to love his forbidden object. In other words, the questing romantic must fear the failure of love's failure. This is always the greater horror, that love might present itself as possible instead of prohibited.

In *Flow My Tears*, Dick stages this very failure through the breakdown of symbolic efficiency via the sci-fi device of alternate futures — or time out of joint. An example of the deleterious effects of this failure of prohibition is found in Ruth Rae's sexual encounter with Jason Taverner.[141] Their sadness after *coitus* — the sadness that prompts Ruth's discussion of the Fusselman rabbit — is not so much a result of their failing to merge meaningfully, although of course this fails, as well. The greater failure at work in this exchange is the failure of prohibition that would keep them from merging. Taverner and Rae are literally out of step with each other as they come from different times and different futures; consequently, they should not be able to encounter each other. However, owing to the disruption of the space-time continuum, the greatest prohibition, they are able to come together. Each is free to do as she or he chooses, and there is nothing stopping them from continuing their relation save for a lack of desire — which is to say a lack of a prohibition of one kind or another. This is the point of Rae's post-coital recitation of the story of the rabbit. Sadly, for Rae and Taverner, Achilles effectively catches up to the tortoise.

This failure of prohibition in the sexual relationship is most evident in the incestuous union of Felix and Alys Buckman. It is of course no coincidence that objects, and the question of collecting, become the mediating factor in this relation. As Alys says of her brother, "Between us we have a good deal of interesting objects" (*FMT* 145). Unfortunately, these objects are in the end insufficient, for in their incestuous union, exclusion is strictly impossible. What becomes necessary for Felix, and perhaps for Alys as well, is the collection of cultural artifacts to instantiate the symbolic order that is in disarray. Conceivably, it is punishment for this incestuous union that the greater circumvention of the symbolic order is visited upon all of the primary characters of the text. As the reader discovers, this temporal overlap is triggered by Alys' use of the experimental drug KR-3, which pulls her brother Inspector Buckman, Jason Taverner, and numerous other individuals into *her* own delusional world. A wonderfully Dickian psychotropic trope, the drug apparently unbinds individuals from their own temporal sequences, bringing them within the sway of another's delusion. To be caught within the symptom of another is all too common. Indeed, this might very well be the basic requirement of love, in the very specific sense that has been discussed in this chapter. Presumably, to be caught within the psychosis of another remains a quite different thing, though Dick's work challenges us to consider the uncanny similarity of these two possibilities.

To conclude this discussion, as is clearly shown in *Flow My Tears*, the basic paradigm of the science fiction plot, namely, the "time warp," scripts the possibility of the impossible.[142] As Zupančič has argued, the category of the Lacanian Real is far too often confused with the impossible, or that which can neither be experienced nor symbolized. On the contrary, the entire point of the Real is that the impossible happens — "The Real happens as the impossible."[143] In her reading of love, this is precisely what occurs insofar as one meets the sublime object of the beloved in everyday reality, yet somehow manages to maintain this transcendence in its accessibility.[144]

In this way, we see the significance of the discourse of love in the context of anti-detection. The detective narrative — which, I am suggesting, is libidinally quite similar to romantic love — is built upon a series of prohibitions that will forever foreclose an encounter with the object sought — be this *rara avis* or the beloved. In opposition to this entrenchment, the anti-detective impulse, and the love of sublimation (i.e., the second variety described by Salecl) thwarts prohibition and confronts the lover and detective with the impossible. In *Time Out of Joint*, there is clearly a plea for a new intimacy. However, in the end, the possibility of the impossible truly occurring is far too anxiety provoking, and the text concludes, privileging the romantic love described by Ruth Rae. This is true despite the fact that Alys Buckman and Jason Taverner represent, in effect, the coincidence of two impossible worlds, for their "relationship" remains entirely solipsistic — and unrecognized — in each case. It is not incidental, then, that one of the key scenes of the conclusion of the text features Felix Buckman, the policeman, embracing a stranger at a gas station. Failing to catch his quarry, Taverner — that is, failing at detection — the policeman longs for human contact. However, as his incestuous relation with his sister makes clear, it is not a lack of proximity that keeps individuals in this world from "connection." Quite the opposite, with the failure of symbolic efficiency, others become threateningly proximate though intimacy remains wanting.

Love and the Mechanical Woman

These difficulties inherent in such symbolic confusion, particularly as these relate to the relation between the sexes, are all the more apparent in the 1969 texts *Do Androids Dream of Electric Sheep?* and "Notes on *Do Androids Dream of Electric Sheep?*" — the latter written by Dick as guide for the (then potential) filming of his novel. As Scott's brilliant film version *Blade Runner* (1981) translates so well, *Do Androids Dream?* is a hard-boiled tale projected into a dismal, post-apocalyptic, sci-fi future. The detective, Richard Deckard, is charged with finding a group of runaway androids and "retiring" (i.e., destroying) them before their presence causes widespread panic on Earth. As was true for the hard-boiled detective, along the way he will be confronted with the ultimately indeterminate boundaries that separate not merely the detective and criminal, but the human and inhuman, as well. Concomitantly, Dick's written texts for *Do Androids Dream?* emphasize the return of *the* Woman as the impossible that happens in reality, a disruption that here directs the anti-detective impulse of Dick's project.

What I wish to show in this concluding section is that the misogyny — something that is for the most part downplayed in Scott's film version — of these two texts is actually in keeping with the overarching logic of Philip K.

Dick's work, bound as it is to the hard-boiled ethic discussed in Chapter Two. Nevertheless, Dick's work in this way offers a compelling assessment of the question of love in a time of the foreclosure of symbolic efficiency. If Lacan's final understanding of love privileges a relationship with the drive — indeed, if analysis itself has this very goal in mind[145] — the question becomes is it more or less possible to achieve such a love in the age of the foreclosure of the Name-of-the-Father? *Do Androids Dream?* and the "Notes" for the filming of this work indicate both a hope and a fear that this is the case, an ambivalence that I have been arguing is common to the author's work as a whole.

As has been well documented, *Do Androids Dream?* revolves around the question of the double and the crippling impotence that the emergence of this figure always visits upon the unsuspecting. Far from presenting a "new" variety of double that requires us to reconsider the concept from a more modern context, the "replicants" of the film — and, presumably, the "andys" of the novel — underscore the horror that is the uncanny itself.[146] The very point of the double, as Freud demonstrated, is that the figure is always "unnatural," all the more so because of its concomitant familiarity. What Dick's fiction does so brilliantly is to underscore the similarly uncanny nature of that most familiar and intimate experience — love. Indeed, there is always something decidedly "unnatural" accompanying the love relation in the Dickian world, difficulties that are always strategically exacerbated by the devices of science fiction. In *Do Androids Dream?*, such a genre-specific derangement is achieved when the protagonist, Deckard, falls in love with an android. Lacan claimed that love makes up for the fact that there is "no such thing as a sexual relation," in that, when in love, the subject is able to assume that there is a symbolic script that ensures the relation between the sexes.[147] When in love, things suddenly "make sense," as all lovers know. However, this does not entirely cover over the uncanny aspects that are basic to the experience. Falling in love with an android, then, is not so novel or problematic as one might first assume. Indeed, the romantic lover is always falling in love with a piece of "machinery," or the lifeless object — the other as object.[148] Only under love's spell is it possible to imagine otherwise.

However, this failure of the romantic lover to truly encounter his partner (i.e., apart from a reduction to object) does not stop the subject from assuming the existence of *the* Woman who would make the sexual relationship possible. Indeed, this prospect guides the man's search of love and has everything to do with his relationship to the phallus. For example, in the essay "The Signification of the Phallus," Lacan describes this as the "centrifugal tendency of the genital drive in love life" that will always make his own desire for the phallus (i.e., for love) move in a "residual divergence towards 'another woman' who may signify this phallus in various ways, either as a virgin or as a prostitute."[149] The man is, then, given to the tendency of seeking the Woman through a series of women. By completing the series, by providing it with both start and finish, it is possible, so the man imagines, to at last provide a meaning for this vexed question, "What is Woman?"

Even a cursory reading of Dick's notes to the possible filming of his novel reveal such a fascination with *the* Woman. Leaving aside the author's own psychopathology — though this project so readily demands to be written — one finds two items of preoccupation: 1) a deliberate meditation on the question of *the* Woman taken in a series; and 2) the issue of anxiety and impotence in the sexual act. This anxiety is necessary when one considers the fact that *the* Woman is, in effect, the structural equivalent of the Anal Father of Enjoyment, as each is not subject to the law of castration and is, therefore, the violent mediator of all enjoyment for the subject. Following Dick's reliance on the hard-boiled tradition, both structurally and aesthetically, we encounter a *femme fatale* figure in this android that promises to be all for the detective. As the characterization of the *femme fatale* is inevitably inhuman — she appears only as savage animal or succubus — the literal mechanization of this figure is no great innovation. Indeed, with the android Rachel, Dick simply works the logic of the *femme fatale* to its uncanny conclusion, a focus that is perhaps inevitable given the make-up of his fictional worlds. Without the paternal metaphor to successfully break up the mother-child dyad by naming the mother's enjoyment — and thereby opening a symbolic space in which the subject might emerge — the violent return of the un-castrated Woman becomes a reality.

In both the book and film versions of *Do Androids Dream?*, this unfettered, total *jouissance* is presented in the perversity of the creating a "basic pleasure model" of "replicant," a mechanized, and therefore inhuman, source of enjoyment. As the android Rachel jokes, the shorted lifespan of replicants is to keep men from forsaking flesh and blood women altogether in favor of running off and living with "artificials." The "short circuit" that would result from such a choice would of course bypass the prohibitions of desire that guarantee the traditional detective's researches. Naturally, in the anti-detective space of *Do Androids Dream?*, Deckard is not interested in maintaining desire's obligatory caution, a fact that recalls but one of the many felicities of the film's title, *Blade Runner*. Though the detective is married in the novel (he is not in the film), he seems perfectly willing to forsake this union by daring to enjoy Rachel sexually. After consummating his relation with the machine, Deckard assures Rachel that "If I could, I would marry you right now," a gesture that immediately reminds one of Marlowe's use of desire as a defense against *jouissance* in *The Big Sleep*.[150] Yet, in keeping with the romantic form of Chandler, Rachel is inaccessible as both she and Deckard are from different worlds, her job will not permit their union, and he is already married. This is of course to say nothing of the more fantastic hindrances to their union (i.e., she is a renegade replicant, she possesses only a limited lifespan, etc.). While these facts are formidable, there remains something much more troubling about Rachel, something beyond even her admittance that she only slept with Deckard to keep him from continuing his hunt for her compatriots.

Rachel's greater menace might in part be understood in the literal doubling of her character with the replicant Pris (played by Daryl Hannah in Scott's film). The reader of Dick's novel is told that each replicant is the same model and is therefore identical in appearance. Rachel herself could, then, very easily have been the "pleasure model" that is Pris. In his "Notes," Dick is quite pleased by the "possibilities" that are offered by this doubling, going so far as to sketch a montage that cuts between Deckard and the character Isodore making love to identical women, during which the author foresees Isodore "fouling it all up, a la Peter Sellers."[151] No mention is made as to how Deckard will "foul it up," leaving us free to conjecture that his own failure would be a result of the male side of sexuation. This assumption bears itself out well as Dick describes Deckard's sexual experience with the "andy" both in terms of impotence and series.

Far from boldly showing the way to a novel arrangement between the sexes, Dick's fascination with the dilemma of a man who falls in love with a woman who is not, as she readily admits, "alive," reveals an anxiety that is all too common:

> Isn't this, this sexual union between Rick Deckard and Rachael Rosen — isn't it the *summa* of falsity and mechanical motions carried out minus any real feeling, as we understand the word? Feeling on each of their parts. Does in fact her mental — and physical — coldness numb the male, the human man into an echo of it?[152]

The fear of succubae is even more manifest in the following:

> His relationship, by having intercourse with her, has melded him to — not an individual, human or android — but to a whole type or model, of which, theoretically, there could be tens of thousands. To whom, then, has he *really* given his erotic libido to? An army of rachel rosens, a horde of them, all identical? This undermines the meaning of love — at least sexual, erotic love — because the basic parity is undermined, one man for one woman (at least one at a time). But he has, in effect, made love to them all![153]

The "cold," inhuman numbness of the android is of course the necessary result of the reduction of one's partner to object in romantic love. In other words, the Tyrell Corporation (the company that builds replicants) hardly has a monopoly on this industry, as the man is always involved in the manufacture of women. The same is true of the troubling question of series suggested in the second quotation. Though the construction of a total series is one of the strategies through which the man will continue to imagine *the* Woman exists, the completion of this project can only bring about the sort of anxiety that Dick is here expressing. Reading the notes and text together, then, it is easy to conclude that Dick has used the artifice of the science fiction story arc — that is, the impossible that happens — to de-realize the impossibility of the sexual relationship to which all who align themselves with the male side of sexuation are themselves subject. In other words, Deckard meets an impossible Woman, as it were.

The fear of having one's "libido drained" off by some monstrous female, as Dick represents it here, is a wonderfully straightforward elaboration of the difficulty produced by such a meeting. For, in meeting the object-cause (i.e., *the* Woman) in reality, the man will truly be rendered impotent, no longer able to maintain his desire according to a dialectic of lack. Here again, the *femme fatale* character, with all her plundering attributes, is a useful model for this threat. In a like fashion, Rachel amusingly chides Deckard before the consummation of their relation, telling him, "If you think too much about it too much — then you can't go on. For, ahem, physical reasons."[154] Although this may be true of any sexual encounter for the man, the distraction to which Rachel refers is the fact that she is a replicant: "*I'm not alive!* You're not going to bed with a woman," as she insistently reminds him (*DA* 169; italics in orig.). However, the point to be taken is the romantic lover is never going to bed with a "real woman." He only ever lies with the object. The replicant, that tailor-made object of desire, uncannily foregrounds this basic process, all the while belying the hysteric demand of the Dickian universe — the longing for and the terror at potentially finding *the* Woman that would complete the sexual relationship. This is the ambiguity of Rachel who sexually defeats Deckard with the "tireless core of her electronic being," which at the same time potentially allows her to be the partner that Deckard seeks (*DA* 160).

Deckard does indeed "fall in love" with Rachel, and the andy professes to have done the same, although her intentions in the novel are, apparently, for the worse. At the end of Dick's "Notes," the author indicates that what is to be emphasized is the not only the abyss that an "electronic" Rachel is — sexually or otherwise — but likewise to show how each partner might "force back the artificial and mechanical and smother it in their mutual yearnings" (*DA* 160). Like Emily Fusselman's rabbit, both android and man are, potentially, capable of throwing off their limitations and truly embracing the other. Still Dick seems more terrified at this possibility. Continuing to side with romantic desire, in the "Notes" he asks, "Will desire successfully be maintained" or will disappointment be the end result at the end of Deckard's union with Rachel (*DA* 160)? Here again, Dick's emphasis on sustaining desire belies his penchant for romantic love. Importantly, in the novel, Rachel remains in collusion with the other andys, despite the fact that none have empathy, as such, for the other. This is why Rachel professes to sleep with Deckard — to render him incapable of killing the other andys. Unfortunately, her action does not yield the desired results, and it seems that her profession to love Deckard may in fact be genuine after all. This is evident when, after Deckard has successfully killed the remaining androids, he arrives home to discover that Rachel has killed his electric sheep. (In this post-apocalyptic world, nuclear fallout has killed nearly all the animals, requiring pet lovers to own *ersatz* versions such as Deckard's sheep.) It seems that despite her treachery, she remains resentful of the fact that Deckard could love an artificial animal more than he could love her, or, as she conjectures, even his own wife (*DA* 177).

This privileging of the love of an animal is a curious point of fascination within Dick's fiction, a detail that must not be separated from a similar privileging of the handcrafted objects of the artisan. In the individual's relation to each object, there is a reciprocity that is unavailable elsewhere in the hyper-alienated futures presented by the author. It is of course commonplace to describe the love of a pet as a "pure love," or more simply, a love devoid of love's vicissitudes, which necessarily includes hate. Deckard's fetishizing of the animal, or "life" itself — even in an artificial form — is comprehensible given the condition of radical entropy, death, and loneliness of the post-apocalyptic landscape of his world. The "love" of an animal would seem to offer the desired vivification that remains out of reach with the human partner. For example, the animal is not limited by language in the manner that we are, allowing them an (imagined) immediacy with instinctual life that Dick seems to have found quite enviable. This claim itself becomes quite appealing when one acknowledges that Dick, for better or worse, was attempting to think how the subject continues to function despite the failure of the governing Other. As animals care nothing of this Other — they are not subject *to* language — they perhaps provide an ideal point for imagining just this dilemma.

When Rachel kills Deckard's electric sheep, she seems to understand this quite well. However, what remains misunderstood by Rachel is the necessary role of lack within the love relation. The emotional immaturity of the androids is emphasized both within the film and novel, despite the radically different portrayal of the androids in each text. After Deckard sleeps with Rachel, she is described twice in just these terms: she is as "human as any girl he had known" (*DA* 173).[155] Given her murder of Deckard's sheep, this is not to be taken as entirely *ersatz* frailty, for Rachel does indeed suffer from a sort of jealousy, that most human of emotions.

Bearing this in mind, my former reading of the text might be supplemented. Rather than Deckard alone bent upon the construction of *the* Woman that will allow the sexual relation to be fulfilled at last, what if the android likewise believes in the sexual relation, particularly as a passage to (complete) subjectivity? Rachel, in both the novel and the film, seems to imagine that love will in fact make her "more human," and therefore allow her to fill that void that she senses so palpably within her. The constant description of her infantile aspects seems to support this. The phallic nature of this gesture is apparent, for here Dick offers a woman that truly desires the man, rather than something beyond him.[156] In seeking her humanity solely through man's love, the electric woman remains all the more a masculine fantasy.

It is for this reason that I find readings of both *Do Androids Dream of Electric Sheep?* and *Blade Runner* that offer the possibility of thinking of new configurations of sexuality as deeply problematic. What is central to each text are very banal crises characteristic of the male side of sexuation. I would argue that this is true in each of the releases of the film *Blade Runner*, as well as within Dick's novel itself. The original release of the film is perhaps illustrative of this point. Dick's initial distaste for Scott's film is well known. In addition to his outrage at the fact that the director had, apparently, not read his novel, Dick was disappointed with the sympathetic representation of the androids within the film.[157] This is no doubt true of all the androids, but of the character Rachel in particular. She is not, as his notes of 1968 imagined, cast as identical to the more sexually predatory character, Pris. In the conclusion of the 1981 release of *Blade Runner*, Deckard and Rachel are shown speeding into the countryside, in order to enjoy the indeterminate amount of time that they will have together. As Harrison Ford's voice-over at this point indicates, "We didn't know how much time we'd have together, but, then again, who does?"[158] This happy ending is, supposedly, corrected in the director's cut of the film, which was released in 1995, by removing this drive into the sunset and including details that suggest that Deckard is himself a replicant.[159] The latter suggestion is a hard-boiled gesture that has much in common with the anti-detective project, in that the distinction between the detective and criminal is never so clearly drawn. Given this, a similar coincidence must occur when the futuristic detective hunts replicants. Indeed, a reader attentive to the aesthetics of Dick's story would be tempted to make the assumption that Deckard is himself an "artificial" even without the inclusion of these more explicit indications. In any case, given Dick's ambivalent preoccupation with the successful completion of the sexual relationship, the ending to the first release of the film is not so un–Dickian as has been imagined. The "completed" relationship, based as it is upon an impossible future—that is, an inevitable failure—is Dickian through and through.

Indeed, that Deckard "gets the (artificial) girl" at the end of the first version of *Blade Runner* is not so very far removed from the discovery at the end of the novel that the toad found in the desert is in fact a forgery. Deckard finds the toad — a prized animal thought to be extinct — in the uninhabited wasteland north of San Francisco. Feeling lost, in a number of respects, he drives there into wilderness after completing his mission, hoping to make sense of things.[160] As Deckard explains, "what I've done ... that's become alien to me. In fact everything about me has become unnatural; I've become an unnatural self" (*DA* 204). Finding such a rare example of life there in the desert for an instant offers the possibility of authenticity reclaimed. However, this is illusory, as the toad itself proves to be unnatural — it is an electric toad that had somehow wondered into the desert. Appropriately, Deckard's wife, Iran, discovers this before he does. She is, as is most often the case, more adept at the mediation of love and desire in the sexual relationship. At the very conclusion of the novel, we find Iran calling the service department of the local electric pet retailer inquiring about the maintenance of the family's new mechanical addition. As she says, "I want it to work perfectly. My husband is devoted to it" (*DA* 216).[161] The human woman proves herself to be far more capable of supporting the fantasy of the man. Interestingly, Rachel, the object manufactured for this very purpose (i.e., supporting the man's fantasy), is not up to the task. In the novel, the insight Iran is privy to and the replicant Rachel is not, is that there is little of herself that is forsaken in this gesture, as there is not a signifier for the place of woman.[162] In the end, it is Iran, and not the artificial woman, who more readily takes up the masquerade that is woman. (In each of the versions of the film, Iran's exclusion allows Rachel to approach this insight more closely.) Again, the technological aspect of the union of man and machine does not confront us with an artificiality that is new, or anything that might resemble an original *re*-configuration of the sexual relationship. Rather, what we are uncannily confronted with in Rachel and Deckard's union is that driving, alien factor that leaves each of us forever removed from the Other we seek — by bringing us painfully close to this same figure.

Hysteria, Paranoia, and the Loneliness of Love

In conclusion, the psychoanalytic reading of love as a structure that, potentially, bonds one individual to another via the mechanism of the drive must be understood as the logical outcome of the Dickian opus, though this possibility is never, in the end, fully embraced given the nostalgia of Dick's hysteric demand. This is true insofar as Dick's science fiction documents the increasingly tenuous symbolic structure that only fleetingly guarantees its own authority. In response to this recognition, we find indecision. The author both revels in the possibility of this situation and laments the loss of former models of relation. In the former instance, one finds the anti-detective impulse that always appears in Dick's work; in the latter, one finds a hysteric demand informed by the hard-boiled ethos that is Dick's response to this unbearable anxiety. As has been shown, the failure of conventional institutions, and the symbolic trust through which we participate in and create their authority, by no means results in a liberation of any sort. When symbolic efficiency falters, the result is not a return of all that was formerly forbidden — be this the relation behind prohibition or the reality behind ideology. Rather, what occurs with the failure of symbolic efficiency is the return of the tyrannical Other that hordes enjoyment from the subject who is no longer the beneficiary of a pact made with the now lost father. The subject is left to the hysterical search for a new "father" — a new Other — that will again orient the subject's psychical economy. Little has perhaps changed from the former situation, and as Žižek and others have shown, even the helicon days of Oedipus contained the seeds of its demise. However, though this basic search for the recognition from the Other has not altered significantly, the failure of the symbolic guarantee that once allowed us to "believe the Other's words" in spite of the lie results in an increasingly hysterical journey for the subject, a journey that necessarily has frequent exchanges with paranoia.

This is the legacy of Philip K. Dick, whose work provides both a prolepsis of the symbolic failure that is now so evident, as well as an indication of a strategy of response that has likewise itself become quite common. The hesitation of Philip K. Dick and the underlying indecision is remarkably timely today. So too is this privileging of love and empathy, when the very mechanism that might have allowed one to gauge the nature of each has gone missing. As Verhaeghe has said, "Love is a remedy in a time of loneliness."[163] What love offers, particularly love of the romantic variety, is the possible production of a limit that might define the subject, a directive that is lacking in Dick's fictional worlds and, no doubt, our own. But with the failure of symbolic authority, this relation becomes increasingly difficult, as the impossible threatens to happen in actuality. In several respects, then, we travel to the future only to return to the desiring economy of the hard-boiled detective.

FOUR

Remembering, Repeating, and Working Through: Traumatic Narrative in the Hard-Boiled Fiction of Marcia Muller

Introduction

Despite the fact that Marcia Muller is perhaps the most important figure at the "origin" of the female hard-boiled detective, she has remained largely a footnote within criticism. A nod to the importance of her work and the obligatory quotation of Sue Grafton's proclamation that Muller was the "founding 'mother' of the contemporary female hard-boiled private eye" are typically the extent of Muller scholarship, even within histories of the genre.[1] Of course, Grafton is quite right when she speaks of Muller's parentage of the female hard-boiled detective. In 1977, with her publication of *Edwin of the Iron Shoes*, Muller creates a sub-genre that revitalized the mystery genre and compellingly recast the hard-boiled detective popularized by Chandler and MacDonald — two of Muller's acknowledged influences.[2]

This early work paved the way for Sue Grafton and Sara Paretsky, fellow pioneers who are perhaps more readily associated with the modern tough female detective.[3] As Grafton's alphabet series and Paretsky's V. I. Washarski novels achieved cult status in the 1980s — Muller's work of the time fares well, but not as well — the female hard-boiled detective became a beloved and lucrative force on the mystery-publishing scene.[4] Popular and academic responses to this new sleuth celebrated the tantalizing paradox at the heart of the gendered transformation, which was at the same time the key to its success.

Women, formerly reduced to the *femme fatale* or even less-interesting objects of the (male) detective's search, were suddenly cast as detectives. And not just any detective. This new brand of investigator was not a genderless matriarch solving cozy mysteries in the British countryside. Neither was she a wife or sidekick to a more famous private dick. On the contrary, she was herself a tough, lone wolf operative, with nothing but her gut and gun — and perhaps a little female intuition — to aid her in her own quest. This role reversal clearly required a great deal of artistry and finesse, a circumstance that was perhaps best summarized by early critics who plainly asked, "How is it possible to produce a female hard-boiled detective without winding up with something akin to Philip Marlowe in drag?"[5]

In an interview given in 1997, Marcia Muller discussed her careful, gendered appropriation of the hard-boiled genre. She recalled being immediately cognizant of the danger of a straightforward translation of a woman into a masculine space. She refused to script her new character as either a banal "hard-bitten" loner or, to err on the side of womanly modesty, make her an unobtrusive observer, a "camera," as Muller said, who neither responds nor engages with the world around her.[6] Avoiding such pitfalls, the author resolved to take the advice offered in Chandler's "The Simple Art of Murder": she will make it real, taking up the feminist literary imperative that Munt describes as "telling it like it is."[7] For Muller, this meant she had to "create a woman who would be a fully developed individual" living in the real world, and carrying on believable interactions with supporting characters so as to provide the raw material for a long-lasting series.[8] Unlike the "ideal man" spoken of by Chandler in his hard-boiled manifesto (i.e., the man who will maintain his consistency in this or any world), Muller decided that her detective would be open to the "full range of human emotions" and "her reactions and interactions with others."[9] On this point, Muller spoke to the organic process of her own writing, going so far as to claim that the character, Sharon McCone, had actually suggested the larger developments of the series. Sharon McCone herself, averred Muller, would take the author and reader to spaces that Philip Marlowe and Lew Archer never dreamed of going.

This is not to say that there are no female predecessors to Sharon McCone. In a short article entitled "What Sharon McCone Learned from Judy Bolton," Muller describes the influence of Margaret Sutton's Bolton novels on the McCone series. Sutton's novels, which featured a plucky and resourceful girl detective, date to the 1930s. In addition to being a favorite from Muller's own childhood reading, Sutton's work contained many of the issues at stake for a female detective that interested Muller. Perhaps most important among the usual traits of the successful detective (i.e., courage, decision, independence), male or female, are Bolton's faults. She is not superwoman. She is a woman, as well as a first-rate detective. As Muller has described, "People [were] constantly telling her to stop being unladylike. But what the hell — the chief of police frequently consulted with her, and she couldn't even go on her honeymoon without becoming involved in a mystery."[10] As was true for Sutton during the 1930s, a key concern for Muller's series will be this question of what is in fact "ladylike."

As was also the case for Sutton, addressing these issues from a position that had been traditionally occupied by men (i.e., the detective) necessarily critiques the more conventional position of "woman" in contemporary society. Because of this, the female hard-boiled detective immediately drew the interest of feminist critics working with popular culture. Indeed, the criticism that first welcomed the female hard-boiled detective in the 1980s was ebullient, lauding the difficulties of this generic appropriation and the effectiveness of its political gesture.

In this chapter, I wish to reassess such framings of this fiction by reading female hard-boiled detection from the psychoanalytic structure of hysteria. As hysteria is fundamentally a query to the Other regarding the sexed being of the subject, the hard-boiled genre, from this perspective, is not so straightforwardly read as either masculine or feminine. Rather, it is a narrative structure that necessarily interrogates sexed identity, an inquiry that is consonant with Muller's project. Additionally, I wish show how Marcia Muller's hard-boiled fiction strategically uses the hysteric's greatest critical insight, the desupposition of knowledge and authority, as a paradigm of inquiry. Finally, beginning with these assumptions, I wish to consider the orienting binary of the McCone series: nostalgia and trauma. From the beginning, the hysteric taught the psychoanalyst about the indelible trauma that is at the core of the subject, a trauma that remains beyond either translation or transformation. Muller's fiction offers a sophisticated meditation upon this insight and interestingly (re)positions the work of detection when there is no longer a definitive mystery to be solved. This opacity is, as much of this study has endeavored to show, the threshold the hard-boiled world. These various desuppositions of knowledge in Muller's fiction confront us with the trauma of gender, identity, and history, as such.

Hysteria and the Either/Or of the Female Hard-Boiled Detective

Muller, Paretsky, and Grafton emerge at an especially propitious moment for the academy in the 1980s, as research and curricula are opened to popular texts featuring formerly marginalized figures. Given that the very notion of the female hard-boiled detective is subversive — at the level of genre and, more generally, in terms of basic gender expectations — it is hardly surprising that the sub-genre received a tremendous amount of critical attention.

One of the earlier and most significant additions to this body of criticism was Kathleen Gregory Klein's *The Woman Detective: Gender and Genre* (1988). This brilliant and expansive work surveys the history and pre-history of American and British female sleuths, beginning with the earliest examples of this figure in the nineteenth century and concluding with the hard-boiled writers of the 1980s. As the secondary title of the work suggests, Klein is interested in the implications for gender and generic conventions when a female character is written into a space that had almost exclusively been occupied by men. While the contentious relation between gender and genre is certainly galvanized by contemporary versions of the female hard-boiled detective, such concerns of course long precede this new form. Klein's conclusion is not an optimistic one: detective fiction remains a conservative genre incapable of providing fertile ground for a feminist project of any kind. Though Klein in subsequent work relented from this extreme position,[11] I would suggest that this argument continues to inform literary criticism that engages the female hard-boiled detective.

Fundamental to Klein's claim is a simple either/or: either the female detective genre is in all ways subversive — that is, aligned with and helpful to the feminist cause — or it is not. In other words, if the genre is not wholly radical, it can only be conservative and, therefore, anti-feminist in nature. Klein begins from the assumption that the detective genre is necessarily traditionalistic and unprogressive, a generic imperative that has everything to do with the relation of the sexes during the nineteenth and twentieth centuries, the rise and development of women's suffrage during the nineteenth century playing a crucial role in this genealogy.[12]

Certainly, it is not difficult to imagine a feminist-inspired criticism of the structural necessity of always "getting your man." At the level of plot, the resistive aspect of the detective narrative seems undeniable: The detective encounters an anomaly that must be reduced to knowledge so that normalcy can again be established. At the conclusion of the story, the final (often implied) action of the detective (amateur or professional) is to turn the criminal over to the authorities, letting justice dole out punishment as is necessary. This leap of faith is always a tacit approbation of things as they are. Though the narrative begins from the perspective of rupture, the status quo is in the end always served and reified.

Obviously, throughout the history of the genre, the detective is most often a man and it goes without saying that the status quo that is defended primarily serves the interests of men. Quite simply, then, detective fiction serves the patriarchal social order. Change — generic or social — is unlikely to be represented precisely because the genre is not built, so to speak, for such endeavors. Indeed, its task is just the opposite: to keep things as they are. The recalcitrance of the genre, and its parochial tendencies against "other" representations (of the social, self, knowledge, etc.), is doubled by the fact that it is formula fiction. As Todorov claimed, where formula literature is concerned, to develop the structure is to violate form.[13] The generic requirements that define a given piece of writing as detective fiction (e.g., the presence of a detective; the occurrence of a significant crime, particularly murder; an emphasis upon problem solving, etc.) must remain largely static. If innovation occurs — for example, by creating a woman detective, by shifting the emphasis from individual to social concerns — we are no longer in the world of detective fiction proper.

This reasoning leads Klein to conclude that genre and gender are at odds in the female detective story: "the detective script and the woman script clash because the necessary conditions for each are the inverse and contradiction of the other" (*TWD* 57). Here, her thesis draws from the work of Gilbert and Gubar who claim that most literary genres of the West are male dominated and therefore necessarily resist a positive representation of women. According to this argument, literature primarily tells the stories of men for men. To enter a text requires that one enter as a man, a fact that is so much a part of "common sense" that it simply goes without saying. Ideologically, Klein reasons, the detective text serves to mollify both anxiety surrounding historical exigencies that threaten such a world view and its supporting masculine power. At the same time, the genre re-inscribes traditional sex roles that leave women in a subordinate position. She cannot be a professional; she cannot be the site of knowledge; she cannot be an active hero.

Assuming this line of reasoning, it is implausible that a woman appearing as a detective will offer a radical narrative of femininity that is not in the end co-opted by male fantasy. As Klein summarizes this deadlock in fiction featuring a woman detective:

> These authors' representations of a woman detective as protagonist seem to suggest a liberal attitude toward women in new public roles; however, there is a disjunction between that expression and the basic structural designs of the works, their plot form, and numerous telling incidental episodes which undercut and undermine this apparent liberalism. Furthermore, this disjunction, which manifests itself in the diminution of the protagonist, is at odds with the demands of the formula. Emerging from this contest among genre, reality, and nostalgia is a clear vision of the authors' challenges to the dominant form in order to defend explicitly the submissive, secondary position of women [*TWD* 57].

This is one of the more insidious aspects of the female detective, particularly within later varieties. Though these texts draw the reader in with innovative and radical positioning of woman as something more than the object of detection (sexual or otherwise), in the end these promises are never delivered. The liberatory gesture fails. And so too, then, does the female detective narrative fail as detective narrative. This thwarting of the hero that results from keeping woman in her place in turn subverts the basic requirements of detective fiction. The conclusion is bleak, to say the least: in the case of the female detective, nothing works, resulting in generic and gendered failure.[14]

A second significant reference in the literary criticism of this new detective is Walton and Jones's *Detective Agency: Women Rewriting the Hard-boiled Tradition* (1999). In this insightful work, the authors take up the opposite extreme of the problematic suggested in Klein's framing of the woman detective. Working primarily with the writers of the female hard-boiled detective (re)naissance of the 1980s,[15] Walton and Jones argued for the political potential of this sub-genre, claiming, "These works also establish the distinctive voice of an empowered female subject, and this, clearly, is not just a formal but is also a political gesture."[16] This is true not only at the level of individual works, the authors argue, but also at the level of the sub-genre itself. Whereas Klein found the woman detective to be politically retrograde, Walton and Jones see something that is inherently subversive in the appropriation of the hard-boiled narrative by (and for) women. Gender remains indisputably related to genre, but here it is an unmistakably positive space for articulating the question of identity. In other words, these texts represent and engender agency for female characters and readers alike, an argument that suggestively engages the questions of feminist politics at the level of narrative, woman's relation to the market, and the trope of autobiography within this female hard-boiled sub-genre.

The authors begin with an analysis of the market boom of female hard-boiled detection, focusing particularly on the series developed by Sue Grafton, Sara Paretsky, and other members of the Sisterhood of Crime group — an organization founded in 1987 by early adherents to provide support for fellow women writers. At nearly every turn, this fiction is read as a strategic infiltration of women into the world of detection that is waged under the banner of empowerment, emphasizing the nostalgia within the genre for the idealism of feminist politics of the 1960s and 1970s (*DA* 34).[17] Unlike the conservative nostalgia of the masculine detective text, what is memorialized here is a demand that has yet to be satisfied, that is, political, economic, and social equity for women.

As the authors argue, the unprecedented success of the genre operating under this program results in a nexus of agency embracing female authors, characters, and readers as well. The efficacy of this force is dependent upon the entrance of women into the market as both producers and consumers, an entrance that unilaterally demands more positive representations of women.[18] Naturally, Walton and Jones are careful to hedge their argument and they have no intention of reducing the success of the genre to simple positive images that deny reality, or create simple revenge fantasies of tough women taking power by force. Rather, as they suggest: "The professional female detective character is also a fictional site where the link between gender, capital, and power central to Western economies may be both foregrounded and arbitrated" (*DA* 31). Unlike Klein, the authors conclude that the form of the genre is itself perfectly suited to these ends, as it necessarily entails active arbitration: First, at the level of mystery, insofar as detective and reader must discern the solution to the mystery and its relation to things as they are; secondly, at the level of the detecting subject, insofar as reader and detective must decipher the difference of the female private eye from the expectations of convention. In the process, readers surreptitiously become feminist readers, even those who would not ordinarily align themselves with such politics.[19]

This reading of the various positive agencies that are potentially present in the female hard-boiled text depends upon a drastically different reckoning of the formal structure of the detective narrative. First and foremost, Walton and Jones refuse to take the hard line suggested by Todorov, that innovation equals corruption when speaking of formula fiction. On the contrary, the authors assume that innovation is always already occurring, if for no other reason than there is no "pure" generic form apart from its own examples.[20] This is not to say that certain audience expectations do not exist. However, these prejudices are never quite so clearly delineated as one might imagine — which is not to say that such expectations are diminished because of this fact. Indeed, this lack of an *Uhr*-text of the detective, regardless of sub-genre, is what drives the reading process and its pleasures.

When reading formula fiction, there are at least three primary levels of interpretation. (Of course, it would be foolish to imagine that interpretation occurs only on these three levels.) The first is the surface level of the narrative, that is, the mystery proper, as well as the inevitable false solution that is staged for the eyes of the detective (and reader, as well); the second is the "truth," the second scene behind this dissimulation; the third is the negotiation of the intricate relations between the first two items and the simultaneous assessment of the text's fidelity to, or defiance of, generic principles. In each instance, the reader acts with a discerning eye — much in the manner of a detective as criticism long ago identified — a framing that again underscores a far more adroit interpretative process than might be seen at first glance. In short, to negotiate simultaneously each of these levels of reading, the formula fiction aficionado must possess a tremendous amount of agency, just as the writer of formula fiction must at the same time creatively negotiate these same items. As Walton and Jones conclude: "Indeed, while formula texts must be recognizable to their audience as a 'type' or genre of fiction, they must also add to or strategically alter that genre" (*DA* 48). In this way, subversion actually becomes a requirement of formula fiction.

To be sure, Walton and Jones recognize that some subversions are greater than others. A female hard-boiled detective must speak to a tremendous alteration in the ideologies surrounding the relations of the sexes that, in the 1920s and 1930s, originally scripted the hard-boiled space as a masculine retreat from women and other forces threatening white, male superiority. As social relations change throughout the course of the century, naturally the imaginary representation of these within popular fiction will change as well, a necessity that is evident in the renaissance of the female detective in the 1980s. This is not to say that this later sub-genre suggests a definitive answer to the relation between the sexes and a stable identity for the detecting subject. On the contrary, as is always the case with popular fiction, these texts meditate upon fractured sites of relation rather than represent a consensus fully won. Nevertheless, for the authors, the advent of the female hard-boiled detective is rife with political potential. Walton and Jones have dubbed this more drastic re-visioning as feminist because it demands that readers recognize the artificiality of all genres — including the genre of gender. As they conclude: "Hard-boiled detective fiction written by women can thus merit the label 'feminist' because it admits the possibility of altering 'generic'— and *gendered*— conventions of both literary and social behavior" (*DA* 46).

A final point to be taken from Walton and Jones is their emphasis upon autobiography, what is perhaps the most crucial narrative device at work in this new version of the hard-boiled detective story. Detective fiction itself emerges at roughly the same time as the modern genre of autobiography (and biography, as well) in the first half of the nineteenth century.[21] What these genres share is the assumption that telling the story of a life is not quite so straightforward as one might imagine.[22] Of course, the classical detective more directly evokes such a rupture between an event and its telling, always beginning from the perspective of the "future" in which all has comfortably been resolved. This no less true in the case of autobiography, or in first-person, hard-boiled narration which mimics this gesture, despite the fact that the plainly *ex post facto* nature of the narrative — of all narrative — is often diminished insofar as the text is presented as though the action were happening as it is described.[23] In any case, the contiguity between hard-boiled detective fiction and autobiography inheres and each is, at its most fundamental level, interested in writing the intersection between subject, environment, and history. Indeed, the autobiography effect is in many ways heightened in hard-boiled fiction, as first-person narration allows for a more direct, seemingly unmediated experience of the story of another. As is true with all compelling mysteries, we become the detective in search of the "true" meaning of the life narrated.

In the case of women, the telling of stories is a decisive step toward social recognition and representation, a project with which several female mystery writers align themselves. Through this basic autobiographical gesture, such work underscores the urgency to write the life stories of strong, power women "in their own words." The political import of this documentation is clear: The reader identifies with the unique story documented in the autobiography, taking pleasure in its power, its completeness, and its very existence — a point that was crucial in the 1980s, given the paucity of cultural representations of women as heroes. As Walton and Jones describe the advantage of this intersection of genres:

> As in autobiography, the effect of the private eye novel is predicated on complex relationships of identification, analogy, and even contradiction among author, fictional character, and reader. Shifting the gender of the private "I" is a potentially significant rhetorical and political gesture that reshapes the nature of those relationships, since the refashioned narrative both reflects and resists inherited models of subjectivity [*DA* 154].

In the case of the female hard-boiled detective, women become active heroes. The aesthetics and structural characteristics of these works allow the reader to identify with (or contest, but necessarily engage) these more significant exploits, which in turn produces critical reflection and, again, agency.

In this way, we might take Klein and Walton and Jones as representing the two sides of the either/or suggested above. This Manichean over-determination of these critical works — as tendentious as it may be — galvanizes the identity politics that are part and parcel of the female hard-boiled detective and its scholarship. Writing a space for women in a terrain that was formerly occupied solely by men clearly figures the struggle of women to enter the larger symbolic space of culture as a whole. If the symbolic order, either genre or culture, remains intact, there are, *prima facie*, two possible outcomes: the woman (detective) either succumbs to ideology or gains agency. So runs the endgame of identity politics that demands full representation that is unbound by strictures of any kind, a circumstance that is perhaps unsurprising given the moral absolutism that so frequently informs the genre.[24] As was discussed in chapters two and three, this demand for (complete) recognition by the Other draws us into the psychical structure of hysteria. However, what the hysteric shows us is not merely that all identity is bound to a demand for recognition from the Master, but that this apparent constraint can be both productive and subversive.[25]

It must be immediately recognized that this hysteric component of the hard-boiled discourse is hardly a corruption, or contagion, of the pristine masculine form that emerged during the 1920s and 1930s. On the contrary, as discussed in Chapters Two and Three, the hysteric demand is elemental to the structure of the genre itself. To imagine that the genre is a monolithic expression of a dominant masculinity — that it is a thoroughly masculine genre — is to mistake Howard Hawks and Humphrey Bogart's Philip Marlowe for Chandler's, as it were.

My argument in this chapter will vary slightly from Chapter Two, which read the hystericized, obsessional (male) detective. In the current chapter, I will read the female hard-boiled detective in terms of hysteria proper. This diagnosis is prospective and certainly is not intended to pathologize either women or men according to a symptomatology that reduces its subjects to a given knowledge. Quite the opposite, as will be shown, the structure of hysteria reveals the limits of such presumptions.[26] As I have already discussed Freud and Lacan's understanding of hysteria as the fundamental condition of the split subject, in this chapter, I would like to focus on subsequent development of Lacan's thought on this topic, namely, the discourse of the hysteric, which is discussed in Lacan's *Seminar XVII* and *Seminar XX*.

Reading the Hysteric: The Hysteric and the Master

As is well known, it is the hysteric and not the analyst who has been the driving force of psychoanalysis from its beginnings. This is hardly surprising, as even a cursory reading of the case studies contained in Breuer and Freud's inaugural text *Studies in Hysteria* (1895) indicate that the hysteric's most fundamental demand is for *more* interpretation, a crucial detail that elicited Freud's own idiosyncratic desire for mastery. As recent writings on the topic have indicated, this is precisely why the hysteric cannot be mastered by the psychoanalysis — or by medicine, or any "knowledge," for that matter. This is true because the hysteric's question ultimately concerns the subject's inability to say *it*— to explain the traumatic core subjectivity that must remain elusive precisely because it itself is an effect of every signifying practice.[27]

The structure of hysteria might economically be summarized from a Lacanian perspective by making use of the concepts of alienation and separation. In the developmental drama, the infant arrives and makes a demand upon the parents — it makes a sound or in some way issues a sign with its body. The moment such a sign is issued, the child has entered into a linguistic relation, as its cries, etc., will necessarily be interpreted by the parents as meaningful. Already alienated within the discourse of the Other, the child must take up this alien language if it wishes to articulate its needs better. As Lacan says,

"Demand already constitutes the Other as having the 'privilege' of satisfying needs, that is, the power to deprive them of what alone can satisfy them."[28] The very structure of demand assumes, then, an absolute subject who does not suffer the accident of insufficiency experienced by the demanding subject.

This demand constitutes the Other as potentially possessing that which the child needs, but even prior to this, it is the demand — and not the loss of the imagined fullness of the mother-child dyad — that constitutes the Other, as such. Naturally, the child's demands, which for Lacan is always a request for a lost wholeness, cannot be adequately responded to by the Other. It is this cut of language itself that opened the potential space for demand's fulfillment. The recognition that the Other does not possess the revelatory object requested begins the process of separation, which marks the advent of desire that Lacan equates with the difference that arises from subtracting an "appetite for satisfaction" from "the demand for love," or wholeness.[29]

The emergence of desire is the constitutive trauma of the subject, marking it as lacking by this very inscription in Other. The terms of this equation (i.e., subject, object of desire, and Other) make up the pieces of the fantasy that the neurotic will produce to disavow this lack. As was discussed in Chapter Two, in fantasy, the obsessional will labor on the side of the subject, denying any connection to the Other, thereby eradicating the lack in that space, as well as its delimiting mark upon the subject. Wholeness will be achieved individually, or so the obsessional imagines. The hysteric, on the contrary, will deny the subject position, choosing instead to embody the object of desire for the Other, thereby filling the lack in that imagined space.[30]

This is not to say that in hysteria the subject is reduced merely to a passive object. As Lacan says in *Seminar XX*, "The hysteric makes the man," by which he intends both that the hysteric quite literally makes the man by drawing out his lack and desire, just as she plays the part of man in her own desire, usurping his position.[31] As the hysteric identifies with both the object of the other's desire and with the desiring other, Lacan claimed that the orienting question for this subject was "Am I a man or a woman?" as this subject necessarily asks after the nature of her sexed being.[32] Knowledge is a crucial facet of this relation, as the hysteric attempts to embody the object lacking from the symbolic order itself. In playing this object, the hysteric draws out the Other's desire, asking, even daring, that this aporia be filled with knowledge. Dor describes this split gesture of accommodation and antagonism as a demand that the "phallic attribution" be proven — in other words, the hysteric will demand that the Other prove that he truly has "it."[33]

In *Seminar XVII*, Lacan theorized that this relation to knowledge is one of the four possible discourses linking the subject to the social order. He graphed the "Hysteric's Discourse" as follows[34]:

Four. Remembering, Repeating, and Working Through 183

$$\frac{\$ \longrightarrow S_1}{a \ // \ S_2}$$

As Lacan formalized: In the discourse of the hysteric, the barred subject ($) makes a demand to the Master (S_1), which is at the same time a demand for a Master signifier (also represented by S_1) that will order her symptom. In other words, she requests knowledge that will make her complete.

The result of this demand is indeed the production of knowledge (S_2 in the graph above), which is why Lacan will come to identify true scientific inquiry with the hysteric's discourse. Yet this remains unsatisfying by design.[35] This is the result of an ambiguity in the subject position, as the agent that desires union is a barred subject ($) that demands wholeness, or a removal of that which bars her, and simultaneously a union with this failure. The hysteric seeks the object of demand, but only insofar as it is impossible to meet. It is by maintaining desire as unsatisfied that the hysteric is capable of persisting in the illusion that there is in fact an object to satisfy her desire — as well as the Other's desire. In this, she is able to maintain the belief that the Other is whole, even if this is a wholeness yet to come. Here it will be remembered that obsessional neurosis and hysteria are two strategies for confronting the lack in the Other. The hysteric will accomplish this by becoming the missing object that keeps the Other from completeness. However, this will be done according to her terms, which is to say that she will fill in the Other only by simultaneously marking its lack. (Here, the reader will recall the split gesture of the hystericized hard-boiled detective described in Chapter Two.)

As the hysteric acutely realizes, the signifier lacking in the Other is Woman itself. This brings up the curious place of the phallus for Lacan.[36] The phallus opens a space within language for the subject in its absence. However, at the same time, it serves as a signifier for sexual difference. While Lacan continually warned that the phallus must not be mistaken for the penis, there remains no signifier for "woman" within the symbolic order. Fleshing out the Other, then, the hysteric will attempt to produce this signifier. She "masquerades" as woman, maintaining the illusion that there is indeed some hidden essence of woman that props up her being. From the psychoanalytic perspective, both men and women in effect masquerade in response to the phallic signifier. Men will pretend they *have* "it," whereas women will pretend to *be* "it."[37] While "having" in this sense is alienating for reasons described at length in previous chapters, "being" the phallus will require "that a woman rejects an essential part of femininity, namely, all its attributes, in the masquerade," as Lacan says.[38] This is not to say that there is anything "essential" to femininity. Rather, the point to be taken is that attempting to "be" the phallus requires that the woman bind herself as a signifier to the other. Fortunately, this is not undertaken without protest. As Colette Soler describes this process for the woman: "The masquerade is, to take up Karen Horney's expression, an effect of the veil, but it does not hide; instead, it betrays the desire that orients it. This means that interpretation does not go behind the veil, but concludes with what is sketched out of the demands of the Other with what haunts these demands."[39] In other words, the masquerade is as much as antagonism as it is an enticement.

In the graph above, the limit of this gesture is indicated by the a (standing for the *objet a*) in the lower, left-hand position, what Lacan calls the position of "truth." The truth position is what drives the circuit of the discourse (from the barred subject, $, through knowledge, S_2), but remains unacknowledged. The impasse illustrated in the graph (marked by the //) reveals the inadequacy of the hysteric's query. She demands knowledge as content, S_2, rather than knowledge about the structure of the subject itself, which would require her to contemplate the emptiness of the *objet a* and, therefore, the lack in the Other. From this perspective, the true knowledge of the hysteric structure in question remains inaccessible — the knowledge she achieves, then, is a meaningless barrage of more signifiers.

As with all fantasies, we are assured of a return of the repressed that will interrupt this scripted relation to the Other. This brings us to the question of the third position of the graph in the lower, right-hand corner: the result of the hysteric's discourse is the production of knowledge (S_2). Again, the hysteric cannot be "known" by any knowledge as her truth is incapable of being given an adequate signifier. However, she becomes the *objet a* for any discourse that would seek to know anything about the hysteric. In effect, the hysteric is the blank space upon which a fantasy of mastery is waged. To phrase this another way, she gives body to the absence from which the inevitable question of being-in-language is posed. The hysteric thus engenders the production of knowledge, S_2, which exists as the surplus of this discourse, all the while remaining barred by from this insight.[40] In the end, the hysterical subject asks both "Why is it that I suffer the signifier?" and "Why is the signifier never adequate?" All the Master might offer is the resumption of the metonymic displacement of this a (represented in the graph above) that has for some reason become painfully stuck within a given symptomatic construction.[41] This marks the knowledge of analysis as radically different from any sort of scientific knowledge, the type that has always held a place of authority in detective fiction — even in the hard-boiled world. As we shall see, this apparent devaluation of knowledge is quite productive to the question of reading (and identification) that is engaged by the female hard-boiled detective text.

To these ends, the hysteric's discourse does produce the most fundamental ingredient of analytic insight, what in *Seminar XX* Lacan calls the "desupposition" of knowledge.[42] By unmasking the Master, who can only ever produce more signifiers without providing *it* — thereby illustrating the signifier's "stupidity," as Lacan terms it — the hysteric intuits the basic analytic operation of the dissolution of the fantasy (of definitive knowledge).[43] It is for this reason that Lacan claimed that the subject, regardless of psychical structure, must be hystericized before analytic work can begin.

The hysteric's discourse provides a useful reference point for locating a psychoanalytic response to identity politics generally — that is, a discourse that demands both recognition and wholeness. Communities aligned under such a charge of empowerment and demanding recognition from the big Other must be formed according to a disavowal of the "truth" position of their discourse. As the graph of the hysteric's discourse indicates, there is no definitive content or name that will quell the frustrations of identification. It is not the Master who bars access to the complete identity that is sought. Rather, the Master is an alibi for the structural impossibility of achieving this identity. This is by no means intended to pathologize identity politics, or feminisms that still labor under such directives. The point to be taken is that such interpretive communities, like all interpretive communities, can only function around such a blind spot, a lack of "being" that is the cost of entry into the social order. As is true of all symbolic entrances, access requires that something be given up.

Psychoanalysis's acknowledgment of the hysterical nature of the subject circumvents this impasse by taking as its starting point the impossibility of men or women fully achieving any symbolic identification of sexuality — neither in the name of gender, nor in the name of biology. This is the realm of sexual difference, which is never simply reducible to biological or cultural expectations made upon the individuals. As Wright suggests, "Sexual difference always exceeds, is more than, gender difference."[44] In other words, this difference is both the difference of the categories of "man" and "woman" from each other, as well as the difference of each category from itself. Megan Abbott's description of Philip Marlowe's doomed masculinity is here helpful: "Masculinity is the failure of the binary [of masculine/feminine] to operate as it should. Masculinity is both masculine and feminine by the binary's standards, as is femininity, as the femme fatale figure shows. Gender is ultimately rendered potentially illusory, manipulable, performing, and punishing."[45] The either/or of criticism suggested above denies this question of difference. Further, it denies the fact that, as speaking subjects, admission to the symbolic order demands a sacrifice. As was shown in Chapter Two, at their worst, Hammett, Chandler, and Spillane mourn this loss and await the "cry that will abolish the night," as Pynchon says in a related context.[46] This is the obsessional's strategy *par excellence*. However, as I have suggested, with Chandler guiding the way, the hard-boiled genre becomes structured around the disruption of that very demand. To phrase this in our psychoanalytic vocabulary, the hard-boiled genre responds to the detective's demand with the desire of the Other.[47]

What I am suggesting here is that the hard-boiled text itself is always already a hysteric structure that forces the detective to confront the limits of her or his various identifications — thereby hystericizing the detective — and acknowledge the fundamental emptiness of the Other itself. On this crucial point, I must differ with Klein and others who share her view on the monolithic nature of the detective genre.[48] On the contrary, the hard-boiled fiction of Hammett and Chandler — and those who follow this legacy — does not privilege an essentialism of any kind. Rather, their fiction recounts the anxiety and ultimate failure of such definitive interpretations. Popular texts such as hard-boiled fiction, or mystery and detective fiction generally, may indeed interpellate all readers according to a position of privilege — one that is male, white, heterosexual, etc.[49] Nevertheless, it must at the same time be acknowledged that any hailing — by the social itself, or by the various communities of which we all take part — never fully succeeds.[50] There always remains a portion of the subject that is not fully captured in this identification. The result is what Žižek, in his criticism of Althusser's notion of ideological interpellation, has called the "hysterical response" of the subject.[51]

In Marcia Muller's work we find a strategic appropriation of the hard-boiled hysteric form such that hysteria actually becomes a mode of inquiry. As was demonstrated in the hysteric's discourse, this subject position is at base a demand and a challenge to the Master, interactions that will always be mediated by proxy objects. As Lacan's graph suggests, this transaction begins first with the hysteric fashioning herself as the object of the Other's desire, a skill that will require her to identify both with the Master and his object of fancy. In other words, she will desire both as a man and woman.

In Muller's work, this hysterical mode of inquiry is first evident in the general fascination with objects throughout the McCone series. It is important that these objects must not be mistaken for clues. Whereas, from the time of the classical detective, a clue is a physical residue of the criminal's actual presence, the physical presence of McCone's objects is always in doubt. During each of her investigations, she encounters portentous ruins, fragments, talismans, fetishes, and other such objects that promise a bond between this world and another. While the clue actually signals the presence (in absence) of the criminal, the more ephemeral objects encountered by McCone reference the criminal's relation to the Other itself.[52] In nearly every case, McCone's solution to a mystery will reveal the pathos of the misrecognition of this relation to the Other, a misrecognition that oriented the criminal's actions. This pathos is necessary as McCone will, following the example of Dupin, effectively become criminal herself through the process of identification during her investigations. As a hysteric detective, Sharon McCone is an expert reader of the objects that embody the desire of the other. As such, she has insight into the failure of knowledge (or interpretation) that each of these objects at the same time references. In other words, her work as investigator reveals the difference of each object (and its accompanying subject) from itself.

Identification with the desire of the Other, and an assessment of the accompanying misrecognition (*méconnaissance*) that results, is the *modus operandi* of Muller's detective. Unsurprisingly, her methods consist of insights that have typically been associated with the condition of hysteria, namely, dreams, divinations, and insight into the motivations and desire of others. While the basic approach of the male hard-boiled detective was one of distancing and separation, the female detective McCone has no problems with opening herself to the contagion of the other. Indeed, McCone herself will frequently become this very contaminant, a penchant that immediately reveals the limits of the either/or of the criticism examined above. The female hard-boiled detective does not so much carve her own triumphant space of the individual, but rather, she maintains a split relation to that which is incapable of being reduced to any discourse of identity.

Sharon McCone: The Simple Art of Hysteria

In *Edwin of the Iron Shoes*, the Sharon McCone series appropriately begins with a well-worn, hard-boiled point of departure: McCone is pulled out of bed to visit a crime scene in the wee hours of the morning. Tough and self-sufficient in the manner of her male predecessors (she was once fired for insubordination and has no problems enjoying a bourbon if offered), Sharon at the same time is dissimilar to her male colleagues in significant ways. First and foremost, she is not exactly a "private" investigator. Working as the primary investigator for the All Souls Legal Cooperative in San Francisco, she is bound to an agency — though All Souls is an atypical agency, to be sure. Her "boss" Hank Zahn is her immediate superior and confidant, but he is more of a coordinator in the largely non-hierarchical group of attorneys at All Souls who provide legal assistance to those without the means to afford it otherwise. While Sharon is not above lying to Zahn when the situation warrants, Zahn is hardly the "Old Man" of the Continental Detective Agency found in Hammett. In fact, all members of the cooperative are for the most part friendly associates rather than adversaries, everyone remaining sincerely invested in the political salience of such a differently structured organization. This functional bond to community and the collectivity at All Souls immediately problematizes a straightforward adaptation of the hard-boiled ethos. Though McCone will mime, both with and without irony, various trappings of the hard-boiled ethic that privileges nerve and welcomes loneliness as part of the job, she will always depend upon her personal relationships with others. This sociability is perhaps the most dramatic departure from convention, a variant that is exemplified in the detective's ability to maintain lasting romantic relationships.[53]

In interviews, Muller alternately acknowledges and downplays the influence of the hard-boiled inheritance on her work.[54] Regardless of the author's indications, it is clear there is an ongoing conversation with the past in *Edwin*, both at the level of narrative and at the level of genre convention, as well. Set in the tried-and-true hard-boiled locale of San Francisco, the story revolves around the murder of a recent client of the All Souls Cooperative, Joan Albritton, who ran an antique shop down in the Salem Street Antique district. The list of potential suspects consists primarily of developers who wish to buy up the shops in the district so that they might modernize the space with any number of contemporary developments. Throughout the course of her investigation, McCone is confronted with a variety of modern women — another pressing contemporary development — who will force her to reflect upon her own version of femininity, something she admits is somewhat offbeat.

The use of setting in *Edwin* immediately introduces the reader to the prominence that San Francisco has in the McCone series. Like all hard-boiled fiction, the city becomes a character rather than simply remaining a backdrop, and this is a relation that the detective tends to with great care and affection. The city comes to be known through Sharon's eyes in an exceptionally intimate and detailed fashion. With this focus, every McCone novel foregrounds the necessity of the detective living *with* the city as much as fighting *against* the city. This very personal geography and sense of place is emphasized later in the series when Sharon purchases her earthquake cottage. Always tending to its appearance and interior — and always reminding the reader of its new renovations — the detective is interested in rooting herself within her environment, rather than remaining aloof and dwelling in a more anonymous apartment like Marlowe or Spade, or being literally uprooted and living in a house boat like John D. MacDonald's Travis McGee.

This relation between subject and space is of equal importance to Sharon's investigative methods. Nearly without exception in the series, each suspect and victim is painstaking analyzed according to place. Indeed, McCone insists on beginning each investigation with a trip to the crime scene, even if this space has been irrevocably altered with the passage of time — this distance of a place from itself, as it were, is often all the more helpful to McCone's pursuits. In the later novel *Trophies and Dead Things* (1990), McCone describes this process:

> Often when I'm working on a case I find myself drawn to the places where its key events have occurred, even if it's a long time after the fact. The urge to view these physical settings is more or less instinctive on my part; half the time I'm not even aware of why I'm going there until I arrive. But unscientific and illogical as such behavior might seem, I've come to trust the impulses that prompt it. And while I rarely stumble upon some overlooked clue or receive a blinding flash of insight, just being there gives me a better sense of the individuals involved and their possible motivations.[55]

Far from producing a totalizing knowledge that reads the city as a map, as was the case in Sherlock Holmes's reading of London in "The Red Headed League," McCone's "knowledge" of a given space is felt or intuited. From these viewings, as she asserts, she comes to know something of the individual players in a given crime, but this "knowledge" frequently remains beyond articulation. As will be shown, the success of this interpretative "failure" has much in common with the insight of the limits of interpretation discussed in Chapter Two.

In *Edwin*, the reader is first given a sense of this linkage of character and place in the description of Charlie Cornish, a fellow antique (or junk-) shop owner who was romantically involved with the murdered Albritton. Here, the reader is told that a myth circulates in the neighborhood that "he had sprung full-blown from the pavement of Salem Street twenty years before."[56] The same is said of Joan Albritton, as well, particularly regarding her relation to the interior of her own antique shop. She and the space that she inhabits are one. McCone enters this world proper when she is assigned by All Souls to "take inventory" of the shop for "legal purposes." In actuality, this assignment is a cover story, authorized by Hank Zahn, that will allow Sharon to investigate the murder of her client without the interference of the police. Taking up this task, McCone must literally throw herself into Albritton's world, identifying with every aspect of the murdered woman's life, a practice that will become common for Sharon.

McCone quickly discovers that Albritton's occupation has much in common with detective work. As an antique expert — capable of telling "value and antecedents of any piece in a single glance" (*EIS* 33) — and proficient sales person, Albritton had the great talent of "drawing [a customer] into a fantasy world, where every object in the shop came alive with its own special past" (*EIS* 33). These recollections about Albritton are woven into the reconstruction of a past conversation that McCone (re)presents for the reader as if it were actually happening in the present of the text. Just as McCone brings Albritton to life for the reader, there is a similar temporal dislocation in Albritton's knowledge of antiques and their "antecedents," a knowledge that McCone herself must come to possess during the inventory process.

Importantly, the performative aspect of these narratives of the past is galvanized in Albritton's regular sales pitch. When a customer arrived in her store, Albritton led them through the various aisles, speaking to the objects on display as though they were living beings. The first anthropomorphized object on the tour is "Clothilde," an upholsterer's dummy, followed by a stuffed German Shepherd, and, of course, Edwin of the Iron Shoes, an iron mannequin who is "named for his uncomfortable footgear," as Albritton delights in telling her visitors (*EIS* 34). As McCone reflects later in the novel, Joan would have made a great pagan given her talent to imbue inanimate objects with the qualities of life (*EIS* 80). Indeed, in addition to interesting back stories (e.g., Clothilde, the headless upholsterer's dummy, lost her head over a man), Joan's "friends" have an active life in the present, as well — a fact that will become crucial to the solution of the murder. Edwin in particular is an art lover. He stares (literally) fixedly — his iron shoes bolted to the floor — at various paintings that are hung across the room. Through the power of these stories that in turn give the shop itself life, McCone cannot help but feel Albritton's haunting presence. The detective shares this experience with the reader throughout her narration by describing conversations with the dead woman as though they were happening in the here and now.

Of course, a fascination with objects is absolutely requisite for any detective tale, and it is clear that Muller is intent upon closely examining this and other structural elements of the genre.[57] While this enchantment is frequently downplayed in mystery fiction — often to facilitate better the introduction of red herrings — Muller always privileges this attraction. This accounts for the prominence of the practice of collecting that is seen throughout the McCone series, an always-enlightening hobby that is shared by men and women alike. The collection of antiques is hardly incidental to this over-determined thematic, as the antique is always the nostalgic object *par excellence*; that is, it is a small piece of history pulled from time's narrative to serve as a sort of fetish representing any number of lost golden ages.

As I have discussed in previous chapters, the inherent nostalgia of the detective narrative has been at the center of criticism impugning the conservative elements of the genre. In longing for a golden age in the past, the detective gives tacit support to the status quo of the present, if for no other reason than she or he remains removed from the present, possessing, then, no space from which to engage in criticism of any kind. As charmed as she is by Albritton's sales pitch, which remains nostalgic through and through, McCone is somewhat irritated that she must actually conduct the inventory of the shop, as her cover story demands. This forces her to become an inadvertent expert in antiques, a "womanly pursuit" that takes her away from the more serious investigation — or so she believes. Hence the detective's ire when the police detective Greg Marcus dismisses her assistance to the official case, saying, "You can get back to your antiques," that is, her proper place among such bobbles and trifles (*EIS* 52).

Marcus's ridicule is of course entirely misplaced, for it is by this very drudgery, this "women's work," that Albritton's killer is found. The prominence of antiques in this way serves as a brilliant meditation on the object of detection, a fitting plot point given that the story takes place in the city where Sam Spade's more famous *rara avis* was mistakenly thought to be found. Indeed, the detective is perfectly suited to the inventory process, as she must attach a "meaningful label" to each object within the shop, being attentive to the history that palpably adds heft to each item. The nostalgia of the detective and the collector are in this sense one and the same.

McCone receives her first lesson in the trade from Oliver van Osten, the supplier from whom Joan had purchased much of her inventory, who offers to help her familiarize herself with the world of antiques. A sort of preening Joel Cairo character, he seems to offer a caricature of himself when he suggests that he would like to help with Sharon's investigation because "I always wanted to be a part of a Whodunit. You and I will make a great team of sleuths" (*EIS* 30). His first simple lesson for Sharon is this: most "antiques" — at least those sold around Salem Street — are fake. This results in the greater difficulty of the trade, which is discerning the manufactured items from the real antiques. Indeed, expertise within the field ultimately equals nothing more than this ability. Learning the "lingo" of the profession, then, is not merely the task of learning the names and styles of genuine articles, but also learning to decode the "grandiose titles" that are all too often given to worthless pieces to inflate their "value" (*EIS* 78–79).

While it takes some time for McCone to get her mind around the concept of "manufactured" antiques, the hard-boiled thematic at work here is evident. The detective does not endeavor to bring the "real" into the light of day. Neither does she deal in any sort of historical archeology — though this red herring is repeatedly offered in the McCone series. On the contrary, like her hard-boiled forebears, McCone investigates constructions, confabulation, and conspiracy. Naturally, a solution to such an imbroglio remains simply one story among many. Not so incidentally, this insight immediately undercuts the rescue narrative that seems offered in McCone's assistance to the residents of Salem Street, who are being bullied by unknown agents presumably working on behalf of various urban-renewal projects projected for the neighborhood. Given the deceptiveness of its own products, Salem Street cannot be the authentic experience of old San Francisco that it perhaps at first offers itself to be. If McCone defends the purity of anything, it remains to be seen.

This suggestion that all identity is a manufacture, an *ersatz* representation much like the "artifacts" sold on Salem Street, is repeated in a method of investigation that will become all-important to McCone's characterization: divination through dreams. This method no doubt owes much to the detective's status as "other," as both woman and native. As a woman, she is, presumably, more attune to the alternate realms of reality through her feminine intuition, traits that have made women the keeper of dreams for millennia. (Indeed, in *Edwin*, McCone and the police officer Greg Marcus will have a number of arguments about the benefits of female intuition in practical investigation.) As a native — she is one-eight Shoshone Indian, as she frequently reminds — McCone is imbued with all the obligatory trappings of an indigenous person; that is, she is more in touch with the "unseen" realities of nature and the cosmos. At first glance, connection with this other knowledge may be mistaken for a quasi–New Age integrative identity. In merging with all of creation, the subject finds its true self. However, quite the contrary, McCone's dreams indicate time and time again that connection to this other knowledge results neither in the integration of wisdom nor the completion of the individual.

The first significant dream of the series occurs as McCone sleeps in Joan's shop after a late evening spent taking inventory. As she tells the dressmaker's dummy, Clothilde, "It's a good thing I'm not superstitious ... because I'm sure there must be something about it being bad luck to sleep in a room where a murder's been done" (*EIS* 69). Of course, not only does McCone not believe in ghosts, in this instance, she's not even afraid of them, or so she reasons as she prepares a bed on a settee in the corner of the shop. When sleep at last overtakes the fretful detective, she has the following dream:

> [It was] a great Technicolor dream, of chasing Edwin, the iron-shod mannequin, down into a labyrinth which opened in the antique shop floor. He ran, feet clanking, eluding. The labyrinth was draped with macramé cobwebs, and I tried to avoid them by weaving from side to side, but it didn't help. One of the cobwebs brushed my face with an evil, mocking caress. I screamed in terror [*EIS* 70].

This terrified awakening coincides with an actual robbery attempt at the antique shop. McCone struggles with the would-be burglar, chasing the masked intruder out of the store with great difficulty. This actual threat of violence underscores the way the self becomes imperiled when dreaming. Indisputably, dreams reveal all too well that the self is other, a fact that will be highlighted in the series as McCone will often literally have the dreams of others.[58] When dreaming, one does perhaps encounter a missing part of the self. However, this is not something that might be reclaimed or even interpreted. Reconciliation remains wanting.

This was Freud's conclusion even in the very early text *The Interpretation of Dreams* (1900). Far from providing an index that might be practically applied to any dream — the sort of guide that is widely available in any bookstore — Freud saw in the dream something much more menacing. In his own inaugural dream, the dream of "Irma's Injection," Freud introduces a concept that will undercut the very notion of dream interpretation — the navel of the dream. As he writes:

> There is often a passage in even the most thoroughly interpreted dream which has to be left obscure; this is because we become aware during the work of interpretation that at that point there is a tangle of dream-thoughts which cannot be unraveled and which moreover adds nothing to our knowledge of the content of the dream. This is the dream's navel, the spot where it reaches down into the unknown. The dream-thoughts to which we are led by interpretation cannot, from the nature of things, have any definite endings; they are bound to branch out in every direction into intricate network of our world of thought.[59]

These dream-thoughts are, as Freud suggests elsewhere, "unplumbable"; they grow up relentlessly like a mushroom from mycelium, leaving only more uncanny (and unsymbolized) life instead of a definitive point of origin.[60] Though Freud will continue to uphold the benefits of dream interpretation and the efficacy of this practice within analysis — dream formation is akin to symptom formation, making a translation between these realms largely seamless — in this passage he clearly indicates that interpretation remains powerless when confronted with the navel of the dream. Unfortunately, there are no "definitive endings."

In terms of Freud's own theory of interpretation, what is confronted in the navel of the dream is *avant le lettre*, the turn from interpretation to construction. With the concept of the navel (i.e., Freud's "construction" of the navel), Freud is effectively able to manipulate the limits of his own interpretative strategy, to say something about that which cannot be reduced to sense: the traumatic core of the subject.[61] However, what must be emphasized in the current context is the (literal) pregnancy of the metaphor used for this inevitable breakdown of interpretation — the navel.

The navel of the dream is at the same time the navel of the subject itself. Here, the physical navel is instructive. This mark upon the body references the trauma of birth and, in so doing, provides a linkage to that time before the subject came into being. Obviously, this was time before division from the maternal body and, therefore, a time before the mark of the signifier. It is in this sense that the navel most directly enters into the discussion of hysteria.

The hysteric's demand is ultimately a request for a signifier that would fully account for her entrance into the symbolic order. The conversion symptom — the "classic" hysteric complaint in which a patient's motor-sensory system is affected by a psychical ailment, as in hysterical blindness, for example — in a way performs this task by suturing the body to an idea. Indeed, at base, the symptom is always an "answer" to the dilemma of subjectivity. However, the trauma of the subject is incapable of being bound through any construction, analytic or symptomatic. The "navel" becomes, then, a metaphor for this impossibility. As Shoshana Felman has argued, the theory of the navel marks Freud's own hysteria when confronted with the limits of his own interpretative structure.[62] Like the hysteric subject, he continues to demand an "answer" where there is only darkness. Nevertheless, the recalcitrance of the navel marks the impossibility of addressing the lingering trauma of the body with interpretation — this can only remain "unplumbable," as Freud says in a related context.[63]

While McCone's own use of dreams may at first appear to be a type of integrative interpretation that (re)captures wisdom present in (but unknown to) the subject, I would like to argue that these dreams are at the same time always marked with a navel. This umbilical scar links McCone, the dreamer, to the larger trauma — not only of individual cases, but of the series, as well — that remains beyond the grasp of narrative resolution. The detective's dream interpretation must be understood in just these terms. In other words, though her nighttime visions do at times offer insight into a particular mystery, there inevitably remains a link to the greater unbridgeable trauma of the text itself— something that remains beyond interpretative abreaction of any kind.

Taking McCone's dream of Edwin, for example, it is clear that the mannequin of the iron shoes is a significant clue to the mystery. However, as the iron mannequin pulls her through the labyrinth, Sharon remains blind to this connection — and likely without Aradne's thread to guide her return from the maze. In the end, it is not so much Edwin that is the key to the mystery, but what he looks at — the paintings on the wall across from him. Indeed, he is an "art lover," as Albritton phrased it. He is the cue for art smugglers to purchase stolen artifacts that are being laundered in the shop. What McCone's seeing does not account for is, then, seeing itself— the disembodied gaze of Edwin. (As discussed in Chapter Two, the gaze and voice are privileged "embodiments" of the *objet a* for Lacan. I will return to the importance of these "objects" in Muller's work below.) This blindness is brilliantly figured in the dream via the macramé cobwebs — no doubt, a "cozy" detail drawn from the surroundings of the antique shop — that brush against her as she "weaves" about the halls of the labyrinth trying to avoid them. In her own weaving through the labyrinth, which must be read as her detective work generally, she herself produces more of the macramé entanglements. In other words, even in the first book of the series, McCone's interpretative endeavors are "without definite endings," as Freud would say. Detection, like all interpretation, begets its own entanglements.

Again, far from finding one's true self in the dream, the dreamer encounters a much more disquieting fact: the self is another. This fascination with subjective-dissolution is of course a classic hard-boiled motif, as was illustrated in Chapter Two. Indeed, in many respects, Sharon McCone anticipates and critiques the debate for identity politics that will haunt the female hard-boiled detective, in both fiction and criticism. From the beginning, Muller's work problematizes the more frequently suggested goal of the female detective, that is, writing a space for woman to enter. (This is of course not to say that she dismisses this possibility outright.) In *Edwin*, the complexity of this issue of identity and space is skillfully negotiated in a number of ways, perhaps most notably in Sharon's relation with the text's *femme fatale*, as it were, Cara Ingalls.

Ingalls is a high-powered career woman who runs one of the real estate groups attempting to buy up the shops on Salem Street, and, therefore, an early suspect in Albritton's murder. When Sharon finally meets with the "classically beautiful"—a description that will be repeated throughout the text— real estate mogul, Sharon finds herself enchanted (*EIS* 35). Ingalls is "my kind of woman," say McCone, the sort who has made it "under her own steam" (*EIS* 35–36). Though Ingalls originally went to school to study architecture, like her father and brothers—a detail that will become important—she decided to make a name for herself in another field: real estate. Like many professional women, it was a struggle to find a place for herself, making her success all the more exemplary. However, while casually chatting with McCone, Ingalls admits a more damning detail in that she betrays her lack of empathy for others. For example, after surreptitiously shopping at Albritton's shop to get a sense of her adversary, Ingalls decides to lower her offer on the property because she views the shop owner as "foolish and eccentric" (*EIS* 134). McCone's enchantment is immediately broken, for this is the most damning quality (i.e., heartlessness) for a woman in her eyes. As the detective concludes: "In her [Ingalls'] rush to make, she had left part of her humanity behind" (*EIS* 132).

The professional position achieved by Ingalls is won through the suffering of others, and this is obviously not the type of contemporary woman that McCone wishes to become. On the contrary, she will always champion the disenfranchised, never allowing herself to be cashiered by soulless corporate America. In 1977, gender roles are obviously in a moment of drastic indecision, particularly with women acceding to positions of professional power that were formerly unavailable. To these ends, Ingalls is a ready stock character to figure the wages of success: she becomes a sort of corporate succubus. This device lends itself to some curious popular psychology near the conclusion of the novel, as the real estate developer is painstakingly shown to be unhappy with her success — this quite in spite of herself. Remaining unfulfilled, she longs for companionship and understanding that continue to elude her, despite the many luxuries her lifestyle affords her.

In the final confrontation scene of the text, after McCone has concluded that only Ingalls could have killed Albritton, the detective takes advantage of these insights into Ingalls's character failings. Knowing that Ingalls lacks self-control (this discerned from a series of racist comments she made at their initial lunch meeting) and that she is desperate for the sort of human sympathy that she refuses others, McCone carefully plays upon the killer's weaknesses to overpower her. Struggling to explain the murder, Ingalls recounts her final conversation with Albritton. As she remembers, "She [Albritton] called me a vulture. She said I spent my life feasting off the remains of people I'd destroyed. She said I wasn't human, that I was a sick, disgusting thing to her" (*EIS* 203). Ingalls goes on to tell McCone, "softening" we are told, that this is the worst possible thing to say to another person — that she is inhuman, absolutely without merit or meaning. This, apparently, was the remark that sent Ingalls over the edge. In response to Albritton's comment, Ingalls pulled an antique knife from the display case and killed the stunned shopkeeper. After McCone refuses Ingalls the sympathy and understanding she so desires, the two scuffle, and McCone is wounded — "It's only a small cut, but it's deep" (*EIS* 206). If *Edwin* meditates upon the question "What type of woman is McCone?" the only answer the detective receives is a wound, a physical and psychical trauma that does indeed run deep.

Before concluding my discussion of *Edwin*, I would like to address a final traditional hard-boiled thematic that prominently appears within the text, namely, the question of circulation. McCone's investigation revolves around a piece of stolen art that was still "in transit" at the time of Albritton's murder, a panel from a famous Italian triptych. Appropriately, Ingalls, one of the key figures of the stolen art ring, desires to build a false altar with this artifact. As McCone underlines several times throughout the novel, what is most horrendous about this business of stolen artwork is that it removes from circulation an object that should be shared by all. Per generic convention, this plot point impugns the upper classes (or the new, *nouveau riche* of the corporate world) in a typically hard-boiled fashion. The "haves" hoard their fortunes and objects of culture, while the "have-nots" struggle to get by in daily life.

What is interesting here is that the usual hard-boiled discourse linking plundering women and circulation is reversed. Previously, characters like Dinah Brand or Brigid O'Shaunghnessy were so horrific to the male detective because they wished to open themselves to the market, to become exchangeable. Though this is typically sexualized, the discourse of identity here is clear. A woman, who is dangerously protean in the hard-boiled world, must be kept in her place at all costs. To do otherwise is to prostitute oneself, either literally or symbolically. In *Edwin*, the new career woman who has forsaken her moral groundings functions more like a Harlan Potter character — or, more likely, Mike Hammer's even more insidious nemesis, Berin-Grotin. This position is coded with the ossification of "old money," money that doesn't circulate, despite the fact that it may remain a menacing value behind the scenes. Her desire to keep the assembled altar of stolen artwork away from public viewing and build a massive fortune of stolen money and cultural capital damn her necessarily. However, this occurs in a manner that is entirely different from that of her *femme fatale* forebears. Ingalls should, in effect, get out and circulate, as it were — something that McCone and her cast of humorously supportive friends often suggest as well. Sharon, on the contrary, does not have this problem — again, this is something that her friends will not allow — as she keeps herself in circulation. This goal is met with chauvinistic resistance, to be sure, as nearly each novel includes some man smugly asking McCone what "a pretty little thing" is doing in a "job like this." Nevertheless, she perseveres.

McCone's relation to men throughout the series follows this imperative to circulate, so to speak, and is one of the more compelling departures from the more standard hard-boiled ethic of separation. At issue is the question of desire. Of course, the notion of Philip Marlowe or Sam Spade dating is quite humorous and strictly unthinkable. It is not a coincidence that "marrying off" the detective marked the end of both Hammett and Chandler's careers.[64] It goes without saying that such an ongoing connection with a woman (or women) runs counter to the lone-wolf ethic of the detective and is, psychically, too disruptive to the hard-boiled detective's *modus operandi*. As was discussed in Chapter Two, as either Madonna or whore, the woman must be kept at a distance for the detective's investigative methods to function appropriately. Above all else, the detective must maintain the illusion that he is in no way connected to the Other, and isolation and separation remain key to his method. Unencumbered by this "impossible desire" of the obsessional subject, the woman in this case need not be burdened with this deadlock. As we have seen, the hysteric will in effect do just the opposite: she will become the object (of the desire) for the Other.[66] Structurally, then, the hysteric detective's method is the inverse of her obsessional colleague: it is imperative that she engages the other at the level of desire.

In *Edwin*, this (romantic) engagement begins with the police officer Greg Marcus, a man who will become the first in the series of McCone's boyfriends, or "lovers," as she is wont to describe them. Initially, the police detective Marcus has no patience for a woman encroaching upon his profession. He antagonizes McCone with the obligatory "what's a pretty thing like you doing in a nasty business like this" brand of skepticism. Of course, from the beginning his act is but thinly veiled attraction, and the two find themselves contemplating romance near the conclusion of the novel. Of paramount importance to McCone is Marcus's acceptance of her as a professional equal. Attributing investigative successes to "woman's intuition" will not suffice. Concomitantly, McCone demands that Marcus not view her as a "conventional" woman — she is neither a "homemaker," nor a contemporary "professional woman," as is Ingalls (who Marcus once dated). The detective makes certain that these facts about her are clear by carefully scripting her own hard-boiled character — a "character" that does not necessarily diminish her femininity. When asked how she would improve Marcus's home, McCone suggests putting up a gun collection. Later, when he asks if she has any "womanly skills, like typing," she quips back: "No, but I'm a mean shot with a .38, and I can bake terrific bread" (*EIS* 166; 187). Marcus, who imagines himself unconventional as well, admits that there is much that McCone could teach him. In dialogue that is, for better or for worse, quite straightforward on this point, he suggests that she might teach him "Things about a strong man and a strong woman...." Here he pauses, looking intently into McCone's eyes, and then continues: "about how two such people can be together without diminishing each other or tearing each other apart" (*EIS* 180). Over the course next few books of the series, the possibility that Marcus here promises will prove to be misplaced. However, McCone remains open to romantic entanglements. Appropriately, there can here be no definitive endings, as she seems to suggest when at the conclusion of the novel she agrees with her drunken male colleagues that women are not meant to be understood (*EIS* 213).

The Self Is Another: Identification and the Desire of the Other

For the classical detective, it is imperative that the woman be foreclosed from the symbolic order of the text to insure the efficacy of his investigation — a luxury that is not afforded the hard-boiled detective. From the hysteric's perspective, it is just the opposite: the search for woman must be included. This linkage of desire and woman is crucial, even when working with a heterosexual female detective.[66] Here, one only need recall the fact that the hysteric desires both as man *and* woman. In the hysteric triangle, desire for and of the man must be present, just as desire for and of the woman must be, as well. As has been shown, this process of identification, with all its uncanny returns, is hardly foreign to the detective genre. And, as the discourse of the hysteric reveals, assuming the position of the "object" of desire is anything but passive. In Muller's *The Shape of Dread* (1989) the investigative aspect of this subject position is made manifest, resulting in an interesting twist on the requisite contiguity of the hard-boiled detective's professional and love life.

As *The Shape of Dread* begins, McCone agrees to help an All Souls colleague with an appeal of the conviction of Bobby Foster, an inmate who is on death row for the murder of Tracy Kostakos, a once up-and-coming comedian who disappeared some two years before. As is her custom, McCone begins the investigation by interviewing the people close to the victim, wishing to get a sense of who Tracy was for her friends and family. This practice is not merely to isolate suspects, as one might first expect, but to know who Tracy was for others. This focus upon the place of the individual in relation to others — that is, this appraisal of desire — marks the hysterically structured method of inquiry typical of McCone. The detective's greater interest is always this question of relation.

In several respects, this method of investigation recalls the identification at work in "The Purloined Letter," as Poe demonstrated in the odds/evens game of the clever schoolboy. In that famous antecedent, the hysteric's masquerade of sexuality is present as well in Dupin's presumably visceral identification with the Minister D—.[67] McCone likewise identifies with her adversaries, and thus gets a feel for a criminal's motivations and deceptions. Such insight rarely results in the production of a knowledge that might be quantified, but the vague intuitions that she senses are inevitably helpful to her investigations. Crucially, McCone does not limit the use of this method solely to the identification with the criminal. More often than not, her investigations begin by identifying and empathizing with the victim — a development that is unique to the hard-boiled world.[68] This is true to the extreme in *Pennies on a Dead Woman's Eyes* (1992) when McCone comes to identify so fully with the traumatized daughter of a murder victim that she begins to experience the horrific lost memories from the night of the mother's death. (I will discuss this novel at length below.) The use of this fantastic device dramatizes the perils of McCone's method of analysis. Through such identification, the detective effectively becomes the other.

McCone's initial interviews for the case bring her to Tracy's father, George Kostakos, who had separated from his wife and Tracy's mother, Laura, during the stress of the murder trial. Admitting that she is ready again to attach herself to another in the opening pages of the text — like most hard-boiled novels, the story in this way quickly becomes a hunt for both a man and a woman — an affair is begun with George, while McCone continues her search for the lost daughter. This liaison is not started without some hesitation, as George is still legally married. Naturally, this complication is exacerbated by the fact that his ex-wife, Laura Kostakos, must likewise be a prominent participant in the investigation. McCone, then, doubly enters this inter-subjective triad typical of hysteria: in her identification with the missing daughter, she becomes the object of desire held between the couple, just as McCone herself will come to occupy this place as George's lover.

The refrain of the text is found in Tracy's final words to her mother, in which she admits that she (Tracy) is guilty of the "sin of omission"—a phrase that seems to suggest the betrayal of a friend though its true content remains unvoiced by the daughter. McCone, working on this "no-body" case (the body of the victim has never been found), must give Tracy both body and voice, as it were, yet she herself becomes guilty of her own sins of omission in failing to keep George and Laura Kostakos apprised of the various developments within the investigation. These will come to include some rather unpleasant revelations about their daughter. During her inquiries, McCone discovers that Tracy had become a manipulative and calculating woman focused entirely upon her career in show business. Such demonizing of Hollywood artificiality has, of course, a long history within the hard-boiled genre.

Importantly, Tracy's act involves various impressions of "types" of "contemporary women" and McCone quickly discovers that Tracy's research involved getting close—often intimately—with people solely for the purposes of using their idiosyncrasies as fodder for her caricatures. The enormity of these betrayals reflects upon the realist charge of the genre itself and represents Tracy Kostakos at the extreme experience of hysterical identification: she is nothing but the sum of her base impersonations of others. In the hysteric's masquerade, this is effectively always the case.

The mother, Laura Kostakos, is understandably disturbed by her daughter's disappearance. As the novel begins, she is a woman on the brink of madness in her grief at this loss. She has lost her job, her husband, and all other former connections to the world. Convinced that Tracy is still alive, she actually maintains a weekly vigil at her daughter's apartment, which she continues to finance in hopes of Tracy's return. In carrying on an affair with Laura's husband, McCone on the one hand becomes a usurper of the matriarch's position, a fact that weighs heavily on her mind. However, at the same time, she does act to maintain Laura's fantasy of recovering her daughter by withholding information about the ongoing investigation, an omission that will become quite significant as the case concludes.

McCone does finally find a body and, after the identity is positively confirmed, McCone's own "sin of omission" occurs. After receiving proof positive that the body is Tracy, McCone refuses to call either George or Laura Kostakos with the news. Additionally, she neglects to tell the local police that she will pass this information along in person once she returns to San Francisco. (Tracy's body is found outside of town near their family's cottage on the Napa River.) Rather than confronting the couple with the traumatic truth, she effectively chooses to maintain their desire by supporting the possibility that Tracy is alive, even if just for a while longer. During her conversation with George when she finally confesses this omission, McCone senses that she has committed an act of betrayal that will certainly endanger the future of their relationship. George's long silence after he discovers the truth reveals that McCone's assumption was correct. Understandably, he is hurt by the way Sharon handled the situation, although the greater shock is obviously the certainty that his long-vanished daughter is dead. Further, George speaks of his estranged wife, remarking that the news was "a confrontation with reality that [Laura] didn't need just now" (*SD* 248) — indeed, it landed her in the hospital for psychiatric evaluation. Each of these reactions underscores the detective's failure. Nevertheless, it was by entering the triad of relations of the Kastakos family that McCone was able to conduct her investigation in the first place.

Speaking of Chandler's story "Red Wind," Žižek notes that the detective (a precursor to Marlowe) supports the fantasy of the Other rather than embodying the psychoanalytic ethic that would confront the analysand with the emptiness of such constructions. In this case, the detective refuses to reveal to his female client that a stolen necklace (a family heirloom) was all along fake, as this information would result in the suspension of the woman's fantasy and desire for her lover. Operating in hysteric fashion, in this feign, he supports the Other's desire. Similarly, in *The Shape of Dread*, George Kostakos explicitly asks McCone to maintain his fantasy about his daughter. During her initial interview with him, Kostakos tells McCone that he does not share his wife's hope that their daughter is alive, quite possibly for selfish reasons. If their daughter remained alive it would mean, of course, that she had faked her own death and framed her friend for the crime. As George says: "Because if she's not dead, she has done a monstrous thing. If she's not dead, she is someone I don't want to acknowledge as my own [...] please don't find Tracy alive, Sharon. And if you do don't bring her back to me" (*SD* 81).

While this desire for non-knowledge is perhaps typical of the average client, particularly in hard-boiled fiction, it is all the more interesting given Kostakos's position as a psychology professor. In *I, the Jury*, Spillane, as is his great talent, brings a hard-boiled theme to its perverse conclusion as the analyst, Charlotte Manning, serves as the text's *femme fatale*. As such, she quite literally threatens the detective with subjective erasure — that is, death. From the perspective of the masculine fantasy of completeness, the psychoanalyst necessarily disrupts the detective's subjective consistency, and it is for this reason that, nearly from the beginning, analysis is vilified within the genre. Indeed, in several respects, the hard-boiled detective genre is a protest to the discourse of the analysis.[69]

However, in Muller's reversal in *The Shape of Dread*, it is McCone that actually works to confront the analyst-figure, George, with the emptiness of his own fantasy. Indeed, the self-help manual that he is working on is a transparent psychology of adaptation — the obverse of the most basic psychoanalytic gesture.[70] This work is a sort of nosography of personality types based upon three basic classifications: the action oriented, emotional, or intellectual" (*SD* 78). Each type is defined according to a spectrum of behavior that runs from the healthy to the pathological. Muller does not miss the opportunity to equate the work of the detective and psychologist (in this case), and Kostakos offers the obligatory adequations of his profession with that of McCone's. Both detectives and psychologists must be analytical, logical, and perceptive. As he continues, "I sense you might have what's known in psychological jargon as 'the third ear'— the ability to hear meanings beyond what a person's actually saying. You've got intuitive and emotional qualities. You just don't let them get in the way" (*SD* 78). The meaning beyond what George is actually saying here is, of course, seduction — as George suspects, this is not lost on McCone. However, this conversation begins with an analysis of his daughter, Tracy. He indicates that her personality tends toward the pathological side of her group, the "action oriented." Given the pathos of this discussion, and the self-help ethos of his work, it is clear that he wishes to save if not his daughter, at the very least, her memory.

In the end, McCone perhaps accomplishes this, which would equal a failure of the psychoanalytic and feminist ethic in question. In other words, she supports the other's fantasy of the woman's innocence (i.e., Tracy remains an angelic child), ignoring a much more complex reality. However, the detective's final gesture remains conflicted in hysterical fashion. Tracy's own "sin of omission" involved withholding information about a murderer who she knew as the business partner of her boss at the comedy club. (Tracy randomly discovers this one day when reading an article about an unsolved murder back East. The picture accompanying the article makes the identity of the killer certain.) McCone originally fears that Tracy planned to use this information to further her career, but her final discoveries indicate that Tracy wished to go to the police. Only her murder by a jealous boyfriend prevented her from doing so. This small token would at first seem to be the redemption of the Kostakos' daughter sought by each parent. In discovering this detail, McCone reinstalls the fantasy structure binding the man and woman together. Indeed, at the conclusion of the novel, George moves back in with his wife, though he does this to help her recover from the traumatic breakdown that was, in effect, caused by McCone's handling of the information about Tracy's death. Yet, because of this investigation, the parents are confronted with the harrowing truth of their daughter's improprieties and, as McCone fears, it is for this reason that Kostakos leaves to tend to his wife.

Read as a hysteric structure, the hard-boiled genre necessarily entails an inquiry into the sexed identity of the subject, as it questions the knowledge of the Other from which the subject receives its imagined substance. Nevertheless, this critique is undertaken with the hope of accommodation and a lament for the subject that, quite simply, cannot come into being through knowledge. Not so incidentally, it is for this reason that Lacan viewed the subject itself (regardless of psychical structure) as hysteric in nature. In *The Shape of Dread*, though she remains ambivalent about the results, the hysterical inquiry of McCone has refused to return exactly the object mourned in the traumatic narrative lived by the mother. The result is the still greater trauma of the dissolution of that fantasy. Though McCone herself mourns the loss of the potential offered by George Kostakos, the novel concludes with a hopeful set-up (i.e., blind date) arranged by a friend from All Souls. The fantasy at the core of all traumatic narratives, even that of lost love, is abandoned, allowing for the detective to continue the masquerade.

From Remembering to Construction: The Trauma of Interpretation

Undoubtedly, Muller's most interesting redirection of the hard-boiled genre concerns the question of memory. This focus is perhaps only natural, as hard-boiled fiction has always been a nostalgic project, an arrangement that requires the detective to remain transfixed by memories and an overpowering allegiance to a time gone by. Of course, the basic narrative structure of the detective text always already supposes such a preoccupation. A case begins with the disruption of the peace and plentitude of the city by the criminal, whose crime reverberates throughout the whole of society. The detective, then, always works to reestablish edenic tranquility: in the classical case, he will succeed, more often than not; in the hard-boiled case, he will fail, yet continue to remain illuminated by the dream of this other place. When the hard-boiled detective becomes a woman, there is a marked change in this relation to the past, to be sure. The question remains, what will *she* do when confronted with the pull of history?

Like all great series, Muller's opus reflects and engages issues confronting the cultural climate of which it is a part. In the 1990s, memory becomes a prominent issue, not only in the academy, but throughout popular culture as well, as is evidenced by the output of Hollywood films dealing with the question of memory (e.g., *Shattered, Johnny Mnemonic, The Matrix*). While this cultural fascination with memory and the past obviously has much to do with *fin-de-siècle* anxiety, it is also tied to the interest surrounding recovered memory therapy and the fallout of this method, the so-called "false-memory syndrome."[71]

Recovered memory therapy assumes that a patient suffers an ailment because of a traumatic memory that remains forgotten. By directed free association, the therapist will help the patient recover this memory and, thereby, cure the affliction. As is always the danger with investigation generally, one often finds precisely what it sought. And this was exactly the problem with this brand of therapy. Patients frequently produced intricate stories of abuse (violent and sexual) at the hands of their parents or other authority figures. Several parents were indicted, some even jailed. Yet, as was often later discovered, the accusations could not in several instances be substantiated (e.g., a patient swore abuse occurred at a time when it was impossible, when the parents were out of town). In this way, recovered memory therapy produces recovered or false memory syndrome.

While psychoanalysis was dragged into the public debate surrounding this issue, recovered memory therapy cannot be described as psychoanalytic in nature. Indeed, psychoanalysis confronted this danger of suggestion in the transference over 75 years before the debates of the 1990s. When Freud originally began working with patients near the turn of the century, he was shocked to discover that so many individuals repeated stories of sexual abuse at the hands of a family member. Indeed, the frequency of such narratives suggested an epidemic of abuse.[72] Freud began his career by assuming this testimony recounted actual traumatic events from childhood, that is, he trusts that his patients are telling the truth. This is often termed Freud's seduction theory, as it addresses the literal seduction of children by a trusted loved one. Freud quickly discovered, however, that patients could not be taken at their word. The narratives of abuse that were heard in analysis more frequently recounted events that took place in fantasy. This is of course not to deny the existence of actual abuse. The point to be taken, and this is one of Freud's revolutionary insights, is that children have a sexualized fantasy relation with others long before adolescence. Lacking the knowledge to understand such feelings frequently results in the dilemmas that are presented in analysis. The result is repression, a concept that required Freud to develop an entirely new understanding of remember and forgetting, as these processes played themselves out in analysis.

Freud addressed these issues in the brief essay "Remembering, Repeating, and Working Through" (1914). As the title implies, symptoms of the patient are regarded as a lost memory, which is regained only through the "working through" of the analytic process. The aim of analysis, as Freud explained, is "descriptively, to recover the lost memories" and then "dynamically, to conquer the resistances caused by repression."[73] However, remembering is never simply the process of pulling past images of experience back into the conscious mind. Here, Freud wished to put a finer point on the notion of "remembering," which, as analysis shows, has variety of forms. In the first instance, analysis allows one to understand "purely internal mental activities" (i.e., events that do not take place in reality) that occur outside the observation of the conscious mind, making it impossible for these to be simply "remembered" as they have never been forgotten.[74] Secondly, analysis shows that memory has two components: the memory of a given event, and the affect associated with this particular event. Even if both components of a memory remain present in an individual, forgetting can still occur, as what is "forgotten" in this case is the linkage between these two psychical items. Finally, there are those events "which took place in very early childhood, before they could be comprehended, but which were subsequently interpreted and understood," often in a pathological way.[75]

In each case, the symptom serves as a form of remembering through a writing upon the body (e.g., a hysterical paralysis of the left side of the body) and it is because of this translation that this form of remembering remains barred from the conscious mind. The name Freud gave to this sort of remembering (i.e., the memory at work in the symptom) is "repetition." The analysand in treatment "reproduces [a past experience] not in his memory but in his behaviour he repeats it, without of course knowing that he is repeating it."[76] In effect, the patient repeats in behavior what she or he has yet to understand. Before analysis, this is the patient's sole way of remembering. The goal of analysis is, then, the bringing forth of "a piece of real life" that formerly could express itself only in the form of this repetition. In the analytic session, it is possible to "work through" this trauma by confronting the analysand with its enigma. With this technical goal in mind, Freud makes the following formulation: "The transference [i.e., the space of the analytic session] thus forms a kind of intermediary realm between illness and real life, through which the journey from one to the other might be made."[77] In this way, analysis problematizes the very boundary of reality and fiction.

By the time Freud wrote "Constructions in Analysis" in 1938, a subsequent essay on the transference and remembering, he seemed more prepared to elaborate upon the consequences of the ambiguities found within the formulations of "Remembering, Repeating, and Working Through." Here again, the analytic session is a place where past events express themselves in repetition (e.g., the patient transfers anger at a given parent onto the analyst). This is then translated into a "transference neurosis" that is by definition more pliable during the treatment. In this changed form, the symptom is more susceptible to the working through of analysis. The goal perhaps remains the uncovering of a lost truth about the patient. However, it becomes apparent to Freud that the ambition to uncover the truth of a forgotten and repressed past in analysis is unnecessary. The constructions (i.e., fictional accounts of the past trauma) of analysis operate as well or better than instances recalled from reality. In the session, all that is required of interpretation is that it produce the "assured conviction of the truth of the construction which achieves the same therapeutic result as a recaptured memory."[78] As Freud concluded, "There are no indications of reality in the unconscious, so that one cannot distinguish between the truth and a fiction cathected with affect."[79] Given this lack of distinction, fiction actually becomes a tool of analysis. The patient is not asked to confront the reality of a passed trauma. Rather, they are challenged to author a new construction that allows the pathological reaction to this event (as it existed in fantasy) to be undone.

This arrangement immediately problematizes the status of transference, and here psychoanalysis departs from recovered memory therapy all the more. If the subject is ultimately responsible for the arrangement of her or his memories — that is, she or he must take responsibility for her or his past as it exists in memory — it is clear that he or she is are no longer in a relation of fundamental dependence to some authority figure. This is the very goal of psychoanalysis, to dissolve such a bond and its accompanying demand, while forcing the patient to come to terms with the fact that the definitive meaning she or he seeks (from the analyst, mom, dad, etc.) is equally as illusory.

Recovered memory therapy performs the opposite operation: it demands that the patient follow the suggestion of the therapist to recover a real traumatic memory from the past that implicates an authority figure — of course, this is typically one or both parents — who has either personally wronged or abused them, or sat passively by, allowing another to perform the abuse. As the litigation prompted by recovered memory therapy indicated, the goal of this process was not to confront memories for which the patient was in part responsible, but rather to confront the offending agency. In other words, recovered memory therapy was in sum a demand made to the Other asking that the subject's wholeness be returned, a hysteric project, to be sure.[80]

Among the academic theorists of trauma of the last fifteen years, Cathy Caruth is certainly the most well known, and her work is quite helpful for my current argument. In her *Unclaimed Experience: Trauma, Narrative, and History* (1996), Caruth links the issues of trauma and memory to history, the body and, importantly, literature. As she claims, traumatic experience opens itself to a language that is in some way literary, "a language that defies, even as it claims, our understanding."[81] Following Freud's conclusion that only construction — which is always a type of fiction — can address the trauma (accidental or constitutive) of the subject, Caruth focuses upon various modes of traumatic repetition that are common to our experience. As she argues, trauma is never simply the mark of destruction felt from accident. Rather, it is the "enigma of survival."[82]

Freud most directly addressed this enigma in *Beyond the Pleasure Principle* (1920), a work in which he too famously turns to construction (in the form of mythopoesis) to prop up his understanding of the trauma that is fundamental to life. For Caruth, this question of survival is essential to Freud's theory of the subject. Indeed, in several respects, the object of psychoanalysis becomes the enigma of the survival of consciousness throughout history (be it individual or social history), which is itself nothing more than the history of trauma.[83] As *Beyond the Pleasure Principle* suggests, consciousness acts as a filter, sifting experience, via knowledge, into the experience of time (*UE* 61). In other words, the accident of experience, which is necessarily traumatic, is organized according to the narrative structure of the psyche.[84] The great difficulty of the traumatic experience is that it bypasses this apparatus and is, effectively, experienced out of time. The trauma is never "present" to the subject and, therefore, never fully "known" by the subject (*UE* 62). Traumatic repetition (in dreams, for example) attempts to right this situation by replaying the traumatic event with a better-prepared psyche. In repetition, the event is no longer unexpected. However, in this, repetition forever chases its own tail, as the "time" of the trauma has come and gone, leaving experience forever out of joint.

When Freud speaks generally about the human "organism" and the trauma of life itself, this leaves little doubt that our experience is never present to us. Our experience is at all times mediated by our inability to be fully present to it, and this is always the greater trauma, survival. As Caruth concludes, "If history is to be understood as the history of a trauma, it is a history that is experienced as the endless attempt to assume one's survival as one's own" (*UE* 64). As psychoanalysis concludes, literature remains the most suitable means for addressing this aporia.

There are two connections here that are pertinent for the purposes of this chapter. Caruth analyzes the relation of individual trauma to group trauma — certainly the question of "history" demands this — focusing upon Freud's own analysis of such a convergence in the case of the Jewish people as described in *Moses and Monotheism* (1938). As Caruth writes in a note to this section, the point is to "understand how historical or generational trauma is in some sense presupposed in the theory of individual trauma, which is what I believe is implicit in Freud's texts" (*UE* 136). In other words, the individual's own idiomatic demand to the Other is mediated through a community that collectively experiences the accidents of history. To these ends, Caruth suggests that it may be fruitful to understand Freud's *Beyond the Pleasure Principle* and *Moses and Monotheism* in relation to his own traumas of survival experienced during World War I and II (*UE* 71). The second item of importance in the pivot between individual and historical trauma is the body. If the death drive — understood as the organism's drive to liquidate the trauma of life itself (this through repetition)— represents an experience of death-in-life, of an inability to distinguish between past and present, life and death, and subject and other, this traumatic nexus is centered in the subject's body, as the hysteric's conversion symptom long ago indicated.[85] In the current section, I would like to address the way Muller's work insistently presents the constitutive trauma of the female detective and its relation to memory and history. As will be shown, in the author's inquiry, there is inevitably a traumatic convergence of the issues of gender, genre, and body, as well.

In the 1990s, as both popular and academic debates on the topic of memory continue, Muller will incorporate the *de rigueur* issue of recovered memory in her novel *Pennies on a Dead Woman's Eyes* (1992). At the center of this story is a suitably gothic locale, an old mission-style complex, Sea Cliff, built on a precipice overlooking the Pacific Ocean. Here, in a dovecote on one side of the property, Cordy McKittridge was violently murdered. At the crime scene, her body was found mutilated, her ring finger severed, and, strangely, lead pennies placed over her eyes. Significantly, this traumatic event occurs in the very midst of knowledge production, as the complex houses a renowned think tank that was frequently enlisted by various high-level offices in government and industry after World War II. In this way, the property is an inventive hard-boiled play upon the traditional site of a murder in the cozy English formula, the country estate. In this limited, discrete space, the edifice and inhabitants necessarily represent the social order itself. At the same time, the very purpose of the institution, to advise on policy and political strategy, emphasizes the constructed nature of convention.

The mystery of the text concerns a resident family of Sea Cliff, the Benedicts — Lisbeth, her husband Vincent, and their daughter Judy. The family lived on site, along with a supporting cast of other appropriately eccentric (and sniping) intellectuals. Cordy McKittridge was Mr. Benedict's lover. While Lisbeth Benedict was not initially a prime suspect in the case, she is arrested and convicted of the crime after her daughter discovers Cordy's missing ring among some old clothes in the attic. Naturally, the result is the utter destruction of the family: Lisbeth is sentenced to life in prison; Mr. Benedict dies only a few months after the incident, apparently of guilt; and, curiously, the daughter is adopted by the prosecuting attorney of the murder trial, Joseph Stammeroff.

As the novel begins, due to some deteriorating medical issues, Lis Benedict has been released from prison after serving nineteen years. After her release, she moves in with Judy. McCone is brought in as an investigator at the request of Jack Stuart, the criminal law specialist at All Souls, who just so happens to be dating Judy Benedict. Though the murder has long since passed, and Lis significantly punished, McCone is called in to find new evidence that might exculpate Benedict. This task is largely at the behest of Judy who has, apparently, suffered the most from her mother's incarceration. No doubt, this is a result of the guilt she feels from serving as the key witness against her mother in the original trial. Unbeknownst to McCone, the case will not be retried in an actual court. Rather, it will be restaged in the city's "historical tribunal," a mock court that performs famous cases from the city's past for local history and legal buffs.

When McCone first meets with Benedict, it is clear that the ex-convict has reconciled herself to being a tragic, martyred figure. While she maintains her innocence, McCone is not immediately convinced, and neither does she seem to like Benedict on a personal level. (Naturally, this actually emphasizes a common bond, a fact underscored by the name they share — Sharon's middle name is Elizabeth.) What is most interesting about this initial conversation is the way in which Benedict discusses how her prison sentence has affected her sense of time. She describes herself as "permanently stuck in the past," living a life in which time is truly out of joint because she herself "is history."[86] She is out of step in every sense: as a mother, she has missed the experience of raising her daughter; as a woman, the San Francisco that she knew before has been replaced, often literally torn down. All the landmarks (buildings, parks, etc.) of her youth are gone, "And yet I still see them," she says (*PDWE* 4). It is not so much that she herself is haunted by the traumatic experiences of the night of the murder that transpired long ago. On the contrary, she seems to be entirely reconciled to her fate. However, if her innocence can be "proved"— even after the fact, and in a fictitious court — the trauma that she herself is for her daughter can be obviated. For this, she is willing to undergo all the discomfort and grief of dredging up the long dead past.

The historical tribunal where the case will be tried is a fitting figure for memory construction as this comes to be represented throughout the novel. In the court, a somewhat regular cast of characters (i.e., actors) acts out famous cases in the faux courtroom. For Benedict in particular, the very premise of re-performing demonstrates the function of repressed memory in hysteria. The past is repeated, or reconstructed, with the sole purpose of catching the attention of an authority figure. This reading is appropriate, I would argue, despite the fact that this is a mock trial that will have no real effects, save for in the public perception of a nineteen-year-old case. (This assumption seems to strain the imagination, even when allowing for the status of publicity that is requisite in the hard-boiled world. That is, there is always a danger of scandals "going public," and being written up in the papers. In this way, experience can seamlessly be transcribed into the big Other.) Lis Benedict maintains that the retrial is in the end more for her daughter than for herself or "the public." Quite literally, then, Benedict's case is being retried before an Other that is not there — indeed, an Other that does not exist insofar as the court itself has no agency and cannot, therefore, comprise a "public." Of course, the point to be taken is that an actual court is itself, in several respects, nothing but such empty convention — convention that has typically refused to give women like Lis Benedict a fair chance.

Judy Benedict is so determined to free her mother and herself from the stigma attached to this murder that she agrees to participate in the reenactment, naturally playing herself as a child. This is hardly a stretch for Judy, as she was once a promising actress in New York. Later she made the transition into production, returning home to San Francisco to pursue this new direction. Again, Judy's role in the original trial was the basis for the prosecution's case. As was revealed in the original proceedings, on the night of the murder, she awoke to find her mother coming in from outside, presumably on her way back from the dovecote where the murder took place. Judy recalls seeing blood all over her mother's dress. At the time, Lis maintained that she was simply up late working on calligraphy, a favorite hobby, and that it was impossible for the child to know the difference between ink stains and actual blood. Though this was certainly incriminating, it was not as damning as the second detail linking Judy to her mother's arrest and imprisonment. A few months after the crime, when searching for a Halloween costume in an old trunk in the attic — a detail crucial for her characterization — Judy finds the ring that was taken from Cordy's severed finger. These two pieces of evidence serve as the basis of the prosecution's case, which is handled by Joseph Stammeroff, the man who later adopted Judy.

Clearly, the Benedict family dynamics are complex. Judy's father had betrayed her mother — it is later discovered that he had planned to leave Lis and Judy to marry Cordy — and her mother had in turn betrayed her by committing the heinous crime of killing her father's lover. Stammeroff is a rescuing figure, but he has not been the most affectionate parent and, further, he seems to have something to hide about his own participation in the case. When questioned on the mock trial, he maintains that the past is better left buried, particularly for his adopted daughter Judy, who has suffered so much throughout it all. Now on the California Supreme Court, Stammeroff is not afraid to use his power and influence to guarantee that his wishes are obeyed. He attempts to intimidate McCone in a variety of ways at their first meeting, stating plainly that he refuses to allow the "exhumation of a past that is better left buried" (*PDWE* 107). A familiar hard-boiled patriarch, he rigorously defends his daughter, who he claims is still a child in many respects. At the same time, he obviously represents a sort of "old boy" network of "people who count," as he says (*PDWE* 109). While his rigorous defense of his own participation in the original case is sinister, to be sure — this put him on the fast track to political success — it remains entirely possible that he wishes only the best for Judy, wanting only to protect her from the violent desire of the mother. Like all good fathers.

Judy appreciates this feature of her father's character, yet she remains largely estranged from him. In fact, it is suggested that Judy allowed Lis to move in with her solely to upset Stammeroff. Judy's dramatic personality no doubt plays a significant role in this behavior. She is quite conscious of the antagonisms that she creates (e.g., between herself and her father, herself and her boyfriend), a manipulative aspect of her personality that is not lost on McCone and others at All Souls. Throughout the text, Judy is constantly working herself up into a frenzy, pushing away those who care about her, only to ask quickly that they "come back" to help her deal with the ugliness of her memories.

When McCone first mentions Judy, only one word seems to apply: fey. Here, McCone intends that Judy, like her mother in many respects, seems as though she is from another world. As the term suggests, she seems to McCone to be "under a spell, marked by apprehension of calamity, death, or evil" (*PDWE* 38). Thinking further on the matter, McCone associates it with sadomasochistic fantasies, as well. Of course, this "otherworldliness" is the very experience of a person suffering from traumatic memories. A strong pull from the past is the most obvious component of this condition. However, further, this schism between past and present leaves the subject literally between times and, therefore, never fully present to experience. Again, as psychoanalysis suggests, the great trauma of life is that we are never fully present to it. We are never equal to our experiences, neither in the moment, nor in memory. This distancing occurs all the more frequently for Judy when her mother moves into the apartment. As Judy says of her own recently recovered memories: "Lately, that's been happening a lot [i.e., new memories "appearing"]. Lis will say something, or I'll see something reminds me of childhood, and — bingo! — I'm right back in the past, and it's all so clear" (*PDWE* 44). As the Benedict case progresses, the detective finds that she herself is not immune to such haunting.

For McCone, this intimacy of memory is always experienced as at once welcoming and alien — and, therefore, dangerous. Just as the original hard-boiled sleuths so frequently find themselves personally implicated in a case — this quite in spite of their best efforts — so too does Sharon. However, while the male hard-boiled detective works to defend his life or name, McCone must complete a more difficult task. She must ward off the ill effects of becoming emotionally involved with her work, defending, in this way, her very being. This is her great fear at the start of the Benedict affair. McCone worries that she will become too personally involved in the obviously very disturbing investigation.[87] As she reasons, "I can't risk becoming involved in yet another case where I might get torn emotionally. I used up all my reserves on other clients, other victims. I've got nothing left for you" (*PDWE* 7). Nevertheless, the pull of this danger persists, something that McCone cannot turn her back on. There is always something more that beckons her to continue. Though palpable, this "something" remains just out of sight, as McCone so frequently observes throughout the series.

Of course, McCone's fears will quickly become realized, much beyond the scope of her original apprehension. Indeed, she will come to form what she describes as a "psychic bond" to the events of the night of the murder (*PDWE* 140). Her initial reluctance to take this case owes much to her participation in the events at Tufa Lake described in Muller's previous novel, *Where Echoes Live*—these leave her "newly scarred and tender," as she says (*PDWE* 47). But it seems that these wounds actually make her sensitive to the intricacies of the Benedict case, and she admits that she feels an odd pull to these events after simply reading the original court transcript. "If I could be sucked in by events so many years in the past, would I ever be safe from those of the present?" she worries. It is a concern she elaborates upon elsewhere: "Perhaps the depths that harbored such memories as Judy's were best left unplumbed. Or were they? Which was better — to probe them and risk the pain of unpleasant revelations? Or to keep the lid on and risk the spiritual infection that stems from repressed secrets?" (*PDWE* 47–48).

This aside encapsulates the larger questions of traumatic memory that are at stake in the novel. At first glance, it seems a straightforward translation of the positivistic task of the detective, to exhume artifacts of the past. The term "unplumbed" is appropriate, as the word appears in the English translation of *The Interpretation of Dreams* in the context of Freud's famous discussion of the navel of the dream. As Freud says of dreams, "There is at least one spot in every dream at which it is unplumbable — a navel, as it were, that is its point of contact with the unknown."[88] This more abyssal appraisal of the powers of interpretation seems to escape McCone, at least initially. More terrifying than actually confronting the pain of the past, or refusing to acknowledge such memories, leaving them to return of their own accord in repetition, is the possibility that these two options — this either/or that is by now familiar — are one and the same. In other words, McCone must confront the possibility that the plumbing of such traumatic memories may result in a missed encounter that brings one no closer to revelation, and at the same time results in the contamination that was to be avoided at all costs.

McCone importantly experiences this notion of a more indelible trauma of the subject through the other, that is, both a literal other and the other that she has become to herself in this act of possession. A telling instance of this possession occurs during a nighttime visit to Sea Cliff. Returning to crime scenes, even crime scenes long since altered (the dovecote had been removed shortly after the murder), gives McCone a greater understanding of the case. Yet this "understanding" is never easily quantified. Typically, it is an experience that is better described as an intuition rather than knowledge. As she explains, "Going to crime scenes or places that figure in a case is a habit of mine. It helps me get a feel for what happened" (*PDWE* 88). As the scene continues, it becomes apparent that this "getting a feel" for the place again lends itself toward something of a mystical experience that is in this case perfectly in keeping with the Gothic surroundings. Walking about the moonlit grounds, she asks herself questions about the murder, letting her mind wander, initially with little luck. Suddenly, as she describes,

> The question smashed my mental dam, and images washed over me. A shadowy form of indeterminate sex gliding across the lawn and slipping through the foliage. Finders of light spilling from inside the cote, briefly pulling the mist aside. And inside the cote: rough brick walls across which more shadows fell. Shadows in attitudes of anger, rage, and violence. And the long blades of the garden shears shining ... slashing. Blood flowing ... spattering... [*PDWE* 92].

McCone tries to convince herself that there is no evil in the actual site itself, that the horror of that evening is only a memory now. However, as she muses, "But memories of evil still lived in the minds of some people. Memories of evil still lived in this fog-clotted darkness" (*PDWE* 92). Clearly, memory here splits the individual — or even community — from her own contemporary experience. While the genre often places the detective there at this gap as a redemptive figure, this discourse will prove itself unlikely for McCone.

After this "connection" is made with the actual place — or rather, the nexus of time, place, and memory — the detective comes to be haunted by vivid dreams that seem to focus on the events of the night of the murder. Appropriately, Sharon has the sense that these dreams are actually happening to someone else. For example, waking suddenly from these nightmares, she thinks to herself,

> Call it a morbid preoccupation with the crime; call it a weird psychic link, even. But whatever the label, last night as I'd stood in front of that house in Sea Cliff, I'd *felt* how it had been on June 22, 1956. Altered as the landscape was, I'd *seen* the gardens, the dovecote. And later, in my dreams, I'd sensed what might have gone on there. I knew, and yet I didn't know... [*PDWE* 94].

This frank confession perfectly summarizes the hysteric's relation to knowledge, which is always traumatic. Though she will describe this relation to the case as an "unhealthy obsession" that thwarts her objectivity, it is precisely this indeterminate link that she can only sense, and at times softly *feel*, that guides her investigation. This is hysteric detection *par excellence*. This identification that dissolves the boundaries between the self and other, between past and present, between inside and outside, is the detective's very method for solving the crime. Here, as elsewhere within the McCone series, it is successful — quite in spite of Sharon. The detective summarizes this process near the conclusion of the McKittridge case: "Now the facts enmired [sic] in my subconscious had begun to filter loose and merge with what I'd discovered; soon they would flow freely toward a solution" (*PDWE* 237). While this "subconscious" thought does frequently allow Sharon to reason out connections that remain opaque, the "solution" of which she speaks is never final, and the greater questions raised by her method remain unanswered.

The unconventional nature of this methodology cannot be understated — at least when viewed from the perspective of the more typical hard-boiled ethic based upon radical isolation. Early within the novel, Sharon makes a comment that has wide-ranging significance: "It occurred to me that while I knew a great deal about crime and its immediate effects, I'd given very little thought to its long-range impact, particularly upon parolees" (*PDWE* 38). Though McCone is here thinking of Lis Benedict's experience, the thought and its not-so-implicit criticism must be generalized to detective fiction as a whole. Hammett's Nick Charles was entirely correct to observe that "Murder doesn't round out anybody's life except the murdered and sometimes the murderer's," as his wife Nora was equally correct to conclude that, given this, the solution to a crime is always "all pretty unsatisfactory."[89] As I argued in Chapter Two, it is not insignificant that these words are the final words of Hammett's career as a novelist, nor is it incidental that they are spoken by a woman. Nora understands all too well the futility of the endgame of detection understood in its traditional sense — a tradition that Hammett is already lampooning in 1934. Muller's work addresses this dilemma by focusing not only on the game that is always afoot in detective fiction, but likewise by focusing upon the effects of crime on the individuals in question. Naturally, the trauma experienced by Lis and Judy Benedict is shared in some way by all within the novel. Time has touched each individual involved in the case, and, as is always true, it has been neither kind nor forgiving. In this way, Muller's novel addresses not merely the relevance of the drive for solution and the need for mystery. Further, the work speaks to our inability ever to account for the traumatic effects of time. In other words, Muller's fiction attempts to trace the effects of traumatic experience upon the human condition, what Caruth speaks of as the "trauma of survival."

The mechanics of recovered memory therapy — the "false solution" to the trauma of survival, as it were — are addressed near the conclusion of the text, as McCone questions the wisdom of a still unstable Judy Benedict playing herself in the mock trial. Persevering in spite of McCone's doubts, in this role, Judy does not disappoint. She delivers the "great" performance that always eluded her during her own career as an actress. Before this unfolds, McCone calls a therapist friend, Mary Norton, to discuss Judy's situation and the potential harm that the trial could actually bring about, as well as the actual "reality" of the memories that might be unearthed in this cathartic process. Norton assures McCone that repressed memory is a "fairly common phenomenon" (*PDWE* 153). She suspects that because Judy was a "self-blamer," the trauma of the original event continued forcing Judy to repress these unpleasant experiences. Here, Norton references the famous Susan Nason case, a frequent source in the literature of repressed memory therapy.[90] Less interested in a history lesson, the detective asks what triggers the recovery of such a lost memory. Norton calls this "spontaneous unblocking," which is remarkably reliable, so she says. As the therapist continues, "As for the accuracy of the memories, they're often clearer and far more detailed than ordinary memory, as if they've been frozen or preserved. Sometimes they may have been distorted by shock or fear — in which case it takes some interpretation to get the facts — but most of the time a true memory is easily distinguished because of the richness of detail" (*PDWE* 153). This is clearly a very conventional discourse on memory. The ego psychology at the heart of this view betrays itself in the notion of the subject's "readiness" to recover the past. Norton tells McCone that memory recovery will occur only "when the individual's ego structure can withstand it" (*PDWE* 153).

From the perspective of the trauma theory discussed above, two details from Norton's account of recovered memory should immediately stand out. The first is the "authenticity" of a memory; the second is the subject's "readiness" to recover this traumatic memory. In the first instance, Norton actually maintains that a "real" memory can be distinguished from fabrication by the vividness of the details recalled — details that before were incapable of rising to the subject's conscious memory. Presumably, a memory that is not told with well-described elements is immediately recognized as confabulation made according to the patient's various fantasies constructed in defense of the trauma itself. In sum: fabrication is hazy; reality, on the contrary, is recalled "in living color," as it were. As Carruth indicates, following Freud, this is in part true, insofar as a patient recovering a traumatic memory does "remember for a first time" an event that was so extreme as to escape conscious experience. To put this another way, the traumatic event was so "present" that it escaped being experienced as present. The recovered memory is, then, the experience for the first time of the offending traumatic event. However, gauging the veracity of this memory upon its details seems specious, to say the least.

This suspicion must apply to the second item of interest as well, the timeliness of the recovered memory itself, which only ever occurs when we are "ready." As was evident in the Freud's "Remembering, Repeating, and Working Through," the subject is never ready for the traumatic memory, precisely because the larger point of reference is a trauma for which there is no salve — the trauma that is the very basis of the subject. Not only does a traumatic event occur out of time, insofar as it is not registered within our conscious experience, but in addition, the traumatic event (understood as accident rather than inevitability) underscores the fact that we are always split from our experience. Our memories in fact may not be narratives that comfortably archive our experiences, which arrange our lives in this accessible, human fashion.

The denouement to *Pennies* suggests this more refined insight into memory, as it alludes to a famous antecedent, Balzac's short story "Adieu," a tale whose structure has much in common with detective fiction.[91] As Brooks has suggested, all detective fiction in a way participates in the structure that is found in Balzac's excellent story, as the genre always stages a repetition that attempts to once and for all free the victim from the pull of the past.[92] In Balzac's tale, shortly after the Napoleonic wars, a French soldier comes across the Comtesse de Bandieres, living in the squalid conditions of a country village. The Comtesse had apparently accompanied her husband, a French soldier, on the campaign against Moscow. In his reconstruction of the subsequent events, the soldier assumes that, during the retreat, the Comtesse witnesses the massacre of the troops and the murder of her husband. Unable to shake herself from the shock of this event, she continues to suffer from the traumatic illness that has left her the shell of her former self. Appealing to "modern" ideas of treatment for nervous illness, the soldier constructs a massive mock battle that stages the actual retreat during which the Comtesse was injured. Naturally, the ends are not what the soldier expects: Confronted with the repetition of the original trauma in a near perfect rendering, the Comtesse dies, saying only "Adieu" before her passing.

Balzac's point perfectly exemplifies the psychoanalytic theory of trauma. If the actual object of trauma were to be recaptured and returned to the sub-

Four. Remembering, Repeating, and Working Through

ject, the result could only be death. This is necessary because the greater trauma suffered by the subject is the trauma of being split from its experience and its memories of that experience, by the proxy of the language of the Other, which is always foreign to the extreme. To be sure, this imagined loss creates the sense of epiphany that recovered memory therapy believes to be out there, somewhere on the periphery. Nevertheless, the loss of this "object" is the price of subjectivity. Were that debt to be made good, and the object to be reinstated, the result must be the destruction of the subject.

Fortunately, the conclusion of *Pennies on a Dead Woman's Eyes* stages a more sophisticated version of remembering than the explanation put forth by the therapist Norton. On the night of the trial, Judy is in fine form, delivering the performance of her life, as McCone describes. In other words, Judy delivers an affected version of the events she remembers from childhood, with the inclusion of some new material that had surfaced after the Lis Benedict had been released from prison. As is later discovered, this has all been perfectly calculated by Judy, who had been in therapy for years and has recovered enough of her repressed memories to piece together the events of that evening and her adoptive father's role in the subsequent cover-up. As a child, Judy had found Cordy's murdered body. After this horrific discovery, she had actually taken the severed finger and thrown it over the cliff, taking the ring back up to the attic to hide it where no one would ever find it. Apparently, Stammeroff had made Judy lie about this significant detail throughout the years — at least this is Judy's recollection — and she is resentful for this forced collusion. At the height of the performance, Judy draws a gun and points it at Stammeroff, accusing him of these lies that had, essentially, ruined her life. (This actually occurs at Sea Cliff, the meeting place for the "trial" that evening.) McCone, thinking quickly on her feet, reasons that the best way to address the situation is to make Judy remember even further. At this point, Judy still imagines that her mother had killed Cordy, which is not accurate — as the detective describes, "the memory gap" had not "fully closed" (*PDWE* 282). In traumatic supplement to her previously recovered memories, Judy now has a flash of insight during the reconstruction of the events of the night of the murder. She remembers that she saw Leonard Eyestone, son of the Institute's director, walking out of her mother and father's bedroom — freshly showered and changed after violently killing Cordy. McCone returns Judy's own words to her, and in the midst of the subsequent revelation, McCone jumps on her and takes the gun away from the stunned actress.

Naturally, Judy is apprehended by the authorities and held on attempted murder. Later when McCone speaks with Judy's boyfriend Jack about the situation, he describes Judy as "fuckin' crazy." As he goes on to elaborate, she was completely "obsessed with getting back at Lis for what she imagined Lis had done to her when she was a child" (*PDWE* 293). McCone feels for Judy, to a certain extent, as she says, "having become well acquainted with obsession during the past two weeks. The thought of living in a prolonged state of it was horrifying; being pulled toward something, driven relentlessly by forces you couldn't begin to comprehend..." (*PDWE* 294). Jack and McCone's conclusion sufficiently vilifies Judy's position. She's "so full of hate," as he says. This assessment refuses, then, to fall into the simple discourse of recovered memory that is suggested at various times throughout the narrative. Indeed, McCone will have nothing to do with such therapeutic measures. Judy genuinely did suffer a traumatic experience as a child, and, through recovered memory therapy, actually did recover memories of the offending instance. However, despite the fact that these events are presented as "real" — that is, this traumatic experience actually did occur — Judy's attachment to these events is scripted as entirely pathological. By characterizing Judy in this way, the vilification of some Other (who is responsible for all the subject's problems) is avoided. In other words, Judy's ire at her "parents" (both adopted and actual) does not warrant the hatred that dominates her life. The pennies on the dead woman's eyes symbolize this criticism: the mutilation of another, in fantasy or actuality, is an empty gesture that arrives nowhere, much like the "fake" currency of the leaden pennies left on Cordy McKittridge's eyes.

The political discourse that serves as a subplot to the novel provides a similar commentary at the level of the social, again emphasizing the relation of trauma to history. Surrounding the murder of Cordy was a visit of John Foster Dulles to Sea Cliff, a fitting figure of 1950s demonization of the Soviet Union and concomitant military escalation. The political drama contemporary to the period is similarly found in the primary motive for Leonard Eyestone's murder of Cordy. Apparently, Eyestone had consorted with Communists during his college years. During this time, he met Roger Woods, step-brother to Jane Cardinal, one of Cordy's former roommates. The first explanation of Eyestone's motive is this: Cordy realizes that her family will cut her off financially after she breaks up the Benedicts' marriage. Always thinking of the future, she also realizes that it is in her best interests to keep the Institute from any sort of intrigue involving political radicals. She asks her lover, Eyestone, to break off his friendship with the Communist Woods and to resign from the Institute. In response to this betrayal, he kills her.

They are each left, as are we all, to attempt to experience the past as present for a first time. Woods, McCone discovers, was an agent of the FBI attempting to infiltrate the Institute. This of course nullifies any actual corruption on Eyestone's part, a fact that emphasizes the illusory nature of the Red Scare at the same time that it underscores the pathos for blood that was shed in the name of empty ideology during the Cold War. While the politicization of the love triangle may at first appear to be a stretch, Cordy's body effectively becomes the mark of the trauma between the subject and history. Near the conclusion, Muller includes one of her patented "philosophical asides" on the topic of hate — first the Communists, then Hippies, later Feminists, etc. — saying that "as a nation we don't discriminate in our hatreds..." (*PDWE* 295). However, there is no solution offered to this or any other mystery presented, and the end of the novel begins with a search for McCone's now missing boyfriend, Hy Rapinsky.

Time, Talismans, and Trauma

Trophies and Dead Things (1990) similarly exemplifies Muller's attendance to the lingering effects of traumatic events in America's history, in this case Vietnam and the legacy of the student movements. In this novel, the interest in the idealism of the 1960s-brand of liberal politics common to the series is given a sharper focus, as McCone is confronted with the changing nature of these ideals — even their abandonment — over the course of time. Though Sharon is a bit too young to have experienced the '60s herself — she didn't arrive at Berkeley until the 1970s — she consistently identifies with the politics of that generation, seeing herself as "fighting the good fight," at a time when others had forsaken the struggle.[93] As Walton and Jones have suggested, the nostalgia for the idealism of early feminist politics is at the core of the female hard-boiled detective genre.[94] However, in keeping with Muller's revision of hard-boiled nostalgia, a critical account of such politics (and the longing for those helicon days) is a necessary accompaniment to this remembrance. There will be no return *to* a more responsible political program and reclamation of its dream. Rather, throughout McCone's work, we find a return *of* something that is incapable of being articulated or recognized in any discourse. A traumatic missed encounter that actually opens the subject to history, as such. As was the case in *Pennies on a Dead Women's Eyes,* the sepia-tint of memory always belies something much more sinister. McCone's own sense of the trauma of history, both personal and social, is, appropriately, always tied to the suffering body of another. In this encounter lies the unplumbable nature of the hard kernel of trauma that is at the heart of McCone's inquiry.

The novel begins in the midst of a series of sniper attacks that have occurred, apparently at random, throughout San Francisco. Peter Hilderly, an old associate of Hank Zahn and a leader of the Free Speech Movement at Berkeley during the 1960s, unfortunately becomes one of the victims. As executor of Hiderly's estate, Hank Zahn must get Hilderly's affairs in order. However, as Hank begins this task, he uncovers a newly altered will that mysteriously bequeaths Hilderly's estate to four unknown individuals: Jess Goodhue, Libby Heikknen, D. A. Taylor, and Thomas Grant. Naturally, Hank calls upon McCone to investigate each of these new trustees, and slowly the common thread among them surfaces. This connection seems to be rooted in Hilderly's stint as a reporter for the *New Liberty* newspaper in Vietnam, a time when Hank Zahn and Willie Whelan — Sharon's assistant Rae Kelleher's boyfriend — knew Hilderly through a group of liberal officers who used to meet and discuss politics. Naturally, McCone must at first be drawn to the option that the shootings have something to do with Hilderly and his altered will, a possibility that becomes even more likely when Willie and Hank are each wounded by the sniper.

Though McCone herself later apprehends the sniper — this immediately after Hank is wounded — in the end, the sniper turns out to be a red herring in the larger case. He is simply an old adversary from Vietnam who had, apparently, carried a grudge against the group of liberal army officers of which Hank and Willie were a part. Contiguous with this particular case of mistaken identities (i.e., the sniper's assumed connection with Hilderly) is McCone's own dramatic transformation when she chases down the killer. The detective pins the sniper and holds her gun to his head, telling bystanders who had gathered around to call the police. As she looks up into the crowd, she sees the terror in their eyes: "It was as if I, not the sniper, were the person to be feared."[95] In gesture that is by now common to the series, McCone bears no resemblance to what she thought was her "self." Investigation inevitably results in estrangement for the sleuth. While the violence of the sniper at first offers itself as an obvious explanation for grouping these individuals together — violence, importantly, at the threshold of community — the group of trustees are actually bound by a related, but much more traumatic tie.

The title of *Trophies and Dead Things* is taken from the last stanza of a song by the English playwright John Webster: "Vain the ambition of kings/ Who seek by trophies and dead things/To leave a living name behind,/And weave but nets to catch the wind" (*TDT* 36). McCone recalls this verse after visiting one of the Hilderly trustees, Tom Grant, a ruthless family court lawyer who specializes in defending men in divorce proceedings. Apparently, he is notorious for inventively bypassing community property laws, winning husbands choice settlements, and leaving women and children with little in the exchange. While this characterization is enough to incite McCone's feminist disdain, it is actually his hobby of making fetishes out of animal carcasses that brings Webster's words to Sharon's mind.

As the detective waits to meet Grant in his office, she looks over his collection of "trophies and dead things," what she describes as "primitive folk art," all of which is "unsettling and quite unpleasant" (*TDT* 31). The macabre

Four. Remembering, Repeating, and Working Through 221

nature of these pieces comes to haunt the text generally and in this way comes to be associated with all the particular hauntings of the novel, as well. As she looks over Grant's collection, McCone describes an individual piece that catches her eye: "The framework was a crossed pair of rusted metal spikes, each festooned with mockingbird's feathers. Stretched between the spikes was a swatch of what resembled — but certainly couldn't be — dried human skin" (*TDT* 32). The violence of the piece is clear, and at the same time it invokes mimicry — and, importantly, repetition — in its choice of ornamental feathers, as well as an attendant ossification that any piece of taxidermy necessarily suggests.

This will become important as McCone discovers the significance of the various "charms" that are shared by the group that is brought together by Hilderly's altered will. However, already apparent in this confrontation with Grant's "work" is the ultimate futility of the charm or talisman against the onslaught of time. Grant claims that his pieces are not fetishes in the strict sense, that is, they are not used in religious ceremonies and instilled with magic powers. However, as he goes on, "a fetish is a charm, something with magical powers. These certainly do have the power to disturb" (*TDT* 32). McCone observes that Grant is actually quite pleased with the unsettling effect his fetishes have on her and suspects that these pieces are, in a strange way, seductive props that he uses to take women off guard. When asked where he gets his materials, Grant describes himself as a "scavenger" taking "things on the beach or in parks" (*TDT* 33). His use of the word "things" is particularly unsettling to McCone. The word of course refers to the dead animals or birds, or merely parts of their carcasses, which are incorporated into the fetishes. Speaking of his raw materials in this way seems a perverse betrayal of life itself, particularly given the fact that these have no ceremonial significance and are, so it seems, intended to do nothing more than disturb. Grant's empty totems are clearly an extreme example of violent enjoyment, which immediately categorizes him as a typical hard-boiled "plundering father." However, over the course of the novel, other less monstrous talismans will be shown to be a similar betrayal of life. In this way, the protective power of the charm is a project that inevitably fails, like casting nets to the wind.

As Sharon soon discovers, the greater plot of the novel involves a group of student radicals and a case of failed domestic terrorism. Before going to Vietnam as a reporter, Hilderly had become associated with the group of Berkeley students loosely associated with the larger subversive political organization "The Weather Machine." The core of the group consisted of Libby Heikkinen (later Libby Ross), D. A. Taylor, Jenny Ruhl, and Andy Wrightman. This group of radical students had met at Berkeley and maintained an ongoing campaign against the government and its war efforts abroad. Their most violent protest was to be an actual bombing of a military installation, Port Chicago Naval Weapons Station in Antioch. (The attempt occurred after Hilderly had already left for Vietnam.) This plot was ultimately foiled, and the offenders were apprehended at the base in possession of weapons and explosives.

When active, the "Collective" had fashioned their own talisman, a prop to bind them together as a group and, naturally, to keep them safe from harm. Each member carried a broken portion of a medallion inscribed with single letters. Like the inscribed individual pieces worn around their necks, they were each a part of a larger whole, and were likewise themselves inscribed by the mandate of the group. McCone finds the first piece of the medallion when sorting through Hilderly's things. Later, she finds D. A. Taylor clinging to his, as though the relic continued to hold some sort of power over him. When first questioned by McCone about the pendants, Libby Ross refuses to tell her their meaning, saying only, "It's nothing but a symbol of things that are over and done with" (*TDT* 153). However, later she does admit that the jewelry was part of a larger piece that spelled "Amerika," the "k" taken from Kafka's spelling in the novel of the same title. Ross tells McCone that this transposed spelling was common to the movement, and the (largely empty) reference to Kafka was to indicate the imperialism of the United States (*TDT* 157). As Sharon discovers, this talisman still holds considerable power over D. A. Taylor and Libby Ross; however, the force focused in the piece is no longer what was originally intended. Rather, what holds the two in thrall is the missed relation to that original promise that the object figured, be this "peace," "belonging," "connection," etc. As Ross "ruefully" muses about the significance of their charm:

> From this vantage point, it seems like just one of those silly things that kids do — like sitting around in a clubhouse in a vacant lot and cutting your fingers so you can exchange blood oaths. But at the time it was a big deal: we'd each have a piece of this thing that stood for what we believed in and be connected forever [*TDT* 157].

McCone suggests to Ross that in a way the collective had been connected forever, but this is of course cold comfort, as it is really their failure to remain connected in the way that they imagined that now binds them. The talisman, then, becomes a token of that shared wound.

I would like to suggest that the fascination with the talisman in *Trophies and Dead Things* underscores the subject's fretful relation with language, as well as the failure of the symbolic order to offer a definitive point of orientation. To these ends, Thomas Grant's fetishes are hardly incidental. Indeed, the haunting presence of these pieces is felt throughout the text, a presence that necessarily raises the question of perversion. As was discussed in the case of Spillane in Chapter Two, perversion represents, in several respects, the logic of the hard-boiled ethic worked to its conclusion. Defining the concept in psychoanalytic terms, Fink explains that perversion is a result of "the inadequacy of the paternal function" that keeps the child from distancing himself from the mother's enjoyment through the paternal metaphor.[96] Contrary to the popular notion that this subject enjoys unending transgressive pleasure, the pervert actually works to instantiate the law of the father to defend against the crippling anxiety that accompanies this psychical structure. In this sense, the pervert is the most law-abiding citizen imaginable, precisely because he himself must constantly strive to produce the *No!* of the father. Like the neurotic subject, the pervert wishes above all else to erase the desire of the Other. However, while the neurotic subject will do this through separation and distancing, the pervert will achieve this by engaging the Other's enjoyment.[97] To these ends, the fetishist offers up their compensatory object to fill the lack in the Other (i.e., the Other's desire). The pervert's relation to the Other belies the perverse logic of desire itself, insofar as this relation to the other always occurs through a fetish of one kind or another—be this a high heel, taxidermy, or any object of exchange. As Muller's McCone suggests, the fetish or talisman is thus like a net cast to the wind, a futile endeavor, to be sure.

Returning to Muller's text, it is the failure of what was to have been the defining moment of the Collective at Port Chicago that effectively binds the group together for a lifetime. With this breakdown, the broken pieces of the medallion that all members share reveal their true logic—and, thereby, the logic of the fetish or talisman. They are but small tokens that reference not a whole (i.e., the literal "Amerika" that was the larger medallion, but also the ideal "Amerika" that the Collective imagined) that has been lost, but a whole that has never been. After the group was apprehended at the base, Libby and Taylor each serve prison time for their involvement with the bombing. This experience sours Libby and leaves Taylor broken and on the edge of madness for the remainder of his life. Jenny Ruhl, who is Jess Goodhue's mother, becomes the star witness for the prosecution in the case against her comrades, in exchange for her own freedom. However, wracked with guilt at this betrayal, she commits suicide a few months after the end of the trial, leaving behind a newborn daughter, Jessica. Andy Wrightman, Ruhl's lover, disappears, never to be heard from again, until Sharon discovers that "Wrightman" was an assumed name taken by Tom Grant. Andy Wrightman was the identity he assumed when he worked as an operative for the FBI, as part of that organization's active campaign of infiltrating student political groups. Taylor had suspected such collusion at the time, having had a vague memory of Wrightman simply disappearing into the background at Port Chicago, but it takes McCone to put all the pieces together successfully.

Perhaps the greater loss of innocence for the group concerns the betrayal by one of their own at Port Chicago, a dissention that likewise underscores the imaginary nature of their cooperative. Again, the likely candidate for this is Wrightman (i.e., Grant), but he was a largely peripheral figure, a hanger-on who was not especially liked. In the end, it is discovered that Hilderly is actually the guilty party. He too had infiltrated the group, but as a reporter. While he had liberal sympathies, his greater loyalty was to his work and saving innocent lives. When he became privy to the Collective's plans to commit murder in their raid on Port Chicago, he abandons his story and abandons the group, as well, leaving for Vietnam. This betraying of his friends troubles him until his dying day and this is the reason for the eleventh-hour change of his will. As a more high-profile student radical, Hilderly was a hero to many within the Collective, particularly to D. A. Taylor. The latter will describe Hilderly's complicity as the final loss of heroes from that time and the final loss of his youthful idealism. This loss leads D. A. to kill himself near the conclusion of the text, leaving only the women to continue on.

The traumatic missed relation at the center of the group is duplicated at the level of the couple. Given the prominence of ineffectual talismans throughout the text, this seems to be a general indictment of the sexual relation — a familiar hard-boiled motif. Indeed, the ongoing affair between D. A. Taylor and Libby Ross inspires pathos equal to any of the nets cast to wind throughout the novel. Despite the fact that Taylor is married (to a younger woman), and Libby Ross had been married and then divorced, the two have continued their relationship. Ross describes this as not so much romantic but "just our way of keeping the past alive" (*TDT* 241). Appropriately, it is a connection built upon a by now familiar fracture, both between each other and with the past that each signifies for the other. Ross is quite right to say that Taylor's wife should not be jealous of what she and D. A. have together, for they share nothing but a wound and the absence this references.

To mark this deficiency, Ross holds on to a talisman of her own, a photograph of the collective taken shortly before the Port Chicago debacle. Her attachment to this memento apparently bothered her first husband, who could not understand her desire to keep a token from such a horrible time in her life. However, Libby maintains that she does not mind remembering those days, even given the horrible results. "Those were the best days of my life," she says, "back when we were young and going to change the world. Since then, nothing's been ... anything" (*TDT* 241). As detective fiction has indicated from the start there is something necessarily traumatic about a photograph, that infinitely small, unreal moment violently wrested from the passage of time.[98] As Barthes suggested, the photo marks not simply the distance of the subject from the event represented, but the split that was always already inherent in the photographed subject itself— thus, it serves as a traumatic mark of survival.[99] What Libby Ross mourns is not the loss of an idyllic time — a fact that is made clear with each recovered truth about this history — but the more traumatic insight that the drive to "change the world" was never quite the selfless act of peace that it presented itself to be. Ross and Taylor cling together, then, each as a witness to the repetition of the impossible relation that is history itself.

D. A. is here the more tragic figure. Indeed, one of the most common moral judgments made by McCone is to deem a person too weak to shed the weight of history — or, rather, not persevering in spite of this burden. In *Trophies and Dead Things*, her summation of D. A. Taylor is that he is both pathetic and heroic: "Pathetic because of his drug abuse and inability to let go of the past, but heroic because of what that past had been" (*TDT* 150). This stagnation is figured in D. A.'s dilapidated home and business (a small restaurant), and the decaying dock — a faltering excursion into the liquid abyss — where he spends a great deal of time looking away to an island in the bay, imagining his end. Naturally, as beneficiary of a quarter of a million dollars (his portion of the Hilderly inheritance) it is possible for Taylor to fix his degraded situation, but McCone quickly dismisses this possibility. Taylor is simply incapable of re-envisioning his past and accepting the final emptiness of the various symbols that oriented his youth. His broken body, which after his suicide is splayed out in an eerie tableau, is the final figure of life's excess that remains beyond all symbolic incantations.

Hilderly himself seemed to be aware of time's impasses, a realization that actually prompted the altering of his will. In a telephone conversation shortly after he had made these changes, Hilderly had mentioned something to his son about "guilt and atonement and symbolic acts." In the end, these gestures do not make good on past wrongs or offer therapeutic redemption to the living. Rather, the symbolic act, in its emptiness, repeats the unknown connection to our neighbor and that is the best that we might hope for. This is the wound that is Vietnam. As McCone now understands, the war "didn't discriminate.... All of us were wounded one way or another" (*TDT* 196). In this way, the novel works to demythologize the promise of that time, and this is certainly the result for Sharon, who acknowledges that the case had "stripped away what little remained of the mythic charm of the 1960s for her" (*TDT* 259).

The novel ends with a call from George Kastakos, who, after nursing his wife back to health, was finally beginning his divorce proceedings and wished to continue his romantic relation with McCone. Like many of the novels in the series, *Trophies and Dead Things* ends with a reconnection of McCone with the people who are close to her. However, the detective understands clearly that this is not a "happily ever after": "The pain and anger and disillusionment of the past week fell away from me. Their vestiges would return, I knew. Bad memories would recur — probably for the rest of my life" (*TDT* 265). However, she refuses to become prisoner to such pain. Life goes on, as she says, as does the trauma of survival.

Listening to the Silence

Listen to the Silence (2000) galvanizes many of the issues with which this chapter has dealt and, at the same time, seems to offer the greatest difficulty to my argument regarding the hysteric nature of McCone's detective that always finds identity through the other. Maureen Reddy has compellingly argued that this novel falls back into a discourse of identity based upon biology, a departure within the series that seriously undermines many of Muller's other more radical innovations.[100] While I share many of Reddy's concerns with this text, in this section I would like to propose an alternate reading. To these ends, I will examine *Listen to the Silence* both in terms of the traumatic discourse that I have traced throughout this chapter as well as the discourse of parentage (i.e., the question of the father) that has been pivotal throughout this project. From these coordinates, it is possible to read the novel as a challenge to the more intransigent aspects of the hard-boiled discourses of identity, rather than a confirmation of the conservative aspects of these same thematics.

On the back cover of my mass market copy of *Listen to the Silence* appears the following heading: "This Time It's Personal." Indeed, this is true, as this mystery will require McCone to investigate her family history and her own origins. While "getting personal" has been characteristic of McCone's hysteric method of detection, this personal stake most often occurs through the identification with another — by proxy or through an effigy. In *Listen to the Silence*, the pretense is that the detective at last learns the "truth" about herself. In other words, McCone stumbles into epiphany. The novel begins with the loss of Sharon's father, who dies of a heart attack. Though Sharon has always been something of an outcast, even within her very eccentric family, she has always felt very close to her father. Naturally, the news of his death comes as quite a shock to her. This actual loss of the father will bring about a loss of the symbolic stability afforded by this figure, as well, and though this disequilibrium is obviously a very natural accompaniment of grief, in McCone's case, this experience will be significantly amplified. When going through various papers and accumulated junk in her dad's garage, Sharon happens upon an adoption certificate that has her name on it. She is not her parents' child.

Four. Remembering, Repeating, and Working Through

The reader of the McCone series is well acquainted with the moniker used to describe Sharon in respect to the rest of her family: she is a "throwback."[101] This refers to the one-eighth Shoshone blood that she receives on her mother's side, a heritage that is clearly written upon her face. While her brothers and sisters have nothing "native" about their appearance, Sharon has always been unmistakably of Native American decent. The detective has always understood this as nothing more than an odd genetic accident, like a recessive gene that randomly reappears across the generations. Up until this point in the series, this biological happenstance added to the interstitial nature of her character. Much like that vague sense of "something else" that always haunts her dreams, her Native American heritage was always an opaque connection with another world — an unbounded relation for which even she herself could never account.

In *Trophies and Dead Things*, McCone briefly mourns the loss of this connection with typical hard-boiled sentiment:

> I seldom think of myself in terms of either my Indian heritage or the Scotch-Irish blood that makes up the remainder of my genetic composition. My attitude is a symptom of what's happened to ethnic groups in America, and I suppose in some ways the blurring of differences is a good thing. But on the other hand, there's an inherent sadness in the loss of consciousness of our roots, the loss of touch with history and traditions that make us who we are [*TDT* 146].

Clearly, the revelation of *Listen to the Silence* lends urgency to these issues. Effectively severed from the family that she thought was her own, McCone will more assiduously begin the search for lost "history and traditions." Though she will frequently script this investigation as a quest for the truth about her origins, something that seems very much out of character for the detective, she does at the same time seem to intuit — even in her frantic state — the impossibility of such revelation. After her sister questions what she is ultimately looking for in her search for her "real" family, McCone reflects: "[This was a] question I'd been asking myself. Identity, I suppose. A history. The truth. And something more I couldn't yet put a name to" (*LTS* 65). Importantly, though McCone seems to forsake her general insight into the unnamable trauma that haunts "history" and "truth" generally, this familiar excess — always "something more" — remains in *Listen to the Silence*.

After finding the adoption certificate, Sharon rushes to her mother's house — she and Sharon's father have been divorced for many years — to confront her on the matter. Appropriately, when the mother opens the door, McCone senses something odd about her face. After a handful of moments, Sharon realizes that her mother's uncanny appearance is not simply an effect of the recent discovery: Her mother has had plastic surgery, changing her face for her new life (*LTS* 30). The symbolic loss of her parents that results with the revelation that she is adopted is completed in the actual loss of her father (to death) and her mother's visage (to the surgeon's knife). Understandably, the traumatic circumstances leave Sharon feeling "rudderless" and, in several respects, the hysteric detective is hystericized throughout the remainder of the novel (*LTS* 9). This is tellingly played out in McCone's newfound antagonism with her mother. Her mother implores Sharon to burn the adoption certificate and forget that she has ever seen it, but the detective must, of course, persist. Sharon finds herself obsessively drawn to the name on the adoption certificate, the one indicated before the name change to Sharon Elizabeth McCone: Baby Girl Smith. Asking the hysteric question *par excellence*, Sharon demands: "Who am I, Ma? Who was Baby Girl Smith?" (*LTS* 32). Naturally, her mother is incapable of answering this query. While this demand to the mother ostensibly asks, "Who are my real parents?" its emphatic phrasing reveals that all such questions demand a more definitive account of the subject. Were the Other able to provide definitive knowledge of the subject, this would remedy the more traumatic condition of surviving in the absence of such certainties.[102]

All the more irritating to McCone are her mother's inadvertent silences and hesitations that punctuate each of their conversations after Sharon's "discovery." These are frequently indicated in the text with an ellipsis, a mark that will take on greater significance as the novel progresses. Without the help of her mother, the search must begin with clues culled from her childhood and conversations with her (adopted) family. Hy Ripinski, McCone's current lover (and later husband), suggests that, given everyone's reticence on this very sensitive issue, it will be necessary for her to "listen to the silence" in everyone's speech — "It can tell you everything," he assures (*LTS* 54). With this, Ripinski is effectively telling McCone to remember who she is, for this strategy, listening to the silence, is basic to McCone's methods, a fact that the understandably rattled detective seems to have forgotten. Staying attentive to the unsaid does prove productive. However, at the same time, these ellipses symptomatically mark the demand McCone makes to the Other throughout the novel, a demand that must finally encounter the emptiness of the Other's desire. In other words, this demand for the "truth" about herself, the revelation "behind the silence," is itself strictly impossible.

Nevertheless, McCone will endeavor to put a name to this greater mystery. She begins her *nostos* (i.e., homecoming) proper by investigating the details of the Shoshone people. She finds there is not a great deal of consensus on the tribe; there remains a variety of stories regarding its nature and customs, often one conflicting the other. Not surprisingly, among these varied tales, she finds many attributes that she herself possesses. Dreams and visions, for example, figure prominently in their lifestyle and religion. As she relates, "This religion was said to foster courage, self-reliance, and wisdom. The Shoshones were skilled in dealing with life's problems in a difficult and often hostile environment" (*LTS* 67). The parallels between this and McCone's chosen lifestyle of the private detective are clear. With help from her brother John, who unearths great-grandma Mary's marriage certificate somewhere within all the papers in their father's garage, Sharon is able to identify that her great-aunt Fenella was born on the Flathead Reservation in Montana, where her great-grandmother Mary also lived her "native" life before moving to Flagstaff, Arizona, and becoming a good Catholic.

With this new intelligence in hand, McCone journeys to the reservation where she is directed to Elwood Farmer, a man who knew both Fenella and Mary. She arrives feeling very much out of place, yet knowing that she actually has a quite intimate kinship with the Flathead Reservation. While she has no problems striking up a rapport with complete strangers in her work as an investigator, she senses that her interview with Farmer will be more difficult. It promises to be "deeply personal, perhaps emotional on my side," as she says (*LTS* 77). She explains to Farmer that she is looking for information about her great-grandmother, Mary McCone. When Farmer asks why, Sharon offers the stumbling reply, "Because ... I need to know who I am?" The old man is disappointed by this and he asks the detective simply: "You don't know who you are?" (*LTS* 80–81). After Sharon again fumbles for an adequate response, he tells her to return tomorrow when she has her thoughts in order. The "authentic" native refuses to play any part in McCone's search for origins, just as he challenges her assumption that there is a "true self" to be found there on the reservation. In this way, his comments criticize the poor ethnography that Sharon has made use of to imagine her true identity existing somewhere "out there" among "her people."

Indeed, Sharon discovers that "family" and "self" have quite different definitions on the reservation. Discussing family bonds, Farmer later explains to her, "Our family relationships aren't as clear-cut as whites,' or as formal" (*LTS* 100). Everyone on the reservation is a relative, in a sense. This connection to others startles McCone, who reasons, "While I wasn't exactly a loner, I kept my own family at arm's length and my close friends to fewer than a dozen. Now, by virtue of blood, any number of people might be able to lay claim to me" (*LTS* 101). While she was content with finding "her" family — a narcissistic endeavor, to be sure — she is uncomfortable with less defined kinship. The native structure of family refuses the place McCone sought, further ensuring the experience of the not-at-home that is the order of the day.

Importantly, at the center of these uncanny relations is storytelling, a practice that figures prominently in the Shoshone community. As is always the case, storytelling allows individual experiences to become collective experiences, thereby binding the people together, a practice that makes McCone, the lone wolf operative, all the more uneasy. In his essay "The Storyteller," Benjamin speaks of story's power to unite communities in ways quite different from modern, instrumentalized relations. A story does not transmit information, which is inhuman or uninhabitable. Rather, storytelling connects individuals through shared experience and the transmission of practical knowledge. For Benjamin, stories refuse reduction to "use value" as is demanded of information. The addressee of such information can only be an isolated individual cut off from the social — much like a cog in a greater machine. On the contrary, stories strike the listener most deeply when they possess a "chaste compactness which precludes psychological analysis," a condition that blurs the distinction between memory and forgetting: "The more self-forgetful the listener is, the more deeply is what he listens to impressed upon his memory."[103]

This self-erasure is crucial to Benjamin's insistence on the relation between storytelling and death. As he writes, "Death is the sanction of everything that the storyteller can tell. He has borrowed his authority from death. In other words, it is natural history to which his stories refer back."[104] This "natural history" of life and death underwrites all that the storyteller relates and holds the listener under the spell of narratives that far exceed their own experience. As was the case for Caruth, this "natural history" might be thought of as the traumatic encounter with the impossibility of our own survival. However, for Benjamin, storytelling, and the community that this practice builds, fares far better in the face of this suffering by binding people together through its shared experience. *Arabian Nights* illustrates this purpose all too well, as its story, like all storytelling, always endeavors to hold death at bay, if only for one more night.

As detective, the quintessential figure of the Western individual, McCone is clearly not adept at such forgetting. Indeed, psychological analysis of others is the very compass through which McCone positions herself. The relations among the Native Americans again cast doubt on the plausibility of her quest, as these associations are based upon the amorphous power of storytelling that blurs sharp distinctions between individuals. In fact, "identity," at least as McCone understands it, seems to be out of place on the reservation. Will Camphouse, a local (and therefore a potential relative) who helped her contact Elwood Farmer, assures her that there are more important things than this Western concept of self (*LTS* 106).

During their initial conversation, Elwood Farmer gives McCone a photograph picturing a number of women from the reservation, including Fenella McCone, Shaskin Hunter, and a strange white man. As she later dis-

Four. Remembering, Repeating, and Working Through

covers, the latter is Austin DeCarlo, the son of Joseph Decarlo, a well-known rancher. Further investigation indicates that it is likely that the younger DeCarlo is her actual father, a fact that seems all but assured after Joseph DeCarlo and his security man run her off the DeCarlo ranch when McCone arrives and inquires about Austin. When McCone does finally meet up with Austin DeCarlo, he admits that Shaskin is her mother — the resemblance makes this fact unmistakable — and he shares the story of their time together. When traveling around the country during his wayward youth, Austin had fallen in love with Shaskin and lived on the reservation with her until Joseph DeCarlo, unhappy with his son's dalliances, forced him to return home. The generic import of this act of force is unmistakable, serving as it does to characterize the elder DeCarlo as the bad father typical of hard-boiled fiction. Not surprisingly, the son relents to his father's wishes.

Like Elwood Farmer, Shaskin Hunter, Sharon's birth mother, was educated away from the reservation. After earning a law degree, she came home to open her practice, advocating the rights of Native Americans in Boise, Idaho. The ongoing antagonism between Shaskin and Austin DeCarlo is appropriately figured in a dispute over land. DeCarlo is attempting to develop a plot of land near a small town called Sage Rock, while Shaskin, working on behalf of members of the Medoc tribe, is directing a suit trying to have the development shut down. Acquiring this and other information, McCone heads to Sage Rock to meet her mother, but before the two get a chance to speak, Shaskin is severely injured in a hit-and-run accident. The mother is left in a coma, fading in and out of consciousness. While at her bedside, McCone is given a clue that leads her to the small abandoned Indian town, Cinder Cone.

Cinder Cone was a small Indian settlement that had been abandoned shortly before World War II. It is adjacent to a stretch of desolate lava flats, the area that Austin DeCarlo's real estate firm is interested in developing. Sharon visits the derelict town with Hy Rypinski, looking for what she does not know. During their search, they discover an old boarded-up house that immediately strikes Sharon as significant, even connected with her in some strange way. As they look through the empty house, they find evidence that it had been vacated quickly. An RCA record of the "Theme from *Picnic*," a song that dates to the mid-fifties, leaves no doubts that the house was inhabited after the war, even if the town was not. Like so many of the spaces that she unearths, this house possesses a sadness that seems beyond words. "The atmosphere in the house was more oppressive now: loneliness and abandonment and more. I couldn't shake the notion that something bad had happened here — so bad that even the passage of decades couldn't eradicate its emotional traces" (*LTS* 245). The traumatic pull of this space is clear. However, McCone remains unsure what this means. When McCone returns to Sage Rock, she takes the time to call her Aunt Susan and Uncle Jim to ask them if they recalled Fenella mentioning the Cinder Cone. The dread McCone felt when visiting the place is felt by her Uncle Jim, as well. Though he can't quite describe what it is about the name that is haunting, he claims that the very name of the place gives him an odd sense, like when "you wake from a bad dream and can't remember what it was about, but there's an aura that lingers" (*LTS* 252). Of course, McCone understands exactly what he means.

This sense of dread of course speaks of a trauma shared by her family that occurred in that house in Cinder Cone. Returning to the house after reviewing the telling "silences" of the accounts that surround it, Sharon finds belongings that indicate that Shaskin and her uncle, Raymond Hunter, had been staying there—presumably the house is the very site where her father and mother were split apart by Joseph DeCarlo. As McCone leaves, she remembers an abandoned pick-up truck near the property that she had thought significant when she saw it during her first visit. Looking over the wreck, she finds a registration card belonging to Raymond Hunter on the steering column, and, in a cave cut out of the lava formation a short distance away, she finds a skeleton that can only be that of her great-uncle.

On the drive home, she is apprehended at gunpoint by Jimmy D. Bearpaw, a local who is working for DeCarlo, and brought back to the abandoned house where she is finally confronted by Joseph DeCarlo himself. DeCarlo explains his position to McCone with the murderous bravado typical of his character type. As Sharon recounts, to him, she is not even human, "merely some strange hybrid created by the tainting of his family's blood" (*LTS* 299). She is, then, both to her real and adopted family, a contagion, a figure that is frequently referenced throughout the novel (and the larger series). This emphasis serves a compelling reversal of the standard hard-boiled narrative in which the detective works to stave off contagion at all costs, a modification that is perhaps necessary as McCone has become the object of her own search.[105] As contagion, her confrontation with Joseph DeCarlo, the plundering father, serves as a sort of confrontation with the paternal figures of the hard-boiled motif of inheritance (i.e., "good" and "bad" fathers). DeCarlo laments his strained relationship with his son, speaking ill of Austin's "lack of backbone" (*LTS* 300). He admits to killing Ray Hunter, Sharon's great-uncle, and hiding his body in the lava fields, but he claims that this was in self-defense after Shaskin and her uncle attacked him. In the confusion, Shaskin had run away, never to be seen by DeCarlo again. (Using the knowledge of this murder, Fenella had blackmailed DeCarlo for money to put Shaskin through school.) Sharon suspects that he is behind the Medoc bid to keep the land around Cinder Cone undeveloped, so that the body would not be discovered, allowing his son to piece all of the information together.

However, at this point, DeCarlo gives McCone a surprise: Austin has known of the murder all along. He had found Shaskin a year after the tragic events and, given the change in his behavior after this, Joseph DeCarlo could only conclude that his son had discovered the truth. For years thereafter, Austin had tried to coax a confession out of his father. The land deal around Cinder Cone is just a more recent example of this. In the end, the old man is incapable of killing McCone. Just as he is about to give up his gun to the detective, his son, Austin DeCarlo, breaks down the door and shoots his father once in the chest with a shotgun. Though he will later reason that he did this to save McCone, Sharon knows that this is a fantasy that she will let him confront on his own. As she says, "There are times when the truth must be repressed so that living can go on living, and this was one of them" (*LTS* 309). Like so much of this text, this reprieve seems to betray McCone's basic procedure of confronting the trauma of history found elsewhere in the series. (In the terms used above, this is to support the fantasy of a completed Other, which does not therefore implicate our desire.) This apparent departure becomes all the more complicated when Sharon discovers that Elwood Farmer is her actual father.

Before Sharon comes to this realization, she confronts her biological mother, who has regained consciousness in the hospital and is steadily improving. The encounter is punctuated with all the requisite silences and reproaches, much like McCone's confrontation with her (adopted) mother at the beginning of the novel. At one point, McCone attempts to pull her hand from her mother's grasp, but at that moment she finds that she cannot move, her hand remaining "a limp, unfeeling lump of flesh and bone" (*LTS* 316). This symptomatic response of hysterical paralysis is the perfect figure for "family" relations as these are presented in *Listen to the Silence*. Between mother and daughter there remains only an unformed mass of flesh and bone that exceeds either individual. Incapable of being named or accounted for—or excised, for that matter—this traumatic flesh is the bond of life itself, a connection that marks our uncanny relation to the other and history, as such. In this way, even the biological discourse that has informed McCone's quest for origins must prove to be a failed metaphor, inadequate to deliver on the detective's original hopes. Recognizing this, mother and daughter decide to be "friends" (*LTS* 318).

Though this position is perhaps more difficult to defend, I would like to argue that the same uncanny excess undermines McCone's reconciliation with her real father, Elwood Farmer. In other words, the identity that the detective seeks in this reunion is not entirely underwritten according to its biological determination. When McCone pays Farmer one last visit, she admits that she is no longer concerned with such clear-cut family relations.

However, she still wonders why Farmer did not tell her that he was her father to spare her the circuitous path of her investigation. He responds that he himself did not know that he had a daughter until McCone had walked through his door that afternoon. He admits that he and Shaskin "comforted" each other after each lost a significant other (Austin DeCarlo for Shaskin; Barbara Teton for Farmer). However, when Shaskin went into hiding after DeCarlo killed her uncle, Farmer lost touch with her and therefore could not have known that he was the father of her child — though he admits suspecting this. Much like Sharon's encounter with her mother, there comes a point in the conversation where Sharon and father must decide how they will conceptualize their connection, and the two seem to settle on a somewhat more traditional father and daughter relationship. As Farmer admits, "I've always wanted a child, someone I could pass on the old ways and traditions to," and McCone assures him that she needs "a father who can help me understand them" (*LTS* 329). After this is decided, Elwood suggests that McCone return tomorrow after they have each collected their thoughts.

While McCone does on the one hand reconcile with her biological father, parentage in this case is largely coincidental. Far from being the fantasized father that McCone seeks (i.e., neither affectionately following his daughter's life from a distance, nor remorselessly ignoring his daughter's existence for years), Elwood Farmer has no idea that he is a father. Both father and daughter, then, are very consciously performing these roles as roles in this interaction. Though the notion of a father "passing down the old ways" perhaps comes dangerously close to the poor ethnography for which Farmer had chastised McCone, their conversation ends with a wink given by the old man. The gesture is clearly affectionate, but so too does it seem to offer a criticism of the scripted relations that their conversation had played upon. Farmer will not give McCone the truth about herself, her people, or even the "old ways," as he promises. Rather, what Farmer seems to offer is a bond to others through the process of storytelling. Far from eradicating the "unfeeling lump of flesh and bone" that comes between our relations with others, this bond of story confronts us with the intimacy of this very distance.

Conclusion

To conclude, I would like to return to the theory of reading, and the desupposition of knowledge, that is suggested in Lacan's discourse of the hysteric. As Lacan repeated throughout his seminar, "beware of understanding," a warning that cautions us always to attend to the signifier.[106] Understanding, predicated as it is upon textual closure and a fantasy of mastery, is precisely what cannot abide the shifting nature of the signifier, which always says "something more," as Muller's McCone recognizes. If we are to read well, in either an analytic or literary setting, we must be attentive to the abyssal nature of this supplement, that phantom *a* that drives the hysteric's discourse. As discussed in previous chapters, to read seeking mastery, or "understanding," is to read at the level of demand, a process that assumes an object (be it knowledge, recognition, etc.) that might satisfy the Other. While the hysteric is constantly engaged in the act of reading desire (and thereby embodying such an object of satisfaction), this is always executed with an ambiguity that is perfectly willing to fail. It is this sort of reading, between mastery and poetry, to which the hysteric is privy.[107] The dissonance of her discourse always demands knowledge at the same time that it strives to reveal the masquerade of all knowledge.[108]

In this split gesture, the hysteric marks the literary turn of psychoanalytic interpretation. As Wajcman writes:

> What can be seen from her [the hysteric's] history, then, is not only that the hysteric resists being apprehended as an object of science, but that she cannot serve as such an object because the knowledge she embodies is precisely unknowable. Freud's identification with the hysteric has more than biographical relevance: by putting himself in her place, his knowledge about her was produced like a symptom — a knowledge speaking by itself. Knowledge *about* the hysteric is the knowledge of the hysteric.[109]

The hysteric is the necessary interlocutor of psychoanalysis because she occupies, along with literature, that extimate position of knowledge addressed by psychoanalysis. This is the space of the "fault, hole, or loss" within the Other's locus, indicated in the graph of the hysteric's discourse with the letter *a*.[110] To confront this "hole" is to enter into the realm of the hysteric, which is precisely what Wajcman intends when he says that "Knowledge *about* the hysteric is the knowledge of the hysteric." The hysteric's own interrogation of that space is an action that is inevitably carried out with ulterior motives that seek to reveal the Master — and signifier, as well — as lacking. In this way, the hysteric offers the possibility of a "desupposition" of knowledge, and a reading beyond demand insofar as this is possible.

Lacan himself briefly offers such a theory of reading in *Seminar XX*, speaking of Nancy and Lacoue-Labarthe's reading of his own text, "The Seminar on 'The Purloined Letter.'"[111] He claims that he has never, not by his best adherents, been so "well read — with so much love."[112] Why do they read Lacan so well? Because they "de-suppose" his knowledge. "And why not?" asks Lacan, "Why not, if it turns out that that must be the condition for what I call reading? After all, what can I presume Aristotle knew? Perhaps the less I assume he has knowledge, the better I read him."[113] Leaving the "if" in abeyance here,

Fink's reading of reading well (and of this passage in particular) is based on just this suspicion. As he writes, "Perhaps hate is the condition for a serious reading.... If that is the condition, it had better be preceded by a prolonged period in which the reader loves the author and presumes him or her to have knowledge."[114] I take Fink's proviso here as an expression of the impossibility of a radical desupposition of knowledge. (If I assume a text is utter "nonsense," I have reduced it to a category of knowledge, but I have not "read.") Love must always precede hate and no doubt continue to linger even after the courtship has ended.

In several respects, this is the hysteric's response to the "either/or" of the criticism of the female hard-boiled detective read above. As the hysteric methodology of Muller's McCone indicates so well, the detective is neither fully duped nor fully liberated (nor fully equal to herself). Rather, her *modus operandi* responds to this over-determined choice with a conjunctive "and," which is to say that her reading of love and hate — as Lacan phrases it — both advances and unveils the position of the Master.[115] Sharon McCone, as hysterical reader, embodies just this ambiguity with respect to the position of mastery. Her unwavering attention to the split nature of subject and object repeats the traumatic missed relation to this other space. In so doing, the object (as *objet a*) relentlessly speaks though remains unheard, thereby repeating the trauma of survival. McCone's work reveals the consonance of this hysteric insight with the knowledge of psychoanalysis, an insight that never ceases being posed in her unanswerable question that always exposes "something more."

Afterword

The "*encore!*" in the title of Lacan's *Seminar XX* suggests a number of things. This call for "more!" or "again!" is on the one hand a demand for pleasure beyond the law, a bid that evokes epistemological consequences, as well. Regarding the latter, we might take this as a call for more interpretation, a request that is so frequently made by the patient who remains discontent with the master's (i.e., analyst's) explanation. At the same time, this *encore!* serves as a caution regarding the "beyond" that is always suggested in the appeal for further interpretation.[1] Such a plea will surely reveal the limits of authority. However, it necessarily assumes a greater authority, waiting in some other scene. The hysteric subject remains at this impasse. Though she "knows without knowing," the challenge of her implacable demand is sure to reveal that authority has only words to play with, as it were. It is with this sentiment that I would like to conclude this project.

This hysteric challenge is, I would like to suggest, a suitable way to understand the odd aspect of detective fiction as serial literature, particularly as it is so frequently portrayed as conservative, escapist fare. The argument is by now well known. The detective story begins from the point of Eden, and then suspends this tranquility so that the expert detective might thwart this disruption of knowledge. The reader, then, takes pleasure in the possibility of "things as they are" remaining just that, "things as they are." However, if the detective is to take up the chase again, it is necessary to show that Eden re-won was contingent rather than necessary. Accordingly, knowledge must be defended, repeatedly, a requirement that necessarily denies the possibility that the detective wields a "complete" knowledge.

It is this odd divide (i.e., between certainty and doubt) that has vivified detective fiction from its origins. It should be remembered that this time was marked by the rise of "information," as well as the ascendancy of the discourse of science as the measure of experience. The new metropolis was awash in a sea of data, making it necessary to create an ideal reader capable of mastering and, thus, humanizing this mass. The detective offers this possibility, but this fantasy of course belies the anxiety at its foundation. While this anxiety might be read as the apprehension of disorder, even chaos, this study has argued that the greater fear is that experience might actually be reduced to the knowledge of science. The reader of detective fiction reads not to "tie up loose ends," but rather to make certain that these remain.

In the manner of the hysteric, then, the reader of detective fiction both draws out the master with a faith in interpretative power, while at the same time refusing the possibility that such interpretation will hit its mark. To these ends, we always read detective fiction *encore!* That is, the demand is always for more interpretation, and the failure of interpretation — and, of course, a more capable interpreter.[2] As I have argued, this split gesture remains at the heart of detective fiction. Reading the genre as it develops over the course of the twentieth century, we consequently find a compelling archive of the breakdown of symbolic efficiency and paternal authority. I would argue that the insight of hard-boiled detective fiction on these matters is all the more important today. This is particularly true as so much crime fiction invokes the possibilities of contemporary forensic sciences, indulging in various imagining and identificatory technologies that promise solution without the perniciousness of doubt. In the context of these invasive practices, the hard-boiled mode provides a welcome platform where knowledge might fail.

In articulating the failure of the detective's knowledge, I have read numerous fictional works alongside psychoanalytic texts. However, it was not my intention to reduce detective fiction to the knowledge of analysis, nor was it my intention to illuminate the detective's failure through analytic insight. Speaking of the dangers of applied psychoanalysis and revisiting Freud's frequent use of the metaphor of archeology, Nobus and Quinn present the following distinction:

> For the archaeologist, reconstruction is the primary end in view insofar as she wishes to build an approximation of vanished intersubjective relations out of inert shards of pottery and scattered fragments of bone. The task of the psychoanalyst is almost exactly the opposite; that is, to employ construction in order to expose the lack of cognitive destination and an intersubjective dimension for unconscious knowledge.[3]

The letter thus arrives at its destination, although, as suggested here, this cannot be reduced to teleology. In other words, the subject's narrative coherence is reduced to nonsense by the disruption of the unconscious. Here, one recalls two mottos offered by Poe in his detective stories: "Truth is not always in a well," taken from "The Murders in the Rue Morgue," and the epigraph to "The Purloined Letter," from Seneca, "Nothing is so hateful to wisdom as too much cunning."⁴ In each case, we are cautioned to avoid the lures of depth and meaning. While this is the lesson of the letter, and psychoanalysis generally, we might take this as a comment on applied psychoanalysis, as well. In applying analysis to excavate the hidden truth of a text, or the hidden correspondence of a given discourse with psychoanalysis, we are too cunning. The anti-epistemology of psychoanalysis asks us to confront the ultimate senselessness of such accounts that promise truth (or correspondence) down below — in a well or elsewhere. Attentive to this inevitability, Nobus and Quinn conclude, "Failure and the fall of knowledge are thus the necessary and unwelcome contribution of psychoanalysis to the spirit of epistemological enquiry."⁵

In the ruins of sense, and in lieu of interpretation, Lacan proposes the possibility of poetry, or literature. Fiction, it seems, is a more appropriate way to encounter the object-cause: "Only poetry, as I've said to you, permits interpretation."⁶ As André explains,

> In contrast to the fraudulence of meaning, [Lacan] says, there is poetry, which can accomplish the feat of making a meaning absent. He invites his audience to find in poetry what psychoanalytic interpretation can hope to be. Instead of looking for a new signifier to replace the hole left in the unconscious by the lack of [the Other], the analyst should respond with "an empty word," modeled on poetry, "that is a meaning effect but also a hole-effect."⁷

Returning to the issue of the kinship of the detective and the analyst, if these figures are alike in any significant way, it is because they confront the *objet a*, that abyssal point of non-origin within the subject, with literature itself. Neither interpreter offers the definitive *it*, unveiled at last from the deceptive covering of history. Rather than origin, or cause for effects, the detective and the analyst confront us with the paradoxical logic of the object-cause, which we are then invited to "subjectify," with a poem that both writes and erases — much like detective fiction that both deciphers and equivocates.

Notes

Introduction

1. Quoted in Peter Brooks, *Reading for the Plot: Design and Intention in Narrative* (New York: Alfred A. Knopf, 1987), 269.
2. Sigmund Freud, *Introductory Lectures on Psychoanalysis*, ed. and trans. James Strachey (New York and London: W. W. Norton, 1966), 27.
3. Quoted in Ronald Thomas, *Detective Fiction and the Rise of Forensic Science* (Cambridge: Cambridge University Press, 1999), 32–33.
4. For an elaboration of the distinction between Freud's early and late work, see Paul Verhaeghe, *Does the Woman Exist? From Freud's Hysteric to Lacan's Feminine*, trans. Marc du Ry (New York: Other Press, 1999), 21–32. Peter Brooks has provided a brief introduction to a psychoanalytic reading of Conan Doyle's detective fiction according to such a genealogy. See his *Psychoanalysis and Storytelling* (Oxford: Blackwell, 1994), 61–64.
5. Cawelti nicely summarizes this basic comparison as it appears within criticism: "The curious analogy between the process of dream interpretation and that of detection as represented in the classical formula can be summarized as follows: a brilliant investigator (Dupin, Freud) is confronted with a series of material clues (footprints, tufts of hair, dream symbols, slips of the tongue) that if properly interpreted are signs of a deeply hidden and disturbing truth." See: John Cawelti, *Adventure, Mystery, and Romance: Formula Stories as Art and Popular Culture* (Chicago: University of Chicago Press, 1976), 95.
6. Dany Nobus, "Illiterature," in *Re-Inventing the Symptom: Essays on the Final Lacan*, ed. Luke Thurston (New York: Other Press, 2002), 25.
7. Ibid.
8. Shoshana Felman, "To Open the Question," in *Literature and Psychoanalysis: The Question of Reading: Otherwise* (Baltimore: Johns Hopkins University Press, 1982), 5–10.
9. Ibid., 9–10.
10. Joël Dor, *The Clinical Lacan* (New York: Other Press, 1999), 5–6.
11. Ibid.
12. See Bruce Fink, *A Clinical Introduction to Lacanian Psychoanalysis: Theory and Technique* (Cambridge, MA: Harvard University Press, 1997), 131–134.
13. William V. Spanos, "The Detective and the Boundary: Some Notes on the Postmodern Literary Imagination." *Boundary 2: A Journal of Postmodern Literature* 1.1 (Fall 1972): 54.

Chapter One

1. Arthur Conan Doyle, *The Complete Sherlock Holmes* (New York: Barnes and Noble, 1992), 423. Hereafter, references will be cited in text with the abbreviation, *CSH*.
2. One sees both "classic" and "classical" used to describe the stories of Poe and Conan Doyle, as well as the so-called "Golden Age" of detection during the 1920s and 1930s. Agatha Christie, Dorothy Sayers, and John Dickson Carr, for example, represent the latter time period. Of the many characteristics common to this genealogy, a focus on the use of reason to solve the puzzle of the crime (especially a murder) and answer the question of "whodunit?" rank above others. For an in-depth discussion of this history, see Chapter 5 of John Cawelti's *Adventure, Mystery, and Romance: Formula Stories as Art and Popular Culture* (Chicago: University of Chicago Press, 1976), 106–138.
3. Todorov's terms draw from the Russian

Formalist's *sjuzet* and *fabula*. To avoid the confusion of using these or other untranslated terms, I will use "story" and "plot" throughout this study. Peter Brooks' well-known essay "Freud's Masterplot: Questions of Narrative" is an excellent psychoanalytic reading of the questions suggested by this narrative division. Peter Brooks, "Freud's Masterplot: Questions of Narrative," in *Literature and Psychoanalysis: The Question of Reading: Otherwise*, ed. Shoshana Felman (Baltimore and London: Johns Hopkins University Press, 1982), 280–300.

4. Tzvetan Todorov, "The Typology of Detective Fiction" in *The Poetics of Prose* (Ithaca, NY: Cornell University Press, 1977), 46.

5. Ibid.

6. Whenever the issue of the palliative pleasure of detective fiction is raised, it is customary to note that during the London *blitzkrieg*, Londoners seeking refuge in the tunnels of the Underground would read Conan Doyle's Sherlock Holmes stories.

7. Jacques Barzun, "Detection and the Literary Art," in *The Mystery Writer's Art*, ed. Francis Nevins, Jr. (Bowling Green, OH: Bowling Green University Press, 1970), 248–262. As we shall find, detective fiction is the "romance" of reason in another sense, as well. That is, in the "uncanny" sense the term conveyed to authors like Hawthorne—or Poe.

8. This issue brings up the heart of the debate surrounding all genre literature. Is it possible to develop the formula without betraying it? As Todorov summarizes such logic: "Detective fiction has its norms; to 'develop' them is to disappoint them: to 'improve upon' detective fiction is to write 'literature,' not detective fiction." See: Todorov, "The Typology of Detective Fiction," 43. These issues will become especially important to my discussion of the female hard-boiled detective in Chapter Four.

9. Ibid., 47.

10. Ibid.

11. Ibid.

12. Ibid.

13. Ibid.

14. Edgar Allan Poe, *The Complete Tales and Poems of Edgar Allan Poe* (New York: Vintage, 1975), 144. Hereafter, references will appear in text under the abbreviation, *CEAP*.

15. As Derrida writes, "The center is at the center of the totality, and yet, since the center does not belong to the totality (is not part of the totality), the totality *has its center elsewhere*.... The concept of a centered structure is in fact the concept of a play based on a fundamental ground, a play constituted on the basis of the fundamental immobility and a reassuring certitude, which is itself beyond the reach of free play." Italics in original. See Jacques Derrida, *Writing and Difference*, trans. Alan Bass (Chicago: University of Chicago Press, 1978), 279.

16. See Austin R. Freeman, "The Art of the Detective Story," in *The Art of the Mystery Story: A Collection of Critical Essays*, ed. Howard Haycraft (New York: Simon and Schuster, 1946), 11.

17. See rules 5, 8, 14, and 1, respectively. S. S. Van Dine, "Twenty Rules for Writing Detective Stories," in Haycraft, *The Art of the Mystery Story*, 189–191.

18. For an excellent discussion of the history of this in respect to detective fiction, see Ronald Thomas, *Detective Fiction and the Rise of Forensic Science* (Cambridge: Cambridge University Press, 1999).

19. Van Dine, "Twenty Rules," 192.

20. Ibid.

21. The latter is a general rule of the genre for Dine and not therefore limited solely to the detective. The entirety of rule three humorously reads: "There must be no love interest. The business in hand is to bring a criminal to the bar of justice, not to bring a lovelorn couple to the hymeneal altar" ibid., 190.

22. Given the publication of Agatha Christie's *The Murder of Roger Ackroyd* (1926) only two years prior to Dine's essay, rule four reads as a purist response to both Christie and the audience that embraced this work.

23. This is not to say we are not given many intriguing, yet brief, pieces of insight into these questions throughout Conan Doyle's opus. However, the adventures of Sherlock Holmes certainly cannot be described as an extended reflection on the character of the detective. Indeed, one of the greatest tasks of Sherlockians is to conjecture on details of Holmes' personal life and history.

24. Walter Benjamin, *The Paris of the Second Empire in Baudelaire*, quoted in Ronald Thomas, "Arresting Images in *Bleak House* and *The House of the Seven Gables*," *Novel: A Forum on Fiction* 31:1 (Autumn 1997): 87.

25. See William V. Spanos, "The Detective and the Boundary: Some Notes on the Postmodern Literary Imagination," *Boundary 2: A Journal of Postmodern Literature* 1.1 (Fall 1972): 150.

26. Lacan later formulates this insight: "What comes under the effect of repression returns, for repression and the return of the repressed are just the two sides of the same coin. The repressed is always there, expressed in a perfectly articulate manner in symptoms and a host of other phenomena." See Jacques Lacan, *The Seminar of Jacques Lacan: Book III: The Psychoses, 1955-1956*, ed. Jacques-Alain Miller, trans. Russell Grigg (New York: W. W. Norton, 1993), 12.

27. Michel Foucault, *Discipline and Punish: The Birth of the Prison* (New York: Vintage Books, 1977), 140.
28. Ibid., 220.
29. Ibid., 205.
30. The Sûreté Nationale was founded in 1812 by the former criminal Eugène François Vidocq. It quickly became the model for other intelligence agencies throughout the world. Vidocq's memoirs provide an interesting supplement to detective fiction. Eugène François Vidocq, *Memoirs of Vidocq: Master of Crime* (Edinburgh and London: AK Press, 2003). For a discussion of Vidocq's influence on detective fiction, see Charles Rzepka, *Detective Fiction* (Cambridge: Polity Press, 2005), 59–62.
31. Foucault, *Discipline and Punish*, 184–185.
32. This is said in "The Red-Headed League." Though the detective is referring to geographical knowledge, it is clear that the scope of his knowledge stretches far beyond this limit. I will discuss this story near the conclusion of the current chapter.
33. Foucault, *Discipline and Punish*, 191.
34. Ibid., 192.
35. Franco Moretti, "Clues," in *Popular Fiction: Technology, Ideology, Production, Reading*, ed. Tony Bennett (London and New York: Routledge, 1990), 246.
36. Regarding the issue of the "victim," Moretti points out that in a Sherlock Holmes story, a victim is frequently targeted for past transgressions. The victim is doubly individual in this sense: She or he stepped outside of the stereotype in life and death. Ibid., 240–241.
37. Ibid., 246.
38. Ibid., 248.
39. Ibid., 249.
40. Ibid.
41. Ibid.
42. Ibid.
43. Cuvier's interest in the issue of extinction is another tantalizing detail that supports reading his work as an analogy for the work of the detective. Searching through the clues of the fossil record, Cuvier imagined it was possible to discern the complete story of a lost species, quite literally from beginning to end.
44. To anticipate a later discussion, it should be indicated that Freud frequently likened the practice of psychoanalysis to that of archeology, another discipline that owes its origins to the nineteenth century.
45. See Cuvier's *Discourse on the Revolutionary Upheavals on the Surface of the Globe and on the Changes Which They Have Produced in the Animal Kingdom*. Online Document. www.victorianweb.org/science/science_texts/cuvier/cuvier-e.htm.
46. This reversal of expectations recalls the murders committed by the orangutan in Poe's "The Murders at the Rue Morgue," though Conan Doyle's story lacks the racial elements of Poe's tale. See Charles Rzepka's discussion of this issue in his *Detective Fiction*, 81–86.
47. Even the casual reader can, no doubt, imagine numerous exceptions to the rule that would present problems to the Holmes' reasoning. Perhaps the dog was sick or sleeping, etc.
48. Raymond Chandler, *The Simple Art of Murder* (New York: Ballantine Books, 1950), 5.
49. Poe's letter to Cooke is quoted in Bernd-Pete Lange, "The Detective as Genteel Chess Player: Poe, Conan Doyle, Dibdin," in *The Art of Murder: New Essays on Detective Fiction*, ed. Gustav H. Klaus and Stephen Knight (Tubingen: Stauffenburg Verlag, 1998), 53.
50. These quotations from Peirce appear in Nancy Harrowitz, "The Body of the Detective Model: Charles S. Peirce and Edgar Allan Poe," in *The Sign of Three: Dupin, Holmes, Peirce*, ed. Umberto Eco and Thomas Albert Sebeok (Bloomington: Indiana University Press, 1983), 181–182.
51. Quoted in ibid., 181 italics in orig.
52. Holmes is the greater defender of "science," speaking in its name repeatedly throughout the collected stories and novels. On the contrary, Dupin in several respects maintains more of the detective's gothic influences, a fact that is perhaps not so surprising given Poe's interest in this genre. This distinction between Dupin and Holmes will be discussed at greater length below. For a lengthier discussion of Poe's gothic lineage see: Tony Magistrale and Sidney Poger, *Poe's Children: Connections Between Tales of Terror and Detection* (New York: Peter Lang, 1999).
53. Thomas Sebeok and Jean Umiker-Sebeok, "'You Know My Method': A Juxtaposition of Charles S. Peirce and Sherlock Holmes," in Eco and Sebeok, *The Sign of Three*, 22.
54. On this note, Sebeok and Umiker-Sebeok cite Trevor Hall's brilliant assertion that Holmes' chemical experiments were never themselves of importance beyond the reconfirmation of the action and reaction of a properly functioning causality. These experiments were to "keep him [Holmes] in practical touch with an exact science where cause and effect, action and reaction, followed each other with a predictability beyond the power of the less precise 'science of deduction' to achieve, however hard he might strive toward exactitude in his profession." Qtd. in ibid., 41. The necessity of this exercise should

be clear given the perversion of causality that is at the heart of Holmes' enterprise.

55. As Sebeok shows, all the celebrated Holmesian methods that utilize the observation of bootlaces, shirt cuffs and so forth, were demonstrated by Dr. Bell to his amazed students, Conan Doyle included. The latter was, apparently, quite canny regarding this inspiration, as *The Adventures of Sherlock Holmes* was inscribed to Conan Doyle's former professor. See Sebeok and Umiker-Sebeok, "You Know My Method," 28–46. As Shepherd indicates, Sherlockian societies have been, and no doubt remain, most popular among physicians. See: Michael Shepherd, *Sherlock Holmes and the Case of Dr. Freud* (London and New York: Tavistock Publications, 1985).

56. Seobok and Umiker-Seobok, "You Know My Method," 30.

57. See Carlos Ginzberg, "Morelli, Freud and Sherlock Holmes: Clues and Scientific Method." in Eco and Sebeok, *The Sign of Three*, 81–118.

58. Ibid., 109.

59. Ibid., 92. As Ginzberg suggests, Galileo's science might be summarized with the scholastic saying, "individuum est ineffabile" (we can know nothing of the individual)." Ibid. Of course, for the detective, it is just the opposite — we can know everything of the individual.

60. Ibid., 111.

61. Sebeok and Umiker-Sebeok, "You Know My Method," 47. Watson's use of "necromancer" to describe Holmes can be found in "Study in Scarlet," in *CSH* 23.

62. Such abridged "action" sequences are commonplace in the Holmes stories, a fact that underscores the greater narrative preoccupation with the thought process itself within the classical detective text.

63. This literal name seems to indicate, as later Holmes stories will make clear, that Conan Doyle was well aware of the fantastic nature of his detective, a situation that certainly called for irony such as this.

64. Of course, I recognize the anachronism of moving from Conan Doyle's work back to Poe's fiction, which preceded the former by forty-some years.

65. Conan Doyle's interest in the supernatural is well documented and was even the subject of the film *Fairytale — A True Story* (1997). In 1922, Conan Doyle wrote *The Coming of the Fairies*, a book that expressed his support of the Cottingley Fairies and the supernatural in general. The Cottingley Fairies were supposedly living fairies photographed in the Yorkshire countryside by Elsie Wright and Frances Griffiths.

66. See Nicholas Meyer, *The Seven Percent Solution: Being a Reprint from the Reminiscences of John H. Watson, M.D.* (New York: E. P. Dutton & Co., 1977).

67. Dennis Porter, *The Pursuit of Crime: Art and Ideology in Detective Fiction* (New Haven, CT: Yale University Press, 1981), 220.

68. For example, see Dina Brand, "From the *Flâneur* to the Detective: Interpreting the City of Poe" in Bennett, *Popular Fiction*, 220–237. The thesis that Poe created the detective to stave off both his madness and that of the city is common enough. However, Brand's essay offers insight well beyond this claim.

69. Walter Benjamin, *Illuminations: Essays and Reflections*, trans. Harry Zohn (New York: Schocken Books, 1968), 174.

70. Bruyère's text performs the same operation of the narrator: it reduces types of individuals to their most basic elements, or characters. His work typically mocks the pretensions of the aristocracy and reveals the bankruptcy of the manners of the age.

71. See Brand, "From the *Flâneur* to the Detective," 226.

72. Ibid., 237.

73. Ibid.

74. This story is particularly revealing, as Poe himself hoped to solve the ongoing case of the Mary Cecilia Rogers murder in New York City in 1841 through Dupin's methods. For many years it was held that Poe succeeded at this, though there was no truth to this rumor. The revision of this misconception was a result of the publication of the following text: John Evangelist Walsh, *Poe the Detective: The Curious Circumstances Behind "The Mystery of Marie Roget"* (New Brunswick, NJ: Rutgers University Press, 1967).

75. See Harrowitz, "The Body of the Detective Model," 185.

76. The popularity of Sherlock Holmes is truly the beginning of modern series literature. From this perspective, an interesting reading of the mania surrounding "The Final Problem" develops. Martin Priestman claims that this response indicates the "raw power of seriesicity itself, flexing its emotional and financial muscles for the first time." See Martin Priestman, "Sherlock's Children: The Birth of the Series," in *The Art of Detective Fiction*, ed. Warren Chernaik, et al. (New York: St. Martins, 2000), 54.

77. Given this emphasis upon measurement, one is reminded of Copjec's claim that detective fiction as a genre is impossible before the rise of statistics as a diagnostic tool for the study of populations. In other words, detective fiction emerges with the rise of the actuary table. See Chapter Seven of Joan Copjec, *Read My Desire: Lacan Against the Historicists* (Cambridge, MA: MIT Press, 1994), 163–200.

78. Here again, see Magistrale and Poger, *Poe's Children*.

79. A later story, "The Adventure of the Illustrious Client" (1924), again features Watson and Holmes in an act of burglary. Here, too, it is a matter of a woman's (or women's) honor that is at stake.

80. See especially Jacques Derrida, "The Purveyor of Truth," and Barbara Johnson, "The Frame of Reference: Poe, Lacan, Derrida," in *The Purloined Poe: Lacan, Derrida, and Psychoanalytic Reading*, ed. John P. Muller and William J. Richardson (Baltimore: Johns Hopkins University Press, 1988), 173–212, 213–251.

81. Mladen Dolar, "I Shall Be with You on Your Wedding-Night: Lacan and the 'Uncanny,'" *October* 58 (1991), 7.

82. Ibid., 17.

83. Ibid.

84. Ibid.

85. Ibid., 20. Italics in orig.

86. See Bruce Fink, *The Lacanian Subject: Between Language and Jouissance* (Princeton, NJ: Princeton University Press, 1995), 140–141, 165–172.

87. Jacques Lacan, *The Seminar of Jacques Lacan: Book XI: The Four Fundamental Concepts of Psychoanalysis*, trans. Alan Sheridan (New York: W. W. Norton, 1977), 22. Hereafter, this text will be referred to as *Seminar XI*.

88. Sigmund Freud, "The 'Uncanny,'" in *Sigmund Freud: The Collected Papers, Vol. 4*, trans. Joan Riviere (New York: Basic Books, 1959), 376.

89. Jacques Lacan, *Écrits: The First Complete English Edition*, trans. Bruce Fink (New York: W. W. Norton, 2006), 76.

90. Ibid.

91. Freud, "The 'Uncanny,'" 387.

92. Ibid.

93. Ibid.

94. See Chapter Three in Magistrale and Poger, *Poe's Children*, 45–56.

95. In addition to Freud and literary criticism generally, Lacan also takes great pains to distinguish his reading of Poe from Marie Bonaparte's work. In 1933, Bonaparte published *The Life and Work of Edgar Allan Poe: A Psychoanalytic Interpretation*, with a preface written by Freud. This work is the sort of psychobiography that Lacan repudiates.

96. Jacques Lacan, "Seminar on 'The Purloined Letter,'" in *The Purloined Poe: Lacan, Derrida, and Psychoanalytic Reading*, ed. John P. Muller and William J. Richardson (Baltimore: Johns Hopkins University Press, 1988), 33. Subsequent references will appear in-text with the abbreviation *SPL*.

97. See Jacques Lacan, *The Seminar of Jacques Lacan: Book II: The Ego in Freud's Theory and in the Technique of Psychoanalysis, 1954-1955*, ed. Jacques-Alain Miller, trans. Sylvanna Tomaselli (New York: W. W. Norton, 1988), 175–205. (Henceforth, *Seminar II* in notes.)

98. As Lacan says plainly in his discussion of "The Purloined Letter" in *Seminar II*, "for each of them [i.e., the characters in the story] the letter is his unconscious." See Lacan's *Seminar II*, 197.

99. Jacques Lacan, "The Instance of the Letter in the Unconscious or Reason Since Freud," in *Écrits*, 418.

100. Ibid., 419.

101. See Ferdinand de Saussure, *Course in General Linguistics* (Chicago: Open Court, 1972).

102. Fortunately, this demonstration is typically reduced by critics — and by Lacan himself in the case of his reading of the game odds and evens — to only two terms as in the toss of a coin, heads or tails. See Bruce Fink, "The Nature of Unconscious Thought or Why No One Ever Reads Lacan's Postface to the 'Seminar on "The Purloined Letter,"'" in *Reading Seminars I and II: Lacan's Return to Freud*, ed. Richard Feldstein, Bruce Fink and Maire Jaanus (Albany, NY: State University of New York Press, 1996), 173–191. See also Lacan, *Seminar II*, 175–190.

103. Fink, "The Nature of Unconscious Thought," 182. My presentation of Lacan's experiment here is entirely indebted to Fink.

104. Ibid., 18–19.

105. Ibid., 186.

106. Lacan, *Seminar II*, 9.

107. Lacan, *Écrits*, 694.

108. In addition to describing the larger implications of Lacan's seminar on Poe as a whole, John Muller and William Richardson provide a thorough discussion of the structure of these repeated scenes in their "'The Purloined Letter': Overview," in Muller and Richardson, *The Purloined Poe*, 55–76.

109. Lacan, *Seminar II*, 180.

110. Ibid., 187.

111. Slavoj Žižek, *Looking Awry: An Introduction to Jacques Lacan through Popular Culture* (Cambridge, MA: MIT Press, 1991), 56–57.

112. Ibid., 54.

113. Copjec, *Read My Desire*, 177.

114. For a discussion of this concept in Lacan's thought, see Chapter Three in Dany Nobus, *Jacques Lacan and the Freudian Practice of Psychoanalysis* (London: Routledge, 2000), 106–153.

115. Žižek, *Looking Awry*, 59.

116. Ibid.

117. Slavoj Žižek, *Enjoy Your Symptom!*

Jacques Lacan in Hollywood and Out (New York and London: Routledge, 1992), 9–23.

118. Barbara Johnson, "The Frame of Reference: Poe, Lacan, Derrida," in Muller and Richardson, *The Purloined Poe*, 248.

119. Žižek, *Enjoy Your Symptom!*, 18–19.

120. Ibid., 19.

121. Ibid.

122. Ibid., 22.

123. Fink, "The Nature of Unconscious Thought," 185.

124. For an excellent discussion of these concepts in Lacan's work, see Paul Verhaeghe, "Teaching and Psychoanalysis: A Necessary Impossibility," in *Beyond Gender: From Subject to Drive* (New York: Other Press, 2001), 35–48.

125. Lacan, *Seminar II*, 103.

126. Jacques Lacan, *Television* (New York: W. W. Norton, 1990), 4.

127. Nobus, *Jacques Lacan and the Freudian Practice of Psychoanalysis*, 135.

128. Johnson, "The Frame of Reference," in Muller and Richardson, *The Purloined Poe*, 245.

129. Ibid. Italics in orig.

130. Žižek's discussion of the differences between classical and hard-boiled payment is helpful in this discussion. See Žižek, *Looking Awry*, 49–66.

131. For a reading of this development, see Chapter Two in Nobus, *Jacques Lacan and the Freudian Practice of Psychoanalysis*, 56–105.

132. Ibid., 70–71.

133. Jacques Lacan, *Seminar XI*, 20–23.

Chapter Two

1. Dashiell Hammett, *The Thin Man* (New York: Vintage Books, 1992), 201.

2. Importantly, Williams is also quick to state that he is "no knight errant." Writing years before Chandler, Daly acknowledged the potential "courtly" aspects of this new detective, a demeanor from which he wished to distance his detective. See Carroll John Daly, "The False Burton Combs" (1922), in *The Hard-Boiled Detective: Stories from Black Mask Magazine, 1920–1951*, ed. Herbert Ruhm (New York: Vintage Books, 1977), 3–20.

3. Regarding the latter, in "The False Burton Combs," Williams concedes that he takes a "straight" job with the paternal James B. Burton—whose son he has been impersonating—so that he might marry Marion St. James, the latter's testimony having acquitted him of murder. As he says at the story's conclusion, "That's all, unless to warn you that it would be kind of foolish to take too seriously anything I said about keeping clear of women" ibid., 30. The relation between Race Williams and the various paternal figures he encounters, as well as the mediating role this plays in his relations with women, deserves serious attention.

4. See Mickey Spillane. *Fan Letter to John Carroll Daly*. Online Document. http://www.thrillingdetective.com/trivia/triv29.html.

5. The passionate dislike of Spillane was so great as to prompt the assertion that the writer was responsible for the increased crime and moral decay in the early 1950s. For examples of this exaggerated criticism of Spillane, see, notably, Malcolm Cowley, "Sex Murder Incorporated," *New Republic* (11 Feb. 1952), 11–12, and Christopher La Farge, "Mickey Spillane and His Bloody Hammer," *Saturday Review* (6 Nov. 1954): 54–59.

6. Spillane, *Fan Letter to John Carroll Daly*.

7. The final Sherlock Holmes story to be published individually was "The Adventure of Shoscombe Old Place," published first in the U.S. magazine *Liberty* in March of 1927. The story was published in England a month later in *The Strand*.

8. Again, this is to dismiss Daly's work, as his *Snarl of the Beast* (1927) appears two years before Hammett's novel. For a more recent history of the genre that examines Daly's contribution, see Sean McCann, *Gumshoe America: Hard-Boiled Crime Fiction and the Rise and Fall of New Deal Liberalism* (Durham, NC: Duke University Press, 2000). See also Lewis Moore, *Cracking the Hard-Boiled Detective: A Critical History from the 1920s to the Present* (Jefferson, NC: McFarland & Co., 2006).

9. Raymond Chandler, *The Simple Art of Murder* (New York: Ballantine Books, 1950), 16. Subsequent references will appear in text under the abbreviation *SAM*.

10. Ibid., 20.

11. It is worth noting that in France, following World War II, there was an anxious consumption of these "darker" American detective texts, in both fiction and film, as exemplary of existentialist philosophy. Irwin discusses the marketing aspects of this gesture, as well as the limits and merits of this adequation, particularly in regard to Hammett's *The Maltese Falcon*. The basic gesture of such work is to read the hard-boiled text as a parable describing the detective's eventual acceptance of the chaos that surrounds him and the ultimate meaningless of existence. See John Irwin, "Unless the Threat of Death is Behind Them: Hammett's *The Maltese Falcon*," *Literary Review* 2.3 (2000): 341–374.

For an example responded to by Irwin, see Steven Marcus, "Dashiell Hammett and the Continental Op," in *Representations: Essays on Literature and Society* (New York: Random House, 1975), 311–331.

12. Cawelti's work remains one of the most frequently cited taxonomies of detective fiction. For his discussion of the hard-boiled detective, see John Cawelti, *Adventure, Mystery, and Romance: Formula Stories as Art and Popular Culture* (Chicago: University of Chicago Press, 1976), 139–161.

13. Ibid., 149.

14. See Plain's reading of Chandler's "The Simple Art of Murder" in respect to his own fiction. Gill Plain, *Twentieth-Century Crime Fiction: Gender, Sexuality, and the Body* (Edinburgh: Edinburgh University Press, 2001), 56–86.

15. Of course, I do not intend to make a biological argument regarding obsessional neurosis. For the sake of simplicity, the personal pronouns used when discussing the psychical structures throughout this study are chosen in acknowledgement of percentages daily affirmed in clinical practice. A majority — but certainly not all — obsessionals are men. This is likewise appropriate as the detectives discussed in this chapter are exclusively male.

16. Here one is reminded of such actions made by the so-called "Rat Man" in Freud's primary case study of the obsessive neurotic. In an episode emphasized by Freud, the Rat Man feels urgently that he must clear a stone he had kicked onto a road a short while before, apparently absentmindedly. He imagines this necessity, as his "lady" was to travel by this same path on her ride home. Recalling this, he becomes worried that she will be injured on this return trip. Of course, the point is that the stone was not so innocently tossed onto the path. This gesture was actually an act of aggression that must be undone by the obsessive, given the desire (and potential pleasure) contained therein. See Sigmund Freud, *Three Case Histories*, trans. Philip Rieff (New York: Touchstone, 1963), 1–82.

17. In this process, the obsessive is, often only briefly, confronted with the Other's desire and, therefore, his own. The difficulty of maintaining this new openness will be of great importance to my discussion. Regarding this, Fink has written, "The problem is that 'hysterization' is fragile and short-lived: the obsessive often reverts quite quickly to shutting out the Other and denying any kind of dependence. If analysis is to have any effect on the obsessive, the analyst must foster hysterization; cast in the role of the Other by the analysands, the analyst must continually bring to bear his or her desire ... in order to thwart the otherwise inevitable 'obsessionalization' or shutting off of the obsessive" (131). See Fink's explanation of this concept in the eighth chapter of his text, Bruce Fink, *A Clinical Introduction to Lacanian Psychoanalysis: Theory and Technique* (Cambridge, MA: Harvard University Press, 1997), 131–134.

18. Sigmund Freud, *Inhibitions, Symptoms, and Anxiety*, trans. James Strachey (New York: W. W. Norton, 1989), 45.

19. Ibid., 47.

20. Ibid., 48.

21. In the analytic session, this aspiration will take the form of the incessant talking of the obsessional, who will all too often provide both free association — which is even less free in his case — in addition to the interpretation that should, presumably, come from the analyst. Darian Leader tells the amusing story of an analytic session that Lacan was conducting with an obsessional patient. During the course of the analysand's ceaseless talking, Lacan got up to leave the office for one reason or another, saying matter-of-factly, "Don't hesitate to continue the session during my absence." The patient was, apparently, quite dismayed by this action, but the point to be taken, as Leader explains, is that Lacan's intervention was to call attention to the obsessional's desire that the analyst in fact not be present at the session, that he disappear. See Darian Leader, *Why Do Women Write More Letters Than They Send? A Meditation on the Loneliness of the Sexes* (New York: Basic Books, 1997), 127.

22. As Lacan writes: "Demand already constitutes the Other as having the privilege of satisfying needs, that is, the power to deprive them of what alone can satisfy them. The Other's privilege here thus outlines the radical form of the gift of what the Other does not have — namely what is known as its love." See Jacques Lacan, *Écrits: The First Complete English Edition*, trans. Bruce Fink (New York: W. W. Norton, 2006), 580.

23. To quote the famous passage from Lacan's "The Signification of the Phallus": "This is why desire is neither the appetite for satisfaction nor the demand for love, but the difference that results from the subtraction of the first from the second" (287). See Lacan, *Écrits*, 580.

24. See note 15. The same is true — but again not exclusive — in respect to women and the category of hysteria.

25. Paul Verhaeghe, *Beyond Gender: From Subject to Drive* (New York: Other Press, 2001), 159.

26. See Bruce Fink's distinction between the Name-of-the-Father and the phallus in Bruce Fink, *The Lacanian Subject: Between Language*

and Jouissance (Princeton, NJ: Princeton University Press, 1995), 57–58.

27. Ibid., 98–113.

28. Lacan, *Écrits*, 694.

29. See Serge Leclaire, "Philo, or the Obsessional and His Desire" in Stuart Schneiderman, *Returning to Freud: Clinical Psychoanalysis in the School of Lacan* (New Haven, CT: Yale University Press, 1980), 123.

30. Here again, Freud's exemplary case study of the obsessional, the "Rat Man," offers a sound illustration of this experience. As a child, the Rat Man is clearly a substitute satisfaction for his mother, compensating her for the failure of her marriage. Importantly, the mother is openly unsatisfied with the father, making the child's assumption that the father has what the mother desires—that mythic moment of separation made according to the law of the father—largely impossible. This situation exhibits well the often smothering nature of the mother in the formative years of the obsessional. The Rat Man's mother wishes her son to give her all that her husband had not, namely, his love. In defense against this, the son needs the interruption of the father to limit safely and to name the desire of the mother, which threatens to engulf the subject—a possibility that remains both terrifying and tempting for the obsessional at the same time. Later in life, because the mother bears an (implicit) grudge at her son's potential choice of brides, she threatens to place the Rat Man in a similar position of derision as his father, who likewise chose his bride for the wrong—that is, pecuniary—reasons. See Sigmund Freud, "Notes Upon a Case of Obsessional Neurosis" in *Three Case Histories*, 1–82.

31. Fink, *The Lacanian Subject*, 91–92.

32. Ibid., 91.

33. Ibid.

34. Ibid., 92.

35. See for example, Lacan, *Écrits*, 691.

36. See chapters 28 and 29 in Raymond Chandler, *The Big Sleep* (New York: Vintage, 1992), 190–203. All subsequent references to this novel will appear in text under the abbreviation *TBS*. Even while recovering from a concussion, and then essentially bargaining for his life, Marlowe carefully observes and admires the beautiful Mona Mars. For a further discussion of the way in which romantic love might be used as a defense against *jouissance* (and emergent desire), see my reading of the work of Philip K. Dick in Chapter Three.

37. The term *jouissance* expresses sexual pleasure and pain, as well as the wholeness (or the "whole" pleasure assumed to have been) lost when the subject entered language. It is this issue of pain that greatly complicates the concept. While pleasure is experienced as agreeable for the subject, there is always something foreign, painful, and destructive in the experience of *jouissance*. As Dylan Evans has succinctly defined the term: "*Jouissance* thus nicely expresses the paradoxical satisfaction that the subject derives from his symptom or, to put it another way, the suffering that he derives from his own satisfaction." See the Dylan Evans, *An Introductory Dictionary of Lacanian Psychoanalysis* (London and New York: Routledge, 1996), 92.

38. Raymond Chandler, *The Long Goodbye* (New York: Ballantine Books, 1976), 165. Hereafter, all references to this novel will appear in the text, designated by the abbreviation *TLG*.

39. See, for example, Paul Verhaeghe, *Does the Woman Exist? From Freud's Hysteric to Lacan's Feminine*, trans. Marc du Ry (New York: Other Press, 1999). See also Juan-David Nasio, *Hysteria from Freud to Lacan: The Splendid Child of Psychoanalysis* (New York: Other Press, 1998).

40. Here, the Dora case must be taken as an exemplary impasse that requires Freud to rethink his understanding of the hysteric. For the hysteric, it must be acknowledged that the signifying matter in question was, particularly in the time of Freud, the body itself. Currently, the nature of the hysterical symptom is undergoing a transformation, owing, no doubt, to a disruption in the transferential nexus between patient and doctor. The hysteric no longer presents medical symptoms precisely because she is, more often than not, no longer speaking to a medical doctor. As clinical work has shown, because of this, the true conversion symptom is somewhat *passé*, and is becoming an increasingly less frequent complaint in clinical practice. As Wajcman has argued, this phenomenon itself illustrates the power of transference and the subject's deference to the Other of the moment. In the Middle Ages, hysterical symptoms took the form of demonic possessions, symptoms of which were directed towards priests. In the late nineteenth century and for much of the twentieth, conversion symptoms written upon the body were rendered in a form immediately comprehensible to the hysteric's new interlocutor, namely, the physician. In our own time, such symptoms have been directed at the more pharmacologically-minded psychiatrist, becoming in this case pharmacological symptoms proper. See Gérard Wajcman, *Le Maitre et L'hysterique* (Paris: Navarin, 1982). See also Sigmund Freud, *Dora: An Analysis of a Case of Hysteria*, trans. Philip Rieff (New York: Touchstone, 1963).

41. Such a stance is suggested in Todorov's work, discussed in Chapter One.

42. See, for example, Felman's well-known essays "To Open the Question" and "Turning the Screw of Interpretation," in Shoshana Felman, *Literature and Psychoanalysis: The Question of Reading: Otherwise* (Baltimore, MD: Johns Hopkins University Press, 1982), 5–10, 94–207. As should be evident, these perspectives privilege hysteria in their analysis of the relationship between literature and psychoanalysis in the way in which I have been speaking.

43. Jacques Lacan, *Television* (New York: W. W. Norton, 1990), 3.

44. Jacques Lacan, *The Seminar of Jacques Lacan: Book II: The Ego in Freud's Theory and in the Technique of Psychoanalysis, 1954-1955*, ed. Jacques-Alain Miller, trans. Sylvanna Tomaselli (New York: W. W. Norton, 1988), 244. (Henceforth, *Seminar II* in notes.)

45. Lacan, "Subversion of the Subject," *Écrits*, 678. As Lacan indicates later in this same essay, the obsessional imagines his own consistency "inasmuch as he negates the Other's desire, forming his fantasy in such way as to accentuate the impossibility of the subject vanishing." Ibid., 698. For the subject's confrontation with an "ever purer" signifier, see also my discussion of "The Purloined Letter" in Chapter One.

46. Colette Soler, "Hysteria and Obsession," in *Reading Seminars I and II: Lacan's Return to Freud*, ed. Richard Feldstein et al. (Albany, NY: State University of New York Press, 1996), 270.

47. See note 17.

48. See Verhaeghe, *Beyond Gender*, 159.

49. For a reading of Hammett's use of third-person narration, see Chapter 1 in Greg Forter, *Murdering Masculinities: Fantasies of Gender and Violence in the American Crime Novel* (New York: New York University Press, 2000), 11–45. Forter's basic premise is that Hammett makes use of this narrative strategy to augment the masochistic will to dissolution that, in his reading, always accompanies "tough," hard-boiled masculinity.

50. While speaking of the American novel of the 1930s and 1940s, and of detective fiction in particular, Camus made the apt observations that these texts "claim to find [their] unity in reducing man either to elementals or to his external reactions and to his behavior.... [This fiction] rejects analysis and the search for a fundamental psychological motive that could explain and recapitulate the behavior of a character.... Its technique consists in describing men by their outside appearances, in their most casual actions, of reproducing without comment everything they say down to their repetitions, and finally by acting as if men were entirely defined by their daily automatisms." Quoted in David Madden, *Tough Guy Writers of the Thirties* (Carbondale, IL: Southern Illinois University Press, 1979), 94.

51. In his brilliant essay, "Tough Talk and Wisecracks: Language as Power in American Detective Fiction," Christianson, reacting to Porter's reading of the detective's use of language, makes the distinction between "wisecracks" and "hard-boiled conceit." In using the exaggerated metaphors of "hard-boiled conceit," the detective's use of the power of language to "create something new" is most evident (159). For Christianson, it is through this idiosyncratic use of language that the detective gains autonomy and is capable of (re)ordering his world. However, in the end, these novels remain doubtful about the viability of this — decidedly masculine — use of language and subjective posturing. The results can only be loneliness and isolation. See Scott R. Christianson, "Tough Talk and Wisecracks: Language as Power in American Detective Fiction," *Journal of Popular Culture* 23:2 (Fall 1989): 152–162.

52. In Chandler and Hammett, there is a more carefully maintained boundary between violence and speech. Violence does, as Christianson indicates, offer a final guarantee of "tough talk," but even in this genre of "action," this is always a last resort. In Spillane, violence and sex are of course unmistakably paired. Interestingly, though Spillane's detective Mike Hammer will narrate at length his sexual encounters, he frequently indicates that "words do not suffice" to explain such pleasure. Eerily, the language of violence seems to fill that void for the detective.

53. Žižek is here speaking of the classical detective story. We might say that the impossibility of story in the classical case becomes manifest with the hard-boiled detective. Slavoj Žižek, *Looking Awry: An Introduction to Jacques Lacan through Popular Culture* (Cambridge, MA: MIT Press, 1991), 60.

54. As is well documented, the time period in question is rife with historical examples of the increasing uncertainty, even failure, of masculine authority. This is evident in the passing of the 19th Amendment in 1920, granting women the right to vote, and to the inter-and post-war malaise. The market crash of 1929 is equally significant, as not only is the individual ignored in favor of "imaginary" transfers of capital, but so too is physical industry. The impotence of authority and, further, its complicity with the criminal was a daily — and importantly un-repressed — reality during the Prohibition Era, ushered in by the 18th Amendment to the Constitution, passed in 1919. As it was possible to purchase alcohol readily, despite the Volstead

Act, the empty threat of government's assault on crime was all too clear. It is hardly surprising, then, that the hard-boiled text is preoccupied with questions of class and the tacit plutocracy of America at that time. Subsequently, masculinity was devalued by the success of the post-war economic boom and the emergence of the "company man" in all his banal, conflicted mythology.

55. Dennis Porter, *The Pursuit of Crime: Art and Ideology in Detective Fiction* (New Haven, CT: Yale University Press, 1981), 176–177.

56. This span refers to the publication dates of Hammett's *Red Harvest* and Spillane's *I, the Jury*, respectively.

57. See William Marling, *The American Roman Noir: Hammett, Cain, and Chandler* (Athens, GA: University of Georgia Press, 1995), 39–92.

58. Ibid., 125.

59. The larger question of Marling's work is the coherence of the social order represented within Hammett's fiction. This line of questioning must be placed alongside Marcus' assertion that Hammett, as early as *Red Harvest*, no longer defers to a social consensus of any kind. In place of this, the Continental Op will substitute the productive force of fiction. See Marcus, "Dashiell Hammett and the Continental Op" in *Representations*, 311–331.

60. As a concrete example of such "abstraction," Paul Virilio argues that the use of fingerprints to determine a criminal's identity, which began around the turn of the century, "marks the decline of story." In other words, eyewitness accounts (i.e., stories) become less and less useful to investigation. Of course, this decline of "story" has been crucial throughout the history of detective fiction. Paul Virilio, *The Vision Machine* (Bloomington: Indiana University Press, 1994), 42.

61. Marling, *The American Roman Noir*, 46.

62. Slavoj Žižek, *The Metastases of Enjoyment: Six Essays on Women and Causality* (New York: Verso, 2005), 206.

63. Paul Verhaeghe, "The Collapse of the Function of the Father and Its Effect on Gender Roles," in *Sic 3: Sexuation*, ed. Renata Salecl (Durham, NC: Duke University Press, 2000), 138.

64. Mickey Spillane, *The Mike Hammer Collection Volume 1: I, the Jury, My Gun Is Quick, Vengeance Is Mine!* (New York: New American Library, 2001), 175. Subsequent references will appear in the text under the abbreviation *MHC*.

65. When such a virginal figure does not immediately present herself, Hammer's secretary Velda, whom he promises to marry throughout the early novels, fills this place. However, it should be noted that though Velda does indeed maintain this place within Hammer's fantasy, she is not limited to this role in the Hammer opus as a whole. She also possesses a private detective's license and is, on more than one occasion, called upon to carry on an investigation when Hammer's own license is revoked. This unique characterization, unheard of for either Hammett or Chandler, deserves further attention.

66. In several cases, the Madonna is shown to be the whore, an unveiling that requires, in Spillane's well-known misogynist manner, her execution. More will be said of this in the conclusion to this chapter.

67. Though his work brilliantly distills numerous hard-boiled conventions, often taking these to a humorous extreme, Spillane's interest in the detective's *jouissance* perhaps marks his greatest — and most frequently repudiated — innovation to the genre. More will be said below regarding the placement of this apparently antithetical trait within the structure I have been describing.

68. Serge Leclaire, "Jerome, or Death in the Life of the Obsessional," in *Returning to Freud: Clinical Psychoanalysis in the School of Lacan*, ed. Stuart Schneiderman (New Haven, CT: Yale University Press, 1980), 107.

69. Dating back to the earliest of the author's short stories written during the 1920s, the Continental Op is Hammett's first serial character, drawing upon much of Hammett's own experience as an operative working for the Pinkerton Detective Agency in both Baltimore and San Francisco.

70. Dashiell Hammett, *Red Harvest* (New York: Vintage, 1992). Subsequent references to this work will appear in the text under the abbreviation, *RH*.

71. Porter is correct in indicating that the Op here acts in conformity with Hammett's own radical politics. He is not only a detective; he is also a "muckraker" and "racket buster." See Porter, *The Pursuit of Crime*, 173.

72. I would argue that there is an anti-detective element to this disruption of the quest narrative here, and elsewhere within the hard-boiled genre. I will discuss this possibility in Chapter Three. For this notion of the "anti-detective," see especially William V. Spanos, "The Detective and the Boundary: Some Notes on the Postmodern Literary Imagination." *Boundary 2: A Journal of Postmodern Literature* 1.1 (Fall 1972): 147–168. See also Stefano Tani, *The Doomed Detective: The Contribution of the Detective Novel to Postmodern American and Italian Fiction* (Car-

bondale, IL: Southern Illinois University Press, 1984).

73. The novel ends, then, with a more familiar form of the "whodunit?" importantly surrounding the murder of a woman. However, per hard-boiled convention, in this case the detective works to clear himself from blame. By the conclusion of the text, it is clear that such exculpation — regardless of whether he actually killed Brand or not — is impossible.

74. Dashiell Hammett, *The Maltese Falcon* (New York: Vintage, 1992), 214. All subsequent references to this work will be indicated in the text with the abbreviation *MF*.

75. Verhaeghe, *Beyond Gender*, 158.

76. Joan Copjec, *Read My Desire: Lacan Against the Historicists* (Cambridge, MA: MIT Press, 1994), 199.

77. See Slavoj Žižek, *The Plague of Fantasies* (New York and London: Verso, 1997), 113–117.

78. Ibid., 116.

79. Here again, Forter's reading of Hammett is instructive on this issue. See Forter, *Murdering Masculinities*, 11–45.

80. Franco Moretti, "Clues," in *Popular Fiction: Technology, Ideology, Production, Reading*, ed. Tony Bennett (London and New York: Routledge, 1990), 242.

81. *The Maltese Falcon*, DVD, directed by John Huston. CA: Warner Studios, 1941.

82. Of course, the scar is a representation of that trauma, but it is, like all scars, a sign that is made up of disorganized flesh. As such, the scar speaks to the impossibility of the representation of its origin. Obviously, the navel is the first mark of this kind upon the body. See my discussion of "the navel" in Chapter Four.

83. Irwin suggests that Spade himself uses the strategy of randomness as "a psychological tool to disrupt his opponents' settled plans and keep his enemies off balance, a method that must be occasionally and unpredictably applied, since random action loses its psychological effect if it becomes expected and routine." Though Irwin does not move his argument in this direction, I would offer that this is actually a helpful description of the analyst's task in maintaining the analysand's "hystericization" during the session. Such pointed (or random) disruptions of the patient's discourse are difficult to maintain, to be sure. See John Irwin, *Unless the Threat of Death Is Behind Them: Hard-Boiled Fiction and Film Noir* (Baltimore, MD: Johns Hopkins University Press, 2006), 24.

84. In Spokane, Flitcraft assumes the name Charles Pierce, which seems, as various critics have indicated, to be a play upon the name of the contemporary American semioticist, Charles Peirce. This underscores the randomness that Flitcraft imagines he uncovers in his brush with death, as the philosopher was interested in the arbitrary, or at least descriptivist, nature of language itself.

85. This motto is actually the title of the unpublished *Seminar XXI, Les non-dupes errant*, given during the years of 1973-1974.

86. See Chapter 1 of Slavoj Žižek, *The Sublime Object of Ideology* (New York: Verso, 1991), 11–54.

87. Slavoj Žižek, *The Ticklish Subject: The Absent Center of Political Ontology* (New York: Verso, 1999), 327.

88. The size — and therefore plausibility — of "communities of symbolic efficiency" is diminishing, as the father function is increasingly suspect. In other words, we no longer believe in the fiction of the big Other. See Paul Verhaeghe, "The Collapse of the Function of the Father and Its Effect on Gender Roles," in *Sic 3: Sexuation*, ed. Renata Salecl (Durham, NC: Duke University Press, 2000), 131–156.

89. For a superb reading the "Flitcraft Parable" and its cycle of repetition, see Irwin, "Unless the Threat of Death is Behind Them," 341–374. See also the author's more recent book of the same title.

90. This doubling of partners is common to the hard-boiled genre. Like any bad relationship, the situation allows Spade the requisite distance from his partner to maintain his desire — which must then lie elsewhere — as impossible. Effie Perrine, who is cast in many ways as the ideal woman (ideal certainly for a detective), likewise fuels this impossibility. She is an employee and, despite her perfection, is effectively off limits. For a discussion of the doubling of partners that is not unrelated to the hard-boiled context, see Renata Salecl, "Love and Sexual Difference: Doubled Partners in Men and Women," in Salecl, *Sic 3: Sexuation*, 297–316.

91. For an introduction to this notion of "woman as the symptom of man," see Chapter 8 of Fink, *The Lacanian Subject*, 98–123.

92. Though I have no interest in making a psychobiographical argument about Raymond Chandler, the author's relationships with women are perhaps telling in light of my current argument. Chandler was famously devoted to his mother, living with her nearly until the age of thirty. At this point in his life, Chandler then married Cissy Hulbert, who was eighteen years his senior. See Tom Hiney, *Raymond Chandler: A Biography* (New York: Atlantic Monthly Press, 1997).

93. In her brilliant work *The Street Was Mine: White Masculinity in Hardboiled Fiction*

and Film Noir (New York: Palgrave, 2002), Megan Abbott describes the "hysterical" Marlowe. I am greatly indebted to the insight of her study in this current section.

94. See Raymond Chandler, *Farewell, My Lovely* (New York: Vintage, 1992), 140, 244, 100, 64. Additional references to this work will be cited in text under the abbreviation, *FML*.

95. For an interesting reading of Marlowe's hysterical preoccupation with this question, see Chapter 2 of Abbott, *The Street Was Mine*, 21–65. My argument is greatly indebted to her insights.

96. Of course each of the neurotic positions ask both questions of being ("Am I alive or dead?") and sexuality ("Am I a man or woman?"). The point of Lacan's privileging these questions is to illuminate the nature of the psychical structures in question. In the case of hysteria, the subject behaves as an object, a position that requires that she pay careful attention to the Other's desire. In other words, gender confusion arises because the hysteric must desire as a man in order to fill out that object more perfectly. The obsessional denies both object and Other, embracing a radical separation that leaves the subject incapable of desiring. This immobilization necessarily leads the obsessive to question his being: "Am I alive or dead?" See Bruce Fink, *A Clinical Introduction*, 122–123.

97. As Plain has observed, the "father" most often frames Chandler's novels, appearing at or near the beginning of the text with a certain mandate for the detective, subsequently arriving at the end to pass judgment—and often to be judged—on the detective's own efficacy. See Plain, *Twentieth-Century Crime Fiction*, 57–58.

98. As Plain writes, "The father is instead an unseen power who must, paradoxically, be both defended and defied." See ibid., 57–58.

99. Plain likewise makes the excellent point that Marlowe is not the ideal detective spoken of in Chandler's essay, "The Simple Art of Murder." He is by no means that whole or complete man who is neither mean nor tarnished, etc. Rather, as is evident in the beginning of *The Big Sleep*, *The Long Goodbye*, and in an only briefly deflected way in *Farewell, My Lovely*, he looking for this very man. See ibid., 63–65. Plain's assessment of the character of Marlowe is quite illuminating. However, I at times find her reduction of Marlowe's quest to Kristevean terms, read largely through the work of Butler, as problematic. The symbolic framework of the hard-boiled texts is, to be sure, largely called into question in Chandler's work; nevertheless, this function is never abandoned entirely, and one should be skeptical of the detective's impulse to accomplish such a thing. As I am endeavoring to show, the name for this action that immediately undoes itself is obsessive neurosis.

100. Her flagrant infidelities and betrayal of her husband, the judge, recall Žižek's discussion of the "non-dupes errant." The duplicitous woman, who is in this case literally protean, is not duped by the authority her husband embodies as either judge or spouse. Marlowe's behavior after the murder of Moose Malloy in many ways works to indicate (violently) the fallacy of this position. I will later discuss the nature of Marlowe's "knowledge" and address whether he is ultimately either "duped" or "non-duped."

101. Žižek's reading of paternal power as being predicated upon its failure to satisfy its own mandate (i.e., of being all-powerful) is here important. Marlowe identifies with Lennox not in spite of his failure as a man, but because of his failure. The detective seeks a figure through which he might model his own masculinity, and Lennox's struggle with his own manhood here offers a point of identification. However, in the end, he proves himself even to fail inappropriately, as he runs away to Mexico City to hide from the inevitable suspicion of the murder of his wife Sylvia, which he in fact did not commit. I will say more of this failure at the end of this section.

102. Forter, *Murdering Masculinities*, 13.

103. As Plain argues in her discussion of the homosexual undercurrents of the Marlowe-Lennox relationship, the entire text might be read as Marlowe's attempt to find an acceptable object of desire to replace Terry Lennox. See Plain, *Twentieth-Century Crime Fiction*, 80.

104. These statements are repeated throughout all of Chandler's novels. An especially colorful example from *The Long Goodbye* reads, "Hard little men in hard little offices talking hard little words that don't mean a goddam thing." See Raymond Chandler, *Raymond Chandler: The Lady in the Lake, The Little Sister, The Long Goodbye, Playback*, Everyman's Library Edition (New York: Alfred A. Knopf, 2002), 519.

105. Such details are given greater weight in *Farewell, My Lovely*, a text that is perhaps the most homoerotic of all the Chandler novels. For a related discussion of eyes and the issue of the gaze, see Abbott, *The Street Was Mine*, 50–56.

106. *Playback* (1958) is the final published text written entirely by Chandler, but this is a novelization of a film script that the author had been in the process of writing. Interestingly, the unfinished Chandler novel *Poodle Springs*, ultimately completed by Robert B. Parker in 1989,

begins with Marlowe marrying Linda Loring, a woman whom he meets in *The Long Goodbye* and, uncharacteristically, spends the evening with. That Chandler wished for his detective to be married raises significant questions as to how Marlowe would carry on. Given the reciprocal distancing at the base of relations within genre, the "solution" of marriage to the impasses of the detective's personal mythology is perhaps not so banal as it may first appear. Hammett ended his career in a similar manner with *The Thin Man*, a text that detailed the exploits of the husband and wife detective team of Nick and Nora Charles. The result in this case was not only a return to the more traditional ploys of investigation and the "whodunit," but also a rewriting of the genre in terms of comedy.

107. Plain's reading of the homoerotic relationship between Marlowe and Malloy offers an interesting supplement to this claim. See Plain, *Twentieth-Century Crime Fiction*, 66–78.

108. For the "Rat Man" case study, see Sigmund Freud, *Three Case Histories*, 1–82.

109. Of course, in *The Long Goodbye*, Linda Loring, daughter of Harlan Potter, is the greatest exception. See note 106.

110. This distinction is best made by comparing Carmen with Brigid O'Shaughnessy from Hammett's *The Maltese Falcon*. The latter is considerably more conniving, taking careful inventory of the man's desire and using it against him. On the contrary, Carmen Sternwood is described in terms of animal-like violence. Taking this as a definition, it would be productive to read the Sternwood sisters as two sides of the *femme fatale*. Vivian in this case represents the charming cunning of this figure, while Carmen, of course, represents the violent danger of these very charms. See William Marling, "The Hammett Succubus," *Clues: A Journal of Detection* 3:2 (1982): 66–75.

111. See Alexander Howe, "The Detective and the Analyst: Truth, Knowledge, and Psychoanalysis in the Hard-boiled Fiction of Raymond Chandler," *Clues: A Journal of Detection* 24.4 (Summer 2006): 15–30.

112. Though the argument is infrequently made through the position of obsessional neurosis, this claim is not as surprising as it may at first appear. Indeed, the resistances of the hysteric have, since the infancy of analysis, been used to demonstrate the workings of analytic knowledge.

113. The Lacanian analyst demands subjective erasure, a process that might be expressed by the cannibalistic imperative that concludes Lacan's "Seminar on 'The Purloined Letter'": "Eat your *dasein*." What the analyst devours is the analysand's fantasies of wholeness or knowledge. See Slavoj Žižek, "In His Bold Gaze My Ruin Is Writ Large," in *Everything You Always Wanted to Know About Lacan (But Were Afraid to Ask Hitchcock)* (New York: Verso, 1992), 262–263.

114. See note 17.

115. See note 111.

116. As suggested at the end of Chapter One, the adequation I am suggesting depends upon Lacan's repositioning of the analyst from the place of the Other to the that of the analysand's object-cause. For a reading of this development, see Chapter Two in Dany Nobus, *Jacques Lacan and the Freudian Practice of Psychoanalysis* (London: Routledge, 2000), 56–105.

117. Analysis from a position of mastery was a practice disastrously utilized by Freud in his early work. He himself ultimately became aware of this inherent difficulty, particularly when presented with the hysteric patient. Such patients are capable of producing a volume of symptoms that outrun the master's interpretative capacities. See my discussion of this issue in Chapter One.

118. Here again, see Chapter One.

119. Jacques Lacan, *The Seminar of Jacques Lacan: Book XI: The Four Fundamental Concepts of Psychoanalysis*, trans. Alan Sheridan (New York: W. W. Norton, 1977), 276. (Henceforth, *Seminar XI* in notes.)

120. This motto has of course been popularized throughout Žižek's work. What one finds here is, essentially, the movement from symptom to *sinthome*, a concept that Lacan develops in the unpublished *Seminar XXIII*. Rather than functioning as veiled message to the Other, in which case enjoyment is taken in renunciation, the symptom as *sinthome*, comes to be enjoyed in itself. To put this in the simplest terms, the symptom moves from the register of demand — or thwarted desire — to that of drive. As Lacan writes: "It is in as much as the analyst's desire, which remains an x, which tends in a direction that is the exact opposite of identification, that the crossing of the plane of identification is possible, through the mediation of the separation of the subject in experience. The experience of the subject is thus brought back to the plane at which, from the reality of the unconscious, the drive may be made present." Ibid., 274. I address the issue of drive in Chapter Three.

121. The question of the serial nature of detective fiction has yet to be adequately addressed from the perspective of psychoanalysis. As I hope I have indicated in the current study, it would be quite productive to begin such a venture from the question of repetition and isolation, and

their necessary failures, in terms of the structure of obsessional neurosis.

122. Of course, unlike Hammer's murderous ethic, analysis does not operate according to the *lex talionis* or any logic of simple exchange. When the analysand identifies with the cause of their desire, the very notion of equivalence (e.g., an eye for an eye) is shown to be an effect of the transference.

123. Importantly, the crucial difference between these figures is the pleasure that is taken by Hammer both in confronting criminals with their crimes and then executing them. As has been indicated, in such scenes, one finds the remarkable assimilation of both speech and violence, as Hammer has a special penchant for narrating (to both the reader and criminal) the violence that is about to unfold. As will be shown, the possibility of this combination speaks to change in the psychical structure of the detective.

124. Even within Spillane, the ideal woman remains, in effect, a man, as Charlotte's last name, "Manning," and athletic build indicate. This coincidence is taken a step further in *Kiss Me, Deadly*, in which the *femme fatale* turns out to actually be a man. Even critics of Spillane must concede the intelligence, and novelty, of this literal combination of the figure of the father of enjoyment and the *femme fatale*. Indeed, it is physical combination of the Rat Man's forbidden couple: the father and his beloved.

125. See Bruce Fink, "Perversion," in *Sic 4: Perversion and the Social Relation*, ed. Molly Anne Rothenberg, Dennis Foster, and Slavoj Žižek (Durham, NC, and London: Duke University Press, 2003), 48–54.

126. Ibid., 54–57.

127. Verhaeghe, *Beyond Gender*, 47.

128. Ibid., 47.

129. Žižek, *Looking Awry*, 66.

130. Ibid.

131. Christian Kupke discusses this uncanny aspect of the obsessional neurotic, as well as the typically regressive turn back towards systematization that analysis with such patients often takes. As Kupke writes, speaking of an individual analysis, "In [the patient's] lack of knowledge about himself, as already mentioned, he seemed to possess an unconscious knowledge about psychoanalysis, a knowledge about its lack of knowledge. But the effects of such a wish for comprehending and regulating became obvious to me: the obsessional neurotic becomes a hindrance to analysis not only because the 'analytic basic rule' (free association) is a horror for him, but also — and first of all — because he is absolutely able to infect us analysts, who can't totally delete the significant of knowledge too, with his will for knowledge and with his 'knowledge-plague.'" Christian Kupke, "The Conflicts of the Obsessional Neurotic: A Lacanian Dream-Interpretation," *The Symptom: The Online Journal for Lacan* 1 (Autumn 2001). http://www.lacan.com/kupef.htm.

132. Raymond Chandler, *The High Window*, Vintage Edition (New York: Vintage, 1992), 262.

133. Quoted in Serge André, *What Does a Woman Want?*, trans. Susan Fairfield (New York: Other Press, 1999), 327.

134. Ibid.

135. For a lengthier discussion of Marlowe's own analysis in *The High Window*, see Howe, "The Detective and the Analyst."

Chapter Three

1. Fredric Jameson is well known early supporter of Philip K. Dick's work. For an excellent discussion of the history of scholarship on Philip K. Dick, see Istavan Csicsery-Ronay, Jr., "Pilgrims in Pandemonium: Philip K. Dick and the Critics," in *On Philip K. Dick: 40 Articles from Science Fiction Studies*, ed. R. D. Mullen et al. (Terre Haute, IN: SF-TH Inc., 1992), v–xviii.

2. The issue of paranoia is a frequent topic of Dick's conversations with Paul Williams in the interviews collected in Paul Williams, *Only Apparently Real* (New York: Arbor House, 1986).

3. Stanislav Lem, "Philip K. Dick: A Visionary Among Charlatans," in Mullen, *On Philip K. Dick: 40 Articles*, 57–58. Interestingly, Lem is speaking specifically of science fiction and the question of dark agents. In most fiction, argues the author, it is clear that Evil is perpetrated either by people or by "blind forces of matter." In Dick, this cannot be clearly distinguished.

4. This deception of love is spoken of, for example, in Lacan's *Seminar XI*: "What better way of assuring oneself, on the point on which is mistaken, than to persuade the other of the truth of what one says! Is not this a fundamental structure of the dimension of love that the transference gives us the opportunity of depicting? In persuading the other that he has that which may complement us, we assure ourselves of being able to continue to misunderstand precisely what we lack." See Jacques Lacan, *The Seminar of Jacques Lacan: Book XI: The Four Fundamental Concepts of Psychoanalysis*, trans. Alan Sheridan (New York: W. W. Norton, 1977), 133. Henceforth, *Seminar XI* in notes.

5. The recent work of both Alenka Zupan-

čič and Slavoj Žižek emphasizes that the impossible *does* happen. This is perhaps most evident in the experience of love as understood by psychoanalysis. See especially Slavoj Žižek, *On Belief* (London and New York: Routledge, 2001), 39–42. See also Alenka Zupančič, *Ethics of the Real: Kant and Lacan*, ed. Slavoj Žižek (London and New York: Verso, 2000).

6. The non-existence of the sexual relation is obviously a vast question in Lacan's work, one that is taken up over the course of many years. For a discussion of this that is related to my current purposes, see, for example Jacques Lacan, *The Seminar of Jacques Lacan: On Feminine Sexuality: The Limits of Love and Knowledge: Book XX, Encore 1972-1973* (New York and London: W. W. Norton, 1998), 12. Hereafter, *Seminar XX* in notes.

7. As in previous chapters, gendered pronouns are used only as a convenience. It is therefore important to emphasize that Lacan's distinction between the masculine and feminine side of "sexuation," a distinction that will be used throughout this chapter, is not based upon the biological differences between the sexes. As he outlines in *Seminar XX*, the masculine and feminine sides of sexuation refer to the position taken by the subject in respect to the lack within the Other. For the graph of sexuation, see Lacan, *Seminar XX*, 78.

8. As infamous as Lacan's statement that "there is no such thing as the sexual relation" is his comment that "The Woman does not exist," a perplexing remark when taken out of context. Of course, Lacan is not denying the actual existence of women. Rather, the point is that there is no signifier in the symbolic order for "woman" — she is represented only by a lack of a signifier, the phallus, which she does not possess. This will be taken up at greater length below.

9. Dick's insight on this score lies in the fact that this sublime object of fantasy frequently is found in the simplest of female characters, that is, in the most abject, ordinary figure. As will be shown, this object choice far from denies the sublimity of the fantasy.

10. Dick claimed that this method was taken from writers working in the French Department at the University of Tokyo. Naturally, the historian of detective fiction must call attention to Wilkie Collins's use of this device in his famous *The Moonstone* (1868), what is typically regarded as the first detective novel — though obviously not the first detective short story. See the Introduction in Philip K. Dick, *What If Our World Is Their Heaven? The Final Conversations of Philip K. Dick*, ed. Gwen Lee and Elaine Sauter (Woodstock, NY: Overlook Press, 2000).

11. This "paranoiac knowledge" of the subject must be contrasted with the "knowledge" of psychoanalysis. Lacan preferred to speak of the latter using the purposely inflammatory term "truth." This distinction between truth and knowledge, spoken of in previous chapters, will be taken up below. Regarding paranoia in this context, see Paul Verhaeghe, "The Desire of Freud in His Correspondence with Fliess: From Knowledge to Truth," *Umbr(a): A Journal of the Unconscious* 1 (1996): 103–108.

12. However, the psychotic subject is by no means comfortable within this carefully scripted symbolic space for reasons that will be discussed at length below. For a discussion of psychotic "certainty," see Jacques Lacan, *The Seminar of Jacques Lacan: Book III: The Psychoses, 1955–1956*, ed. Jacques-Alain Miller, trans. Russell Grigg (New York: W. W. Norton, 1993), 75–76. (Henceforth, *Seminar III* in notes.)

13. See Russell Grigg, "From the Mechanism of Psychosis to the Universal Condition of the Symptom: On Foreclosure," in *Key Concepts of Lacanian Psychoanalysis*, ed. Dany Nobus (New York: Other Press, 1998), 48–74.

14. For a fascinating discussion of Freud's relation with Wilhem Fliess, see Chapter 2 of Serge André, *What Does a Woman Want?*, trans. Susan Fairfield (New York: Other Press, 1999), 27–42. Fliess, a rhinolaryngologist, authored a kind of sexual cosmology that puts forth a nosography of the "nose-genital." As a trusted friend and colleague, Freud was the first reader of this work, which was entitled *The Relation Between the Nose and the Female Sex Organs, Presented in their Biological Significance* (1897). As André argues, initially Freud had difficulty avoiding the seduction of Fliess's "paranoid science."

15. For an encyclopedic account of Lacan's career, see Elisabeth Roudinesco, *Jacques Lacan* (New York: Columbia University Press, 1997). Lacan's thesis is available in French: Jacques Lacan, *De La Psychose Paranoiaque Dan Ses Rapports Avec La Personnalité Suivi De Premiers Écrits Sur La Paranoia, Champ Freudian* (Paris: Editions du Seuil, 1980).

16. Sigmund Freud, *Three Case Histories*, trans. Philip Rieff (New York: Touchstone, 1963), 154.

17. Sigmund Freud, "Constructions in Analysis," in *Sigmund Freud: Collected Papers, Vol. 5*, ed. James Strachey (New York: Basic Books, 1959), 371. Freud is, in effect, speaking of a missing signifier that the subject presumes to be available. The form of this presumption of course varies between the neurotic and the psychotic patient and is, in the end, the difference of experiencing either certainty or doubt.

18. Ibid.

19. Sigmund Freud, "The Loss of Reality in Neurosis and Psychosis," in *Sigmund Freud: The Collected Papers. Vol. 2* (New York: Basic Books, 1959), 279.

20. Ibid.

21. Ibid., 280.

22. Ibid.

23. Jacques Lacan, *Écrits: The First Complete English Edition*, trans. Bruce Fink (New York: W. W. Norton, 2006), 95.

24. Lacan, *Écrits*, 91–92.

25. Bruce Fink, *The Lacanian Subject: Between Language and Jouissance* (Princeton, NJ: Princeton University Press, 1995), 103.

26. Jacques Lacan, *Écrits*, 579.

27. Slavoj Žižek, "The Seven Veils of Paranoia, or Why Does the Paranoiac Need Two Fathers?" *Constellations* 3, No. 2 (1996): 139–140.

28. Freud, *Three Case Histories*, 125.

29. See Lacan, *Seminar III*, especially pages 195–207.

30. See my discussion of the discourse of hysteria in Chapter Four.

31. Freud writes, for example, "The second step in a psychosis is the attempt to make good the loss of reality, not, however, at the expense of a restriction laid on the *id*—as in neurosis at the expense of the relation with reality—but in another, a more lordly manner, by creating a new reality which is no longer open to the objections like that which has been forsaken" (279). See Freud, "The Loss of Reality in Neurosis and Psychosis," 279.

32. See Lacan, *Seminar III*, 12–13. As Nobus describes the psychotic's ex-centric relation to language: "The foreclosure of the Name-of-the-Father in psychosis thus means that an individual has been excluded from the possibility of substituting a culturally determined symbolic pact, including injunction, prohibitions and allowances, for an unblemished yet chaotic natural condition. In Lacan's view, the psychotic is literally an outlaw, because she has not assimilated the cultural laws of language.... This foreclosure of the Name-of-the-Father and the ensuing absence of quilting points between the signifier and the signified also entail that the meaning of words no longer shifts, but solidifies to the point where it becomes petrified on the level of the code itself." In other words, without the possibility of a meaning postponed (i.e., the neurotic's relation to language), the psychotic experiences the signifier's demand as immediate and traumatic. With no symbolic buffer, this demand returns in the Real. Dany Nobus, *Jacques Lacan and the Freudian Practice of Psychoanalysis* (London: Routledge, 2000), 17.

33. Lacan here indicates Jakobson's use of Jesperson's term to designate "code" as that which syntactically takes on meaning from the content of a message. That is, the "code" is composed of "shifters" (I, you, him, her, etc.). As Lacan writes, "Personal pronouns are the best example [of the shifter]: the difficulties involved in their acquisition and their functional deficiencies illustrate the problematic generated by these signifiers in the subject" (485). See Note 1, Lacan, *Écrits*, 485.

34. For an excellent reading of the Schreber case, and the cultural and philosophical history that surrounds it, see Eric Santer, *My Own Private Germany: Daniel Paul Schreber's Secret History of Modernity* (Princeton, NJ: Princeton University Press, 1996).

35. Lacan, *Écrits*, 452.

36. Lacan makes a similar suggestion in "The Signification of the Phallus." See Lacan, *Écrits*, 581.

37. This is the "double twist" of metaphor, or "double elbow" in Fink's translation. This is an elision doubly made, the second of which establishes the subject as subject of the signifier. See Jacques Lacan, "The Instance of the Letter in the Unconscious or Reason Since Freud," in ibid., 430.

38. Grigg, "From the Mechanism of Psychosis," 59.

39. It will be remembered that the Name-of-the-Father, which is inoperative for the psychotic, distances the subject from the overpowering enjoyment of the mother by breaking up the mother-child dyad. Without this step, the child does not become a subject (of the signifier), as such, and remains an object of the mother's *jouissance*.

40. See Žižek's discussion of this fantasy construction in Žižek, "The Seven Veils of Paranoia," 139–156.

41. Stefano Tani, *The Doomed Detective: The Contribution of the Detective Novel to Postmodern American and Italian Fiction* (Carbondale, IL: Southern Illinois University Press, 1984), 40.

42. William V. Spanos, "The Detective and the Boundary: Some Notes on the Postmodern Literary Imagination." *Boundary 2: A Journal of Postmodern Literature* 1.1 (Fall 1972): 154.

43. Of course, there are anti-detective elements already at work in the hard-boiled school. Indeed, as discussed in Chapter Two, the hard-boiled world assumes a basic disunity within the social order, and it remains exceptionally difficult to articulate the boundary between detective and criminal. Copjec's discussion of the world of noir, which is entered when the detective becomes criminal, as in James M. Cain's

work, is helpful on this score. Joan Copjec, "Locked Room/Lonely Room: Private Space in Film Noir," in *Read My Desire: Lacan Against the Historicists* (Cambridge, MA: MIT Press, 1994), 163–200.

44. I would suggest that Spanos's criticism on this point is not directed against psychoanalysis as such, but at ego psychology and applied psychoanalysis.

45. See Michel Foucault, "Nietzche, Genealogy, History," in *Language, Counter-Memory, Practice: Selected Essays and Interviews*, ed. Donald F. Bouchard (Ithaca, NY: Cornell University Press, 1977), 139–164.

46. Jacques Barzun, "Detection and the Literary Art," in *The Mystery Writer's Art*, ed. Francis Nevins, Jr. (Bowling Green, OH: Bowling Green University Press, 1970), 250.

47. I realize that in this section I come dangerously close to an applied psychoanalytic criticism of the author. I do not wish to argue that Dick's mental state provides the "truth" of his fiction. However, accounts of his afflictions are especially illustrative of the concepts I am discussing. Additionally, such accounts figure prominently in work done on the author, making a detour through psychobiography at times necessary when looking at P. K. Dick criticism.

48. This "conversion" took the form of a quasi-religious experience in February and March of 1974, during which time Dick maintains that he was transported back to the early Christian era where he received wisdom regarding the "true" nature of the universe. Afterwards, he believed that he was in contact with a benign force that he named VALIS (Vast Active Living Intelligence System). This entity would, apparently, frequently visit the author in the form of a comforting pink light, advising him in all aspects of his life. See Dick, *What If Our World Is Their Heaven?*, 8.

49. Jeet Heer, "Marxist Literary Critics Are Following Me! How Philip K. Dick Betrayed His Academic Admirers to the FBI," *Lingua Franca* (May/June 2001): 27–31.

50. Williams, *Only Apparently Real*, 154.

51. Heer, "Marxist Literary Critics Are Following Me!," 30.

52. Nobus, *Jacques Lacan and the Freudian Practice of Psychoanalysis*, 17.

53. See Fink's chapter on the treatment of psychotic patients in Bruce Fink, *A Clinical Introduction to Lacanian Psychoanalysis: Theory and Technique* (Cambridge, MA: Harvard University Press, 1997), 79–111.

54. Peter Fitting, a central figure in this "conspiracy" and an early supporter of Dick's work as subversive, has himself admitted to just this difficulty: "It is harder to find a radical vision in his work." Quoted in Heer, "Marxist Literary Critics Are Following Me!," 31.

55. See Fink's discussion of the "forced choice" of the subject, Fink, *The Lacanian Subject*, 49–53.

56. Williams, *Only Apparently Real*, 161.

57. Ibid., 162.

58. Ibid., 162–163.

59. Slavoj Žižek, "Whither Oedipus?" in *The Ticklish Subject: An Essay on Political Ontology* (New York Verso, 1999), 325. In this work, Žižek is discussing three separate pairs of fathers—and, thus, three separate murders. I am limiting my discussion to the loss of symbolic efficiency that occurs in the second case, the murder of the symbolic father by the father of enjoyment.

60. Ibid., 323.

61. Slavoj Žižek, *The Metastases of Enjoyment: Six Essays on Women and Causality* (New York: Verso, 2005), 206.

62. This concept of the "aesthetics of ambivalence" is borrowed from Brooks Landon, *The Aesthetics of Ambivalence: Rethinking Science Fiction and Film in the Age of Electronic (Re)Production* (Westport, CT: Greenwood Press, 1992). See also Istavan Csicsery-Ronay, Jr., "Gregg Rickman and Others on Philip K. Dick," *Science Fiction Studies* 22:3 (1995): 430–438.

63. Palmer describes the split in Dick's fiction (his short stories, in particular) in a way that is useful to my argument: Dick inevitably had problems "reconciling existential openness, or relativity, with political or ethical discourse." See Christopher Palmer, *Philip K. Dick: Exhilaration and Terror of the Postmodern* (Liverpool: Liverpool University Press, 2003), 32.

64. Ibid., 102.

65. Ibid., 108.

66. One only need remember the famous Dora case to underscore the appropriateness of this characterization. An ill, impotent, and philandering father was at the root of several of the girl's difficulties. Sigmund Freud, *Dora: An Analysis of a Case of Hysteria*, trans. Philip Rieff (New York: Collier Books, 1963).

67. Paul Verhaeghe, "The Collapse of the Function of the Father and Its Effects on Gender Roles," *Sic 3: Sexuation*, ed. Renata Salecl (Durham, NC: Duke University Press, 2000), 137.

68. Ibid.

69. This latter phrase is taken from the dust jacket of the original edition. See Williams, *Only Apparently Real*, 89. Obviously, the lack of traditional sci-fi accoutrements made the book well suited for a larger demographic, allowing Dick to obtain his first major contract with a hard-

cover publisher. Unfortunately, the novel was not a success. Williams has likened the style of the text to the unpublished "literary" novels that Dick had written in the early 1950s. These failed attempts at breaking out of the genre of science fiction into more "serious" literary realms were repeated throughout Dick's career. Only his last published work, *The Transmigration of Timothy Archer* (1982), another foray beyond the sci-fi genre, crossed this border, though this success was achieved, unfortunately, only posthumously. Regarding this struggle, see the introduction to Dick, *What If Our World Is Their Heaven?*, 7–12.

70. Williams, *Only Apparently Real*, 83.

71. This plot structure, which came to be a staple in *fin de siècle* Hollywood film (e.g., *The Truman Show, The Matrix*), originates in Dick's *Time Out of Joint*. Speaking of *Time Out of Joint* specifically, Žižek has gone so far as to claim that such a paranoid fantasy is fundamental to American culture: it is not that we continue to live our daily lives in spite of these presentiments of an ominous world beyond from which ours is controlled; rather, we continue *because of* this very fantasy. Here, see the final chapter in the revised edition of Slavoj Žižek, *Enjoy Your Symptom! Jacques Lacan in Hollywood and Out* (New York and London: Routledge, 2001).

72. As Freud observed, the psychotic's fantasy projections are all made in an attempt to get well or, rather, in an attempt to reestablish an agreeable connection to the world. "Agreeable" is here the operative word, as the psychotic does not *share* a bond to a common symbolic system. In *Time Out of Joint*, Ragle Gumm moves from a largely solitary to a shared symbolic system, but this is not usually the case in the author's work. *A Scanner Darkly* (1977) gives a version of psychosis more typical of Dick's fiction, as Fred-Bob Archer's psychosis presumably lingers beyond the conclusion of the novel. The character's inability achieve a clearly shared social bond is far more "Dickian" in nature, especially given Dick's comments indicated here. A Linklater-directed film of *A Scanner Darkly* was released in 2006.

73. See Fredric Jameson, "Nostalgia for the Present" in *Postmodernism, or, The Cultural Logic of Late Capitalism* (Durham: Duke University Press, 1991), 279–289. See also Peter Fitting, "Reality as Ideological Construct" in Mullen, *On Philip K. Dick: 40 Articles*, 92–110. From a related perspective, a more recent essay by Krabbenhoft reads *Time Out of Joint* as an illustration of the "freedom" madness might offer against such ideological forces. As will be shown through the course of my discussion, this position is hugely problematic. See Kenneth Krabbenhoft, "Uses of Madness in Cervantes and Philip K. Dick," *Science Fiction Studies* 27:2 [81] (July 2000): 216–233.

74. Fitting, "Reality as Ideological Construct," 98–99.

75. Ibid., 99.

76. See Slavoj Žižek, *The Sublime Object of Ideology* (London and New York: Verso, 1989), 43–47.

77. See Louis Althusser, "Ideology and Ideological State Apparatuses (Notes Towards an Investigation)," in *Mapping Ideology*, ed. Slavoj Žižek (New York: Verso, 1994), 100–140.

78. As Althusser writes, "[T]he individual is interpellated as a (free) subject in order that he shall submit freely to the commandments of the Subject, i.e., in order that he shall (freely) accept his subjection, i.e., in order that he shall make the gestures and actions of his subjection 'all by himself.'" Ibid., 136.

79. For Žižek's "correction" of Althusser, see Slavoj Žižek, "How Did Marx Invent the Symptom?," in Žižek, *The Sublime Object of Ideology*, 43–53.

80. For the Lacanian armature of this argument, see Lacan's chapter entitled, "The Subject and the Other: Alienation" in Jacques Lacan, *Seminar XI*, 203–215. Here, Lacan discusses why these holes in the big Other are responsible for producing the sexed being. In other words, Lacan discusses the necessary relation of the failure of the big Other to the failure of the sexual relation.

81. For a clearer sense of Žižek's interest in their work, see his introduction to Ernesto Laclau and Chantal Mouffe, *Hegemony and Socialist Strategy: Towards a Radical Democratic Politics* (London: Vero, 1985), 1–5. Though their argument is vast, making adequate summary impossible, the following statement may be helpful for indicating Laclau and Mouffe's use of the Lacanian concepts at stake here: "But if, as we have demonstrated, the social only exists as a partial effort for constructing society—that is, an objective and closed system of differences—antagonism, as a witness of the impossibility of a final suture, is the 'experience' of the limit of the social. Strictly speaking, antagonisms are not *internal* but *external* to society; or rather, they constitute the limits of society, the latter's impossibility of fully constituting itself." Ibid., 125. In other words, antagonism is extimate (i.e., both internal *and* external) to the social because of the necessary misrecognition (*méconnaissance*) of any identification with a social group. To anticipate a subsequent argument from this terminology, the failure of the father undoes the previous extimacy of the social and its fundamental

impossibility, by actualizing this antagonism in the form of the demon Other — of race, religion, etc.

82. Žižek, *The Sublime Object of Ideology*, 45.

83. It should be said that Fitting's later work does begin to offer such a reading of ideology within the Dickian opus. As he says of *The Three Stigmata of Palmer Eldritch*, one finds a "need for illusion" in each of the characters of the novel. However, his reading in this specific case is without the emphasis upon the paradoxical linkage between this need for illusion and with "reality" as such. See Fitting, "Reality as Ideological Construct," 101.

84. Philip K. Dick, *Time Out of Joint* (Philadelphia: Lippincott, 1959), 32. Hereafter, this work will be cited in text by the abbreviation, *TOJ*.

85. See my discussion of Freud's "navel" in Chapter Four.

86. In *Beyond the Pleasure Principle*, Freud describes the *fort da* (German for "gone" and "there") game that his grandson played. When the mother left the child, he would throw a toy away and say "*fort*," or "gone." This game was frequently played with a reel on a string that allowed Freud's grandson to pull the toy back, at which point he would say "*da*," or "there." As Freud theorizes, his grandson was mastering events beyond his control (i.e., his mother leaving) by staging them through the game. This illustration is given in a discussion regarding repetition and trauma. See Sigmund Freud, *Beyond the Pleasure Principle*, trans. and ed. James Strachey (New York: W. W. Norton, 1961), 13–15.

87. At the story's conclusion, the presence of the "Chris thing" and "Mother thing," these unformed patches of both excessive life and decay, speak to the *jouissance* that returns unbound with the loss of the father in Dick's tale.

88. Philip K. Dick, "The Father Thing," in *The Collected Stories of Philip K. Dick: The Father Thing, Vol. 3* (Los Angeles: Underwood and Miller, 1987), 105.

89. Ibid., 104.

90. We are, no doubt, on the far edge of the continuum of the father's failure. Indeed, the larger theoretical question that has come into view is what happens when there is no father to fail. In other words, is the subject's relation to the social still presided over by both an identificatory and prohibitive referent? As is often indicated, psychoanalysis owes its origin to the crisis of the father, as it was this very situation that both created and fueled the hysteric's demand for a master. For a discussion of this genealogy, see Žižek, "Whither Oedipus?," 313–400.

91. Žižek gives the contrasting example of aboriginal tribes who imagined that their "real" father was a stone or a spirit. In such a situation, the actual and symbolic fathers are obviously separate entities. Ibid., 313.

92. The father that returns is the "anal" father, insofar as this figure indicates a moment before (complete) Oedipalization. As Žižek and Verhaeghe argue, this must be thought of in terms of the two myths Freud produced regarding the primal father. See Ibid. and Verhaeghe, "The Collapse of the Function of the Father," respectively.

93. Žižek, "Whither Oedipus?," 316. In *Seminar VII*, Lacan speaks of *das Ding* (i.e., "the Thing") as the original object of desire left over from the imagined union of the child with the mother. Though Lacan uses this term in a variety of ways, insofar as it marks the forbidden "object" in the real (i.e., outside of the symbolic order, beyond symbolization) we might take this as the "object-cause" as I have described elsewhere in this study. As this is described in *Seminar VII*, *das Ding* requires that "to follow the path of his pleasure, man must go around it." In other words, the subject must keep a proper distance from *das Ding* because it is the object forbidden after subjectivization. See Jacques Lacan, *The Seminar of Jacques Lacan: The Ethics of Psychoanalysis. Book VII, 1959–1960*, ed. Jacques-Alain Miller, trans. Dennis Porter (New York and London: W. W. Norton, 1992), 95.

94. Verhaeghe, "The Collapse of the Function of the Father," 138.

95. Žižek, "Whither Oedipus?," 315.

96. Dick, "The Father Thing," 109.

97. In many respects, this is similar to Jameson's reading of this text in "Nostalgia for the Present." In this essay, the author argues that during the 1950s, for a variety of socio-political reasons, it becomes impossible to imagine ourselves participating in a continuous history of any kind. We are unable to imagine our past as belonging to ourselves, leaving the mechanism of *Time Out of Joint*, the reconstruction of Old Town, impossible. Such a hermeneutic reading of history (i.e., the production of "Old Town") is no longer possible.

98. See Verhaeghe, "The Collapse of the Function of the Father," 140. It should be noted that Žižek's own text on the decline of the Father Function (i.e., "Whither Oedipus?") is quite indebted to Verhaeghe's work.

99. Ibid.

100. Shortly after 9–11, Žižek published an online article responding to the tragedy. His use of the Dick's *Time Out of Joint* to understand the irreducible paranoid fantasies of the American

psyche is helpful for placing this discussion in a larger context. See Slavoj Žižek. "Welcome to the Desert of the Real." 15 Sep. 2001. Online document. http://web.mit.edu/cms/reconstructions/interpretations/desertreal.html.

101. The point to be taken is not that outside the support of the big Other one is caught and left motionless, forever attempting to move forward. Rather, this is the very position of the subject *within* the symbolic order. The "movement" of desire, or even love as we shall see, is only apparent, for what in fact occurs is simply the coming and going of objects to that same place within our fantasy constructions. It is in this respect that "every step out is a step right back in," as I have been discussing. The paranoia that Dick spoke of in the above discussion is, then, neurotic paranoia, a necessary component to knowledge production.

102. Here Žižek's discussion of narrative representation of drive and desire is quite helpful. The space of the drive is a closed space. The constitutive gap (i.e., opening) that is the foundation of the subject of desire is effectively closed, resulting in a claustrophobic, insular space. It is for this reason that the experience of the drive is always accompanied by anxiety — the object has indeed come too close, as with the drive any object can become the formerly prohibited object of desire. See Slavoj Žižek, *The Plague of Fantasies* (New York and London: Verso, 1997), 33–35.

103. Here one need only think of the conclusion of *The Three Stigmata of Palmer Eldritch* (1964). The character Leo Bulero asserts his freedom from Palmer Eldritch, a menacing father of enjoyment. He does this by identifying with the intimate kernel of his being that he imagines is untouchable; however, in the midst of this assertion, Leo forgets his name, indicating that he remains psychically possessed by Palmer Eldritch. Intimacy thus becomes extimacy. As Leo says, "So in a sense it isn't me; it's something *in* me that even that thing Palmer Eldritch can't reach and consume because since it's not me, it's not mine to lose." Philip K. Dick, *The Three Stigmata of Palmer Eldritch* (New York: Vintage, 1964), 229.

104. Lacan, *Seminar XX*, 45.

105. I would like to thank Josefina Ayerza and Jorge Jauregui, editors of *Lacanian Ink*, for granting me permission to reproduce this image of Lacan's graph of sexuation in Figure 1. The original can be found in Slavoj Žižek, "Woman is One of the Names-of-the-Father," *Lacanian Ink* 10 (Fall 1995): 24–39. This article was subsequently published on *Lacan dot com* in the Spring of 2005. See: http://www.lacan.com/ zizwoman.htm. Lacan's original graph can be found in *Seminar XX*, 78.

106. Lacan, *Écrits*, 696.

107. Alenka Zupančič, "The Case of the Perforated Sheet," in *Sic 3: Sexuation*, ed. Renata Salecl (Durham, NC: Duke University Press, 2000), 292.

108. This misdirection is duplicated on the feminine side of the graph, as indicated in the arrow running from the barred Woman to the Phi suggests. The woman does not desire the man himself. Rather, she is focused upon his (potential) symbolic authority represented in the Phi on the masculine side of the graph.

109. Fink, *The Lacanian Subject*, 110–111.

110. As Fink writes, "But while men are wholly castrated, there is nevertheless a contradiction: that ideal of noncastration — of knowing no boundaries, no limitations — lives on somewhere, somehow, in each and every man." Ibid., 111. Attempting to create a "full" set of Woman is one of the strategies for imagining this ideal.

111. For an in-depth discussion of the nonexistence of Woman, see Chapters 4 and 5 in Paul Verhaeghe, *Does the Woman Exist? From Freud's Hysteric to Lacan's Feminine*, trans. Marc du Ry (New York: Other Press, 1999), 55–76.

112. Lacan, *Seminar XX*, 10.

113. See Lacan's discussion of courtly love in Lacan, *Seminar VII*, 139–154.

114. Hence Salecl's appeal to the famous passage from Edith Wharton's *The Age of Innocence*: "I can't love you unless I give you up."

115. Renata Salecl *(Per)Versions of Love and Hate* (New York: Verso, 1998), 19.

116. See Verhaeghe's account of such distancing in the case of the obsessional: Paul Verhaeghe, *Beyond Gender. From Subject to Drive* (New York: Other Press, 2001), 160–162.

117. Salecl *(Per)Versions of Love and Hate*, 48.

118. Lacan, *Seminar XI*, 181. Žižek has indicated the accompanying feeling of paranoia that emerges with the "experience" of the drive. The driven subject, like the psychotic, is enjoyed by an other without gap. See Žižek, *The Plague of Fantasies*, 30–35. As Salecl indicates, the drive is "solipsistic," partially severing the connection between the subject and the Other. Salecl *(Per) Versions of Love and Hate*, 52.

119. See Miller's "On Perversion" for a reading of the similarity between the enjoyment of the drive for the neurotic subject and enjoyment in the case of the pervert. See Jacques-Alain Miller, "On Perversion," in Richard Feldstein, Bruce Fink, and Maire Jaanus, *Reading Seminars I and II: Lacan's Return to Freud* (Albany: State University of New York Press, 1996), 306–322.

120. Lacan, *Seminar XI*, 167.
121. Ibid.
122. Zupančič, *Ethics of the Real*, 243.
123. Alenka Zupančič, "On Love as Comedy," *Lacanian Ink* 20 (2002): 77.
124. Lacan, *Seminar VII*, 110.
125. Alenka Zupančič, "On Love as Comedy," 77.
126. Quoted in ibid., 62.
127. Salecl *(Per)Versions of Love and Hate*, 52.
128. Jacques Lacan, *The Seminar of Jacques Lacan: The Other Side of Psychoanalysis. Book XVII*, ed. Jacques-Alain Miller, trans. Russell Grigg (New York and London: W. W. Norton, 2007), 207.
129. I am greatly indebted to the work of Paul Verhaeghe in this section, particularly his discussion of these issues in Paul Verhaeghe, *Love in a Time of Loneliness: Three Essays on Drives and Desires* (New York: Other Press, 1999).
130. Quoted in Zupančič, "On Love as Comedy," 62.
131. *Time Out of Joint* is brilliant insofar as it presages 1950s nostalgia from the vantage point of the 1950s itself. See Jameson, "Nostalgia for the Present," 279–296.
132. Freud called attention to this coincidence in the Schreber case, a conclusion that is based upon the *totalizing* structure of both the lover's and the psychotic's world view. It is for this reason that Verhaeghe states that the lover has no sense of humor. However, as Zupančič reminds, love itself is in the end a comic in form, as its process plays at both veiling and unveiling. Unfortunately, in Dick's work, this insight regarding the relation between love and psychosis is not maintained unilaterally. See Verhaeghe, *Love in a Time of Loneliness*; and Zuzpancic, "The Case of the Perforated Sheet."
133. See Chapter 11 of Philip K. Dick, *Flow My Tears, the Policeman Said* (New York: Vintage, 1974), 107–114. All subsequent references to this novel will appear in text under the abbreviation *FMT*.
134. What one encounters here is what Lacan describes as "phallic desire." Such a lover is doomed to engage with the beloved solely at the level of the (forbidden) object. It can be assumed that the beloved is no closer during the initial stages of the relationship. Indeed, the other may in fact be all the more distant. The desirer in this instance, approaches the other "*une par une*," or piece by piece, never reaching the whole of the other. See Lacan, *Seminar XX*, 10.
135. As Lacan describes the vase: "If it really is a signifier, and the first of such signifiers fashioned by human hand, it is in its signifying essence a signifier of nothing other than of signifying as such or, in other words, of no particular signified," and elsewhere, "I posit the following: an object, insofar as it is a created object, may fill the function that enables it not to avoid the Thing as signifier, but to represent it." See Lacan, *Seminar VII*, 119–120.
136. Here again, my presentation is entirely indebted to Zupančič's illuminating discussion of Lacan's formulas of sexuation from *Seminar XX*.
137. Lacan, *Seminar XX*, 8.
138. Zupančič, "The Case of the Perforated Sheet," 292.
139. Lacan, *Seminar XX*, 8.
140. Lacan, *Écrits*, 583.
141. This failure of prohibition is likewise evident in the "free love" of late-1960s California. The whole point of "love," despite its serial nature, is that is anything but "free." The subject, particularly the male subject, gives up that which is most intimate to his make-up, that is, his distance from the forbidden object. Dick's own anxiety at this sacrifice was even more apparent in his "Notes to the Filming of *Do Androids Dream Electric Sheep?*" which will be discussed at length below.
142. See Zupančič, "On Love as Comedy," 76. This reading of the sci-fi story arc, though parenthetical in her essay, provided a great deal of direction to this section of my text.
143. Ibid., 74.
144. Ibid., 72.
145. For example, in the final paragraph of *Seminar XI*, Lacan suggests that analysis ends when the analysand subjects him- or herself to the emptiness of the "primary signifier." "There only may the signification of a limitless love emerge, because it is outside the limits of the law, where alone it may live." See Lacan, *Seminar XI*, 276. Again, the drive is outside the limits and prohibition of the law of desire.
146. For an example of a reading of the replicant as a novel double, see Joseph Francavilla, "The Android as *Doppelganger*," in *Retrofitting Blade Runner: Issues in Ridley Scott's* Blade Runner *and Philip K. Dick's* Do Androids Dream Electric Sheep, ed. Judith Kerman (Bowling Green, OH: Bowling Green University Press, 1991), 9.
147. As Lacan states, "What makes up for the sexual relationship [as nonexistent] is, quite precisely, love." Lacan, *Seminar XX*, 45.
148. Žižek's reading of the tamagotchi, the Japanese "virtual pet" popular during the mid-1990s, is instructive here. See Slavoj Žižek, "Is It Possible to Traverse the Fantasy in Cyberspace?," in *The Žižek Reader*, ed. Elizabeth Wright and

Edmond Wright (Oxford: Blackwell, 1999), 102–124.
149. Lacan, *Écrits*, 583.
150. See my discussion in Chapter Two regarding "desire as a defense against *jouissance*" in Chandler's *The Big Sleep*.
151. Philip K. Dick, *The Shifting Realities of Philip K. Dick: Selected Literary and Philosophical Writings* (New York: Vintage, 1996), 158.
152. Ibid.
153. Ibid., 159.
154. Philip K. Dick, *Do Androids Dream of Electric Sheep?* (New York: Ballantine, 1968), 169. All subsequent references to this work will appear in text, indicated by the abbreviation, *DA*.
155. Shortly after Rachel's explanation that she has slept with Deckard to leave him incapable of hunting down the remaining androids, she is described, parenthetically, as "it." Dick, *Do Androids Dream?*, 175.
156. Criticism that reads Deckard's seduction of Rachel in terms of "rape" misses what comes across so well in Scott's film: just as no one can give us our "humanity" — as this is in the end nothing more than an empty space — neither can anyone give us our pleasure. Deckard does not dominate Rachel's desire in any respect, as this is quite impossible; rather, if anything, he initiates her into the masquerade of the sexual relationship, in which doubt forever reigns. On this question of sex, desire and pleasure, see Brett Levinson, "Sex without Sex, Queering the Market, the Collapse of the Political, the Death of Difference, and AIDS: Hailing Judith Butler," *Diacritics: A Review of Contemporary Criticism* 29, no. 3 Fall (1999): 81–101.
157. See Gregg Rickman, "Philip K. Dick on *Blade Runner*: They Did Sight Simulation on My Brain," in *Retrofitting Blade Runner: Issues in Ridley Scott's Blade Runner and Philip K. Dick's Do Androids Dream of Electric Sheep?*, ed. Judith Kerman (Bowling Green, OH: Bowling Green State University Popular Press, 1991), 103–109.
158. *Blade Runner*, VHS, directed by Ridley Scott (1982; Hollywood, CA: Warner Brothers).
159. The most prominent detail in the director's cut that perhaps indicates that Deckard is a replicant is his dream of the unicorn. Importantly, this occurs as Deckard briefly drifts off to sleep shortly after Rachel's piano playing — a skill which she cannot take as her own, despite the fact that she does remember lessons. Just before the conclusion of this version of the film, Deckard finds an origami unicorn, presumably made by Gaff, the character played by Edward James Olmos. This coincidence, it is assumed, indicates that Gaff, Bryant, and others have access to the memories that have been manufactured for the replicant Deckard.
160. Importantly, Deckard decides to drive into the wilderness after he learns that Rachel has killed his electric sheep and that Mercerism, the state media-based religion, has been debunked as a fraud (*DA* 201).
161. Dick's subtle brilliance is here quite evident as the concluding sentence of the novel reads: "And, feeling better, [Iran] fixed herself at last a cup of black, hot coffee" (*DA*, 216). One artificial stimulant demands another.
162. As Lacan states in "The Signification of the Phallus," unlike the man who will experience a depreciation in the sphere of love, the woman will behave as follows: "Paradoxical as this formulation may seem ... in order to be the phallus — that is, the signifier of the Other's desire ... woman rejects an essential part of femininity, namely, all its attributes, in the masquerade." Lacan, *Écrits*, 583.
163. Verhaeghe, *Love in a Time of Loneliness*, 2.

Chapter Four

1. This omnipresent quotation appears, for example, on the back cover of my Mysterious Press edition of Muller's *Pennies on a Dead Woman's Eyes* (1992).
2. Jan Grape, "A Visit with Marcia Muller," in *Deadly Women: The Woman Mystery Reader's Indispensable Companion*, ed. Jan Grape, Dean James, and Ellen Nehr (New York: Carroll & Graf Publishers, 1998), 307–312.
3. Sara Paretsky's first V. I. Warshawski novel, *Indemnity Only*, and Sue Grafton's first Alphabet Series novel, *'A' is for Alibi*, were both published in 1982.
4. For a discussion of the market forces involved in the creation and success of the female hard-boiled detective, as well as an excellent history of the sub-genre, see Priscilla Walton and Manina Jones, *Detective Agency: Women Rewriting the Hard-boiled Tradition* (Berkeley, CA: California University Press, 1999). References will subsequently appear in the body text under the abbreviation *DA*.
5. This issue is raised by a number of critics. See, for example, Ann Wilson, "The Female Dick and the Crisis of Heterosexuality," in *Feminism in Women's Detective Fiction*, ed. Glenwood Irons (Toronto and London: Toronto University Press, 1995), 148–156.
6. Marcia Muller, "Partners in Crime," *The Writer* 110.5 (1997): 7–10, 46.

7. Sally Munt, *Murder By the Book? Feminism and the Crime Novel* (London: Routledge, 1994).

8. Muller, "Partners in Crime," 8.

9. Ibid.

10. Marcia Muller, "What Sharon McCone Learned from Judy Bolton," in *Deadly Women*, 67–69.

11. For a revision of this position, see Kathleen Klein, "*Habeas Corpus*: Feminism and Detective Fiction," in Irons, *Feminism in Women's Detective Fiction*, 171–190.

12. Klein's implication here is one of the more interesting theses of her work: detective fiction is a conservative response to women's suffrage. See Kathleen Klein, *The Woman Detective: Gender and Genre* (Urbana and Chicago: Illinois University Press, 1988), 16–17, 77–78. Subsequent references will be made with the abbreviation *TWD*.

13. The author's famous pronouncement reads: "Detective fiction has its norms; to 'develop' them is also to disappoint them: to improve upon detective fiction is to write 'literature,' not detective fiction." Tzvetan Todorov, "The Topology of Detective Fiction," in *The Poetics of Prose* (Ithaca, NY: Cornell University Press, 1978), 43.

14. Though Klein's position remains largely uniform, she does indicate a certain optimism in respect to the new women writers of detective fiction of the 1980s: Muller, Grafton, and Paretsky. Klein is most optimistic about Paretsky, particularly regarding Warshawski's complex relation with the police. In other words, faith in the social order, represented by the police and the judicial system, is criticized concomitantly with the gendered position of the detective. Klein, *The Woman Detective*, 200–222.

15. Admittedly, Walton and Jones work primarily with authors whom Klein thought to be working in a positive direction (e.g., Muller, Paretsky, and Grafton). See Walton and Jones, *Detective Agency*, 124.

16. Ibid., 4.

17. Though this may at first seem oxymoronic, a progressive appropriation of the nostalgia endemic to the hard-boiled narrative is essential for understanding the complexity of Muller's work. This will be taken up at length below.

18. Here it should be noted that the male hard-boiled detective story typically presents a more hostile relation between the detective and the market—indeed, the profession serves to provide the male detective safe distance from that circuit of exchange, a desire that is in all ways supported by the detective's "ethic." See my discussion of this in Chapter Two. In the case of the female hard-boiled detective, the desire is precisely the opposite: to be recognized by the market. This distinction will be crucial for the current chapter.

19. On this score, Walton and Jones make a claim that is in all ways opposed to Klein's conclusions: Female hard-boiled detection actually "normalizes" a certain type of feminism and feminist reading. Walton and Jones, *Detective Agency*, 60.

20. The metonymic structure of the hard-boiled detective narrative, so described by Marling, defends this insight. On the "mean streets," the failure of knowledge based upon types and their indexes (i.e., genres) privileged by the classical detective, underscores the fact that the whole exists only as the (imaginary) sum of its parts. See William Marling, *The American Roman Noir: Hammett, Cain, and Chandler* (Athens, GA: University of Georgia Press, 1995), 39–92.

21. For an excellent history of biography, see Scott Casper, *Constructing American Lives: Biography in Nineteenth-Century America* (Chapel Hill, NC: University of North Carolina Press, 1999).

22. Here, Walton and Jones cite the work of Glenn Most. See Glenn Most and William Stowe, *The Poetics of Murder: Detective Fiction and Literary Theory* (New York: Harcourt, 1983).

23. The genre of memoir takes this to the extreme by dwelling upon the process of memory and its (in)ability to capture successfully the lives and stories of its tellers. Paul de Man has suggested that the basic trope of autobiography is that of prosopopoeia, as the genre's endeavor to grant life always encounters a greater, inhuman silence. Further, the author argues, this prosopopoeia is present in all literature. De Man's description of this vain address has much in common with the discourse of hysteria that will be described at length in this chapter. See Paul de Man, "Autobiography as De-Facement," *Modern Language Notes* 94 (1979): 919–930.

24. Though the possibility of sharp distinctions between good and evil that would support such absolutism remains in doubt, these questions of morality remain necessary in the hard-boiled case. See John Cawelti, *Adventure, Mystery and Romance: Formula Stories as Art and Popular Culture* (Chicago and London: Chicago University Press), 146.

25. Though they do not frame their discussion in terms of hysteria, Walton and Jones often suggest the same necessary conjunction, such as when they describe Muller's *Wild and Lonely Place* as both giving women a sense of empow-

erment as well as a sense of oppression. Walton and Jones, *Detective Agency*, 208. Marianne Noble also speaks of the benefits of thinking such an ideological breach in her reading of domestic fiction as at the same time repressive and subversive, specifically in her reading of Harriet Beecher Stowe's *Uncle Tom's Cabin*. See Marianne Noble, "The Ecstasies of Sentimental Wounding in *Uncle Tom's Cabin*," in *The Masochistic Pleasures of Sentimental Literature* (Princeton, NJ: Princeton University Press, 2000), 126–146.

26. This has been true from the "origin" of hysteria in modern medicine. Of course, over the past century, psychoanalysis has been at the forefront of this conversation with the hysteric subject. For a discussion of this history, see Elizabeth Bronfen, "Medicine's Hysteria Romance: Is It History or Legend," in *The Knotted Subject: Hysteria and Its Discontents* (Princeton, NJ: Princeton University Press, 1998), 101–138.

27. For more extensive discussions of the hysteric and epistemology, see Paul Verhaeghe, *Does the Woman Exist? From Freud's Hysteric to Lacan's Feminine*, trans. Marc du Ry (New York: Other Press, 1999); Serge André, *What Does a Woman Want?*, trans. Susan Fairfield (New York: Other Press, 1999); Gérard Wajcman, *Le Maitre et L'Hyerique* (Paris: Navarin, 1982).

28. Jacques Lacan, *Écrits: The First Complete English Edition*, trans. Bruce Fink (New York: W. W. Norton, 2006), 580.

29. Ibid.

30. See Bruce Fink, *A Clinical Introduction to Lacanian Psychoanalysis: Theory and Technique* (Cambridge, MA and London: Harvard University Press, 1997), 120.

31. Ibid., 126.

32. See Note 96, Chapter Two.

33. Joël Dor, *Clinical Introduction to Lacanian Psychoanalysis* (New York: Other Press, 1999), 73.

34. For the graphs of the four discourses, see Jacques Lacan, *The Seminar of Jacques Lacan: The Other Side of Psychoanalysis. Book XVII*, ed. Jacques-Alain Miller, trans. Russell Grigg (New York and London: W. W. Norton, 2007), 29. My version of the hysteric's discourse follows Paul Verhaeghe's notation. See: Verhaeghe, *Does the Woman Exist?*, 116.

35. For a discussion of this convergence of the hysteric's discourse and science, see Bruce Fink, *The Lacanian Subject: Between Language and Jouissance* (Princeton, NJ: Princeton University Press, 1995), 141–142.

36. See my discussion of the phallus and phallic function in Chapter Three.

37. As is often mentioned, the phallus as a signifier of power is contingent. Psychoanalysis makes no prescriptions regarding this fact. It merely describes a fantasy structure that frequently plays itself out in analysis.

38. Lacan, *Écrits*, 583.

39. See Collette Soler, *What Lacan Said About Women*, trans. John Holland (New York: Other Press, 2006), 32.

40. A "disjuncture" appears between the terms at each level of the discourses, keeping the demand and surplus of each exchange from reading its intended destination. On the upper level we find the disjunction of impossibility; on the lower, the disjunction of impotence. The disjunction of impossibility represents the failure of communication between subject and addressee. In the hysteric's discourse, for example, the barred subject ($) addresses the Master (S1). However, it is impossible for the subject to articulate fully its desire, resulting in the disjunction of subject from the other, as well as from itself. The disjuncture of impotence is related to the disjunction of impossibility, as the subject's message to the other fails, resulting in a product (S2) that has nothing to do with the truth position of the discourse (a). Verhaeghe, *Does the Woman Exist?*, 102–104.

41. This is by no means to belittle the praxis of psychoanalysis. Though the analyst remains incapable of answering the question that is posed by the analysand's symptom, the analyst does offer the possibility of reprieve. The patient comes to the analyst hurting, in pain, and may find there the means to "get well"—in all the ambiguity that this term must imply given my current discussion.

42. Jacques Lacan, *The Seminar of Jacques Lacan: On Feminine Sexuality: The Limits of Love and Knowledge: Book XX, Encore 1972–1973* (New York and London: W. W. Norton, 1998), 67. (Henceforth, *Seminar XX* in notes.)

43. The signifier is "stupid" because it is always an empty, arbitrary placeholder though the analysand continues the search for that one revelatory signifier that is not split from itself. The analyst, then, actually labors on behalf of the stupidity of the signifier, always confronting the analysand with the emptiness of this transferential faith in its fullness. As Lacan says in *Seminar XX*, "Why do I so strongly emphasize the function of the signifier? Because it is the foundation of the symbolic dimension that only analytic discourse allows us to isolate as such.... The question of import here concerns the fact that analytic discourse introduces an adjective made into a noun, 'stupidity,' insofar as it is a dimension of the signifier at work." Lacan, *Seminar XX*, 21.

44. Elizabeth Wright, *Lacan and Postfeminism* (Lanham, MD: Totem Books, 2000), 34.

45. Megan Abbott, *The Street Was Mine: White Masculinity in Hardboiled Fiction and Film Noir* (New York: Palgrave, 2002), 63.

46. Pynchon's *The Crying of Lot 49* is an outstanding study in anti-detection and, I would argue, hysteria. See Thomas Pynchon, *The Crying of Lot 49* (New York: Harper Books, 1965), 118.

47. Of course, in the masculine version of the hard-boiled detective, the detective in turn attempts to reduce this aporia by pathologizing—and sexualizing—this desire in the figure of the *femme fatale*. Not surprisingly, for reasons that will be made clear throughout the remainder of the chapter, the same is not true in the case of the female hard-boiled detective.

48. Here again, it should be said that Klein's position on these issues is subsequently revised. For example, when speaking of the issue of "coming out" for the lesbian detective in a later essay, Klein seems to suggest the limits of identity politics. Though an "outing" brings the conflict inherent in "cultural norms and expectations" into the open, it can result, admits Klein, in "unwanted exposure," fully reducing the subject to the Other's recognition. "Just as identity politics requires self-disclosure, detective investigations reveal what would be kept secret: detecting is like 'outing.'" See Klein in Irons, *Feminism in Women's Detective Fiction*, 179. Hammett's Nora Charles offered perhaps the best hysteric response to such "outings" (i.e., solutions to mysteries) when she described these as "unsatisfactory."

49. Maureen Reddy concludes that the hardboiled genre is itself this privileged subject position—the white, male, and heterosexual consciousness—a determination that applies, to a greater or lesser extent, to all versions of crime fiction. See Maureen Reddy, *Traces, Codes, and Clues: Reading Race in Crime Fiction* (London: Routledge, 2003), 41, 115.

50. Using the theoretical moorings of Althusser, hooks, and Hall, Reddy's work provides a very compelling theoretical account of the difficulties of marking hegemony (i.e., showing that common sense is in fact arbitrary and constructed) while remaining within that same space. However, while she acknowledges that it is possible to resist such hailings—this, through the reader's agency—she seems to suggest that the hard-boiled fiction of Hammett and Chandler remains especially resistant to such a possibility. The rhetorical necessity of this gesture is clear, yet it seems as clear that such a "hysterical response" to the mandate of "detective," "man," and even "white," is of tremendous interest to both Hammett and Chandler. This is not to deny an underlying racism to their work, or even to the genre generally, but only to say that this very anxiety surrounding the performance of these subject positions accounts for the genre itself. See ibid.

51. See my discussion of this concept in Chapter Three. Žižek's point is that, far from thwarting ideological interpellation, this failure actually facilitates the process. In ideological interpellation, there always remains a "residue, a leftover, a stain of traumatic irrationality and senselessness sticking to it, and that *this leftover, far from hindering the full submission of the subject to the ideological command, is the very condition of it:* it is precisely this non-integrated surplus of senseless traumatism which confers on the Law its unconditional authority...." (Italics in orig.) Slavoj Žižek, *The Sublime Object of Ideology* (New York and London: Verso, 1989), 43.

52. Joan Copjec has spoken of such a relation between detective, clue, and other. For Copjec, the clue never fully presents the criminal; rather, the clue opens the question of desire, which is always a lack of presence. As she writes, "The detective does not refute the belief that the criminal author reveals himself completely and exclusively in his criminal works; he simply, but critically, denies that the evidence itself can account for the way it gives evidence. There is a gap, a distance, between the evidence and that which the evidence establishes, which means that there is something that is *not* visible in the evidence: the principle by which the trail attaches itself to the criminal." (Italics in orig.) Joan Copjec, *Read My Desire: Lacan Against the Historicists* (Cambridge, MA: MIT Press, 1994), 177.

53. For example, *Edwin of the Iron Shoes* lays the foundations for McCone's future relationship with the police detective, Greg Marcus.

54. For example, see Jan Grape, "A Visit with Marcia Muller," 307–313.

55. Marcia Muller, *Trophies and Dead Things* (London: Women's Press, 1990), 208. Hereafter, references will appear in text under the abbreviation *TDT*.

56. Marcia Muller, *Edwin of the Iron Shoes* (New York: Mysterious Press, 1977), 13. References will subsequently appear in text under the abbreviation *EIS*.

57. Of course, this has been a focus throughout this study. Again, Barzun's well-known pronouncement reads: "What happens in modern detective fiction is that objects—and more than one in each tale—are taken literally and seriously. They are scanned for what they imply,

studied as signs of past action and dark purpose. This search for history in things is anything but trivial. It reflects the way our civilization thinks about law and evidence, nature and knowledge." See Jacques Barzun, "Detection and the Literary Art," in *The Mystery Writer's Art*, ed. Francis Nevins, Jr. (Bowling Green, OH: Bowling Green University Popular Press, 1970), 250.

58. See especially *Pennies on a Dead Woman's Eyes*. This will be discussed at greater length below.

59. See Sigmund Freud, *The Interpretation of Dreams* (New York: Avon Books, 1965), 564.

60. Ibid.

61. For an extensive account of this change in interpretative strategy, see Paul Verhaeghe, "Freud's Second Theory of Hysteria," in *Does the Woman Exist? From Freud's Hysteric to Lacan's Feminine*, trans. Marc du Ry (New York: Other Press, 1999), 123–148.

62. See Shoshana Felman, "Postal Survival, or the Question of the Navel," *Yale French Studies* 69 (1985): 49–72.

63. As Felman remarks, "To ask a question at the level of the navel is to ask a question at the level of a certain birth and of a certain scar: the question is posed out of a certain wound, a certain severance, a certain impossibility of asking" (ibid. 69). Later in the essay, quoting de Man, she adds, "To ask a question at the level of the navel is to ask a question at the level of 'the wound of a fracture that lies hidden in all texts'" (ibid.). As will be argued throughout this chapter, the greater question(s) asked by Muller's McCone is always asked at the level of the navel.

64. From antiquity on, the comic form frequently concludes with a wedding. This of course marks the end of the *agon* that drove the narrative, a terminus marked through the penultimate figure of synthesis: the completed sexual relation. As the detective story is predicated upon the fissure of disunion, a wedding must indeed signal the conclusion of his story. In *The Thin Man* (1934), Hammett inventively and humorously plays upon such assumptions. Near the end of this career, Chandler was likewise tempted by the challenge of marrying off Philip Marlowe. At the time of his death in 1959, Chandler was working on *The Poodle Springs Story*, a novel that was to feature Philip Marlowe married to Linda Loring from *The Long Goodbye*. Chandler completed only four chapters (what amounts to only about a dozen pages), but Robert B. Parker "completed" the story in 1989, publishing it under the title *Poodle Springs*. Though there are significant problems with Parker's project, he perhaps gets it right when he has Marlowe and Loring split up at the conclusion of the story.

65. As has been true throughout this work, the use of pronouns when describing psychical structures does not refer to an individual's biological sex. The use of the feminine pronoun merely recognizes that a majority — but not all — hysterics in analysis are women. See Fink, *A Clinical Introduction to Lacanian Psychoanalysis*, 119. This practice is likewise helpful in the current chapter, as the detective of interest is a woman.

66. On the issue of sexual orientation in the female hard-boiled detective, see Ann Wilson, "The Female Dick and the Crisis of Heterosexuality," 148–156; Rebecca Pope, "'Friends Is a Weak Word for It': Female Friendship and the Specter of Lesbianism in Sara Paretsky," in ibid., 157–170; and Klein, "*Habeas Corpus*," 171–190.

67. Here, I would suggest that the purloined letter raises the issue of the "masquerade" as no character *is* or *possesses* the letter, just as no subject *is* or *possesses* the phallus. See Fink's discussion of the phallic function and sexual difference in Fink, *The Lacanian Subject*, 101–125.

68. To be sure, the male hard-boiled detective often feels sympathy for the "little man," but I would argue that this is all too often a narcissistic identification.

69. For a further discussion of this, see Alexander Howe, "The Detective and the Analyst: Truth, Knowledge, and Psychoanalysis in the Hard-boiled Fiction of Raymond Chandler," *Clues: A Journal of Detection*. 24.4 (Summer 2006): 15–30.

70. For an in-depth discussion of the distance of psychoanalysis from practical, American ego-psychology, see Paul Verhaeghe, *On Being Normal and Other Disorders: A Manual for Clinical Psychodiagnostics*, trans. Sigi Jottkandt (New York: Other Press, 2004), 1–148.

71. This is itself, no doubt, in turn a function of *fin-de-siècle* anxiety. Also, we might think of this issue of memory as concerning the failure of symbolic efficiency that I have been describing throughout this study. I will attempt to develop this linkage throughout the remainder of this chapter.

72. For an extensive account of Freud's seduction theory, see Chapter 2 of Verhaeghe, *Does the Woman Exist?*, 21–32.

73. Sigmund Freud, "Further Recommendations in the Technique of Psychoanalysis: Recollection, Repetition and Working Through," in *Sigmund Freud: The Collected Papers, Vol. II* (New York: Basic Books, 1959), 376.

74. Ibid., 367–377.

75. Ibid., 368.

76. Ibid., 369.

77. Ibid., 375–375.
78. Sigmund Freud, "Constructions in Analysis," in *Sigmund Freud: The Collected Papers, Vol. 5*, ed. James Strachey (New York: Basic Books, 1959), 368.
79. Quoted in Verhaeghe, *Does the Woman Exist?*, 27.
80. Again, this is not to say that actual abuse does not occur. However, what analysis confronts the analysand with is the fantasized relationship with trauma.
81. Cathy Caruth, *Unclaimed Experience: Trauma, Narrative, and History* (Baltimore and London: Johns Hopkins University Press, 1996), 5.
82. Ibid., 58.
83. Ibid., 60.
84. For a further elaboration of this point, see the well-known essay Peter Brooks, "Freud's Masterplot: Questions of Narrative," in *Literature and Psychoanalysis: The Question of Reading: Otherwise*, ed. Shoshana Felman (Baltimore and London: Johns Hopkins University Press, 1982), 280–300.
85. Freud develops his notion of the death drive (*Thanatos*) in opposition to the life drive (*Eros*) in *Beyond the Pleasure Principle*. In this text, Freud openly engages in *mythopoesis*; the theory of death and life drives is an excellent example of this. The death drive represents the conservative aspects of all organisms (humans included), which seek a return to inanimate matter. To these ends, Freud made the controversial assertion that "the aim of all life is death." See Sigmund Freud, *Beyond the Pleasure Principle*, trans. and ed. James Strachey (New York: W. W. Norton, 1961), 46.
86. Marcia Muller, *Pennies on a Dead Woman's Eyes* (London: The Women's Press, 1992), 4, 7. Hereafter, references will appear in text under the abbreviation *PDWE*.
87. Here, Sharon refers to the cases described in the two previous novels: *Where Echoes Live* (1991) and *Trophies and Dead Things* (1990). The latter will be taken up below.
88. Sigmund Freud, *The Interpretation of Dreams*, 143.
89. Dashiell Hammett, *The Thin Man* (New York: Vintage Books, 1962), 201.
90. In a high-profile case during the early 1990s, George Franklin was convicted of murder based upon the testimony of recovered memory. This testimony was given by his daughter, Eileen Franklin, who swore that she witnessed her father murder her playmate, Susan Nason, some twenty years before. The conviction was later overturned due to insufficient evidence. For an interesting account of this case, and recovered memory generally, see Marita Sturken, "The Remembering of Forgetting: Recovered Memory and the Question of Experience," *Social Text* 57 (Winter 1998): 103–125.
91. One frequently finds allusions to this story within the genre. For a recent example, see Dennis Lehane, *Shutter Island* (2003).
92. For Brooks's reading of "Adieu," see Peter Brooks, *The Melodramatic Imagination: Balzac, Henry James, Melodrama, and the Mode of Excess* (New Haven, CT: Yale University Press, 1995).
93. The politics of the 1960s is a diffuse political program, to be sure. In the early novels of the McCone series, such a discourse is directed against the corporatization of American experience and the loss of 1960s counter-culture ideals, as we see here in *Trophies and Dead Things*. It should be noted that later in the McCone series, Sharon actually becomes a corporation by opening her own detective agency, allowing Muller to further explore the intricacies of the female detective's relation to the status quo.
94. Walton and Jones, *Detective Agency*, 34.
95. Muller, *Trophies and Dead Things*, 193.
96. See Bruce Fink, "Perversion," in *Sic 4: Perversion and the Social Relation*, ed. Molly Anne Rothenberg, Dennis Foster, and Slavoj Žižek (Durham, NC, and London: Duke University Press, 2003), 47–48.
97. For a discussion of the psychical structure of perversion as it is understood by psychoanalysis, see Joël Dor, *Structure and Perversions*, trans. Susan Fairfield (New York: Other Press, 2001).
98. For a discussion of the place of the photograph in the history of detective fiction, see Part II of Ronald Thomas, *Detective Fiction and the Rise of Forensic Science* (Cambridge: Cambridge University Press, 1999), 111–200.
99. For example, see Roland Barthes, "The Photographic Message," *Image. Music. Text* (New York: Hill and Wang, 1977), 15–31.
100. Reddy, *Traces, Codes, and Clues*, 172–175.
101. Marcia Muller, *Listen to the Silence* (New York: Warner Books, 2000). Subsequent references will appear in text under the abbreviation *LTS*.
102. In his famous *The Uses of Enchantment*, Bettelheim discusses the frequent childhood fantasy of being a "foundling," that is, the fantasy of imaging one's "true" parents are elsewhere. Discovering one is adopted has perhaps the detriment of providing ground for the basic fantasy of the "Mirror Phase," that is, that one's true self lies elsewhere. This is certainly McCone's initial reaction to such news. See Bruno

Bettelheim, *The Uses of Enchantment: The Meaning and Importance of Fairy Tales* (New York: Vintage Books, 1976).

103. Walter Benjamin, *Illuminations: Essays and Reflections*, trans. Harry Zohn (New York: Schocken Books, 1968), 91.

104. Ibid., 94.

105. This reversal of structure does not afford her the safe distance usually maintained by the detective from personal harm and implication. Of course, the obligatory distinction between the hard-boiled and classical detective revolves around just this question. The classical detective solves crimes from the safety of the study, never risking any bodily harm. On the contrary, the hard-boiled detective risks life and limb at every turn. However, as discussed in Chapter Two, this ever-present threat to the detective's life does not threaten his more ideal sense of self that always remains safely elsewhere—always yet to come. McCone suggests a similar situation when she discusses the increased difficulty of this personal investigation in *Listen to the Silence*. Though in other cases she risks losing the boundary between herself and the other, this always leaves room for an identity in reserve, an identity that remains elsewhere.

106. For example: "Because they understand a lot of things, analysts on the whole imagine that to understand is an end in itself, and that it can only be a 'happy end'.... To think, it is often better not to understand; and one can gallop along, understanding for miles and miles, without the slightest thought being produced." Lacan, *Écrits*, 514.

107. André's discussion of the hysteric in terms of semblance, or literature, emphasizes the play of veils that is at stake here: "To put it more precisely, femininity cannot be reached or designated except as semblance. To be a woman is, whether one likes it or not, to pretend to be a woman." André, *What Does the Woman Want?*, 303.

108. Regarding this notion of masquerade, see ibid., 303–329. The woman (as hysteric) is of course intimately aware of the nuances of this game of knowledge and semblance because she has always masqueraded *as* a woman.

109. See Gérard Wajcman, "The Hysteric's Discourse," *The Symptom: The Online Journal for Lacan* 4 (Spring 2003). http://www.lacan.com/hysteric.htm.

110. Lacan, *Seminar XX*, 28.

111. See Jean Luc Nancy and Philippe Lacoue-Labarthe, *The Title of the Letter: A Reading of Lacan*, trans. Francois Raffoul and David Pettigrew (Albany, NY: SUNY Press, 1992).

112. Lacan, *Seminar XX*, 65.

113. Ibid., 67.

114. Fink, *The Lacanian Subject*, 151.

115. To read well, then, demands a mixture of both "love" and "hate" (i.e., a supposition and desupposition of knowledge) from the reader, but a hate that is not a response to the Master's failure, as this is simply to repeat the demand.

Afterword

1. Serge André, *What Does a Woman Want?*, trans. Susan Fairfield (New York: Other Press, 1999), 246.

2. To be sure, there are limits to the application of hysteria to the practice of reading. Indeed, it is because the hysteric awaits a greater authority that she suffers. Nevertheless, the hysteric's protest has proved productive throughout the history of psychoanalysis. See, for example, Verhaeghe's account of this history in Paul Verhaeghe, *Does the Woman Exist? From Freud's Hysteric to Lacan's Feminine*, trans. Marc du Ry (New York: Other Press, 1999).

3. Dany Nobus and Malcolm Quinn, *Knowing Nothing and Staying Stupid: Elements for a Psychoanalytic Epistemology* (New York and London: Routledge, 2005), 196.

4. Edgar Allan Poe, *The Complete Tales and Poems of Edgar Allen Poe*, Vintage Ed. (New York: Vintage Books, 1975), 153, 208.

5. Nobus and Quinn, *Knowing Nothing and Staying Stupid*, 197.

6. André, *What Does a Woman Want?*, 327.

7. Ibid., 327.

Bibliography

Abbott, Megan E. *The Street Was Mine: White Masculinity in Hardboiled Fiction and Film Noir.* New York: Palgrave, 2002.

Althusser, Louis. "Ideology and Ideological State Apparatuses (Notes Towards an Investigation)." In *Mapping Ideology*, ed. Slavoj Žižek, 100–140. New York: Verso, 1994.

André, Serge. *What Does a Woman Want?*, trans. Susan Fairfield. New York: Other Press, 1999.

Barthes, Roland. "The Photographic Message." In *Image. Music. Text*, trans. by Stephen Heath, 15–31. New York: Hill and Wang, 1977.

Barzun, Jacques. "Detection and the Literary Art." In *The Mystery Writer's Art*, edited by Francis Nevins, Jr., 248–262. Bowling Green, OH: Bowling Green University Press, 1970.

Belsey, Catherine. "Deconstructing the Text: Sherlock Holmes." In *Popular Fiction: Technology, Ideology, Production, Reading*, edited by Tony Bennett, 277–287. New York and London: Routledge, 1990.

Benjamin, Walter. *Illuminations: Essays and Reflections*, trans. Harry Zohn. New York: Schocken Books, 1968.

———. *The Paris of the Second Empire in Baudelaire*. Quoted in Thomas, Ronald. "Arresting Images in *Bleak House* and *The House of the Seven Gables*." *Novel: A Forum on Fiction* 31:1 (Autumn 1997): 87–113.

Bennett, Tony, ed. *Popular Fiction: Technology, Ideology, Production, Reading*. New York and London: Routledge, 1990.

Bettelheim, Bruno. *The Uses of Enchantment: The Meaning and Importance of Fairy Tales.* New York: Vintage Books, 1976.

Blade Runner, VHS, directed by Ridley Scott. Hollywood, CA: Warner Brothers, 1982.

Bonaparte, Marie. *The Life and Work of Edgar Allan Poe: A Psychoanalytic Interpretation*, 1933.

Brand, Dana. "From the *Flâneur* to the Detective: Interpreting the City of Poe." In *Popular Fiction: Technology, Ideology, Production, Reading*, edited by Tony Bennett, 220–237. New York and London: Routledge, 1990.

Bronfen, Elizabeth. *The Knotted Subject: Hysteria and Its Discontents*. Princeton, NJ: Princeton University Press, 1998.

Brooks, Peter. "Freud's Masterplot: Questions of Narrative." In *Literature and Psychoanalysis: The Question of Reading: Otherwise*, edited by Shoshana Felman, 283–300. Baltimore and London: Johns Hopkins University Press, 1982.

———. *The Melodramatic Imagination: Balzac, Henry James, Melodrama, and the Mode of Excess*. New Haven, CT: Yale University Press, 1995.

———. *Psychoanalysis and Storytelling*. Oxford: Blackwell, 1994.

———. *Reading for the Plot: Design and Intention in Narrative*. New York: Alfred A. Knopf, 1987.

Caruth, Cathy. *Unclaimed Experience: Trauma, Narrative, and History*. Baltimore and London: Johns Hopkins University Press, 1996.

Casper, Scott. *Constructing American Lives: Biography and Culture in Nineteenth-Century America*. Chapel Hill, NC: University of North Carolina Press, 1999.

Cawelti, John G. *Adventure, Mystery, and Romance: Formula Stories as Art and Popular*

Culture. Chicago and London: Chicago University Press, 1977.

Chandler, Raymond. *The Big Sleep*. New York: Vintage, 1992.

———. *Farewell, My Lovely*. New York: Vintage, 1992.

———. *The High Window*. Vintage Edition. New York: Vintage, 1992.

———. *The Little Sister*. New York: Ballantine, 1949.

———. *The Long Goodbye*. New York: Ballantine Books, 1976.

———. *Raymond Chandler: The Lady in the Lake, The Little Sister, The Long Goodbye, Playback*, Everyman's Library Edition. New York: Alfred A. Knopf, 2002.

———. *The Simple Art of Murder*. New York: Ballantine Books, 1950.

Chernaik, Warren, et al., eds. *The Art of Detective Fiction*. New York: St. Martins, 2000.

Christianson, Scott R. "Tough Talk and Wisecracks: Language as Power in American Detective Fiction," *Journal of Popular Culture* 23:2 (Fall 1989): 152–162.

Conan Doyle, Arthur. *The Complete Sherlock Holmes*. New York: Barnes and Noble, 1992.

Copjec, Joan. "The Anxiety of the Influencing Machine," *October* 23 (Winter 1984): 43–59.

———. "Locked Room/Lonely Room: Private Space in Film Noir." In *Read My Desire: Lacan Against the Historicists*, 163–200. Cambridge, MA: MIT Press, 1994.

———. *Read My Desire: Lacan against the Historicists*. Cambridge, MA: MIT Press, 1994.

Cowley, Malcolm. "Sex Murder Incorporated," *New Republic* (11 Feb. 1952): 11–12.

Csicsery-Ronay, Istavan, Jr. "Gregg Rickman and Others on Philip K. Dick," *Science Fiction Studies* 22:3 (1995): 430–438.

———. "Pilgrims in Pandemonium: Philip K. Dick and the Critics." In *On Philip K. Dick: 40 Articles from Science-Fiction Studies*, edited by R. D. Mullen et al., v–xviii. Terre Haute, IN: SF-TH Inc., 1992.

Cuvier, Georges. *Discourse on the Revolutionary Upheavals on the Surface of the Globe and on the Changes Which They Have Produced in the Animal Kingdom*. Online Document. www.victorianweb.org/science/science_texts/cuvier/cuvier-e.htm.

Daly, Carroll John. "The False Burton Combs." In *The Hard-Boiled Detective: Stories from Black Mask Magazine, 1920–1951*, ed. Herbert Ruhm, 3–20. New York: Vintage Books, 1977.

de Man, Paul. "Autobiography as De-Facement." *Modern Language Notes* 94 (1979): 919–930.

Derrida, Jacques. "The Purveyor of Truth." In *The Purloined Poe: Lacan, Derrida, and Psychoanalytic Reading*, ed. John P. Muller and William J. Richardson, 173–212. Baltimore: Johns Hopkins University Press, 1988.

———. *Writing and Difference*, trans. Alan Bass. Chicago: University of Chicago Press, 1978.

Dick, Philip K. *The Collected Stories of Philip K. Dick: The Father-Thing, Vol. 3*. Los Angeles: Underwood and Miller, 1987.

———. *Do Androids Dream of Electric Sheep?* New York: Ballantine, 1968.

———. *Flow My Tears, the Policeman Said*. New York: Vintage, 1974.

———. *The Three Stigmata of Palmer Eldritch*. New York: Vintage, 1964.

———. *Time Out of Joint*. Philadelphia: Lippincott, 1959.

———. *What If Our World Is Their Heaven? The Final Conversations of Philip K. Dick*, ed. Gwen Lee and Elaine Sauter. Woodstock, NY: Overlook Press, 2000.

Dick, Philip K., and Lawrence Sutin. *The Shifting Realities of Philip K. Dick: Selected Literary and Philosophical Writings*. New York: Vintage, 1996.

Dolar, Mladen. "I Shall Be with You on Your Wedding-Night: Lacan and the 'Uncanny.'" *October* 58 (1991): 5–23.

Dor, Joël. *The Clinical Lacan*. New York: Other Press, 1999.

———. *Structure and Perversions*, trans. Susan Fairfield. New York: Other Press, 2001.

Dove, George N. *The Reader and the Detective Story*. Bowling Green, OH: Bowling Green State University Popular Press, 1997.

———. *Memories & Adventures*. London: Greenhill Books, 1988.

Eco, Umberto, and Thomas Albert Sebeok. *The Sign of Three: Dupin, Holmes, Peirce*. Bloomington: Indiana University Press, 1983.

Evans, Dylan. *An Introductory Dictionary of Lacanian Psychoanalysis*. London and New York: Routledge, 1996.

Feldstein, Richard, Bruce Fink, and Maire Jaanus, eds. *Reading Seminars I and II: Lacan's Return to Freud*. Albany: State University of New York Press, 1996.

Felman, Shoshana. *Literature and Psychoanaly-*

sis: The Question of Reading: Otherwise. Baltimore, MD: Johns Hopkins University Press, 1982.

_____. "Postal Survival, or the Question of the Navel." *Yale French Studies* 69 (1985): 49–72.

_____. "To Open the Question." In *Literature and Psychoanalysis: The Question of Reading: Otherwise*, 5–10. Baltimore: Johns Hopkins University Press, 1982.

Fink, Bruce. *A Clinical Introduction to Lacanian Psychoanalysis: Theory and Technique.* Cambridge, MA and London: Harvard University Press, 1997.

_____. *The Lacanian Subject: Between Language and Jouissance.* Princeton, NJ: Princeton University Press, 1995.

_____. "The Nature of Unconscious Thought or Why No One Ever Reads Lacan's Postface to the 'Seminar on "The Purloined Letter."'" In *Reading Seminars I and II: Lacan's Return to Freud*, edited by Richard Feldstein, Bruce Fink and Maire Jaanus, 173–191. Albany, NY: State University of New York Press, 1996.

_____. "Perversion." In *Sic 4: Perversion and the Social Relation*, edited by Molly Anne Rothenberg, Dennis Foster, and Slavoj Žižek, 38–67. Durham, NC, and London: Duke University Press, 2003.

Fitting, Peter. "Reality as Ideological Construct." In *On Philip K. Dick: 40 Articles from Science Fiction Studies*, edited by R. D. Mullen et al., 92–110. Terre Haute, IN: SF-TH Inc., 1992.

Forter, Greg. *Murdering Masculinities: Fantasies of Gender and Violence in the American Crime Novel.* New York: New York University Press, 2000.

Foucault, Michel. *Discipline and Punish: The Birth of the Prison.* New York: Vintage Books, 1977.

_____. "Nietzsche, Genealogy, History." In *Language, Counter-Memory, Practice: Selected Essays and Interviews*, edited by Donald F. Bouchard, 139–164. Ithaca, NY: Cornell University Press, 1977.

Francavilla, Joseph. "The Android as *Doppelganger*." In *Retrofitting Blade Runner: Issues in Ridley Scott's Blade Runner and Philip K. Dick's Do Androids Dream Electric Sheep?*, edited by Judith Kerman, 4–15. Bowling Green, OH: Bowling Green University Press, 1991.

Freeman, Austin R. "The Art of the Detective Story." In *The Art of the Mystery Story: A Collection of Critical Essays*, edited by Howard Haycraft, 11–12. New York: Simon and Schuster, 1946.

Freud, Sigmund. *Beyond the Pleasure Principle*, trans. and edited by James Strachey. New York: W. W. Norton, 1961.

_____. *Dora: An Analysis of a Case of Hysteria*, trans. Philip Rieff. New York: Touchstone, 1963.

_____. "Further Recommendations in the Technique of Psychoanalysis. Recollection, Repetition and Working Through." In *Sigmund Freud: The Collected Papers. Vol. II*, trans. Joan Riviere, 366–376. New York: Basic Books, 1959.

_____. *Inhibitions, Symptoms, and Anxiety*, trans. James Strachey. New York: W. W. Norton, 1989.

_____. *The Interpretation of Dreams.* New York: Avon Books, 1965.

_____. *Introductory Lectures on Psychoanalysis*, trans. and edited by James Strachey. New York and London: W. W. Norton, 1966.

_____. "The Loss of Reality in Neurosis and Psychosis." In *Sigmund Freud: The Collected Papers. Vol. II*, trans. Joan Riviere, 277–284. New York: Basic Books, 1959.

_____. *Sigmund Freud: The Collected Papers. Volumes I–V*, trans. Joan Riviere. New York: Basic Books, 1959.

_____. *Three Case Histories*, edited by Philip Rieff. New York: Collier Books, 1963.

_____. "The 'Uncanny.'" In *Sigmund Freud: The Collected Papers Volume 4*, trans. Joan Riviere, 368–407. New York: Basic Books, 1959.

Gallop, Jane. *Reading Lacan.* Ithaca, NY: Cornell University Press, 1985.

Ginzberg, Carlos. "Morelli, Freud and Sherlock Holmes: Clues and Scientific Method." In *The Sign of Three: Dupin, Holmes, Peirce*, edited by Umberto Eco and Thomas Albert Sebeok, 81–118.

Grape, Jan, Dean James, and Ellen Nehr, eds. *Deadly Women: The Woman Mystery Reader's Indispensable Companion.* New York: Carroll & Graf Publishers, 1998.

Grigg, Russell. "From the Mechanism of Psychosis to the Universal Condition of the Symptom: On Foreclosure." In *Key Concepts of Lacanian Psychoanalysis*, edited by Dany Nobus, 48–74. New York: Other Press, 1998.

Hammett, Dashiell. *The Maltese Falcon.* New York: Vintage, 1992.

_____. *Red Harvest*. New York: Vintage, 1992.
_____. *The Thin Man*. New York: Vintage Books, 1962.
Harrowitz, Nancy. "The Body of the Detective Model: Charles S. Peirce and Edgar Allan Poe." In *The Sign of Three: Dupin, Holmes, Peirce*, edited by Umberto Eco and Thomas Albert Sebeok, 181–182. Bloomington: Indiana University Press, 1983.
Haute, Philippe van. *Against Adaptation: Lacan's "Subversion of the Subject."* New York: Other Press, 2002.
Haycraft, Howard, ed. *The Art of the Mystery Story: A Collection of Critical Essays*. New York: Simon and Schuster, 1946.
Heer, Jeet. "Marxist Literary Critics Are Following Me! How Philip K. Dick Betrayed His Academic Admirers to the FBI." *Lingua Franca* (May/June 2001): 27–31.
Hiney, Tom. *Raymond Chandler: A Biography*. New York: Atlantic Monthly Press, 1997.
Howe, Alexander. "The Detective and the Analyst: Truth, Knowledge, and Psychoanalysis in the Hard-boiled Fiction of Raymond Chandler." *Clues: A Journal of Detection*. 24.4 (Summer 2006): 15–30.
Irons, Glenwood, ed. *Feminism in Women's Detective Fiction*. Toronto: Toronto University Press, 1995.
Irwin, John T. "Unless the Threat of Death is Behind Them: Hammett's *The Maltese Falcon*." *Literary Review* 2.3 (2000): 341–374.
_____. *Unless the Threat of Death Is Behind Them: Hard-Boiled Fiction and Film Noir*. Baltimore, MD: Johns Hopkins University Press, 2006.
Isherwood, Christopher. *Exhumations: Stories, Articles, Verses*. London: Methuen, 1966.
Jameson, Fredric. *Postmodernism, or, The Cultural Logic of Late Capitalism*. Durham: Duke University Press, 1991.
Johnson, Barbara. "The Frame of Reference: Poe, Lacan, Derrida." In *The Purloined Poe: Lacan, Derrida, and Psychoanalytic Reading*, edited by John P. Muller and William J. Richardson, 213–251. Baltimore: Johns Hopkins University Press, 1988.
Kerman, Judith. *Retrofitting Blade Runner: Issues in Ridley Scott's Blade Runner and Philip K. Dick's Do Androids Dream Electric Sheep?*. Bowling Green, OH: Bowling Green University Press, 1991.
Klaus, Gustav H., and Stephen Knight. *The Art of Murder: New Essays on Detective Fiction*. Tubingen: Stauffenburg Verlag, 1998.
Klein, Kathleen. "*Habeas Corpus*: Feminism and Detective Fiction." In *Feminism in Women's Detective Fiction*, edited by Glenwood Irons, 171–190. Toronto: Toronto University Press, 1995.
_____. *The Woman Detective: Gender and Genre*. Urbana and Chicago: Illinois University Press, 1988.
Knight, Stephen Thomas. *Form and Ideology in Crime Fiction*. Bloomington, IN: Indiana University Press, 1980.
Krabbenhoft, Kenneth. "Uses of Madness in Cervantes and Philip K. Dick." *Science Fiction Studies* 27:2 [81] (July 2000): 216–233.
Krutch, Joseph Wood. *Edgar Allan Poe: A Study in Genius*. New York: Russell & Russell, 1965.
Kupke, Christian. "The Conflicts of the Obsessional Neurotic: A Lacanian Dream-Interpretation." *The Symptom: The Online Journal for Lacan* 1 (Autumn 2001). http://www.lacan.com/kupef.htm.
Lacan, Jacques. *De la Psychose Paranoiaque dan ses Rapports avec la Personnalité Suivi de Premiers Ecrits sur la Paranoia, Champ Freudian*. Paris: Editions du Seuil, 1980.
_____. *Écrits: The First Complete English Edition*, trans. Bruce Fink. New York: W. W. Norton, 2006.
_____. "Science and Truth." *Newsletter of the Freudian Field* 3:1–2 (1989): 4–29.
_____. *The Seminar of Jacques Lacan: Book II: The Ego in Freud's Theory and in the Technique of Psychoanalysis, 1954–1955*, edited by Jacques-Alain Miller, trans. by Sylvanna Tomaselli. New York: W. W. Norton, 1988.
_____. *The Seminar of Jacques Lacan: Book III: The Psychoses, 1955–1956*, edited by Jacques-Alain Miller, trans. Russell Grigg. New York: W. W. Norton, 1993.
_____. *The Seminar of Jacques Lacan: Book VII: The Ethics of Psychoanalysis, 1959–1960*, edited by Jacques-Alain Miller, trans. Dennis Porter. New York and London: W. W. Norton, 1992.
_____. *The Seminar of Jacques Lacan: Book XI: The Four Fundamental Concepts of Psychoanalysis*, edited by Jacques-Alain Miller, trans. Alan Sheridan. New York: W. W. Norton, 1977.
_____. *The Seminar of Jacques Lacan: Book XVII: The Other Side of Psychoanalysis*, edited by Jacques-Alain Miller, trans. Russell Grigg. New York and London: W. W. Norton, 2007.

———. *The Seminar of Jacques Lacan: Book XX: On Feminine Sexuality: The Limits of Love and Knowledge, Encore 1972–1973*, edited by Jacques-Alain Miller. New York and London: W. W. Norton, 1998.

———. "Seminar on 'The Purloined Letter.'" In *The Purloined Poe: Lacan, Derrida, and Psychoanalytic Reading*, edited by John P. Muller and William J. Richardson, 28–54. Baltimore: Johns Hopkins University Press, 1988.

———. *Television: A Challenge to the Psychoanalytic Establishment*, edited by Joan Copjec, trans. by Denis Hollier, et. al. New York and London: W. W. Norton, 1990.

Laclau, Ernesto, and Chantal Mouffe. *Hegemony and Socialist Strategy: Towards a Radical Democratic Politics*. London: Verso, 1985.

La Farge, Christopher. "Mickey Spillane and His Bloody Hammer." *Saturday Review* (6 Nov. 1954): 11–12, 54–59.

Landon, Brooks. *The Aesthetics of Ambivalence: Rethinking Science Fiction and Film in the Age of Electronic (Re)Production*. Westport, CT: Greenwood Press, 1992.

Lange, Bernd-Pete. "The Detective as Genteel Chess Player: Poe, Doyle, Dibdin." In *The Art of Murder: New Essays on Detective Fiction*, edited by Gustav H. Klaus and Stephen Knight, 50–66. Tubingen: Stauffenburg Verlag, 1998.

Leader, Darian. *Why Do Women Write More Letters than They Send? A Meditation on the Loneliness of the Sexes*. New York: Basic Books, 1997.

Leclaire, Serge. "Jerome, or Death in the Life of the Obsessional." In *Returning to Freud: Clinical Psychoanalysis in the School of Lacan*, edited by Stuart Schneiderman, 94–113. New Haven, CT: Yale University Press, 1980.

Lee, Gwen and Elaine Sauter, eds. *What If Our World Is Their Heaven? The Final Conversations of Philip K. Dick*. Wookstock, NY: Overlook Press, 2000.

Levinson, Brett. "Sex without Sex, Queering the Market, the Collapse of the Political, the Death of Difference, and AIDS: Hailing Judith Butler." *Diacritics: A Review of Contemporary Criticism* 29, no. 3 Fall (1999): 81–101.

Madden, David, ed. *Tough Guy Writers of the Thirties*. Carbondale, IL: Southern Illinois University Press, 1979.

Magistrale, Tony, and Sidney Poger. *Poe's Children: Connections between Tales of Terror and Detection*. New York: Peter Lang, 1999.

The Maltese Falcon, DVD, directed by John Huston. CA: Warner Studios, 1941.

Marcus, Steven. *Freud and the Culture of Psychoanalysis: Studies in the Transition from Victorian Humanism to Modernity*. Boston: G. Allen & Unwin, 1984.

———. *Representations: Essays on Literature and Society*. New York: Random House, 1975.

Marling, William. *The American Roman Noir: Hammett, Cain, and Chandler*. Athens, GA: University of Georgia Press, 1995.

———. "The Hammett Succubus." *Clues: A Journal of Detection* 3:2 (1982): 66–75.

McCann, Sean. *Gumshoe America: Hard-Boiled Crime Fiction and the Rise and Fall of New Deal Liberalism*. Durham, NC: Duke University Press, 2000.

Meyer, Nicholas. *The Seven-Per-Cent Solution: Being a Reprint from the Reminiscences of John H. Watson, M.D.* New York: E. P. Dutton & Co., 1977.

Miller, Jacques-Alain. "On Perversion." In *Reading Seminars I and II: Lacan's Return to Freud*, edited by Richard Feldstein, Bruce Fink, and Maire Jaanus, 306–322. Albany: State University of New York Press, 1996.

Moore, Lewis D. *Cracking the Hard-Boiled Detective: A Critical History from the 1920s to the Present*. Jefferson, NC: McFarland, 2006.

Moretti, Franco. "Clues." In *Popular Fiction: Technology, Ideology, Production, Reading*, edited by Tony Bennett, 238–251. London and New York: Routledge, 1990.

Most, Glenn, and William Stowe, eds. *The Poetics of Murder: Detective Fiction and Literary Theory*. New York: Harcourt, 1983.

Mullen, R. D., et al., eds. *On Philip K. Dick: 40 Articles from Science Fiction Studies*. Terre Haute, IN: SF-TH Inc., 1992.

Muller, John P., and William J. Richardson, eds. *The Purloined Poe: Lacan, Derrida, and Psychoanalytic Reading*. Baltimore, MD: Johns Hopkins University Press, 1988.

Muller, Marcia. *Edwin of the Iron Shoes*. New York: Mysterious Press, 1977.

———. *Listen to the Silence*. New York: Warner Books, 2000.

———. "Partners in Crime." *The Writer* 110.5 (1997): 7–10, 46.

———. *Pennies on a Dead Woman's Eyes*. London: The Women's Press, 1992.

———. *Trophies and Dead Things*. London: Women's Press, 1990.

_____. "What Sharon McCone Learned from Judy Bolton." In *Deadly Women: The Woman Mystery Reader's Indispensable Companion*, edited by Jan Grape, Dean James, and Ellen Nehr, 67–69. New York: Carroll & Graf Publishers, 1998.

Munt, Sally R. "Grief, Doubt and Nostalgia in Detective Fiction or ... Death and the Detective Novel: A Return." *College Literature* 25:3 (1998): 133–145.

_____. *Murder By the Book? Feminism and the Crime Novel*. London: Routledge, 1994.

Nancy, Jean Luc, and Philippe Lacoue-Labarthe. *The Title of the Letter: A Reading of Lacan*, trans. Francois Raffoul and David Pettigrew. Albany, NY: SUNY Press, 1992.

Nasio, Juan-David. *Hysteria from Freud to Lacan: The Splendid Child of Psychoanalysis*. New York: Other Press, 1998.

_____, et al. *Five Lessons on the Psychoanalytic Theory of Jacques Lacan*. Albany, NY: State University of New York Press, 1998.

Nevins, Francis, Jr. *The Mystery Writer's Art*. Bowling Green, OH: Bowling Green University Press, 1970.

Noble, Marianne. *The Masochistic Pleasures of Sentimental Literature*. Princeton, NJ: Princeton University Press, 2000.

Nobus, Dany. "Illiterature." In *Reinventing the Symptom: Essays on the Final Lacan*, edited by Luke Thurston, 19–44. New York: Other Press, 2002.

_____. *Jacques Lacan and the Freudian Practice of Psychoanalysis*. London: Routledge, 2000.

_____, ed. *Key Concepts of Lacanian Psychoanalysis*. New York: Other Press, 1998.

_____, and Malcolm Quinn. *Knowing Nothing and Staying Stupid: Elements for a Psychoanalytic Epistemology*. New York and London: Routledge, 2005.

Palmer, Christopher. *Philip K. Dick: Exhilaration and Terror of the Postmodern*. Liverpool: Liverpool University Press, 2003.

Parker, Robert, and Raymond Chandler. *Poodle Springs*. New York: Berkley Books, 1989.

Plain, Gill. *Twentieth-Century Crime Fiction: Gender, Sexuality, and the Body*. Edinburgh: Edinburgh University Press, 2001.

Poe, Edgar Allan. *The Complete Tales and Poems of Edgar Allan Poe*. New York: Vintage, 1975.

Pope, Rebecca. "'Friends Is a Weak Word for It': Female Friendship and the Specter of Lesbianism in Sara Paretsky." In *Feminism in Women's Detective Fiction*, edited by Glenwood Irons, 157–170. Toronto and London: Toronto University Press, 1995.

Porter, Dennis. *The Pursuit of Crime: Art and Ideology in Detective Fiction*. New Haven, CT: Yale University Press, 1981.

Priestman, Martin. "Sherlock's Children: The Birth of the Series." In *The Art of Detective Fiction*, edited by Warren Chernaik, et al., 50–59. New York: St. Martins, 2000.

Pynchon, Thomas. *The Crying of Lot 49*. New York: Harper Books, 1965.

Reddy, Maureen. *Traces, Codes, and Clues: Reading Race in Crime Fiction*. New Brunswick, NJ: Rutgers University Press, 2003.

Rickman, Gregg. "Philip K. Dick on Blade Runner: They Did Sight Simulation on My Brain." In *Retrofitting Blade Runner: Issues in Ridley Scott's Blade Runner and Philip K. Dick's Do Androids Dream of Electric Sheep?*, edited by Judith Kerman, 103–109. Bowling Green, OH: Bowling Green State University Popular Press, 1991.

Rothenberg, Molly Anne, Dennis Foster, and Slavoj Žižek, eds. *Sic 4: Perversion and the Social Relation*. Durham, NC: Duke University Press, 2003.

Roudinesco, Elisabeth. *Jacques Lacan*. New York: Columbia University Press, 1997.

Ruhm, Herbert, ed. *The Hard-Boiled Detective: Stories from Black Mask Magazine, 1920–1951*. New York: Vintage Books, 1977.

Rzepka, Charles. *Detective Fiction*. Cambridge: Polity Press, 2005.

Salecl, Renata. "Love and Sexual Difference: Doubled Partners in Men and Women." In *Sic 3: Sexuation*, edited by Renata Salecl, 297–316. Durham, NC: Duke University Press, 2000.

_____. *(Per)Versions of Love and Hate*. New York: Verso, 1998.

Salecl, Renata, ed. *Sic 3: Sexuation*. Durham, NC: Duke University Press, 2000.

Santer, Eric. *My Own Private Germany: Daniel Paul Schreber's Secret History of Modernity*. Princeton, NJ: Princeton University Press, 1996.

Saussure, Ferdinand de. *Course in General Linguistics*. Chicago: Open Court, 1972.

Schneiderman, Stuart, ed. *Returning to Freud: Clinical Psychoanalysis in the School of Lacan*. New Haven, CT: Yale University Press, 1980.

Sebeok, Thomas Albert, and Jean Umiker-Sebeok. "'You Know My Method': A Juxtaposition of Charles S. Peirce and Sherlock

Holmes." In *The Sign of Three: Dupin, Holmes, Peirce*, edited by Umberto Eco and Thomas Albert Sebeok, 11–54. Bloomington: Indiana University Press, 1983.

Shepherd, Michael. *Sherlock Holmes and the Case of Dr. Freud*. London and New York: Tavistock Publications, 1985.

Soler, Colette. "Hysteria and Obsession." In *Reading Seminars I and II: Lacan's Return to Freud*, edited by Richard Feldstein, et. al., 248–282. Albany, NY: State University of New York Press, 1996.

_____. *What Lacan Said About Women: A Psychoanalytic Study*, trans. John Holland. New York: Other Press, 2006.

Spanos, William V. "The Detective and the Boundary: Some Notes on the Postmodern Literary Imagination." *Boundary 2: A Journal of Postmodern Literature* 1.1 (Fall 1972): 54.

Spillane, Mickey. *Fan Letter to John Carroll Daly*. Online Document. http://www.thrillingdetective.com/trivia/triv29.html.

_____. *The Mike Hammer Collection Volume I: I, the Jury, My Gun Is Quick, Vengeance Is Mine!* New York: New American Library, 2001.

Sturken, Marita. "The Remembering of Forgetting: Recovered Memory and the Question of Experience." *Social Text* 57 (Winter 1998): 103–125.

Tani, Stefano. *The Doomed Detective: The Contribution of the Detective Novel to Postmodern American and Italian Fiction*. Carbondale, IL: Southern Illinois University Press, 1984.

Thomas, Ronald. "Arresting Images in *Bleak House* and *The House of the Seven Gables*," *Novel: A Forum on Fiction* 31:1 (Autumn 1997): 87–113.

_____. *Detective Fiction and the Rise of Forensic Science*. Cambridge: Cambridge University Press, 1999.

Thurston, Luke, ed. *Re-Inventing the Symptom: Essays on the Final Lacan*. New York: Other Press, 2002.

Todorov, Tzvetan. *The Poetics of Prose*. Ithaca, NY: Cornell University Press, 1978.

_____. "The Typology of Detective Fiction." *The Poetics of Prose*, 45–52. Ithaca, New York: Cornell University Press, 1977.

Van Dines, S. S. "Twenty Rules for Writing Detective Stories." In *The Art of the Mystery Story: A Collection of Critical Essays*, edited by Howard Haycraft, 189–191. New York: Simon and Schuster, 1946.

Verhaeghe, Paul. *Beyond Gender: From Subject to Drive*. New York: Other Press, 2001.

_____. "The Collapse of the Function of the Father and Its Effects on Gender Roles." In *Sic 3: Sexuation*, edited by Renata Salecl, 131–156. Durham, NC: Duke University Press, 2000.

_____. "The Desire of Freud in His Correspondence with Fliess: From Knowledge to Truth." *Umbr(a): A Journal of the Unconscious* 1 (1996): 103–108.

_____. *Does the Woman Exist? From Freud's Hysteric to Lacan's Feminine*, trans. Marc du Ry. New York: Other Press, 1999.

_____. *Love in a Time of Loneliness: Three Essays on Drives and Desires*, trans. by Plym Peters, and Tony Langham. New York: Other Press, 1999.

_____. *On Being Normal and Other Disorders: A Manual for Clinical Psychodiagnostics*, trans. Sigi Jottkandt. New York: Other Press, 2004.

Vidocq, Eugène François. *Memoirs of Vidocq: Master of Crime*. Edinburgh and London: AK Press, 2003.

Virilio, Paul. *Open Sky*, trans. Julie Rose. New York: Verso, 1997.

_____. *The Vision Machine*, trans. Julie Rose. New York: Verso, 1997.

Wajcman, Gérard. "The Hysteric's Discourse," *The Symptom: The Online Journal for Lacan* 4 (Spring 2003). http://www.lacan.com/hysteric.htm.

_____. *Le Maître et L'hystérique*. Paris: Navarin, 1982.

Walsh, John Evangelist. *Poe the Detective: The Curious Circumstances Behind "The Mystery of Marie Roget."* New Brunswick, NJ: Rutgers University Press, 1967.

Walton, Priscilla L., and Manina Jones. *Detective Agency: Women Rewriting the Hard-boiled Tradition*. Berkeley, CA: California University Press, 1999.

Williams, Paul. *Only Apparently Real*. New York: Arbor House, 1986.

Wilson, Ann. "The Female Dick and the Crisis of Heterosexuality." In *Feminism in Women's Detective Fiction*, edited by Glenwood Irons, 148–156. Toronto and London: Toronto University Press, 1995.

Wright, Elizabeth. *Lacan and Postfeminism*. Lanham, MD: Totem Books, 2000.

_____, and Edmond Wright, eds. *The Žižek Reader*. Oxford: Blackwell, 1999.

Žižek, Slavoj. *Enjoy Your Symptom! Jacques Lacan in Hollywood and Out*. New York and London: Routledge, 2001.

———. "In His Bold Gaze My Ruin Is Writ Large." In *Everything You Always Wanted to Know About Lacan (But Were Afraid to Ask Hitchcock)*, edited by Slavoj Žižek, 211–272. New York: Verso, 1992.

———. "Is It Possible to Traverse the Fantasy in Cyberspace?" In *The Žižek Reader*, edited by Elizabeth Wright and Edmond Wright, 102–124. Oxford: Blackwell, 1999.

———. *Looking Awry: An Introduction to Jacques Lacan through Popular Culture*. Cambridge, MA: MIT Press, 1991.

———. *The Metastases of Enjoyment: Six Essays on Women and Causality*. New York: Verso, 2005.

———. *On Belief*. New York: Routledge, 2001.

———. *The Plague of Fantasies*. New York: Verso, 1997.

———. "The Seven Veils of Paranoia, or Why Does the Paranoiac Need Two Fathers?" *Constellations* 3, No. 2 (1996): 139–140.

———. *The Sublime Object of Ideology*. New York: Verso, 1991.

———. *The Ticklish Subject: The Absent Center of Political Ontology*. New York: Verso, 1999.

———. "Welcome to the Desert of the Real." 15 Sep. 2001. Online document. http://web.mit.edu/cms/reconstructions/interpretations/desertreal.html.

———. "Woman is One of the Names-of-the-Father." *Lacanian Ink* 10 (Fall 1995): 24–39.

———, ed. *Mapping Ideology*. New York: Verso, 1994.

———, and F. W. J. von Schelling. *The Abyss of Freedom: Ages of the World, Body in Theory*. Ann Arbor, MI: University of Michigan Press, 1997.

Zupančič, Alenka. "The Case of the Perforated Sheet." In *Sic 3: Sexuation*, edited by Renata Salecl, 282–296. Durham, NC: Duke University Press, 2000.

———. *Ethics of the Real: Kant and Lacan*. New York: Verso, 2000.

———. "On Love as Comedy." *Lacanian Ink* 20 (2002): 77.

Index

"*A" Is for Alibi* 262n
Abbott, Megan 9, 185, 252n
Abduction 27, 28, 29, 34
Achilles and the Tortoise 160–162
"Adieu" 216–217, 267n
Adventure, Mystery, and Romance 241n
"The Adventure of Charles Augustus Milverton" 47–50
"The Adventure of Shoscombe Old Place" 1–2, 246n
"The Adventure of the Empty House" 14
"The Adventure of the Illustrious Client" 245n
"The Adventure of the Second Stain" 47
Adventures of Sherlock Holmes 244n
"Aesthetics of Ambivalence" 138, 257n
The Age of Innocence 260n
Aggessivity (Lacanian concept) 128, 150
Alienation (Lacanian concept) 73, 117, 118, 123, 124, 125, 126, 129, 181
Althusser, Louis 142–143, 186, 258n
Analysand 3, 4, 5, 52, 53, 61, 62, 63, 64, 65, 66, 73, 113, 114, 115, 119, 201, 205, 206, 247n, 251n, 252n, 253n, 254n, 264n, 267n
Analyst *see* Psychoanalyst
André, Serge 126, 239, 255n; *What Does a Woman Want?* 255n
Anti-detection 8, 122, 125, 132–133, 139, 158, 161–163, 165, 169, 250n, 256n, 265n
Anxiety 128, 135, 165, 261n
Applied Psychoanalysis 4, 238–239, 257n
Arabian Nights 230
Archaeology (as figure for analysis) 34, 238, 243n
Autobiography 179–180

Baltimore, MD 250n
Balzac, Honoré de 216; "Adieu" 216–217, 267n
Barthes, Roland 224
Barzun, Jacques 13, 133, 242n, 265n
Bell, Joseph 28, 244n

Benjamin, Walter 17, 37–38, 41, 230; "On Some Motifs in Baudelaire" 37; "The Storyteller" 230
Bentham, Jeremy 18–19, 21
Bettelheim, Bruno 267n; *The Uses of Enchantment* 267n
Beyond Gender: From Subject to Drive 246n
Beyond the Pleasure Principle 207–208, 267n
Bi-Part Soul (of the Detective) 7, 33–34, 41–42
The Big Sleep 76, 93, 103, 110–112, 165, 252n
Black Mask Magazine 67
Blade Runner (film) 163, 165, 169–170
Bogart, Humphrey 181
Bonaparte, Marie 245n; *The Life and Word of Edgar Allan Poe: A Psychoanalytic Interpretation* 245n
Brand, Dana 40–41
Breuer, Joseph 1, 181; *Studies in Hysteria* 1, 181
Brooks, Peter 216–217, 241n, 267n; *Psychoanalysis and Storytelling* 241n

Cain, James M. 93, 256n
California 114, 261n
Camus, Albert 249n
Carr, John Dickson 241n
Caruth, Cathy 206–208, 215, 216, 230; *Unclaimed Experience: Trauma, Narrative, and History* 206–207
Castration 64, 73, 117, 118, 152, 165, 260n
Causality 6, 12, 14, 22, 24, 27–28, 32, 51, 66, 243n, 249n
Cawelti, John G. 241n, 247n; *Adventure, Mystery, and Romance* 241n
Chandler, Raymond 7, 26, 67–72, 76–78, 80, 87, 102–113, 172–173, 186, 197, 201, 249n, 251n, 252n, 253n, 265n, 266n; Philip Marlowe (character) 77, 102–115, 173, 185, 197, 252n, 266n; *The Big Sleep* 76, 93, 103, 110–112, 165, 252n; *Farewell, My Lovely* 102, 104,

110, 127–128, 252n; *The High Window* 121; *The Long Goodbye* 77, 80, 104, 105, 111, 113, 114, 115, 252n, 253n, 266n; *Playback* 252n; "Red Wind" 201; "The Simple Art of Murder" 68–72, 173, 252n

Christianson, Scott 80, 249n; "Tough Talk and Wisecracks: Language as Power in American Detective Fiction" 249n

Christie, Agatha 241n, 242n; *The Murder of Roger Ackroyd* 242n

City (in detective fiction) 17, 21, 32, 37–41, 69, 71, 79, 81, 87, 188, 203

Classical Detective 3, 7, 11–66, 68, 69, 72, 79, 80, 83, 112, 120, 198, 246n, 249n, 268n

Clues 23, 24, 25, 28, 32, 39, 60–62, 79, 90, 132, 186–187, 243n, 265n

"Code" and "Message" (Roman Jakobson) 130–131, 256n

Cold War 8, 135, 218–219

Collins, Wilkie 255n; *The Moonstone* 255n

Comedy (Generic Form) 266n

Conan Doyle, Sir Arthur 1, 2, 3, 7, 11, 12, 14, 24, 28, 34, 35, 42, 56, 243n, 244n; Sherlock Holmes (character) 1, 2, 11, 12, 14, 16, 20–37, 41, 44, 46–50, 56, 68, 69, 189, 242n, 244n 245n, 246n; "The Adventure of Charles Augustus Milverton" 47–50; "The Adventure of Shoscombe Old Place" 246n; "The Adventure of the Empty House" 14; "The Adventure of the Illustrious Client" 245n; "The Adventure of the Second Stain" 47; *Adventures of Sherlock Holmes* 244n; "The Crooked Man" 26; "The Final Problem" 14, 35–37, 51; *Hound of the Baskervilles* 56; "The Red-Headed League" 29–35, 42, 243n; "The Resident Patient" 11, 45; "A Scandal in Bohemia" 46–47, 50; "Silver Blaze" 24, 27; *The Sign of the Four* 27; *A Study in Scarlet* 1, 20

Construction (Freudian concept) 121, 205–207

"Constructions in Analysis" 127, 205–207, 255n

Continental Op (character) 87–92, 105, 115, 250n

Copjec, Joan 61, 93, 94, 111, 244n, 256n, 265n; *Read My Desire: Lacan Against the Historicists* 244n

Course in General Linguistics 58

Courtly Love 153–154

Cowley, Malcolm 246n

"The Crooked Man" 26

The Crying of Lot 49 265n

Csicsery-Ronay, Istavan, Jr. 138, 254n

Cuvier, Georges 23, 32, 42, 243n

Daly, Carroll John 67, 115, 246n; "The False Burton Combs" 246n; *Snarl of the Beast* 246n

Death Drive 106, 208, 267n; see also *Thantos*

Deduction 11, 16, 22, 23–27, 29, 36, 41, 47, 69, 243n

De Man, Paul 263n

Demand 73, 75, 86, 181–182, 247n, 253n

Derrida, Jacques 15, 62, 65, 242n; *Writing and Difference* 242n

Descartes, René 54

Desire (structure of desire) 55, 61–66, 71, 72–84, 95–97, 98, 99–101, 107, 110, 114–115, 144, 150, 155, 161, 167–171, 182–187, 197–199, 252n, 253n, 260n, 262n, 265n

Desupposition of Knowledge 174, 185, 235–236, 268n

Details 18–21, 23, 32, 39, 116 ; see also Clues

Detective *see* Classical Detective; Hard-Boiled Detective

Detective Agency: Women Rewriting the Hard-Boiled Tradition 177–181, 263n, 264n

Detective-Analyst Analogy 1–4, 50, 56, 65, 66, 112, 120–121, 237–239

Detective Fiction 243n

Detective Fiction and the Rise of Forensic Science 241n, 242n, 267n

Diagnosis 4, 6, 28, 85–86, 114, 123

Dick, Philip K. 8, 122–151, 156–171, 254n, 257n, 258n; empathy 8, 123, 145, 151–163, 168, 171; *Do Androids Dream of Electric Sheep?* 8, 125, 163–170, 262n; "The Father Thing" 145–147, 150; *Flow My Tears, the Policeman Said* 8, 125, 158–163; *The Man in the High Castle* 125; "Notes to the Filming of *Do Androids Dream Electric Sheep?* 164–170; *A Scanner Darkly* 258n; *Three Stigmata of Palmer Eldritch* 259n, 260n; *Time Out of Joint* 8, 125, 139–151, 163, 258n, 259n; *Transmigration of Timothy Archer* 258n

Disciplinary Society 18–23, 40

Discipline and Punish: The Birth of the Prison 18, 19, 20

Do Androids Dream of Electric Sheep? 8, 125, 163–170, 262n

Does the Woman Exist? From Freud's Hysteria to Lacan's Feminine 241n, 260n, 266n

Dolar, Mladen 51–53

Dor, Joël 6, 267n

"Dora" (Hysteria Case Study) 248n, 257n

Double (literary figure) 35, 42, 55, 56, 164, 251n, 261n

Dreams 145, 192–195, 228–229

Drive (in psychoanalysis) 154–158, 164, 260n, 261n

Dulles, John Foster 218

Dupin, C. Auguste (character) 7, 14, 21, 23, 26, 27, 33, 40–47, 50, 56, 58, 59, 64, 65, 68, 83, 187, 199, 243n, 244n

Eco, Umberto 26; *The Sign of the Three: Dupin, Holmes, Peirce* 26

Écrits 56, 247n, 256n, 268n
Edwin of the Iron Shoes 8, 172, 187–198
Ego 7, 55, 60, 113, 145
Ego Ideal 84, 102, 106, 109
Ego Psychology 113, 215, 257n, 266n
Empathy (P. K. Dick) 8, 123, 145, 151–163, 168, 171
English Formula 69, 70, 208; *see also* Classical Detective
Enjoyment 63, 64, 79, 81, 83, 84–86, 90, 93, 94, 97, 117, 118, 152–158, 161, 165–170, 221, 256n; see also *Jouissance*
Enlightenment 54, 133
The Erasers 132
Eros (drive) 106, 267n
Evans, Dylan 248n; *An Introductory Dictionary of Lacanian Psychoanalysis* 248n
Extimacy 53, 258n, 260n

"The False Burton Combs" 246n
False Memory Syndrome 204–205
Fantasy 8, 87, 92, 94, 95, 100, 109, 110, 135, 143, 149, 152, 157, 158, 160, 161, 170, 255n, 258n, 260n, 264n; Lacan's graph of fantasy 76, 94, 113, 124, 128, 137, 152, 169, 176, 182, 184, 201, 204
Farewell, My Lovely 102, 104, 110, 127–128, 252n
Father (hard-boiled father) 70, 71, 83–84, 86, 87–95, 103–112, 137, 138, 221, 231–232, 252n
Father (in Psychoanalysis): "anal father" 83, 137, 146–147, 165, 259n; father function 71, 134, 145, 148, 257n, 259n; father of enjoyment 83–84, 86, 87, 94, 137, 146–147, 153, 165, 171, 254n, 260n; law of the father 117, 118, 120, 146, 223; Name-of-the-Father 74, 75, 84, 100, 129, 131, 135, 137, 164, 256n; paternal metaphor 75, 84, 129, 131, 146, 223
"The Father Thing" 145–147, 150
Felman, Shoshana 5, 6, 7, 78, 194, 249n, 266n; "To Open the Question" 78–79, 249n
Femininity 188, 198
Feminism (in detective fiction criticism) 175–187, 263n
Femme fatale 71, 90–98, 101, 110, 112, 119, 120, 132, 165, 167, 173, 195, 197, 201, 253n, 254n, 265n
Fetish 168, 221
"The Final Problem" 14, 35–37, 51
Fink, Bruce 75, 128, 134, 223, 236, 245n, 247n
Fitting, Peter 134, 141–142, 257n, 259n; "Uses of Madness in Cervantes and Philip K. Dick" 258n
Flagstaff, AZ 229

Flâneur 38–40, 244n
Flaubert, Gustave 18, 21
Fliess, William 126, 255n
Flitcraft Parable (*Maltese Falcon*) 97–101, 251n
Flow My Tears, the Policeman Said 8, 125, 158–163
Foreclosure (analytic concept of) 126, 129, 130, 164, 256n
Formula Fiction 178–179
Fort and *Da* game 145, 259n
Forter, Greg 9, 106, 249n; *Murdering Masculinities: Fantasies of Gender and Violence in the American Crime Novel* 249n
Foucault, Michel 18, 19, 20, 40, 133; *Discipline and Punish: The Birth of the Prison* 18, 19, 20; gaze of power 18–23, 76; "Nietzsche, Genealogy, and History" 133; panopticism 18, 19, 21; parodic mode of criticism 133
"Frame of Reference: Poe, Lacan, Derrida" 62, 65
Frankenstein 51, 53
Freeman, Austin 16
Freud, Sigmund 1, 2, 3, 17, 36, 53, 55, 57, 72–74, 77, 110, 112, 114, 118, 121, 125, 126, 128, 130, 145–147, 164, 181, 193, 194, 195, 201, 212, 216, 243n, 247n, 255n, 256n, 258n, 259n, 261n, 266n; *Beyond the Pleasure Principle* 207–208, 267n; "Constructions in Analysis" 205–207; "Dora" 248n, 257n; *Fort-Da* game 145, 259n; *Inhibitions, Symptoms and Anxiety* 72; *The Interpretation of Dreams* 193, 212; *Introductory Lectures on Psychoanalysis* 2; "The Loss of Reality in Neurosis and Psychosis" 127, 256n; *Moses and Monotheism* 207–208; navel 145, 147, 193–195, 212, 251n, 266n; "Remembering, Repeating, and Working Through" 205–207, 216; seduction theory 266n; *Studies in Hysteria* 1, 181; *Totem and Taboo* 145–146, 156–158

Galileo 244n
Gaze (of Power) 18–23, 76
Gender and Genre (female hard-boiled detective) 174–181
Genre Fiction 178–179, 242n, 244n; *see also* Formula Fiction
Gilbert, Sandra 176
Ginzberg, Carlos 28, 29
Gothic Fiction 35, 37, 38, 51, 55–56, 208, 213, 243n
Grafton, Sue 8, 172, 174, 177, 262n, 263n; *"A" Is for Alibi* 262n
Grigg, Russell 131
Gubar, Susan 176
Gumshoe America: Hard-Boiled Crime Fiction and the Rise and Fall of New Deal Liberalism 246n

Index

Hall, Trevor 243n
Hammer, Mike (character) 67, 84–87, 113–119, 197, 250n, 254n
Hammett, Dashiell 7, 67, 70, 72, 80, 81, 87, 95, 96, 98, 102, 103, 115, 185, 186, 187, 197, 214, 249n, 265n, 266n; Continental Op (character) 87–92, 105, 115, 250n; Sam Spade (character) 87, 89, 92–93, 95–101, 115, 191, 197; Flitcraft Parable (*Maltese Falcon*) 97–101, 251n; *The Maltese Falcon* 89, 91, 92, 95–101, 246n; *Red Harvest* 68, 87–92, 96, 250n; *The Thin Man* 89, 253n, 266n
Hard-boiled Detective 3, 7, 8, 9, 66, 67–121, 137, 156, 163, 169, 179, 187, 198, 199, 203, 212, 226, 238, 246n, 249n, 250n, 254n, 256n, 263n, 265n, 266n, 268n; hard-boiled detective's code 69, 71, 82, 88, 92, 94, 97, 104, 105, 106, 109, 246n; hard-boiled ethic 113, 164, 188, 197, 214, 223; hard-boiled ethos 159, 161, 188; hard-boiled genre 80, 86, 89, 118, 121, 173, 174, 186, 200, 203, 210, 265n; hard-boiled language 77, 79, 80, 81, 103, 106, 249n
Hard-boiled Detective (female) 8, 172–187, 199, 219, 246n, 263n, 267n
Harrowitz, Nancy 41
Hawks, Howard 181
Hawthorne, Nathaniel 242n
Heer, Jeet 134–135
Hegemony 265n; *see also* Ideology
Hegemony and Socialist Strategy 143, 258n
The High Window 121
History 203–208, 227, 230, 233, 249n, 266n
Hoffman, E. T. A. 55
Hollywood, CA 158
Holmes, Sherlock (character) 1, 2, 11, 12, 14, 16, 20–37, 41, 44, 46–50, 56, 68, 69, 189, 242n, 244n 245n, 246n
Homoeroticism (in Chandler) 252n, 253n
Hound of the Baskervilles 56
Huston, John 92, 97; *The Maltese Falcon* (film) 97
Hysteria 2, 7, 8, 9, 69, 73, 74, 77, 78, 93, 103, 123, 124, 126, 129, 133, 138, 139, 140, 148, 174, 180–187, 193–194, 198, 206, 210, 226, 234–236, 247n, 252n, 263n, 265n, 266n, 268n; graph of hysteric's discourse 183, 235, 264n; hysteric demand 181, 228, 237, 259n, 268n; hysteric's discourse 181–187, 238–239; hysteric's relation to knowledge 182–187, 214, 235–236; hysteric's relation to master 180, 181–187, 235, 236
Hysteric detection 214, 226
Hystericization 6, 8, 9, 72, 100, 101, 102, 103, 109, 112, 113, 121, 181, 228, 247n, 251n

"I Can't Love You Unless I Give You Up" 153
I, the Jury 85, 113, 116–118

Id (Freudian concept) 127, 256n
Identification 45, 81, 83, 105–106, 108, 113, 114, 120, 146, 185, 199, 266n
Identity Politics 180, 185, 195
Ideological Interpellation 142–143, 186, 258n, 265n; *see also* Althusser
Ideology 142, 150, 180, 258n, 259n; *see also* Hegemony
"Imposter" 122
Imposter (film) 122
Indemnity Only 262n
Individual (structure of) 21, 29, 243n, 244n
Induction 24, 27
Inhibitions 73
Inhibitions, Symptoms and Anxiety 72
The Interpretation of Dreams 193, 212
Intersubjectivity 59, 64
An Introductory Dictionary of Lacanian Psychoanalysis 248n
Introductory Lectures on Psychoanalysis 2
Intuition 29, 34, 189; women's intuition 198, 213
Irony 5
Irwin, John 251n; *Unless the Threat of Death Is Behind Them: Hard-Boiled Fiction and Film Noir* 251n
Isolation (in obsessional neurosis) 72–84, 106, 109, 197, 214, 253n

Jakobson, Roman 130, 256n
Jameson, Fredric 134, 254n, 259n, 261n
Johnson, Barbara 62, 65; "Frame of Reference: Poe, Lacan, Derrida" 62, 65
Johnny Mnemonic (film) 204
Jouissance 77, 79, 93, 94, 111, 118, 132, 135, 151–158, 160, 165, 248n, 250n, 256n, 259n, 262n; phallic *jouissance* 152–153, 261n

Kafka, Franz 222
Kiss Me, Deadly 254n
Klein, Kathleen Gregory 175–177, 180–181, 186, 263n, 265n; *The Woman Detective: Gender and Genre* 175–177
Knowledge (of analyst) 6–7, 59, 64, 78–79, 116, 119, 120–121, 131–132, 181, 234–239, 252n, 254n, 255n, 263n
Knowledge (of detective) 6–7, 18, 19, 20, 21, 22, 25, 32, 33, 35, 36, 40, 78–79, 118, 120–121, 130, 131–132, 234–239
Krabbenhoft, Kenneth 258n
Kupke, Christian 254n

La Bruyère 40, 244n
Lacan, Jacques 4, 5, 7, 8, 50–67, 73–79, 83, 84, 99–100, 114, 119, 121, 125, 126, 128–131, 142, 146, 151–158, 160, 164, 181–187, 203, 234–239, 245n, 249n, 252n, 253n, 256n, 261n, 262n, 264n; *Écrits* 56, 247n, 256n,

268n; graph of sexuation 151, 260n; Imaginary Register 54, 60, 62, 74, 76, 121, 150, 151; "Lituraterre" 5; Mirror Stage 53, 54, 55, 60, 75–76, 128, 142, 143; reading 235–236; Register of the Real 63, 76, 99, 130, 143, 162, 259n; *Seminar II* 59, 64, 78, 245n; *Seminar III* 242n; *Seminar VII* 160, 259n, 261n; *Seminar XI* 52, 63, 66, 154, 254n, 258n, 261n; *Seminar XVII* 181, 264n; *Seminar XX* 7, 119, 124, 151–152, 160, 181–182, 185, 235, 255n, 261n, 264n; "Seminar on 'The Purloined Letter'" 5, 7, 51, 56, 57, 58, 62, 63, 235; sexuation 151–153, 160, 166, 255n; "The Signification of the Phallus" 164–165; Symbolic Register 54, 55, 57, 58, 59, 60, 64, 74, 76, 83, 92, 93, 97, 99–101, 117, 120, 126, 128, 130, 132, 135, 137, 141, 146, 148, 158, 162, 171, 180, 182, 194, 198 260n; *Telelvision* 64, 78

Laclau, Ernesto, and Chatal Mouffe 143, 258n; *Hegemony and Socialist Strategy* 143, 258n

Lacoue-Labarthe, Philippe 235

La Farge, Christopher 246n

Leader, Darian 247n; *Why Do Women Write More Letters Than They Send* 247n

Leclaire, Serge 85

Lehane, Dennis 267n; *Shutter Island* 267n

Lem, Stanislav 123, 134

Lesbian Detective 265n

Letter (in psychoanalysis) 50–66, 83, 95, 107, 199, 238

Libido 117, 166, 167

The Life and Word of Edgar Allan Poe: A Psychoanalytic Interpretation 245n

Listen to the Silence 226–334, 268n

Literature 12, 13, 16, 22, 23, 78, 81, 121, 132–133, 176, 207–208, 263n, 268n

Literature and Psychoanalysis 5, 77, 207, 235–239, 249n, 268n

"Lituraterre" 5

London 20, 47, 189, 242n

The Long Goodbye 77, 80, 104, 105, 111, 113, 114, 115, 252n, 253n, 266n

Looking Awry: An Introduction to Jacques Lacan Through Popular Culture 60

"The Loss of Reality in Neurosis and Psychosis" 127, 256n

Love (romantic) 8, 77, 92, 93, 96, 101, 116, 123, 124, 151–171, 182, 235–236, 248n, 251n, 254n, 261n; love and reading 268n; love as sublimation 153–154, 163

MacDonald, John D. 188

MacDonald, Ross 172

Madonna/Whore Binary 85, 197, 250n

Magistrale, Tony, and Sidney Poger 243n; *Poe's Children: Connections Between Tales of Terror and Detection* 243n

The Maltese Falcon 89, 91, 92, 95–101, 246n

The Maltese Falcon (film) 97

"The Man in the Crowd" 37–40

The Man in the High Castle 125

Marcus, Steven 250n

Market (detective's relation with) 82, 91–92, 150; female detective and market 262n, 263n 267n

Marling, William 81, 250n

Marlowe, Philip (character) 77, 102–115, 173, 185, 197, 252n, 266n

Marx, Groucho 137

Marxist Criticism 134, 141, 143

Masculinity 7, 72, 102, 104, 106, 108–110, 118, 120, 181, 249n

The Masochistic Pleasures of Sentimental Literature 264n

Masquerade (of woman) 122, 170, 183–187, 199, 201, 262n, 266n, 268n

The Matrix (film) 204, 258n

McCann, Sean 246n; *Gumshoe America: Hard-Boiled Crime Fiction and the Rise and Fall of New Deal Liberalism* 246n

McCone, Sharon: character 173, 186–236, 266n, 267n; method of interpretation 194–195

Méconnaissance 54, 55, 62, 94, 126, 128, 142, 187, 258n; *see also* Misrecognition

Medicine (knowledge of) 28–29, 181, 264n

Memoir 263n

Memory 50, 57, 58, 59, 72, 203–208, 211–219, 266n

Metaphor (in analysis) 46, 131, 132, 134, 165, 194, 256n; *see also* Paternal Metaphor

Metonymy: of desire 72, 74, 81, 131, 132, 144, 160 263n; as aesthetic 81–82

Mexico City 252n

Meyer, Nicholas 36; *The Seven Percent Solution* 36

Miller, Jacques-Alain 260n

"Mirror Stage" 53, 54, 55, 60, 75–76, 128, 142, 143

Misrecognition 54, 55, 62, 94, 126, 128, 142, 187, 258n

Montana 229

The Moonstone 255n

Moretti, Frano 20, 21, 22, 23, 27, 29, 37, 43, 96

Moscow 216

Moses and Monotheism 207–208

Mother (in Psychoanalysis) 74, 75, 85, 110, 146, 147, 159–160, 182, 223, 248n, 251n, 252n

Muller, John 245n

Muller, Marcia 9, 172–174, 186–236, 263n, 266n; Sharon McCone (character) 173, 186–236, 266n, 267n; *Edwin of the Iron Shoes* 8, 172, 187–198; *Listen to the Silence* 226–334,

268n; method of interpretation 194–195; *Pennies on a Dead Woman's Eyes* 199, 208–219; *The Shape of Dread* 199–203; *Trophies and Dead Things* 189, 219–227, 267n; "What Sharon McCone Learned from Judy Bolton" 173; *Where Echoes Live* 212
Munt, Sally 173
The Murder of Roger Ackroyd 242n
Murdering Masculinities: Fantasies of Gender and Violence in the American Crime Novel 249n
"Murders in the Rue Morgue" 1, 14, 33, 42, 44, 238, 243n
My Gun Is Quick 84
"Mystery of Marie Roget" 1, 41, 244n

Name-of-the-Father 74, 75, 84, 100, 129, 131, 135, 137, 164, 256n; see also Paternal Metaphor
Nancy, Jean-Luc 235
Narcissism 154
Nason, Susan (Murder Case) 267n
Navel (Freudian concept) 145, 147, 193–195, 212, 251n, 266n
Neurosis 132, 134, 137, 150, 182; neurotic doubt 71–72, 126, 148; see also Obsessional Neurosis; Hysteria
"Nietzsche, Genealogy, and History" 133
Noble, Marianne 264n; The Masochistic Pleasures of Sentimental Literature 264n
Nobus, Dany 238–239, 245n, 253n, 256n
Noir (in film and literature) 93, 94, 120, 246n, 249n
Les Nons Dupes Errent (the non-dupes err) 100–101, 252n
Nostalgia 87, 156, 157, 174, 177, 190–191, 203, 219, 259n, 261n, 263n
"Notes to the Filming of *Do Androids Dream of Electric Sheep?* 164–170

Object-Cause (in psychoanalysis) 4, 51, 52, 53, 63, 66, 75, 76, 111, 114, 119, 120, 121, 167, 239, 253n, 259n
Objet a 63, 76, 93, 94, 111–112, 119, 120, 123, 124, 143, 150, 152, 154, 157, 160, 161, 184, 194, 235, 236, 239
Obsessional Neurosis 7, 8, 71–87, 113, 181, 182, 197, 247n, 248n, 249n, 252n, 253n, 254n, 260n
Odds/Evens (game) 36, 44–46, 60, 199, 245n
Oedipus Complex 62, 73, 74, 83–84, 146–147, 259n
Olmos, Edward James 262n
"On Some Motifs in Baudelaire" 37
Other (Lacanian big Other) 8, 9, 52, 54, 55, 57, 58, 66, 71, 72, 73, 74, 75, 76, 78, 79, 83, 85, 90, 91, 93, 94, 97–101, 107, 112, 113, 114, 115, 118, 119, 126, 129, 131, 132–133, 134–135, 141, 143, 147, 148, 149, 153, 197, 201, 206, 208, 210, 217, 218, 223, 228, 247n, 248n, 251n, 253n, 254n, 258n, 259n; desire of Other 55, 154, 155, 156, 160, 168, 170, 171, 174, 180–187, 201, 223, 247n, 249n, 252n, 262n; gaze of the Other 75–76; Other of the Other in psychosis 137, 144; Supposed-Subject-of-Knowing 61, 114

Paget, Sidney 36
Palmer, Christopher 138, 257n
Panopticism 18, 19, 21
Paranoia 8, 122, 123, 124, 125–133, 134–139, 139–151, 156, 171, 255n, 260n
Paretsky, Sara 8, 172, 174, 177, 262n, 263n; *Indemnity Only* 262n
Paris 14, 17
Parker, Robert B. 266n; *Poodle Springs* 252n, 266n
Paternal Authority 69, 83, 238, 252n; see also Father
Paternal Metaphor 75, 84, 129, 131, 146, 223; see also Name-of-the-Father
Peirce, Charles 27, 243n, 251n
Pennies on a Dead Woman's Eyes 199, 208–219
Perversion 85–86, 117–118, 222–223, 260n, 267n
Phallus 74, 75, 128, 129, 131, 161, 164, 183, 247n, 255n, 262n, 264n, 266n
Photography 17; photograph in detective fiction 224, 267n
Pinhas, Richard 134
Pinkerton Detective Agency 19
Plain, Gill 9, 104, 109, 247n, 252n; *Twentieth-Century Crime Fiction* 247n
Playback 252n
Poe, Edgar Allan 1, 3, 5, 7, 11, 14, 26, 33, 36–47, 56–62, 65, 199, 242n, 243n, 244n; C. Auguste Dupin (character) 7, 14, 21, 23, 26, 27, 33, 40–47, 50, 56, 58, 59, 64, 65, 68, 83, 187, 199, 243n, 244n; "The Man in the Crowd" 37–40; "Murders in the Rue Morgue" 1, 14, 33, 42, 44, 238, 243n; "Mystery of Marie Roget" 1, 41, 244n
Poe the Detective: The Curious Circumstances Behind "The Mystery of Marie Roget" 244n
Poe's Children: Connections Between Tales of Terror and Detection 243n
Poodle Springs 252n, 266n,
Porter, Dennis 37, 81, 250n
Power 18, 19, 21, 28; see also Disciplinary Society
Priestman, Martin 244n; "Sherlock's Children: The Birth of the Series" 244n
Psychoanalysis 1–9, 50–67, 71–84, 85–87, 119–120, 123, 126, 133, 142, 151–158, 174, 181–187, 204, 205–208, 216, 234–236, 237–239, 264n, 266n, 268n; hysteric re-

sponse of subject 142–144, 186, 265n; interpretation in psychoanalysis 52, 57, 63, 114–115, 127, 134, 139, 237–239; letter in psychoanalysis 50–66, 83, 95, 107, 199, 238; subject in psychoanalysis 54, 59, 76, 126, 129, 142, 145, 152–153, 154 160, 181, 183, 203, 207, 217, 224; truth versus understanding 2, 6, 60, 61, 64, 66, 78, 119–121, 122, 255n; woman as ideal 84–87, 96, 122–123, 124, 152, 155, 157, 163–171, 183, 195, 254n, 255n, 260n; woman as series 167–170
Psychoanalysis and Storytelling 241n
Psychoanalyst 1, 2, 4, 7, 8, 50, 56, 57, 60–66, 79, 112–117, 119, 120, 121, 126, 127, 134, 174, 181, 202, 206, 237, 238, 239, 247n, 248n, 253n, 264n, 268n; discourse of the analyst 112, 264n
Psychopharmocology 114
Psychosis 8, 121, 123, 124, 125–133, 134–139, 158, 255n, 256n, 260n, 261n; psychotic certainty 126, 131, 138, 149, 255n; psychotic delusions 128, 131, 141, 145, 157
"The Purloined Letter" 1, 5, 15, 36, 41, 42–46, 48, 63, 64, 107, 199, 238, 245n
Pynchon, Thomas 186, 265n; *The Crying of Lot 49* 265n

Quinn, Malcolm 239

Race (and the detective) 226, 243n, 265n
Rank, Otto 55
"Rat Man" (Obsessional Case Study) 110, 247n, 248n, 254n
Ratiocination 37–50
Read My Desire: Lacan Against the Historicists 244n
Realism 70, 80, 101
Recovered Memory Therapy 204, 206, 208, 215–219
Red Harvest 68, 87–92, 96, 250n
"The Red-Headed League" 29–35, 42, 243n
"Red Wind" 201
Reddy, Maureen 226, 265n; *Traces, Codes, and Clues: Reading Race in Crime Fiction* 265n
"Remembering, Repeating, and Working Through" 205–207, 216
Repetition (in analysis) 57, 58, 60, 63, 65, 72, 73, 103, 112, 120, 205–207, 208, 212, 213, 216, 217, 221, 225, 249n, 251n, 253n; return of the repressed 184
Repression 17, 21, 51–52, 72, 73, 116, 127, 242n
"The Resident Patient" 11, 45
Richardson, William 245n
Robbe-Grillet, Alain 132; *The Erasers* 132
Rzepka, Charles 243n; *Detective Fiction* 243n

Salecl, Renata 153–154, 163; "I Can't Love You Unless I Give You Up" 153

San Francisco, CA 88, 187–188, 192, 210, 219
Saussure, Ferdinand de 58; *Course in General Linguistics* 5
Sayers, Dorothy 241n
"A Scandal in Bohemia" 46–47, 50
A Scanner Darkly 258n
Schreber, Daniel (Psychosis Case Study) 127, 129–131, 256n, 261n
Science 13, 18–20, 22, 23, 27, 29, 34, 35, 183, 235, 238, 243n, 244n, 255n
Science Fiction 123, 125, 137, 141, 156, 163, 254n, 258n, 261n
Scott, Ridley 163, 262n; *Blade Runner* (film) 163, 165, 169–170
Seattle, WA 98
Sebeok, Thomas 26
Sebeok, Thomas, and Jean Umiker-Sebeok 27, 28, 29
Seduction Theory (Freud) 266n
"Seminar on 'The Purloined Letter'" 5, 7, 51, 56, 57, 58, 62, 63, 235
Sentiment (in hard-boiled fiction) 8, 81, 91, 92, 96, 102, 108–109, 116
Separation (Lacanian concept) 73, 74, 75, 85, 87, 90, 97, 104, 117, 156, 181, 197, 252n
The Seven Percent Solution 36
Sexual Difference 9, 74, 94, 120, 185, 266n
Sexual Relation 71, 110, 122, 124, 126, 139, 151, 164–170, 255n, 258n, 261n, 262n, 266n
Sexuation 151–153, 160, 166, 255n; Lacan's graph of 151, 260n
The Shape of Dread 199–203
Shattered (film) 204
Shelley, Mary 51–52, 55; *Frankenstein* 51, 53
Shepherd, Michael 244n; *Sherlock Holmes and the Case of Dr. Freud* 244n
Sherlock Holmes and the Case of Dr. Freud 244n
"Sherlock's Children: The Birth of the Series" 244n
Shutter Island 267n
The Sign of the Four 27
The Sign of the Three: Dupin, Holmes, Peirce 26
"The Signification of the Phallus" 164–165
Signifier 57, 58, 61, 74, 77, 78, 84, 114, 119, 128, 129, 130, 131, 132–133, 182–187, 194, 234–236, 249n, 255n, 256n, 261n, 261n, 264n; stupidity of signifier 185, 264n
The Silence of the Lambs (film) 113
"Silver Blaze" 24, 27
"The Simple Art of Murder" 68–72, 173, 252n
Sinthome 253n
Sisterhood of Crime Group 177
Sjuzet and *Fabula* 242n; *see also* Story and Plot

Snarl of the Beast 246n
Soler, Colette 79, 184
Spade, Sam (character) 87, 89, 92–93, 95–101, 115, 191, 197
Spanos, William V. 17, 132–133, 250n, 257n
Spillane, Mickey 7, 67, 72, 84–87, 103, 107, 113, 116, 117, 118, 185, 223, 246n, 250n; Mike Hammer (character) 67, 84–87, 113–119, 197, 250n, 254n; *I, the Jury* 85, 113, 116–118; *Kiss Me, Deadly* 254; *My Gun Is Quick* 84; *Vengeance Is Mine!* 85
Spokane, WA 98, 251n
Statistics 244n
Story and Plot 12, 13, 15, 72, 80, 130, 242n; see also *Sjuzet* and *Fabula*
"The Storyteller" 230
Storytelling 229–230
Studies in Hysteria 1, 181
A Study in Scarlet 1, 20
Sublimation 153–158, 160, 163
The Sublime Object of Ideology 265n
Succubus 110, 196
Superego 146
Supernatural 16, 51, 244n
Sûreté Nationale 19, 243n
Sutton, Margaret 173, 243n
Symbolic Efficiency 101, 125, 137–139, 145–146, 148, 156, 158, 163, 164, 171, 238, 251n, 257n, 266n
Symptom 1, 3, 22, 28, 53, 61, 78, 79, 94, 99, 115, 119, 120, 183, 205, 248n, 251n, 253n, 264n; conversion symptom 194, 233

"Talking Cure" 1
Tamagotchi 261n
Tani, Stefano 132–133
Telelvision 64, 78
Thanatos (Death Drive) 106, 208, 267n
The Thin Man 89, 253n, 266n
The Thing (*das Ding*, Lacanian concept) 160, 259n
Thomas, Ronald 241n, 242n, 267n; *Detective Fiction and the Rise of Forensic Science* 241n, 242n, 267n
Three Stigmata of Palmer Eldritch 259n, 260n
Time Out of Joint 8, 125, 139–151, 163, 258n, 259n
Time Warp (sci-fi plot device) 158–159, 162
"To Open the Question" 78–79, 249n
Todorov, Tzvetan 12, 13, 15, 62, 176, 178, 242n, 263n; "Topology of Detective Fiction" 12, 13, 242n, 263n
Tokyo 255n
"Topology of Detective Fiction" 12, 13, 242n, 263n
Totem and Taboo 145–146, 156–158
"Tough Talk and Wisecracks: Language as Power in American Detective Fiction" 249n

Traces, Codes, and Clues: Reading Race in Crime Fiction 265n
Transference 61; transference neurosis 206
Transmigration of Timothy Archer 258n
Trauma 174, 182, 194, 206–207, 215; trauma of survival 207–208, 225–226, 230, 233, 236, 211, 215, 216, 217, 233, 251n, 267n; traumatic core of subject 216
Traversing the Fantasy 114, 120
Trophies and Dead Things 189, 219–227, 267n
The Truman Show film 258n
Twentieth-Century Crime Fiction 247n

Uncanny 51, 53, 55, 56, 111–112, 164, 233
Unclaimed Experience: Trauma, Narrative, and History 206–207
Unconscious 5, 6, 57, 58, 65, 78, 133, 245n
Unless the Threat of Death Is Behind Them: Hard-Boiled Fiction and Film Noir 251n
The Uses of Enchantment 267n
"Uses of Madness in Cervantes and Philip K. Dick" 258n

Van Dines, S. S. 15, 16, 31, 242n
Vengeance Is Mine! 85
Verhaeghe, Paul 138, 148, 241n, 246n, 260n, 260n, 266n; *Beyond Gender: From Subject to Drive* 246n; *Does the Woman Exist? From Freud's Hysteria to Lacan's Feminine* 241n, 260n, 266n
Vidoq, Eugène François 19, 243n
Vietnam 219–222, 224–225
Virilio 250n
Voice (as object) 76, 111, 249n
Voltaire 23–24

Wajcman, Gérard 235, 248n
Walsh, John Evangelist 244n; *Poe the Detective: The Curious Circumstances Behind "The Mystery of Marie Roget"* 244n
Walton, Priscilla, and Manina Jones 177–181, 219, 263n; *Detective Agency: Women Rewriting the Hard-Boiled Tradition* 177–181, 263n, 264n
Weber, Max 22
Webster, John 220
Wharton, Edith 260n; *The Age of Innocence* 260n
What Does a Woman Want? 255n
"What Sharon McCone Learned from Judy Bolton" 173
Where Echoes Live 212
"Whodunit?" 12, 13, 130, 251n
Why Do Women Write More Letters Than They Send 247n
Williams, Paul 135
"Wolfman" 2
Woman (as ideal) 84–87, 96, 122–123, 124, 152, 155, 157, 163–171, 183, 195, 254n,

255n, 260n; masquerade of woman 122, 170, 183–187, 199, 201, 262n, 266n, 268n; woman as series 167–170
The Woman Detective: Gender and Genre 175–177
Woman Detective (gender and genre considerations) 177–181
Woman's Suffrage 263n
World War I 208
World War II 89, 125, 133, 208, 231, 246n
Wright, Elizabeth 185
Writing and Difference 242n

Yorkshire 244n

Zadig (Method of) 23–24
Žižek, Slavoj 60–63, 65, 80, 94, 101, 113, 119, 120, 129, 137, 141–143, 146–147, 186, 201, 249n, 255n, 259n, 260n, 261n, 265n; *Looking Awry: An Introduction to Jacques Lacan Through Popular Culture* 60; *The Sublime Object of Ideology* 265n
Zupančič, Alenka 152, 155, 157, 160, 162, 171, 255n, 261n